DATE DUE

Challenging Casanova

Beyond the Stereotype of the Promiscuous Young Male

Andrew P. Smiler

JOSSEY-BASS
A Wiley Imprint
www.josseybass.com

Published by Jossey-Bass
A Wiley Imprint
One Montgomery Street, Suite 1200, San Francisco, CA 94104-4594—www.josseybass.com

Cover photo © Getty Images

Jossey-Bass books and products are available through most bookstores. To contact Jossey-Bass directly call our Customer Care Department within the U.S. at 800-956-7739, outside the U.S. at 317-572-3986, or fax 317-572-4002.

Wiley publishes in a variety of print and electronic formats and by print-on-demand. Some material included with standard print versions of this book may not be included in e-books or in print-on-demand. If this book refers to media such as a CD or DVD that is not included in the version you purchased, you may download this material at **http://booksupport.wiley.com**. For more information about Wiley products, visit **www.wiley.com**.

Library of Congress Cataloging-in-Publication Data
Smiler, Andrew P.
    Challenging Casanova : beyond the stereotype of the promiscuous young male / Andrew P. Smiler.
        p. cm.
    Includes bibliographical references and index.
    ISBN 978-1-118-07266-0 (cloth); ISBN 978-1-118-22246-1 (ebk.);
    ISBN 978-1-118-23639-0 (ebk.); ISBN 978-1-118-26107-1 (ebk.)
    1. Young men–Sexual behavior–United States.   2. Teenage boys–Sexual behavior–United States.   3. Sexual ethics for teenagers–United States.   4. Masculinity–United States.
I. Title.
    HQ27.3.S65 2013
    306.770835'1–dc23

                                        2012026954

Printed in the United States of America

For Rita and Larry, for whom this book was always in the future tense
For Kate, for whom this book was always in the present tense
and
For Esther, for whom this book will always have been in the past tense

Contents

· ·

Acknowledgments

· ·

*C*hallenging Casanova is my work, and over the years, my thinking has been influenced by dozens of other people. This is my first book, so I'll be thanking everyone who influenced my thinking.

I'll start with the teenage boys and their parents from my days as a family therapist. I have no idea how many times I heard some version of "That's what guys do," but it's become a centerpiece of my research. Additional thanks to all the guys who've completed surveys for me or sat through interviews with some seemingly stupid questions. Your honesty has helped me understand what most guys do.

The University of New Hampshire's graduate psychology program played an important role. Carolyn Mebert taught me to recognize, support, and defend my assumptions. Examining assumptions about guys became a central tenet of my work; it's certainly a centerpiece of this book. Liz Stine-Morrow showed me what it means to conduct programmatic research. Ellen Cohn gave more support than I realized at the time, and Vicki Banyard showed me that gender was a viable topic of study. I'll forever be indebted to Peter Fernald and Ken Fuld for helping me understand what it truly means to teach. And a lot of credit to my cohort-mates for helping me get through the day-to-day: Jennifer Feenstra, Tracy Martin, Donna Perkins, Danielle Gagne, and Zorana Ivcevic. Russ Kosits may have done the most to sharpen my thinking, and he was probably the first person to tell me to write a book. In 2003, I said "no way."

From New Hampshire, I had the good fortune to move to Michigan and work with Monique Ward. In Monique I gained a mentor and a friend. My understanding of media comes largely from my work with her. It also provided me with an opportunity to meet and befriend Marina Epstein. My thanks to John Hagan and Toni Antonucci for hiring three people, including me, when they'd intended to hire only one.

I was also fortunate enough to stumble upon something called the Society for the Psychological Study of Men and Masculinity (SPSMM) while attending the annual convention of the American Psychological Association. I'm forever indebted to Ron Levant, Gary Brooks, Jim O'Neil, Joe Pleck, and countless others who recognized that men have gender too, then started doing research on the topic. Fred Rabinowitz, Chris Kilmartin, Sam Cochrane, Michael Addis, Aaron Rochlen, and Larry Beer, among many others, have provided valuable conversation and support over the last decade.

The developmental psychology program at the University of Michigan and the State University of New York at Oswego have also supported me and helped sharpen my thinking. Three labs have also contributed substantially. The first was Deborah Tolman's group at Wellesley College, the second was Monique Ward's lab at the University of Michigan, and the third was my lab at SUNY Oswego. Having knowledgeable colleagues and friends with whom to talk and work through the research has been invaluable. I offer particular thanks to the students who were willing to work on various projects of mine over the years. At Oswego: Nicole Higgins, Kristin Leclair, Jessica Mangold, Sabrina Narad, Christopher O'Brien, Christina Sawyer, Kayla Scalise, James Strail, Leslie Graves, Natsuki Kubotera, and Brennan Payne. At Wake Forest: Rachel Eason, Vincent Ganzon, Abbey Gensch, Brittney Hearon, Courtie Jaffe, Geoff Janssen, Kelsey Meekins, Michelle Murray, Hillary Scudder, and Mandi Yohn.

My thanks also to the Wake Forest Psychology Department, Advancement Office, and the Women's and Gender Studies program, which have offered support throughout the writing. Particular thanks to Dale Dagenbach, Janine Jennings, and Christian Waugh for various forms of support. I'm also indebted to Janice Jennings, Michael Crowe, Miranda Davis, and Brittany Hearon, each of whom commented on drafts of various chapters, helped me find resources, or both. Thanks also to Cheryl Walker, Katie Neal, and Kim McGrath, who put me in contact with a variety of reporters and improved my ability to get my message across.

Serendipity has played a bigger role in my career than I sometimes care to think about. A chance meeting with Judy Chu at a convention led me to an opportunity to work with Deborah Tolman. That, in turn, led to a 2008 journal article on tenth-grade boys' motives for dating and sex, which Tara Parker-Pope of the *New York Times* stumbled upon. Her summary of my work, and subsequent articles by Sharon Jayson of *USA Today*, showed me that there's a substantial audience for the topic and a lot of misinformation. A few years later, this book is the result.

Neil Chethik was kind enough to read my initial proposal, offer his feedback, and ultimately introduce me to his and my agent, Alice Martell, who helped refine the proposal. Alan Rinzler at Jossey-Bass supported *Challenging Casanova* and convinced the powers that be that a book about young men's sexuality was worth the risk. Alan, Kate Bradford, and Michele Jones have helped shape the text and make my message clear. Alan gets extra credit for convincing me to talk about men's bodies in Chapter Seven. A lot of other folks at Jossey-Bass have also helped bring the book to reality; my thanks to all of them.

Throughout the process, I've received input from a variety of folks. This group includes Emily Springfield, Scott Martin, Ken Irwin, Barb Garii, Jack Smiler, Rebecca Plante, Lisa Rinaldi, Tony Goldsmith, Chris Kilmartin, Jay Chang, Marina Epstein, Chris O'Brien, Brennan Payne, Pamela Garnick, Jeffrey Berger, Jobe Lawson, Danielle Gagne, Michael Addis, Sam Buser, Neil Chethik, Fred Rabinowitz, Zev Hechtman, and Maureen Collins Margevich. If I've left anyone's name out of this list, you have my sincere apologies.

I also owe thanks to the folks at the Good Men Project, founded by Tom Matlack. Larry Bean, Henry P. Belanger, and Lisa Hickey, among others, have all helped me become a better writer.

I've also received the support and encouragement of a great many people throughout my writing of this book. Emily has been a boon to my mental health and my ability to remain reasonably sane throughout all this. Thanks also to Judi, Lisa, JoAnne, Karen, Kyndall, Susan, Kevin, Carolyn, Jesse, and the rest of the Wednesday night yoga class.

Finally, my utmost thanks to my partner, Kate, who has been a tremendous support throughout the entire process of developing an idea, pitching it, and ultimately writing the book. She was also kind enough to read it and offer input, much of which was quite helpful. Kate, you remain my beloved.

Introduction

. . . .

In the summer of 2011, men's sexual behavior was all over the news for a few weeks, and not in a good way. The stories were about the sexual misconduct of Rep. Anthony Weiner, actor and governor Arnold Schwarzenegger, and IMF chief Dominique Strauss-Kahn. Men need to learn how to avoid "letting the little head do the thinking for the big head," you say? Eighteen months earlier, we'd learned about the infidelity of Tiger Woods. "Men are dogs," you think? Jon Gosselin. South Carolina governor Mark Sanford. Senator John Edwards. I could go on. The impression I get from the covers of various celebrity magazines in the grocery store is that most Hollywood break-ups happen because he cheats on her—Jesse James and Sandra Bullock, for example. Perhaps you're asking, "What's wrong with men?"

If I pushed, you'd probably acknowledge that "not all guys are like that" and that "there are some good ones out there," but you'd also say they're the minority and that "most guys can't be trusted to control their biological urges." You might even tell me that men are biologically programmed to spread their seed widely because that's their best chance of passing their genes on to the next generation, and therefore "guys can't help it" because you can't defeat biology. Guys who sleep around meet our expectations; guys who are monogamous seem like exceptions.

Many Americans believe that the male sex drive is ever present and barely controlled, and causes guys to be promiscuous. This image forms the basis of some of our most popular mass media. On television, it's young men like Barney from *How I Met Your Mother* and Charlie from *Two and a Half Men*; in movie theaters, it's the young men in *The Wedding Crashers*, as well as the teenage boys in movies like *American Pie, Superbad*, and the not-at-all subtly titled *Sex Drive*. In music videos, it's the male performers in most rap videos, the majority of whom are also young men.

Rampant male sex drive is not just a centerpiece of fiction. Retired basketball players Earvin "Magic" Johnson and Wilt Chamberlain each claimed to have had over a thousand sexual partners. Self-proclaimed pickup gurus like Mystery on VH1's *The Pickup Artist*, who is reputed to have slept with hundreds of women, teach other guys how to score.

Before any of them, there was Giacomo Casanova.

These guys—real and fictional—are the ones boys and young men often look up to. They see these guys as "cool" and "the Man." Well, maybe not the politicians, but the athletes and Hollywood types are certainly cool. Many boys and young men will tell you that if they could sleep with a different woman every week, they would.

But most boys and men don't sleep around in that way, and most don't even try to.

The problem isn't just that there's some group of "bad boys" (and young men) who sleep around; the problem is that we have come to believe that this behavior is normal. This image of young men—I call it the Casanova Complex—has become an all too common expectation of young men's behavior. The Casanova Complex distorts all our perceptions about what's normal for guys. It tells us that guys are primarily interested in sex, not relationships. This contributes to the notion that guys are emotional clods who are incapable of connecting with their partners because, hey, they're just guys, and guys are only interested in sex. As a result, guys shouldn't be expected to achieve any type of "real" emotional intimacy with their partners.

This image has become so accepted and ingrained that this is how young men are described in abstinence-only sex education programs. That's the approach that schools are most likely to use.[1] We teach boys and girls that it's normal and natural for guys to be promiscuous.

It may also help explain why less than half of teenage boys have "the Talk" with their parents.[2] And when parents do talk to boys, they tend to focus on the three don'ts: don't have sex, don't get a disease, and don't get someone pregnant.[3]

The sexuality research is clear: promiscuous teenage boys and young men are the guys who are most likely to have a sexually transmitted infection (STI), and they're the guys who are most likely to get someone pregnant.[4] As I'll explain in Chapter One, that act of personal irresponsibility has costs for us as a nation—it's part of the reason why the United States has teen pregnancy and STI rates that are much, much higher than other industrialized and postindustrialized countries, according to the World Health Organization and the United Nations.[5]

The promotion of the Casanova Complex has other, less obvious costs. When we teach, accept, assume, or infer that this is the normal way for guys to be, then it encourages guys who aren't Casanovas to feel as though they're not normal. Some may start to sleep around or take other risks in order to fit in. If you've seen the movie *Superbad*, then you've seen Seth, a nice but unremarkable guy, talk about needing to get laid before starting college, and spend a day taking some incredible risks in order to do that; he never talks about having a relationship with Jules, just having sex with her.

Our belief in the Casanova Complex lets us hear a story about a cheating husband—whether it be Schwarzenegger, Sanford, Vice President Gore, or Jesse James (husband of Sandra Bullock)—and understand the behavior simply as a guy trying to "get some" on the side. When we go for that simple answer, we don't have to think about the kinds of relationships these men might have had with their wives, and thus we miss out on an opportunity to learn something about what makes a successful relationship.

Imagine what might happen if we improved and expanded our sexual expectations of young men. If we widen the options so that boys and men are encouraged to enjoy relationships, imagine what might happen. If we start expecting boys and young men to be responsible—as the Boys and Girls Clubs of America, Boy Scouts, YMCA, and other character-building organizations do—imagine what might happen. If we stop believing that boys and men are emotional cripples and fly-by-night Casanovas who just want sex, and start believing that they're full, complete human beings who have emotional and relational needs, imagine what might happen.

Challenging Casanova will move us beyond the stereotypical perspective on male sexuality to a conception that is more complex and nuanced, one that acknowledges that most boys and young men want to have relationships and emphasizes that they take a variety of approaches to dating and sexuality. By challenging Casanova, I hope to expand the discussion of boys' and young men's lives and provide all of us with a different way to think about this image; I'm also hoping to make more space for boys who don't fit this particular stereotype of male sexuality, because they're the majority. In part, I'll do this by reminding you of some things you already know—that boys and men want and value relationships and emotional connection. I'll also describe some of the current research and thinking about how boys learn about their sexuality and their gender role.

I'll start by talking about the Casanova Complex. Research tells us that about 15 percent of young men—or about one guy in seven—has three or more sexual partners in any given year. If you look at it over a longer span of time, the number falls to about 5 percent, or one guy in twenty, who has three or more partners per year for three years.[6] No matter which way you look at it, only a small percentage of guys are having multiple partners.

In starting to challenge the Casanova Complex, I'll adopt an approach which emphasizes that sexual development is a natural part of growing up, and I don't just mean puberty. Sure, the vast majority of boys have their first "real" kiss during adolescence, and more than half will lose their virginity,[7] as I'll discuss in Chapter Two. But these firsts occur alongside of, and coincide with, other typical components of adolescence, such as developing an identity and starting to think conceptually. Those things aren't separate from dating and sexual behavior; they are interrelated, and they mutually influence one other. When we put dating and sexuality in the context of other developmental changes instead of thinking about them as things that are separate from any other part of young men's lives, we get a very different, non-Casanova perspective on their sexual development.

Adolescence is also when most boys have their first "real" relationship. Today, most boys have a good friend who is female; she may even be his best friend. This wasn't the case in the 1970s; back then, male-female friendships during adolescence and young adulthood were a rarity.[8] Boys not only hold different perspectives on what makes a good friend as opposed to what makes a good dating partner, they also make distinctions about what makes a good hookup partner.[9] Boys have different motives and priorities when starting a relationship than they do when hooking up; I'll explore these different types of relationships in Chapter Three.

Part Two of the book talks about how the Casanova Complex has become our "basic" understanding of young men's sexuality; it also discusses what we've forgotten or routinely overlook. As recently as the 1950s and 1960s, we thought very differently about boys; we saw them as mostly good, fun-loving, respectful, and responsible. American history tells us that the Casanova-like image of male sexuality has been around for a long time, but that image hasn't always been dominant or even considered "positive" or desirable.

Part of the rise of the Casanova Complex has been the result of some social scientists' attempts to explain current-day behavior using evolutionary rationales. Many people are aware of the evolutionary argument that being a Casanova provides an advantage by encouraging men to spread their seed widely.[10] Yet most people are unaware that research by these same psychologists shows that only about 25 percent of young men say they want multiple short-term partners; 75 percent say they want no more than one partner in the next thirty days.[11] If Casanova-style promiscuity is men's *naturally evolved* state, then why do *most* men want no more than one partner? I'll detail some of the other problems with this approach in Chapter Four. I'll also talk about attachment theory, an evolutionary theory, which argues that male (and female) *Homo sapiens* instinctively seek a single, long-term partner to whom they become very deeply connected.

Or perhaps all this sexual promiscuity is due to boys' trying to prove their masculinity. Globally and historically, boys have had to prove their masculinity in order to be recognized as adults in their society. In those times and places, boys proved their masculinity to the adult males in their community, but now it's other teenage boys and young men who stand in judgment of a guy's "masculinity."[12] If one's friends value promiscuity, then they'll encourage and reward a young man who sleeps around. I'll explore the interactions between proving masculinity, friendship, and self-concept in Chapter Five.

We all know "educational" TV programming can teach us things we don't know, but our kids are influenced a great deal by sitcoms and other shows that address dating relationships and sexual behavior. These shows are also "educational" and highly influential, especially for people who have little or no firsthand experience, such as teens. In Chapter Six, I'll provide an overview of the media's representations of young men's sexuality and how those have changed over the last forty years or so. I'll also give some detail about how and why the media influences us, both positively and negatively.

Over the last few decades, guys have also become more focused on their appearance. And why not? Most of today's male models have six-pack abs, setting a standard many young men think they need to live up to. Convincing guys they'll get laid if they just use the right products or wear the right clothing is a favorite tactic among advertisers, and in many cases—Axe deodorant, Irish Spring, beer commercials—the successful guy gets more than one girl. In Chapter

Seven, I'll talk about how the pressure on guys to look good has increased over the last few decades and how our image of the ideal male body has changed. Although the pressure for guys to be built and to look good isn't quite as intense as the pressure girls face to achieve the so-called thin ideal, many of the same factors are at work.

In Part Three, I'll talk about things that we as parents, teachers, and other members of society can do, starting today, to challenge Casanova. Chapter Eight discusses three other approaches teenage boys and young men adopt in their dating and sexual relationships. These approaches differ from the Casanova Complex in that these boys are thinking about and "doing" dating and sex in a different way. Romantic men, for example, strongly prefer their sexual activities to be with a dating partner. They rarely hook up, and when they do, it's usually with someone they already know, not a stranger. Religious men believe that sex is sacred and reserved for married couples, and they act that way. "Emo" guys are somewhere between Casanovas and romantics. They hook up at fairly high rates, but their hookups typically consist of making out, not sex, and typically occur with people they already know and are interested in dating. And all of these approaches are adopted by both straight and gay men. By recognizing and promoting that these are common and desirable ways for guys to behave, we can challenge the dominance of the Casanova Complex.

Extracting a theme from that chapter, I'll talk in Chapter Nine about the importance of meaning—the values we develop during adolescence and how they shape our behavior. The research on adolescent sexuality, and much of the research on parenting, tells us that parents who talk about, explain, and live out their values are most likely to produce children who have similar values.[13] They're also less likely to have teenage sons who have sex, are promiscuous, get an STI, or get a girl pregnant.[14] This research demonstrates that it's vital that parents talk to their sons about dating and sex, and do more than have just a one-time "Talk." Teenage boys and young men need to have accurate knowledge about sex, even if it's embarrassing to talk about with Dad or Mom. I'll help by giving some suggestions about what to talk about, and how to do it, in Chapter Nine. I'll also mention some things you can leave out of the conversation.

Knowledge about relationships is very important, and even though we often don't discuss this subject with boys, it's the focus of Chapter Ten. After all, many of the dynamics important in dating and sexual relationships—trust, honesty, long-term perspective, balance, sharing—are things that boys experience in their friendships, with their family members, and probably also with their teammates and coworkers.

Finally, in Chapter Eleven, I'll talk about how we can respond to the media and other large-scale cultural phenomena. In the 1970s, women's groups were able to change the way that lawmakers, employers, television executives, and the general public thought about women. We can use some of those same strategies to change the way that people think about the sex lives of young men. Of course, we also have the Internet. We can develop new content (Web sites, videos) and use a variety of networking tools to help get the word out.

Throughout the book, I've included quotations from some of the boys and young men I've interviewed over the years. Their names—and the names of the people they talk about—have all been changed to protect everyone's anonymity. You should also know that the research was conducted under the supervision of the Institutional Review Board of the university with which I was associated when I conducted the research.

I hope that *Challenging Casanova* will help you look beyond the stereotype of promiscuous male sexuality by providing information you don't already have, reminding you of things you already know, and, most important, giving you a new way to think about young men's sexuality. I won't overwhelm you with facts and figures, but I will include some essential information. I hope the result will be a greater understanding of boys' sexuality and the influences upon it.

Part I

Approaches to Boys' Sexual Development

1

The Casanova Complex and
Its Inaccuracies

A lex* (not his real name) was a college senior when he agreed to be interviewed for my study of young men's sexual lives. About a year earlier, he'd completed a paper-and-pencil survey on the same topic. On that survey, he said that he'd had sex with four girlfriends and that he'd had hookup sex with about twenty other girls and young women. I asked him to tell me about his most recent hookup; he told me a story from three months earlier.

> It happened during winter break. A couple buddies and I rented a cabin at a ski lodge and were up there for about a week. There was one night when we had a party. Some of the guys were there with girlfriends, but I wasn't seeing anyone at the time. We also invited some girls that we'd met while we were there.
>
> I started talking to this one girl, Jess, and it was going pretty well. We'd both had a lot to drink. At some point, I asked if she wanted to go some place quieter to talk. She said OK, and we went back to my room. I guess we didn't really talk very much at that point, maybe five or ten minutes. Then we started making out, and eventually we had sex.

*All interviewee's names, and the names of those they talk about, have been changed to protect everyone's anonymity.

We fell asleep together, and when I woke up, Jess was gone. I never saw her again. But we both knew that this would be a one-time thing. I was fine with that, and she was too.

I asked him why he chose Jess; she wasn't the only girl in the room, after all. Alex told me there was no particular reason he picked Jess, that it was really serendipity—he happened to have been talking to her earlier while waiting to get another drink, and the conversation seemed to go well. He couldn't remember what they'd talked about, but he was sure it was along the lines of small talk—favorite bands, college likes and dislikes, possibly college football, because her school might have been in a bowl game. Whatever it was, the conversation was easy enough. That was it. It wasn't because Jess was hot or had been dancing suggestively or had been flirting with him all night. It was just because they happened to have started a conversation that went smoothly, and (Alex believed) Jess understood that this would be a one-time thing.

Alex never knew Jess's last name and never asked for her cell number, email address, screen name, or any other contact information. She didn't ask him either.

I've heard similar stories from many guys over the years. Most of those guys were looking for a girl to hook up with, but some were looking for another guy. The stories all share the same basic features: a bar or party with alcohol and possibly other drugs, an intention to spend just one night of being together, and little effort to get to know the other person or his or her sexual history.

When I think of someone like Alex, I sometimes think about famous—or infamous—men like Rep. Anthony Weiner and golfer Tiger Woods. They were both married and had children, yet they kept sleeping with people who weren't their legally wedded wives. It was almost as though they just couldn't stop having sex with new people. Retired NBA players Magic Johnson and Wilt Chamberlain each claimed to have slept with hundreds, if not thousands, of women.

Maybe that's what you think all guys are like. Reports like these contribute to the widespread belief that guys just want to have sex and don't care about relationships. In other words, "Men are dogs."

Alex's hooking up (in current slang) or casual sex or having a one-night stand is not uncommon, and it's what many people expect guys to do.[1] In American culture, we are often encouraged to believe that guys think about sex all the time. According to popular culture, it's every seven seconds. Or maybe you heard the recent report that half of young men think about sex at least nineteen times per day?[2] That's a lot less often than every seven seconds, but it still sounds like a lot.

Likewise, you may "know" that boys are always horny and that they don't care much whom they have sex with—although we think they have a real preference for good-looking or "hot" girls. We think that guys "make the moves" and start all sexual encounters, from kissing through coitus, and we're not entirely sure they'll stop when a girl says no. Sometimes we even joke that teenage boys get a hard-on every time the wind blows. And many people believe that guys really aren't interested in relationships.

Our cultural beliefs also tell us that boys and young men aren't concerned about the consequences of hooking up and that they'll take some pretty substantial risks in order to do so. This perception of young men is the central idea behind a subgenre of movies known as sex comedies. You may recognize some of the titles: *Porky's* (1982), *American Pie* (1999), and *Superbad* (2007). There's also the directly titled *Sex Drive* (2008). The common story line is about a boy or a group of boys who want or "need" to get laid. The boy or boys usually aren't cool or popular.

Alex could be called a player (in current slang) or a Casanova, stud, Don Juan, or a variety of other names. Whatever you call him, he certainly fits some of the prevalent expectations about young men's sexual behavior. And he's often looked up to by other guys; Joe, a college junior, told me that he was "impressed [by players] because they know how to play the game."

But let's take a step back and view this from a different angle. Many Americans believe that boys and young men—especially those between about fifteen and twenty-five years old—are primarily, if not exclusively, interested only in this kind of hookup behavior. Let me say that again: we think this is *normal*. When we act as though this is normal, we may very well be creating a self-fulfilling prophecy. Just before I started writing this book, my wife and I were shopping for our infant daughter at a national retail store. I noticed a blue bib that said "Chick Magnet." Do we really want our baby boys to wear this message?

The Casanova Complex

In *The Casanova Complex,* Peter Trachtenberg analyzed fifty men whom he referred to as "compulsive lovers."[3] He defined the complex as the "compulsive pursuit and abandonment of women" and said these men were able to have so many sexual partners because they were good at seduction, not because they were physically attractive or had lots of money. Following Freud, Trachtenberg traced the cause back to Mom and Dad.

I'm going to expand this definition of the Casanova Complex by tapping into Deborah David and Robert Brannon's 1976 description of the "Jet Set Playboy" as someone who is "usually sighted in expensive restaurants or fast convertibles, accompanied by a beautiful woman (whom he's ignoring)."[4] When asked to describe the stereotype of a player, the current version of the term, undergraduates say players are attractive, flattering, flirty, self-centered, well groomed and well dressed (in a casual style), involved in their college's social scene, and not expected to be known for their academic prowess.[5] David and Brannon also described the "Don Juan" as smoldering and irresistible to women, but this seems to be the only use of this term in the research literature.

In an early stage of my dissertation work, I asked 106 university undergraduates to provide a brief description of "players" and "Don Juans," among other terms.[6] Both were described as being interested in women, being physically attractive, attending parties, and drinking alcohol regularly. Players, much more so than Don Juans, were seen as using women, as focused on status (financial or social), as jerks, as not-nice, as self-centered, and as loudmouths. Students indicated that *Playboy* founder Hugh Hefner was a good example of a player, as were various rap performers who were popular at the time. Of course, this was still a study about stereotypes and expectations.

I've also asked people how much they see themselves as a player, using a 1–4 scale where 1 meant "not at all like me" and 4 meant "very much like me." "Player" was included in a list of ten to twelve terms; other terms in the list included "airhead," "jock," "prince/princess," "nerd," and "rebel." In a series of studies, I posed this question to the 2006, 2007, and 2008 senior classes of a rural northeastern high school, under the supervision of my Institutional Review Board. (The high school's name will remain confidential.)

The more strongly a guy saw himself as a player, the younger he was when he had his first sexual experience and the more people he'd had sex with. Not surprisingly, players averaged more sexual partners per year. Further, the more strongly a guy saw himself as a player, the younger he was when he started dating, the more dating partners he'd had overall, and the more dating partners he had each year.

But being a player is also about a set of beliefs, not just a set of dating and sexual behaviors. Not surprisingly, self-described players were more accepting of sexual promiscuity. They also described themselves as competitive, taking risks, and, to a lesser extent, making sure others know they're heterosexual. One would think that the last point wouldn't have been an issue for the handful of gay youth in the study, although it's possible some of them weren't comfortable with their sexual orientation and therefore slept with a number of girls in order to "prove" they were straight. Self-described players were also more sexist. In some ways, you might consider players to be more stereotypically masculine.

Self-described players don't see themselves only as players. They also identified themselves as "jocks," "populars," "princes," "toughs," "criminals," and "rebels." They were explicitly not "loners" or "nerds." The first three—jock, popular, and prince—tell us something about self-presentation and social status. Players see themselves as having high social status, and it may be part and parcel of being a jock, popular, or prince. They're certainly not in the categories that don't have status: loner or nerd. Being a player might tap into a "bad boy" image and thus coexists with being a tough, a criminal, or a rebel. Although adults may see these kinds of identities negatively, they play well and provide a different form of status during adolescence.[7] I'll talk more about status and these kinds of identities in Chapter Five.

School isn't exactly for players. Or, more specifically, academics aren't for players. They tended to have somewhat lower GPAs than others and were less likely to be members of academically oriented extracurricular activities, such as math club. At the same time, they were more likely to be members of sports teams or to participate in service activities such as student council; these activity choices line up nicely with some of those other identities, such as that of jock or popular. Players' nonacademic focus doesn't seem to hurt their subsequent goals; there was no connection between seeing oneself as a player and a guy's future academic goals.

There was no connection between being religious and being a player. It would be nice to think that players weren't religious and non-players were, but that wasn't the case. It's also possible that there wasn't a clear connection because players were wrestling with their beliefs in the same way the real Casanova described in his memoirs; he alternated between a desire to be devout and a sense of himself as someone above conventional morality.[8] The reality is that these high school students didn't see themselves as particularly religious. As a group, they averaged just over 2 on a 1–5 scale where 1 was "not at all" religious and 5 was "very" religious.

This pattern of results isn't unique to high school students. Among almost 350 men ages eighteen to eighty-three who participated in the main part of my dissertation work, men ages eighteen to twenty-nine who described themselves as players were more likely than non-players to think that having multiple sexual partners was a good—or at least acceptable—thing.[9] Players also said they'd had more sexual partners overall and averaged more partners per year. In fact, about half of self-described players averaged more than one sexual partner per year compared to about 20 percent of non-players.[10]

Adult players also reported holding a number of other attitudes. Most prominent among these was a set of sexist beliefs, as well as a strong desire to be dominant in general. In addition, they believed in taking risks, were somewhat more competitive than others, and placed greater emphasis on being seen as heterosexual. In many ways, the teenage boys and adult men offered very similar profiles of what it means to be a player.

The Casanova Complex and American Culture

The Casanova Complex is a culturally based image that says guys just want promiscuous sex, not relationships, and that almost any behavior, no matter how rude, crude, risky, or destructive, is OK if it'll get him laid. The Casanova Complex includes a set of beliefs that support, justify, and explain the image. Together, the image and the beliefs create and describe a set of expectations about male behavior, as well as a backstory that explains why Casanova-like behavior exists. There are many different pieces of the backstory, and you might believe or accept some of them but not others.

Following Trachtenberg, I'll also use the Casanova Complex to refer to boys and men who are trying to live up to this image. In that way, it parallels such terms as "inferiority complex" or "Napoleon complex."

As a cultural phenomenon, the Casanova Complex requires that most people approve of hooking up, or at least don't disapprove. It doesn't matter if we call it a one-night stand or casual sex or friends with benefits or some other name; what's important is that the general public is on some level OK with this behavior and views it as normal or typical. Indeed, many Americans, perhaps most, will tell you that they're OK with premarital sex and even hooking up. At least that's what the majority of adolescents and undergraduates tell us, and that sentiment has become increasingly common since the 1970s. Some people have begun to describe college as being dominated by a "hookup culture."[11]

At the cultural level, we've learned to love at least some Casanovas. If you watch television programs from the 1950s and 1960s, Casanova-like behavior was rarely present, and when it was, it was limited to the bad guys—the characters you weren't supposed to like or from whom you were supposed to learn lessons about improper behavior. But that seems to have started to change in the 1970s, and two of the biggest "change agents" were named Arthur Fonzarelli and Benjamin Franklin "Hawkeye" Pierce. Both characters were among the most popular of their time.[12]

Set in the 1950s, *Happy Days* aired from 1974 through 1985. From 1976 through 1980, it was a perennial top 20 show. The plots originally focused on clean-cut Richie Cunningham. Fonzie started as a minor character; a greaser with a bad reputation, he was sometimes used as a bad example. The character was very popular from the beginning, and when Ron Howard decided to leave the show at the end of the sixth season (and Richie was sent away to college and then the army), the Fonz became the star. Already somewhat cleansed of his greaser ways by that time, Fonzie got his GED, became a small business owner (motorcycle repair, of course), then a high school teacher and, eventually, dean of boys. We also discovered that he had a heart of gold; he helped straighten out his wayward nephew, Spike, and then took in his cousin Chachi.[13] In other words, he went from bad-example delinquent to reclaimed and lovable stepson who fit reasonably well into a 1950s white-bread family. And no matter what his status, the girls and women on the show were always attracted to the Fonz, who could get whomever he wanted by standing next to the jukebox and banging on it in his trademarked fashion.

Across the dial and on a different night, wise-cracking Hawkeye Pierce slept with about half the nurses serving in Korea. MASH was produced from 1972 to 1983 and was a top 20 show almost every year it aired. The final episode was watched by an incredible 77 percent of all viewers the night it aired. A doctor, Hawkeye repeatedly flaunted the directions of his head surgeon (Major Burns) and followed just enough of the rules to avoid getting in trouble with either of his commanding officers, Lt. Colonel Henry Blake or Colonel Sherman T. Potter. A nice guy and very intelligent, Hawkeye repeatedly questioned orders and challenged the U.S. purpose for being in Korea, paralleling cultural events regarding Vietnam.[14] And no matter what else was happening on screen, Hawkeye could always get laid.

Hawkeye and the Fonz showed us that you could sleep with a lot of women and (almost) everyone would still like and admire you. To kids, teens, and young adults in the late 1970s and early 1980s, Fonzie defined cool. To all of us, laid-back Hawkeye said it's not just the macho guys who can get the girls. More important, we'd gone from "promiscuous characters are bad" to "good guys can be promiscuous too."

The cultural change isn't due just to TV, of course. These shows tapped into and played off messages from the so-called sexual revolution of the 1960s. The TV shows were important because they reached a mass audience. I'll give more details on the importance of mass media in Chapter Six, but when you think about the 1960s, you may remember that not everyone supported the revolution. The people who expressed their disapproval of "long-haired hippy freaks" weren't in favor of things like "free love." Yet Fonzie and Hawkeye were the central characters on the most popular TV shows of their time and dominated the ratings. While the Fonz taught the kids that promiscuity was cool, Hawkeye spoke to the adults, including those adults who'd served in Korea and many folks who disapproved of the hippies and their counterculture. In the days before cable TV, VCRs, and ubiquitous reruns, we made time to invite these guys into our living rooms every week; their portrayals of casual sex were witnessed and approved by a broad swath of American households.

Today, you can find shows like *The Pickup Artist* on VH1. On the show, "best-selling author and ultimate pick-up artist" Mystery (real name: Erik von Markovik), along with his assistants Matador and J-Dog, teach young men on the show how to woo and seduce women. In this so-called reality show, the winner gains the title of Master Pickup Artist.

Pickup artistry isn't limited to TV. There's a pickup artist (PUA) community that consists of thousands of Web sites. There are several well-known gurus, guys like VH1's Mystery, who provide coaching, write books, and run "boot camps." There are even conventions. The most popular gurus may make over a million dollars per year.[15]

Who Was Casanova?

There is no doubt that a man named Giacomo Casanova lived during the eighteenth century, and most historians agree that his published memoirs seem to be mostly factual. In his memoirs, Casanova reported having 116 distinct sexual partners over a forty-year span, or about three partners per year. Reviewers are clear that some of these were likely fabricated, possibly to shock readers of the day and possibly to help maintain the confidentiality of some of those who aren't specifically named.[16] Biographer John Masters observed that Casanova didn't report any homosexual behavior and speculated that, given his sexual appetites and desire for at least some novel sexual experiences, this seems unlikely. Some have suspected that Casanova's public promiscuity was a cover for his same-sex preferences, a pattern called "Don Juan-ism" in the 1950s and 1960s.[17]

Casanova's memoirs also make clear that he didn't sleep with just anyone he came across. He explicitly appears to have avoided women he thought might "trap" him into marriage, and he didn't try to seduce women who were clearly "out of his league"—those who were rich or very beautiful. Although he did engage in some sexual risk-taking—he slept with several married women, and some of his encounters occurred in public spaces—he was very careful about which risks to take.[18]

We also learn about other aspects of Casanova's character from his memoirs. He comes off as something of a spendthrift and never amasses a fortune of his own, but at the same time, he's not poor, and he travels frequently. He routinely spent money on the women he was wooing, and he also gave freely to others, including his brother. He was quite intelligent: he spoke several languages and was able to maintain a reasonable knowledge of political and economic conditions in the days before there was a twenty-four-hour news cycle or an official currency exchange rate.[19]

Casanova's biographers consistently comment on his morality, taking their cue from his writings on the topic. Casanova saw himself as above conventional morality, thus allowing his sexual adventures. He also described himself as Christian (or Catholic, using current distinctions), and repeatedly seemed to be struggling to reconcile his faith with his promiscuous behavior.[20]

The Casanova of the memoirs sounds a lot like the self-described players from my surveys. There's nonrelational (hookup) sex, of course, as well as some risk-taking. Casanova was popular, or at least well-connected, and he was reasonably smart.

Research on Promiscuous Youth

The federal government has been funding research on adolescent sexual behavior since the 1960s, primarily to find ways to prevent teen pregnancy and prevent the spread of HIV/AIDS.[21] It's fairly uncommon for a teenage boy or young man to get someone pregnant or get a sexually transmitted infection (STI).[22] Almost one-third of young men become fathers by age twenty-six, and about one-third of those pregnancies were probably unplanned.[23] Between 5 and 10 percent of eighteen- to twenty-nine-year olds, about nine million people, will contract a new STI in any given year; this age group accounts for almost half of all new STIs.[24] Although those totals include a lot of people, most research studies include only a few hundred participants at most, which means that the typical study has only a small number of people who had an unplanned pregnancy or an STI. As a result, researchers have often focused on three other sexual behaviors that are more common and are also good predictors of pregnancy and disease: (1) having multiple partners, (2) poor or inconsistent use, or nonuse, of protection, especially condoms, and (3) first experience of intercourse at age fifteen or younger.

When you read these studies, you learn that the problem is largely due to the behavior of the kids we'd expect to be causing the problem: kids from low-socioeconomic-status households, children of divorced or single parents, kids who live in urban areas, kids who are black and possibly kids who are Hispanic, kids who hit puberty earlier, and kids who appear older.[25] These factors are all associated with greater odds of being promiscuous, but there's nothing about any of these things that explains why some kids who fit into these categories are promiscuous and others aren't.

The research also tells us that these kids tend to have poor-quality relationships with their parents, don't do well in school, are more likely to drop out before completing high school, don't have good-quality relationships with teachers or other school officials, are more likely to be delinquent, and are more likely to have delinquent friends. They're also more likely to drink alcohol and use other illicit drugs and are more likely to have been arrested.[26] But for many of these factors, it's not clear which comes first—the behaviors or the promiscuity.

Although these findings may—or may not—fit with your conception of who the "bad kids" are, they don't give us a complete picture of which kids get pregnant in high school. We've all heard stories about otherwise nice, respectable, white teenage girls who get pregnant by their nice, respectable boyfriends. Some of these girls—and boys—carry their or their partner's pregnancies responsibly, but there are plenty of stories of teenage girls who hide their pregnancies and then deliver the child on their own in the school bathroom. Your image of the bad kids probably doesn't include the nice, white, middle-class Gloucester, Massachusetts, high school girls who made a pregnancy pact in 2008, either.[27]

We need a different, more complete explanation, and the Casanova Complex helps do that. Not all Casanovas are "bad kids," after all.[28] If you found out that the quarterback of your high school's football team had sex with a different girl before every game last season, would you be surprised? Would you start thinking of him as a bad kid? Or would you smile and think "Atta boy"? In any case, he's doing the same thing those so-called bad kids are doing, and the odds that he'll get someone pregnant or get a disease don't change just because he's the quarterback.

Casanova as Part of the Teen and Early Adult Years

Living up to the Casanova Complex may well be an age-related phenomenon. Although we may accept this behavior in teenage boys and young adult men, we tend to look askance at forty-year-olds who are doing it. In *Guyland*, Michael Kimmel points to demographic changes indicating that the transition from adolescence to adulthood now averages about ten years, bookended by high school graduation at eighteen and first marriage in the mid- to late twenties.[29] He argues that during this transitional time, and in a variety of ways, we encourage guys to be Casanovas.

Take David, for example. His last relationship ended early in his senior year of college. I interviewed him in the spring, about three months before graduation. He knew he'd be moving at the end of the school year, and after his breakup, he decided that a relationship "wasn't going to be worthwhile finishing, so I haven't dated seriously." His explanation was straightforward: he didn't want to make decisions about a first job or where he'd be moving after college because of a relationship that probably wouldn't lead to marriage. So he intentionally didn't date. But he did hook up.

Earlier, I mentioned a study I conducted in which I asked approximately 350 men, ages 18 to 83, how strongly they identified themselves as players. There were 142 undergraduates ages 18 to 23 and another 65 young men ages 18 to 29 who were not currently in college. Among the young men, 12 percent of the undergraduates and 11 percent of the others described themselves as a player at least some of the time. For the 60 men ages 30 to 49 and the 70 men ages 50 and older, the percentage of self-identified players fell to 7 percent and 3 percent, respectively.[30] To me, those numbers say that adhering to the Casanova Complex is mostly relevant for guys under thirty.

Because my focus is on younger guys, I'll spend very little time talking about marriage in this book. But I will tell you that among the 350 men in this study, adults who described themselves as players reported fewer marriages than non-players. Players and non-players reported about the same number of divorces.

Casanova's Problems

As long as guys like Alex are finding willing partners and nobody's in a monogamous relationship, what's the problem? For some, sex with strangers sounds like fun.

On some levels, there may not be a problem, especially if everyone really is being honest about what he or she wants and about what else is going on in his or her life, and if Casanova and his partner truly have equal say.

Yet there are costs, for Alex and his partners and also for you and me. Some of these, like unplanned pregnancies and STIs, are fairly obvious. The research tells us that Casanovas are less likely than other guys to use condoms,[31] which means they're regularly at risk of catching or passing on an STI. In the year 2000, approximately nine million Americans aged eighteen to twenty-nine contracted an STI, with an estimated direct cost of at least $6.5 billion (in the year 2000).[32] As you might expect, the odds of contracting an STI increase with each new partner; one study reported that 27 percent of men who'd had eleven to twenty partners since age eighteen, and 37 percent of men who'd had twenty-one or more partners, knew they'd contracted an STI at some point.[33] This means that even though only a minority of young men contract STIs, Casanovas are among those at greatest risk for doing so.

If these young men aren't using condoms and if their female partners aren't using contraception correctly, then these guys are also running the risk of getting their partners pregnant. According to a 2004 World Health Organization report, the United States had sixty pregnancies for every thousand female teenagers, the highest rate of teenage pregnancies of any industrialized or postindustrialized nation.[34] The WHO used figures from 1998, not quite ten years after the fall of the Berlin Wall. We were doing worse than every country in Europe, including the countries that had been behind the Iron Curtain. We were worse than the average of fifty-six pregnancies per thousand girls among the countries of the Middle East and North Africa and of the East Asia–South Asia–Pacific region. In fact, our rates of teen pregnancy were so high that if the United States were in sub-Saharan Africa, a region wracked by poverty, numerous wars during the last hundred years, and poor development, we'd be only third best.

Those unwanted pregnancies have long-term financial costs for us as a nation. When a teenage girl gets pregnant, the likelihood that she'll graduate from high school drops substantially,[35] especially if she's not yet in her senior year. If a teenage boy is the father of that child, the odds that he'll finish high school also plummet dramatically, whether the boy intends to help raise the child or not.[36] Over the last thirty years, one of the best indicators that someone will end up on welfare or in prison is whether he or she completes high school by age twenty. Regardless of your moral stance, your tax dollars pay the costs of those welfare checks and that jail.

There's also a loss of human capital. As a nation, we tend not to look kindly on teenage parents. They're not particularly likely to graduate from high school, and many never get their GED. Without that, it's very difficult to get a job, which means it's difficult to become a "productive" member of society. What might those people have contributed to society if they had waited even two years before becoming pregnant?

Some costs are less obvious, such as those related to development and personal growth. What happens if you're a guy and everyone keeps saying you should have sex with lots of girls, but you don't think that's right, or you prefer other guys? Do you start to feel as though you're not normal? Do you change your image so that people think you're sleeping around? Do you take other risks, like the guys from the TV show and movie *Jackass*, in order to prove that you're "the Man" so that everyone will ignore the fact that you're not screwing a different girl every week?

Several gay athletes told sociologist Michael Messner that part of the reason they pushed themselves to excel at sports during high school was to gain some protection against charges of homosexuality.[37] After all, when those guys were growing up in the 1970s and 1980s, "everyone knew" you couldn't be gay and be good at sports.

Teaching people that all or most guys are Casanovas also has bad implications for women, and not just the women who sleep with these guys. One problem is that you can't sleep with a horde of strangers (or try to) and genuinely respect them. Again, the research tells us that adolescent boys and undergraduate young men who demonstrate or believe in Casanova-like promiscuity tend to be more sexist and to have a lower opinion of women in general than other guys.[38] Although sexism isn't the only factor or even the biggest factor, research shows that it contributes to the idea that sexual assault and rape may be justified if the girl was provocatively dressed or "leading the guy on."[39] However, these results coexist alongside data indicating that the average college male has become less sexist over the last few decades,[40] one of many contradictions between the stereotype and the reality of young men and their sexuality.

Further, when we teach girls and women that all guys are Casanovas and only interested in sex, we encourage girls to develop what researcher Deborah Tolman calls a "defensive sexuality."[41] This means we teach girls that sex is about saying yes or no instead of teaching them that sexuality should be about their own desires and pleasure. In other words, we teach girls to ignore their own desires in order to keep boys' sexual desires in check.

By teaching girls that all guys are Casanovas, we mislead girls into thinking that there are few "good" guys who will be monogamous. There's little doubt that young men are more likely to cheat on their partners than are young women,[42] and guys who adhere to the Casanova Complex are the ones who are most likely to cheat.[43] But when we behave as though *all* boys and young men are Casanovas, we're teaching the girls the wrong odds.

The idea that male sexual desire is powerful, ever present, and barely controlled has been a part of American culture for at least two centuries.[44] Taken to the extreme, it contributes to the possibility that *any* guy could be a rapist, child molester, or some other type of sexual predator. On some levels, that's absurd; we know that very few guys commit sexual crimes. Yet if we believe that male sexual desire is just that common and that powerful, then the idea that *any guy* could be a rapist or a child molester does seem to make sense.

The idea that "any guy could do that" appears in various elements of our culture. Fear of sexual molestation was used against African Americans during the Jim Crow and civil rights eras.[45] Similar claims have been made about gay men raping straight men in the last few decades.[46] When the Riverview Center, a rape crisis center, ran a video campaign against child sexual abuse under the title "It Could Be Him" a few years ago, the ad was criticized for tapping into this belief.

How Many Guys Are Promiscuous?

Alex, whose story opened the chapter, reported that he'd had twenty-four partners (twenty in hookups, four in relationships), and he was only twenty-one years old. It's possible that he'll continue to behave in this manner and have more than a hundred partners by the time he reaches fifty. But it's also possible that he'll "settle down" and have one partner for most of that time and have "only" twenty-five partners in his lifetime.

Alex is hardly unique or exceptional. Since 1991, the federal government has surveyed approximately fifteen thousand high school students, grades 9 to 12, every other year, to get a sense of the risky behavior they're engaging in. The Youth Risk Behavior Survey (YRBS) asks adolescents to report on a variety of things adults don't want them to do, most notably using alcohol and drugs. The YRBS also asks a variety of questions about sexual behavior and sex education, including age of first sex and total number of sexual partners. For number of partners, the possible responses are zero, one, two, three, and four or more. Over the last twenty years, the percentage of twelfth-grade boys who said they'd had four or more total partners has ranged from about 21 percent, or one boy in five (in 1995 and 1999), to as high as 31 percent, or nearly one boy in three (in 1993). In 2009, it was about 23 percent, or almost exactly two boys in nine.[47]

The YRBS statistics are the highest percentages I'll give you, but I think they're overestimates. Many guys have sex for the first time around age sixteen, as I'll discuss in Chapter Two, so that'd be his first partner. If he has another partner at seventeen and two more at eighteen, that's four partners. But it doesn't sound as though he's trying to get in bed with every girl he meets.

A better estimate of the number of guys who adhere to the Casanova Complex comes from the research team of Daniel Offer, Marjorie Kaiz Offer, and Eric Ostrove.[48] In *Regular Guys: 34 Years Beyond Adolescence*, they described a group of guys born between 1946 and 1949. Looking at men who had originally been part of a large study of high school students, the research team identified a group who were statistically average during high school. The researchers talked to them four years after the original survey, and again thirty-four years after that original survey. At middle age, 3 percent said they'd had one hundred or more sexual partners; those are our Casanovas.

Another 13 percent claimed to have twenty-one to ninety-nine partners, and it's less clear if they're Casanovas, in part because there's a vast difference between twenty-one and ninety-nine partners. Think about it this way: if your first sexual experience was at age eighteen and you're being asked about the last thirty-four years of your life, having a hundred partners means you've averaged three partners per year, about the same as Casanova claimed in his memoirs. If you've had twenty-one partners in that time period, you've averaged almost two partners in any given three-year span. Although two partners in three years add up to twenty partners over three-and-a-half decades, it doesn't mean you had a new partner every week, and it may mean that every partner is part of a yearlong relationship. That's not exactly in keeping with the Casanova Complex or our stereotype of young men's sexual behavior.

Those studies are all focused on the total number of partners a guy has had in his lifetime. Casanovas are expected to have multiple partners in any given year, if not at the same time. Estimates vary somewhat, but between 5 and 15 percent of young men report they've had four or more partners in the last year.[49] Most guys don't sustain that pace, but some clearly do. About 3 to 5 percent of young men averaged four or more partners per year over a four-year span.[50]

By reputation, Casanovas are expected to cheat on their partners. This "extradyadic" sex—that is, having simultaneous or concurrent partners—is more common among those who consistently have five or more partners per year. Not surprisingly, as the number of partners per year increases, so do the odds that the guy will have extradyadic intercourse. These guys also have the longest stretches of time with multiple partners.[51]

As you can see, it's only a minority of guys who really follow the dictates of the Casanova Complex. Offer et al. reported that 12 percent of their middle-aged men said they'd had exactly one sexual partner in their life, and another 33 percent said they'd had two to four partners.[52] Together, that's 45 percent of middle-aged men who can count their sexual partners on one hand. That's about three times more than the number of Casanovas and nearly half the sample. Researchers who study promiscuous guys consistently note that the majority of guys have only a small number of partners in any given year, usually zero, one, or two, and that the majority of guys have only one sexual partner at a time.[53] As Edward Laumann, John Gagnon, Robert Michael, and Stuart Michaels, authors of The Social Organization of Sexuality, note, "The vast majority of men and women report that they are monogamous while married or living with a partner. Over 90 percent of women and over 75 percent of the men report[ed] fidelity within their marriage, over its entirety."[54]

Even on VH1's *The Pickup Artist*, the "students" talk about wanting to learn how to talk to girls, and their goals are to start dating and have relationships. That's right—the guys trying to earn the title Master Pickup Artist are really trying to find girlfriends.

You also see that pattern among the young men, and not-so-young men, who make up most of the PUA community. Mark Manson, one of the biggest names on that circuit, estimates that only about 10 percent of the guys who attend workshops, buy books, and appear on discussion boards are interested in being Casanovas. The majority, about 75 percent or so, are guys looking for girlfriends (and possibly wives) and have little or no experience or success in dating.[55]

As you can see, the Casanova Complex describes only a minority of men. In any given year, that might be as much as 15 percent, but when we look at men's behavior over a period of several years, we see that Casanova-like promiscuity drops to no more than 5 percent of the population. This means that Casanova-like promiscuity is in fact not the norm and does not reflect the way most boys or young men really feel.[56] Throughout the book, I'll provide you with a variety of perspectives to help you understand and think about the reality of young men's sexuality. When we develop sex education curricula based on the assumption that Casanova is the norm and when we act as though Casanova is the reality for all boys and men, we're giving our kids incorrect information.[57] That's irresponsible behavior by the adults.

We as a nation haven't always approved of young men's promiscuity. If we've changed our expectations once, to promote the Casanova Complex, we can change our expectations again. And change means *change*; it doesn't mean going back to the 1950s. We can return to emphasizing responsibility, honesty, caring, and respect as male traits without sending women back home to care for the house and family. And we can do this while holding onto such "traditional" male values as independence, loyalty, and hard work.

2

. . . .

Sexual Behavior During Adolescence

Before you read any further, let me ask you a question: What do you think qualifies as "normal" teenage sexual behavior?

When I ask people this question, there are some common answers. Crushes, the first kiss, and the first date or relationship always make the list. Prom and "the Talk" are also common answers. "Petting" or "groping" or something else that means fondling a girl's breasts usually gets mentioned. The first experience with sexual intercourse may or may not be included; that depends a lot on who's in the audience. People don't usually mention Spin the Bottle and other kissing games, but if I suggest it, most nod in agreement. Oral sex may be on the list, and when I ask for details, people usually admit that they think blow jobs are fairly common and cunnilingus is rare. Masturbation may also make the list, but that tends to be our expectation of boys but not girls. Anal sex, pregnancy, and sexually transmitted infections (STIs) rarely get mentioned.

Marriage and getting engaged aren't common answers, but once upon a time, they may have been. Through the 1950s and 1960s, the median age of first marriage for American men was around twenty-two or twenty-three, and around twenty for women. This means that a lot of folks were getting engaged and married in their teens. Today, the median age for first marriage is about twenty-seven for men and twenty-six for women.[1] This older age at first marriage may help explain why approximately 90 percent of people have sex before they're married.[2] At the same time, chastity became less valuable and desirable in a marital partner during the twentieth century.[3]

In this chapter, I'm going to talk about sexual development as it occurs for most boys. Understanding what's typical—what most boys do—will help clarify how much the Casanova Complex distorts our thinking about boys' sexuality.

The Standard Markers

Most people expect adolescents to follow a particular pattern of sexual firsts: first kiss, then fondling of (female) breasts, followed by touching below the waist, and then intercourse. Adolescents also expect this sequence of behaviors.[4] When I was growing up, we boys used a baseball metaphor; each of these steps was a base, and sex was a home run or scoring a run. This metaphor was sufficiently well known to show up in popular media, perhaps most notably Meatloaf's "Paradise by the Dashboard Lights," in which the baseball announcer tells us what's happening in the backseat of the car.

I'm going to start here as well. The Casanova Complex tells us that the important part of sexuality is getting laid and having more partners than other guys. And if there's one thing the baseball metaphor is especially good at, it's keeping score.

Kissing (First Base)

Most guys have their first real kiss in early adolescence. By "real," I mean that it's occurring with someone who is considered to be a girlfriend or boyfriend, at least for a few hours.[5] You might also call it a French kiss or tongue kissing or something of the sort. My favorite expression is "tonsil hockey."

Estimates can vary quite a bit, but it seems reasonable to assume that about two-thirds of fifteen-year-olds have had their first kiss.[6] About 90 percent of undergraduates, if not more, tell us they've had at least one such kiss, typically around age fourteen or fifteen.[7]

It's a little different for guys who are attracted to other guys. Although some of them are doing exactly what their female-attracted friends are doing, a fair number of young men have their same-sex first kisses later, pulling the average up to about seventeen.[8]

Groping (Second Base)

From there, it's on to groping. Initially, that's about touching a girl's breasts over her shirt, but eventually those hands will find bare skin. Researchers have paid less attention to this behavior, especially in surveys of undergraduates. Some of that is practical: you can probably name the person with whom you had your first kiss and who your first sexual partner was (if you've had sex). You can probably provide other details about those experiences, including some of the when and where. After all, those are important events in general and within a relationship.[9] But if I asked you about your first groping experience, how much could you remember, and how certain would you be?

The research we do have on first groping experiences indicates that it's almost as common as kissing, but not quite. Among younger teens, a much higher percentage have kissed than groped. But by the time we're talking about high school seniors or college students, the percentages are quite similar. On average, age of first groping is around sixteen, putting it one to two years after the first kiss.[10] And that seems to be true whether we're talking about boys with female partners or with male partners.[11]

Hand Jobs and Blow Jobs (Third Base)

I'm mostly going to skip third base and go right home. There are two reasons for that. One is that third base isn't always defined the same way by teenagers. Some insist that it's being brought to orgasm by another person's hand, also known as a hand job or, for guys, being jerked off. Jargonistically, it's "manual-genital contact." For the vast majority of adolescents and young adults, hand jobs do not qualify as sex; if that's as far as you've gotten, you're still a virgin.[12]

Other people insist that third base is oral sex. Among adolescents and young adults, that's much more likely to mean that a guy has received a blow job than it is to mean that he's performed cunnilingus.[13] Although a majority of teens and young adults believe that a guy can have oral sex with a girl and still be a virgin, a fair number consider oral sex to be sex.[14] And in male-male couples, oral sex often qualifies as sex.

In their history of the "genital kiss," sociologists Alan Hunt and Bruce Curtis said that categorizing oral sex as not-sex has become particularly popular because of the emphasis on abstinence over the last few decades.[15] They also pointed out that oral sex is considered less intimate than intercourse among adolescent and young adult couples, but more intimate than sex among (married) adults.

The other reason I'm skipping third base is that most of the research that includes hand jobs and oral sex has simply noted that adolescents and undergrads do these things. In fact, most boys and young men say they've had some experience with these behaviors prior to having intercourse. However, very little of the research specifies who receives manual or oral sex or whether it's mutual, which means that it's not always clear what's being measured. As a result, I'm not comfortable giving you percentages or ages here.

Intercourse (Home!)

Adolescents and young adults often talk about first intercourse as a rite of passage.[16] As do many adults. The Web site myfirsttime.com is devoted to it, and managed to create an off-Broadway show based on the stories people submitted.

A lot of adolescents are having sex. Data from the Youth Risk Behavior Surveillance Survey (YRBS), which I described in Chapter One, are considered to be the standard. In every odd-numbered year since 1991, the Centers for Disease Control and Prevention have surveyed approximately twelve thousand to fifteen thousand adolescents in grades 9 through 12 as part of the YRBS. Smaller studies typically generate numbers that are very similar.

According to YRBS data collected in 2009, 46 percent of high school boys reported they'd voluntarily had sexual intercourse at least once. This percentage has changed very little since 2001, ranging from a low of 46 percent in 2009 to a high of 50 percent in 2007, and around 48 percent most years.[17]

As you'd expect, the older the boys, the more likely they are to have had sex. During the last ten years, between one-third (2009) and four-tenths (2001) of ninth-grade boys told us they'd had sex; among twelfth-graders, it's approaching two-thirds, ranging between 60 and 64 percent.[18]

Among high school students, the average age of first sex is closely linked to the grade they're in, and often works out to be at the lower end of students' ages for that grade. After all, if the vast majority of tenth-graders are fifteen or sixteen, there's no real way the average can be higher than sixteen. Among the approximately 40 to 45 percent of tenth-grade boys who've had sex, the typical age of first sex is four-teen or fifteen years.

It's similar for high school seniors. Most of them are seventeen or eighteen years old, and their average age of first sex is typically a little over sixteen for boys (and a little under seventeen for girls).

When we ask undergraduates, most of whom are eighteen or nine-teen when surveyed, or when we ask adults, the average age of first sex is typically around seventeen, with young men reporting an average that's about six months younger than young women.[19] Among under-graduates, it's not unusual for 67 to 80 percent of the participants to say they've had sex.[20]

For undergraduate men who have sex with men, the average age of first sex seems to be a little younger than it is for men who have sex with women. Their average age of first sex is closer to sixteen than seventeen, reflecting a difference of about six to eight months.[21] This difference may be due to the fact that among this group, oral sex is generally considered to be sex. It may also be due to the fact that these guys are dating guys, who've been taught to say yes to sex, in contrast to guys who date girls, who are taught to say no.[22]

We also know that adolescents who are having sex by age fifteen aren't doing very well in general. They're more likely to report other problems, from bad home environments to substance abuse to delinquency, as well as relatively poor relationships with their parents.[23] Given all that, it's little surprise that the relationships they're having are less stable and the couple less committed to each other than couples who aren't having sex at age fifteen.[24]

Extra Innings?

Now that a guy has scored his first run, all that's left is to keep scoring, right? That's certainly what the Casanova Complex tells us, but the baseball metaphor starts to break down once a guy has scored his first run. Like any metaphor, it's only an approximation, and I think it's important to understand the limits of that metaphor.

For one thing, baseball is a competition in which your goal is to score more runs than the other team, but it's not exactly clear who the other team is here. The competition seems to be a guy's male buddies; having more partners—being a Casanova—gives you higher status than other guys.[25]

In baseball, you play a game against an opponent. If your framework for sex is that a guy's role is to push for more sexual contact and try to get around the bases, and that a girl's job is to be a sexual "gatekeeper" and say no,[26] then you've got a scenario where the people who are having sex together are also opponents. Guys who endorse "traditional" notions of masculinity, including the Casanova Complex, tend to adopt this kind of adversarial description of romantic relationships.[27] Of course, that's consistent with our cultural conception of a "battle of the sexes," even though 90 percent of us are sleeping with—and will marry—the "enemy."

The baseball metaphor also ignores everything that happens before a guy gets up to the plate. We know that professional baseball players have spent thousands of hours and many years working on their baseball skills. But the metaphor doesn't tell us anything about the preparation necessary for sexual contact.

Around the Bases out of Order?

According to our metaphor, and according to the rules of baseball, you have to go in order. Looking at the average ages and the percentages, there's reason to believe that most people do: first kiss at thirteen or fourteen, followed by groping a year or two later, possibly a hand job or blow job, and then first sex around sixteen or seventeen.[28] Studies from Norway and the Netherlands that explicitly focused on the sequence tell us that most boys do follow this sequence; those who don't were more likely to be less educated, from an ethnic minority group, or both.[29]

Working with colleagues Loren Frankel and Ritch Savin-Williams, I focused on this kind of sequencing among undergraduates and a few graduate students; most participants were white.[30] There were 141 young men whose sexual experience was limited to women and another 81 who had some kind of sexual experience with both women and men. Among all of these guys, 211 of 222 (95 percent) were following the expected sequence; this includes the guys who reported a first kiss but hadn't had sex yet. Ten more reported that they had their first kiss and first sex at the same age, so they were probably following the sequence, but moving much faster than other guys. Exactly one guy was out of sequence; he reported having intercourse with a girl and that he'd never kissed anyone. To me, it sounds as though that guy hooked up with someone in order to lose his virginity.

Things were a little different among the young men with male partners. There were thirty-three whose experiences were limited just to men, and eighty-one who had both male and female partners. Just over one-third of this group were on the standard path and clearly had their first kiss before first sex. Almost half had their first kiss and first sex at the same age, so we'll say they're on the standard path around the bases, just as we did for the guys with female partners. Overall, this means that most young men with male partners were going in the expected order. But about 10 percent said they'd had first sex before first kiss, and about 6 percent said they'd had sex but hadn't yet kissed another guy.

A Broader Framework

Theories of normative or "healthy" sexual development give us a broader perspective on adolescent sexual behavior. These theories use an expanded definition of sexuality that includes dating and romantic relationships, as well as sexual behaviors like kissing and hand-holding that we expect to occur before intercourse. They also emphasize the fact that dating and sexual behavior are a normal part of growing up. Unless you said that there is nothing that qualifies as normal sexual behavior and disagreed with everything in the beginning of this chapter, you already think that some degree of sexual behavior is typical or "normative."

Throughout the book, I'll use the terms *sexuality* and *sexual behavior* to refer to this broad variety of behaviors, not just intercourse or coitus. After all, isn't kissing sexual? Fondling? Don't we expect some of these behaviors to be a normal part of adolescents' dating relationships? At the end of the movie *Footloose*, Reverend Moore decides not to interfere with the prom after his wife reminds him that when they were teens, all it took to get them (sexually) excited was looking at each other.

By adopting a normative framework, it gives us a different way to think about what our boys are doing and gets us away from the Casanova Complex. It moves us—and our boys—away from keeping score and lets us think about other aspects of sexuality, including how sex feels and what it means when sexual behavior is part of a romantic relationship (or not). It also gives us a way to think about a boy's early dating and sexual experiences as opportunities to learn about himself and others, his values, and all the things necessary to make a relationship work.

What's It Like: The Subjective Experience of First Sex

Casanova's emphasis on scoring has obscured boys' perceptions and interpretations of their first sexual experience. There's been some research into this topic, and you may have heard about the results:

boys' first sexual experiences are usually positive, whereas girls' first coital experiences are usually negative. If that summary is all that you've heard, then you've been misinformed.

The research on first sexual experiences shows that it's true that boys describe their first coital experience more positively than girls do, and girls describe their first sex more negatively than boys do; however, what gets obscured is that for most boys and girls, the overall experience is more positive than negative. The positives, for both boys and girls, include pleasure, satisfaction, and excitement.[31]

The negatives include tension, guilt, and anxiety. Some of those feelings are typical of doing something important for the first time, and some of the anxiety is about not being able to get an erection. Guys also report some embarrassment; girls aren't the only ones who are worried about what someone else will think about their naked body.[32]

You should also know that boys and girls both tend to describe first sex as "loving" or about being in love, and there's no difference between the genders here.[33]

What's the Score: Number of Partners

The Casanova Complex tells us that the score is important. It also tells us that what's important is the number of people you've had sex with, not the number of times you've had sex with any particular person. As we saw in Chapter One, the YRBS tells us that for twelfth-grade boys surveyed in 2009, about 23 percent reported four or more partners. The YRBS also told us that about 40 percent never had sex, and about 37 percent reported one to three partners.[34]

If you believe in the Casanova Complex, you may find those numbers surprising because they tell us that most guys have few partners. Take a look at the figure on the following page. It illustrates the number of partners that guys claim they've had sex with. These data come from 207 men ages eighteen to twenty-nine from a study mentioned in Chapter One; I've omitted the men thirty and older. Across the bottom, the numbers range from zero to twenty-five (or more) partners. The height of each bar tells how many young men gave that answer.[35]

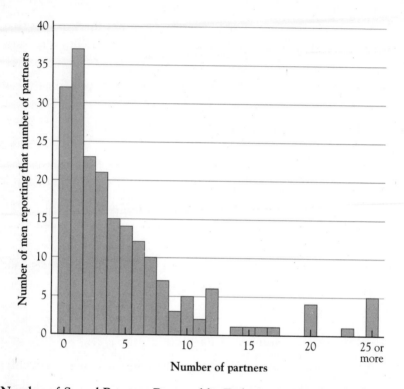

Number of Sexual Partners Reported by Eighteen- to Twenty-Nine-Year-Old Men.

Five guys in the survey, 2.5 percent of the total, said they'd had twenty-five or more partners. Another twenty-two, or almost 11 percent, said they'd had ten to twenty-four partners. These two groups, about 13.5 percent of the total, are the guys most likely to be Casanovas. As the figure shows, the two most common answers were zero partners (16 percent) and one partner (18 percent). Together, that's about one-third of eighteen- to twenty-nine-year-olds. More than half of guys have had three or fewer partners.

This pattern of results is typical. In survey after survey, we find that most guys, whether they are fifteen- or fifty-year-olds, are on the left-hand side of that graph; most guys have only a small number of sexual partners, and a small number of guys have a lot of partners.

Getting in the Game: Puberty and First Ejaculation

Puberty is typically positioned as the beginning of adolescence and consists of changes in both physical and sexual maturity for boys. Physical maturity includes increased height and weight, development of body hair, and other aspects of growth that are not directly related to reproduction. Sexual maturity includes those changes that prepare the body for reproduction, particularly maturation of the male reproductive system. Because the changes occur together, we know that a boy who is becoming more physically mature is also becoming sexually mature.

Historical research tells us that the age at which girls hit puberty has fallen over the last three centuries. In 1800, for example, menarche occurred around age seventeen or eighteen. As a result of better nutrition, better health care, and better public sewage systems (which reduce disease), the average age of menarche has gotten about two years younger in each of the last two centuries, according to official statistics and medical records. Although the evidence is indirect, the average age at which boys enter puberty seems to have gotten younger as well.[36]

The visible components of puberty are important. Research tells us that physical maturity is related to the age at which an adolescent starts dating.[37] However, the research is less clear when it comes to connections between physical maturity and age of first sex. A few studies have found such a connection, but most studies find none.[38]

Menarche marks an important rite of passage for girls and has been well studied by researchers. Its complement—called either "spermarche" or "semenarche," depending on whom you ask—has been only minimally studied. (That shouldn't be a surprise; you're almost certainly familiar with the term menarche, but you may not have heard of spermarche or semenarche.) The database I use for academic research, called PsycInfo, tells me there were exactly ten references to that topic between 1985 and 2011. There were 669 articles that addressed menarche in one way or another during this same time period, 85 in 2010 and 2011 alone.

Menarche is typically shared with parents, if for no other reason than the need to purchase feminine hygiene products. (One of the most embarrassing moments I remember from my work as a therapist was at the beginning of a session with a fourteen-year-old girl and her family. Everyone was saying hello and taking his or her seat, when the mother told us her daughter had "become a woman" over the past weekend. The mother was very pleased and proud; the daughter was mortified that her mother was telling everyone.) In contrast, according to the research, first ejaculation is typically a private and often secretive experience.[39]

Spermarche almost always happens as either a wet dream or as the result of masturbation, with these two "methods" being about equally common.[40] Young men report that they were often surprised by the event, especially if it occurred as part of a wet dream. They also tend to be excited and pleased about having reached this milestone. Although they see spermarche as more positive than negative, boys do report some confusion, embarrassment, and feelings of being out of control.[41]

Even though boys and their parents think it's an important milestone, they rarely talk about first ejaculation when it happens,[42] even when the parents presumably know (whether because they see stained sheets or note their son's sudden interest in doing laundry at 2 AM). Parents often say they're uncomfortable talking to their sons about ejaculation because they think it's strictly about sex and not about physical maturation. Most also think there's nothing to discuss.[43] I think that this belief is the result of the Casanova Complex's emphasis on promiscuous male sexuality and its disregard of relationships. In Part Three of this book, I'll help you figure out what you might talk about with your son, and provide some suggestions for how to have those conversations.

Just because boys aren't talking to their parents doesn't mean they're not talking. Most boys tell their friends.[44] This seems to be mostly about status: boys who can ejaculate have reached a developmental milestone.

Sexual Development as Part of Adolescent Development

Adolescence isn't just about physical and sexual development; it's a time of many changes, including the development of an identity, changes in the way adolescents think about and understand the world, and increased autonomy. Sexual development occurs alongside these other changes, is influenced by them, and may also help drive some of them.

Identity and Self-Knowledge

Early dating and sexual experiences help a boy figure out who he is, what he enjoys, and what's important to him. If you're an adolescent and you're in the process of figuring out who you are, a romantic relationship may help you. After all, many of those early conversations with a new partner are about finding common ground and exploring topics that are important to the two of you.[45] In conversation with your girl- or boyfriend, you may need to think about and explain why you like this type of book, music, movie, or TV show, and especially why you like this one and not that one. You'll probably also talk about how well you get along with your family and what your reputation is in comparison to who you "really" are, among other topics. This all qualifies as "identity work," a central task of adolescence and early adulthood.[46]

Complex Thinking

The beginning of adolescence is also marked by new, or at least more obvious, use of complex thinking, including the ability to think abstractly, to manipulate ideas, to understand and deal with multiple perspectives, and to use relative (as opposed to absolute) standards.[47] Adolescents are less black-and-white thinkers and more conscious of the gray areas. For example, younger children understand that "drugs are bad," but adolescents are able to recognize that prescription medications are also drugs. They understand that some drugs, like crack cocaine, are worse than others, like alcohol. Adolescents know there's a difference between a champagne toast at a wedding and having a drink with dinner every night. They may drive you nuts by asking about, or arguing about, every inch of this gray space with you.

Developing an Interest in Dating and Sex

For the most part, ten-year-olds aren't interested in dating or having sex. But as kids get older, they do develop an interest. In a study of eleven- to fourteen-year-olds, Mary Ott and her colleagues found a stagelike progression in how young adolescents' thinking about and interest in sexual relationships changed. At first, the kids viewed sexuality as distasteful and to be avoided; one participant said it was "nasty." You might think of this as the "cooties" stage of sexual development. These kids tended to see sex as inherently risky and almost certain to lead to pregnancy, disease, or both, and from there to a ruined life.[48]

Of course, adolescents don't stay in this mental space forever. Some of the teens in this study had moved on and were curious. In this stage, they tended to view abstinence positively and saw sex as something that was only appropriate within a committed, exclusive relationship or marriage. Many of these adolescents saw sex as risky, but they were less certain that it automatically led to bad outcomes. They also talked about the social pressure to appear sexually experienced, and acknowledged the double standard: sexual experience is good for boys, but it's a double-edged sword for girls, sometimes providing social benefits but sometimes bearing social costs.

Many of the teens in this study had passed through both of these stages and had begun thinking about dating and sexual behaviors, including coitus, as a normal part of their lives. Most of the young adolescents in this stage had at least some sexual experience, ranging from kissing to foreplay to coitus. They were also more realistic about the outcomes of sex and continued to acknowledge the double standard that praises boys for losing their virginity while giving mixed messages to girls. In this stage, they routinely referred to the earlier stages as "abstinence."

Understanding Sexual Risks

In another study, Dr. Ott and her colleagues interviewed forty-two adolescents from a local clinic serving the low-income area in which they lived.[49] Twenty-two of the adolescents were 11 to 14 years old, and the remaining twenty were 15 to 17 years old. Again, the younger adolescents talked about pregnancy as a virtually inevitable outcome of having sex, even just once, and believed there was also a high likelihood of being infected with HIV.

The older participants, some of whom had already experienced intercourse, were more nuanced and realistic in their views; they could draw and deal with finer distinctions. The older teens acknowledged that having sex meant there was some chance of pregnancy or an STI, but they also knew that pregnancy and disease were preventable. Unlike the eleven- to fourteen-year-olds, the older teens also talked about the social costs and benefits of sex; the older adolescents said that having sex was one way a guy could improve his social standing.

Autonomy

In the United States, adolescence is also a time of increasing autonomy and responsibility. As our children move through these years, we adults give them more control over their lives. Adolescents become increasingly responsible for their schedule and develop better time management skills. At ten or twelve, this is mostly about balancing homework, household chores, some scheduled activities or practices, and free time within a relatively narrow number of hours bounded by the end of the school day and parentally instituted bedtime. With kids this age, we often help them figure out that scheduling, and we may actively remind them about things to help them stay on time. By the time our kids are seventeen or eighteen, reminders tend to be limited to making sure the kids get to school on time and that they're aware of family events. Some older teens also hold down part-time jobs, which adds complexity to their weekly schedule. Most of us don't keep track of their work schedules, and as long as they're in their rooms and quiet, we don't really enforce bedtime.

From Ott's research, we know that adolescents experience a stage in sexual development when they lack interest and are abstinent, followed by a time of being ready for intercourse, then finally doing the deed. Deciding to have sex is usually an autonomous decision, and in some ways, it may be the most important decision a boy will make without direct parental input. Sex happens when teenagers want it to happen; they don't have to wait until the state or their parents say they are old enough, they don't have to pass a test, and they don't have to graduate high school or reach some other milestone.

Yet adolescents' notions of what it means to be "ready" tend to be somewhat vague and romantic; many talked about meeting the right person or knowing it was the right time, but they couldn't really specify what made it "right."[50] Even among those who see themselves as ready, they may lack a willing partner.[51]

A minority of adolescents make a different choice: abstinence. They see it as the only appropriate choice prior to marriage, drawing from religious descriptions of abstinence and marital relationships.[52]

Broader Factors

As long as we're thinking about more than just going around the bases, let's talk about some other things that influence how we think about sex. You might think of these as "background" factors because they're the kinds of things that don't immediately come to mind when we talk about why people do some of the sexual things they do.

Ethnicity

Ethnic group membership is one of the factors that influences boys' sexuality. Research routinely demonstrates that boys who are African American, and possibly boys who are of Latino descent, have their first intercourse at a younger age and tend to have more partners during adolescence.[53] But it's unclear if that's really about ethnicity or if that's part of growing up in poverty, which is also a factor in those kinds of sexual behaviors.

One study compared roughly equal numbers of male European American ("white"), African American, Latino (or Hispanic), and Asian American undergraduates on their age of first kiss, first serious relationship, and first intercourse.[54] Regardless of the students' ethnicity, going on a date and kissing were the most commonly reported behaviors and had the youngest average age. Intercourse was the least commonly reported behavior, but the first serious relationship had the oldest average age. And each of the four groups had an average age of about 17.5 years for their first experience of being in love.

Some differences were also evident. For almost every dating and sexual behavior the research team asked about, white youth tended to outnumber their Asian peers by 10 to 20 percent and were about two years younger. Youth of Latino or African descent were almost always between these two groups in both percentage and age.[55] The lower rates of behavior and older ages for Asian Americans are likely due to parental discouragement of dating,[56] combined with a parental focus on academics that leaves little time for dating.[57]

Culture

Ethnic differences are really about cultural differences, as the aforementioned description of Asian parents suggests. Different cultures give different messages about what's appropriate and when.[58] American culture tells us that dating is expected, at least for high school students if not middle school students.[59] After all, isn't that one of the implicit messages of school dances and proms, especially when tickets are sold only to couples?

In a transnational comparison, Geert Hofstede created two broad classifications, even though there's a fair amount of variability within each category.[60] The group that included the United States tended to emphasize frequency of sex, male promiscuity, number of partners, female chastity, moralistic sexual attitudes, and female sexual passivity. The other group, which included Finland, Sweden, Thailand, and South Korea, was characterized by beliefs that premarital sex was socially acceptable, a focus on personal feelings and interpretations of sexual behaviors, and minimal emphasis on chastity. Those cultures also expect girls to ask boys out and initiate sexual behavior, instead of simply waiting for boys to ask them out or start sexual behaviors. If you've read the books in Stieg Larsson's Girl with the Dragon Tattoo series, you may have noticed the matter-of-fact way in which the adults ask each other for sex, their reactions to those requests, and the reactions of the other adults. For example, there's little shock, no scandal, and few hurt feelings when Mikael Blomkvist has sex with different members of the Vanger family.

Religion

Followers of the more conservative sects of their religion—whether they are evangelical Christians, Orthodox Jews, or devout Muslims—typically teach their kids that dating is not a recreational activity; it's a purposeful one that's intended to lead to marriage. The only sexual activities that are allowable before marriage are relatively chaste: holding hands and possibly some kissing (often without parental knowledge or approval).[61] You may think of religious youth as atypical, but they make up about 15 percent of all adolescents and young adults, which means there are at least as many of them as there are Casanovas. We'll meet a religious young man in Chapter Eight.

Social Class

We know that kids who grow up in or near poverty are more likely to have sex and tend to be younger when they have their first sex.[62] On average, they also have more total partners during adolescence, but we've already seen that a boy's "number" isn't reliable evidence that he's following the Casanova Complex. It may surprise you to hear it, but the percentage of guys who are Casanovas is pretty stable across social classes.[63]

One marker of middle-class status in the United States is college attendance immediately following high school. Approximately 40 percent of American youth do not enter college immediately after high school,[64] so they're usually left out of studies that rely on undergraduates. Some don't attend college for "good" or "understandable" reasons, such as needing to care for an ailing parent or needing to work full-time in order to help pay the family's bills. But boys who have gotten someone pregnant, are juvenile delinquents, have run away, or have other behavioral problems are much less likely to attend college at age eighteen, even if they have finished high school. Research indicates that adolescents who fall into these categories are more likely to have begun having sex, and may have begun dating, earlier than the general population of adolescents.[65] Again, that does not necessarily mean they adhere to the Casanova Complex.

The 40 percent who don't attend college also includes millions of children who don't really have a family to raise them. In the movie *The Blind Side*, for example, we saw the story of Michael Oher, who was basically raising himself. If he hadn't been adopted by the Tuohy family, he probably would not have finished high school or gone to college. Even though these kids have raised themselves, they're no more likely to follow the Casanova Complex than others.

Sexual Orientation

Many adolescents come out as gay, bisexual, queer, and so on,[66] and public opinion polls indicate greater acceptance of homosexuality than ever before.[67] The research on gay youth indicates that many know they're attracted to members of their own sex before they realize that this makes them "different." Those first attractions often occur during childhood (for example, before age ten), with the recognition of difference coming during early adolescence.[68] They then actively choose to tell—or not tell—others.[69]

If it works this way for youth with same-sex attractions, then you'd expect it to work similarly for youth with other-sex attractions. However, there's been very little research on the development of a "straight" sexual orientation, so we don't really know. In one of the few studies that explicitly asked young men when they first knew they were straight or if they'd thought about the implications of being straight, most reported that they'd never really considered it.[70]

It's also unclear how much flexibility there is among men regarding sexual attractions and behavior; some women certainly demonstrate this flexibility.[71] It's not unusual for gay men to report that they've kissed or had sex with a woman, for a variety of reasons. We typically assume that straight guys aren't attracted to other guys, but we've started to discover that some are.[72] In the research with Frankel and Savin-Williams I mentioned earlier, 14 of 141 men whose sexual experiences were with female partners reported becoming more attracted to men since puberty; at the same time, 11 of 140 men reported greater attraction to women since puberty (and the remainder reported no change).[73] If you look at personal advertisements, especially the ones that are really about sex and not relationships, you can find any number of "straight" or "str8" or "bi-curious" men who are looking for male sexual partners. And then there are the straight guys J. L. King refers to as being "on the down low": men who are almost always married or have a girlfriend, and many with children, but who are surreptitiously having sex with other men.[74]

When we consider the totality of adolescent sexuality, the Casanova Complex presents a very limited picture. If that's the only way we think about the sexuality of boys and young men, then we are forcing them—or at least encouraging them—to get into a narrow box that positions sexuality as something that's separate from the rest of their lives and promotes some bad habits. I think we owe it to boys to think about their sexual development in a different, more holistic way.

3

The Importance of Romantic Relationships

We often think of girls and women as wanting relationships and of boys and men as wanting sex. That idea fits nicely with the Casanova Complex, which relies on that sexual focus for boys and men. It also fits nicely with the idea that men and women are fundamentally different and come from different planets.

The idea that women just want relationships and men just want sex isn't entirely true. As I mentioned in Chapter Two, most boys and young men date. But you probably knew that from real life without my telling you. And if you've ever tried to get a teenage boy to do something he doesn't want to do, then the idea that these guys are dating against their will just sounds absurd.

You probably also know that about 90 percent of men will get married at some point. And even if their first marriage doesn't work out, many of them will get married again. Although it's entirely possible that all these relationships are just about sex and everything else is secondary, I doubt it. I think guys want, and mostly enjoy, having a romantic partner.

From a different perspective, you might think of sex as a cooperative endeavor and that the goal is usually for everyone to win by having an orgasm. Using the baseball metaphor, this means that your partner is your teammate, not your opponent. Most of us want to like and help our teammates.

No matter how you look at it, relationships are important. In this chapter, I'm going to focus on three types of relationships that are important to a young man's sexual development: dating, hookups, and friendship. I'm not saying that all of these necessarily include sexual contact, just that they're all important for understanding what's going on.

Romantic Relationships

Romantic relationships are very important, especially to the adolescents having them. We might not expect a teenage boy to marry the first girl he kisses or falls in love with, but that doesn't mean his relationships should be trivialized as "cute" or can be ignored because we don't expect them to affect the rest of his life.[1] We don't expect a boy to mow lawns, work in fast food, or stock shelves for the rest of his life either, but we often talk about those jobs as helping build important skills: time management, money management, responsibility, the ability to get along with coworkers, and the like. These early dating experiences provide boys with opportunities to recognize their own wants and needs and to learn about balancing their own wants and needs against their partner's, about managing time, and about differences between friends and romantic partners.

Among teens fifteen and under, anywhere from 50 to 90 percent say they've been on at least one date.[2] Then again, some of those couples don't see or talk to each other outside of the school day, and fewer than half of boys say they've been out together as a couple. At this age, many couples spend more time together with their other friends than they spend alone together, although about three-fourths of boys have told their friends they had a girlfriend or boyfriend, and about two-thirds have told their partner they love her or him. Fewer than half of boys have introduced their parents to their sweetie.[3]

Regardless of whether we ask teenagers or undergraduates, boys' average age at first date is around fifteen, with fourteen and sixteen also being quite common.[4] I don't think it's a coincidence that this is about the same age as first kiss. It's also a year or two younger than first sex, which means there's a whole lot of dating that doesn't include intercourse.

Adolescent dating relationships can vary substantially in length. In one sample of ninth-graders, half of the relationships lasted twelve weeks or longer.[5] In a separate study of high school students, grades 9 through 12, one boy in six reported being in a relationship of eleven months or longer at the time of the survey.[6] Although the point may be obvious, it's worth noting that the longer a relationship lasts, the more important it is to the adolescent.

Among undergraduates, at least 80 percent said they had at least one "serious" or "real" dating relationship before they graduated from high school.[7] These relationships include spending time alone with the other person and talking to the other person outside of school, and typically require a young man to balance sweetie time with friend time; there's also a clear expectation of monogamy.[8] Among older teens and young adults, more than 70 percent of guys say they've been out as a couple in public, about two-thirds have told their partner they loved her or him, and more than half have introduced their parents to their partner.[9]

When asked about their first "serious" relationship, young men report an average age of around seventeen or eighteen.[10] This means that first serious relationships occur, on average, two or three years after first date and first kiss, and a year or two after first intercourse.

When asked about their first "important" relationship, average age drops to sixteen for boys who date girls and stays around eighteen for boys who date boys.[11] For guys who date girls, that's about the same as first intercourse, which suggests that those first sexual encounters are occurring within relationships the boys value. Admittedly, the value may come from the fact that they had sex, but even then, the boys are not saying that the relationship was meaningless or unimportant.

Among guys who date other guys, age of first important relationship is older than age of first sex. I suspect that this is because that relationship is a form of coming out, "confirms" he's gay, or both. By contrast, sex at age sixteen may be surreptitious "experimentation" and thus may not require a boy to come out.[12] And because sex for these guys might be oral sex, which teenagers often see as less intimate than other forms of sex, it can also be dismissed as "fooling around."

Why Date?

It's pretty clear that the majority of boys and young men date, and most have at least one girlfriend or boyfriend during high school. But let me ask you a question: Why date, especially if you haven't finished your education? And I don't mean why date person A instead of person B; I mean why date at all? Most guys will have their first date and their first serious relationship during high school, but won't get married until they've finished their education.[13] Men's age at first marriage has gotten older over the last half century, rising from just under twenty-three in 1950 to a little over twenty-seven at present.[14] On average, we're talking about a decade of dating before marriage, only some of which is likely to be with his long-term partner. Why bother?

Lots of reasons, it turns out. And often more than one; when researchers ask guys why they're dating or why they've gotten into their most recent relationship, they often give multiple reasons if they're allowed to do so.[15] This means that their motives are complex and multifaceted, and I'll describe them next.

Regardless of whether we ask adolescents to describe an actual romantic relationship, discuss their ideal relationship, tell us their motives for dating, or give them a series of scales that assess different components of relationships, we get the same answers time and time again. Those same answers also appear whether they date girls or date boys. And for the most part, it doesn't matter if we're asking fourteen-year-olds or twenty-year-olds; when age matters, I'll mention it.

Companionship and Connection

Companionship is consistently identified as one of the most important aspects of dating. As you might expect, boys "like the person" they're dating and enjoy spending time with that person.[16] In the early stages of a relationship, the wording is slightly different; guys tell us they "want to get to know the person better" or they were "curious" about their partner.[17] As David explained, "the more I talked to Steph, the more I liked her."

But dating isn't just about having someone to spend time with; it's also about intense feelings. Teenage boys and young men repeatedly identify this as a major component of dating. The intensity of the relationship, call it passion or connection if you like, is a central and important part of the relationship.[18]

Emotional Support and Intimacy

Support and general friendship are also common reasons to date. Guys tell us they like having someone to talk to and someone to be heard by, as well as someone to hang out with.[19] This is exemplified in Mike's reaction to doing poorly on an AP calculus exam, and his girlfriend's response:

> I would be thinking to myself, like you know, wow, I'm really not that intelligent or whatever, and she would be like, "Yeah you are. You know, you are taking these difficult courses and for the most part you do well." She just, you know, make[s] you really look at the big picture instead of focusing on one little setback.

As you might expect, the more supportive the relationship, the longer it tends to last. In fact, adolescents who have romantic relationships that last for a year or more often describe their dating partner as more supportive than either their best friend or their parents.[20]

Emotional intimacy is also a factor in boys' dating, and it refers to something beyond the support I've just talked about. A guy's girlfriend, or his boyfriend, is someone trusted with his deeper secrets, especially the things he's worried about. The specialness of the relationship provides guys with someone who will share their most private thoughts, feelings, and dreams. Although most adults view emotional intimacy as central to a romantic relationship, it's only mentioned by a minority of boys (and girls) at age fifteen.[21] But as young men get older and have more experience with relationships, intimacy becomes more important.[22]

Physical Intimacy

Guys tell us that physical intimacy and opportunities for sexual behavior—kissing, fondling, coitus, and so on—also influence their decision to date. After all, these are behaviors that require a partner and are expected to be part of a romantic relationship. Kissing and holding hands are almost exclusively limited to dating relationships and serve as public indicators of that relationship.[23] But when asked why they're dating, only a minority of boys tell us that physical intimacy is a factor in their decision, making this a secondary reason to date. To put it differently, most guys may see sexual behavior as a result of dating and not the reason to date.

Peer Groups and Dating

Peers also play a part in the decision to date. Young men sometimes tell us that they started dating because they "didn't want to be the only person without" a partner or "felt like they should be in a relationship,"[24] or even to improve their social status.[25] I often think of this as "peer conformity" because it's really about the adolescent's choice to fit in; to me, that's different from "peer pressure," which seems to be about other people actively encouraging an adolescent to do something he might not otherwise do.

When adolescents are asked to report on various dimensions of dating—the whole list of characteristics I've described here, for instance—peer-related reasons usually get the lowest scores. They are rarely the only reason to date, although there are a small number of boys who date just to fit in. More often, peer conformity is reported alongside other reasons, such as connection to or interest in the partner.[26]

This is important because the research tells us that once someone in a guy's friendship circle starts dating for the first time, the odds of dating increase for everyone else in the group.[27] Over time, some guys may feel that they need to date someone in order to remain in their circle of friends, especially if everyone else in the group has a girlfriend or boyfriend.

Dating's Downsides

It's not all good, of course, and guys know that. Adolescents tell researchers that relationships sometimes have problems and include negative interactions. One big disadvantage to being in a relationship seems to be the commitment that comes with it, in terms of time, decreased spontaneity, and the loss of freedom.[28]

The other big risk is related to *no longer* being in a relationship. Boys and men are aware that dating carries risks of "being rejected," "invest[ing] feelings and getting hurt," and "having a broken heart."[29] These, of course, are downsides to emotional intimacy.

At times, and especially among younger teens, guys will also mention the financial cost of dating. Despite living in a culture that is evermore egalitarian,[30] the conventional expectation is that the guy will pay for the first date, pick up the check more often than the girl, and buy the girl gifts on a regular basis.[31] With increased age, and probably with input from their female friends, many guys start to understand that girls and women also put money into the relationship, but less obviously. For example, sexually active couples that have been together for more than three months are much more likely to be using chemical contraceptives such as the pill or the ring, instead of condoms;[32] those prescriptions are almost always paid for by the young woman.

Whom to Date?

Given that most guys date, it seems safe to assume that the benefits outweigh the costs. Those benefits are primarily about connection and emotional intimacy, with sexual pleasure and peer conformity adding a little to the mix. Once a guy has decided that dating will be part of his life, he needs to find a partner.

Contrary to the directives of the Casanova Complex, most boys don't give high priority to girls' appearance. Among younger adolescents and those with the least experience, appearance is one of the primary factors in choosing whom to date, but it's a secondary reason for older and more experienced boys.[33] Older adolescents and young adults, as well as those with more dating experience, understand that appearance doesn't actually help you achieve any of the relational "whys" we've just discussed, with the possible exception of peer status. The hottest girl may or may not be a good companion or someone with whom you can be emotionally intimate or who is consistently supportive, and there's nothing about her appearance that's going to tell you any of this.

The characteristics that teenage boys and young men do look for in a dating partner include being funny, nice, outgoing, understanding of others, able to make decisions, and reasonably self-confident. Having some similar interests is also important.[34] These characteristics help the couple achieve the "whys" we've already discussed: companionship, support, emotional intimacy, and possibly even passion.

Turnoffs include stubbornness, bossiness, and a sense of superiority. Being highly competitive or too independent are also characteristics that make guys wary, especially when those characteristics get in the way of companionship and intimacy. Boys also say that frequent fighting, nagging, and jealousy are undesirable.[35]

Although it's not necessarily what guys focus on or talk about, most partners in adolescent and young adult couples are similar in age and have the same ethnic background.[36] That makes a certain amount of sense: people who share your demographic profile are more likely to just "get" what you're talking about without your needing to explain it in detail, as compared to people who don't share that background.

The Most Desirable Characteristics

A team of researchers lead by David Buss was able to examine the characteristics desired in a long-term partner, or "mate," by building on a study originally conducted in 1939. The same survey was used again in 1956, 1967, 1977, 1984–85, and 1996. The survey was given to undergraduates at a variety of institutions over these fifty-seven years, presumably depending on where the researchers were. Even though the campuses changed over the years, the survey was exactly the same for each group of undergraduates, regardless of year or campus.[37]

In this survey, male and female participants were given a list of eighteen characteristics and asked to rate each one on a 0–3 scale, where 0 indicated that it was "irrelevant or unimportant" and 3 indicated that it was "indispensable." An average was computed for each characteristic, which was then placed in order from most desired to least desired.

In each of the six survey periods over the fifty-seven years, men's top four characteristics were the same:

- Dependable character

- Emotional stability or maturity

- Pleasing disposition

- Mutual attraction or love

The ranks of these characteristics varied slightly over time, with mutual attraction or love shifting from fourth in 1939 and 1956 to first in 1984–85 and 1996. Dependable character fell from first before 1970 to third after 1970. Given what we've already seen about the primary reasons for dating—companionship, support, and emotional intimacy—these characteristics are right on target. Good health and ambition-industriousness were always in the top half of the ratings. Their scores placed them anywhere between fifth and ninth.

Other Desirable Characteristics

The next few characteristics reveal a fairly clear generational and historical change, consistent with the broader culture's transformation of women's roles. In the three rounds of surveying prior to 1970, desire for home and children, refinement and neatness, and being a good cook and housekeeper all placed fifth through ninth. After 1970, they fell by a few slots, ranking no better than ninth. They were replaced in the fifth-to-ninth slots by education and intelligence, sociability, and good looks.

In other words, from 1939 until 1967, men wanted a dependable, mature, healthy, industrious domestic servant with a good personality whom they could fall in love with. From 1977 to 1996, they wanted a dependable, mature, healthy, industrious, educated, and physically attractive wife with a good personality who would be a good companion whom they could fall in love with. That's really not what the Casanova Complex tells guys to do.

There were two characteristics on the list that fit into the Casanova Complex: physical attractiveness, which I've just mentioned briefly, and chastity. Good looks didn't crack the top half of the ratings until the 1977 survey; prior to that it had been in the bottom half. And even after 1977, it was near the middle, not the top. Female chastity was always in the bottom half of the ratings, and its ranking got even worse after 1970. These responses are consistent with the other findings on boys' motives: appearance and sexual behavior are secondary concerns when choosing a partner.

Collectively, these studies tell us that the characteristics young men consider important are related to companionship and love, mirroring the reasons they date in the first place. Good looks, and perhaps even chastity, play a role, but they're not the primary characteristics that guys seek in a longer-term partner.

Why Have Sex?

Sex is sex, right? Physically, yes. But it's also clear that sex within a relationship carries a different set of meanings than hookup sex.[38]

The reasons boys have sex are strikingly similar to the reasons they get into dating relationships. In fact, boys and young men tend to respond with the same kinds of motives for sex as for dating. And as we saw with dating, boys usually report multiple reasons, not just one.[39]

Love and Relational Concerns

The most common reason that guys have sex is to connect with their partner or maintain or increase the intimacy of the relationship. Their motives are things like "being in love," "showing their love," "deepening the connection to their partner," "strengthening the relationship," and even "my partner wanted to."[40] These reasons run parallel to, and are consistent with, dating motives like emotional intimacy and intense feelings.

In American culture, we often talk about sex as a physical expression of love, and these reasons are consistent with that notion. For example, David told me, "You combine the physical with the emotional and you care about this person and you are in love with them and you are sharing more than your physical body; you are sharing your emotional side as well." Along the same lines, Matthew said that sex with a boyfriend was "almost more and more [an] emotional than physical kind of concept."

Not all relationship-related reasons are positive, however. It's unusual to hear it, but some guys acknowledge that they're having sex in order to keep their partner happy and are afraid that if the sex ends, so will the relationship.[41]

Physical Intimacy

Physical pleasure also factors into a boy's decision to have sex, but it's rarely the primary motive. Then again, guys are more certain that sex leads to physical pleasure than they're certain that it increases either intimacy or social status.[42]

Peers

Peers also play a role in boys' decisions to have sex, and in the same ways they affected boys' decisions around dating. A minority of teenage boys tell us they've had sex "to get it over with or not be a virgin anymore," because "I thought I had to," or "to fit in with my friends." As you might expect, boys who endorsed peer conformity reasons for sex also endorsed peer conformity reasons for dating.[43]

In one of my analyses of tenth-grade boys' reasons for sex, every boy who endorsed peer conformity reasons for sex also endorsed at least one reason that wasn't related to peer conformity. No boy in that study said he'd had sex *only* for peer conformity reasons.[44]

Other Sexual Motives

A small number of boys provide more idiosyncratic reasons for sex. In some cases, it's about being "ready" and seems to be about proving something, either to themselves or others. In other cases, guys tell us that their most recent sexual experience "just happened"; they weren't intending to have sex, yet there they were, doing it.[45] Although not common, neither of these motives really sounds like what we might expect from the Casanova Complex.

Collectively, these reasons suggest that sex often occurs as part of a caring, connected, loving relationship. But that's hardly the only time sex happens.

Hooking Up

Today it's called hooking up. We used to call it casual sex or having a one-night stand. Whatever you call it, it's about having sex with a person you're not dating and with whom you don't have any real emotional connection. That person is usually a stranger (or was at the beginning of the night), and any contact between the two of you is expected to be limited to that night;[46] breakfast together the next morning is a possibility, but don't count on it.

This isn't just my definition; it's the one that young men typically use. I conducted an interview-based study in which male undergraduates were asked to define the terms "dating" and "hooking up," among others. My colleagues Marina Epstein and Jerel Calzo analyzed the guys' responses.[47]

They found that guys' answers were pretty consistent when it came to the definition of hooking up, but they weren't in complete agreement with each other. When asked for more detail, several of the guys acknowledged that even though intercourse was assumed, the reality of hooking up might be limited to making out, but could also include oral sex or, among male-male pairings, anal sex.[48] BD explained it this way:

> Well, to me, a hookup does not have to be sex. Some people say it is, but to me a hookup could be anything from, you know, making out to having sex, but it's not *necessarily* sex. So like for me hooking up would be, you know, just kissing a girl or it could be going to second base or anything in there. It doesn't really matter. . . . Anything [physically] intimate counts as a hookup for the sake of conversation.

The definitions of a hookup didn't usually say anything about alcohol or drugs. In the actual stories the young men told us about hookups, alcohol or some other substance was almost always present.[49]

How Common Is Hooking Up?

As we know, some guys just want to hook up. There's reason to believe that most guys will hook up at least once in their lifetime.[50] The research team of Wendy Manning, Monica Longmore, and Peggy Giordano analyzed data from the National Longitudinal Study of Adolescent Health, also known as Add Health.[51] The study consisted of nearly nineteen thousand adolescents who were surveyed for the first time when they were in grades 7 through 12 and then surveyed again about eighteen months later. The researchers used data from about seventy-five hundred students who were fifteen or older when the first survey was completed and who completed the survey both times.

About one teen in four reported that he or she had sexual intercourse outside of a romantic relationship in the first round of surveying, and one in seven reported intercourse outside of a romantic relationship in the eighteen months between surveys. Although hooking up is certainly part of the Casanova Complex, it's a fairly small number of guys who really subscribe to the Casanova Complex and hook up several times per year.[52]

Why Hook Up?

Given guys' descriptions of sex with a dating partner as merging the physical and the emotional, you might be asking why guys hook up at all. Some guys are like David, whom I mentioned in Chapter One. He was a few months from graduating college, expected that he'd be moving for his first job, and didn't want his options constrained by a relatively new relationship that might not last very long.

Matthew told me about a time when a hookup "just happened." He'd been at a bar drinking with friends, and one of his friends happened to know the bartender. Matthew found the bartender attractive, and near the end of the evening, the bartender invited the group back to his apartment. Matthew hooked up with him, and he explained to me,

> That night was weird because I wasn't going out to find anybody. I was just going to have fun with my friends. We were just going to do all these fun things, have "gay night." And yeah, I wasn't really looking for it.

A recent study by Carolyn Bradshaw, Arnie Kahn, and Bryan Saville asked male and female undergraduates if they'd prefer to hook up with someone or be in a traditional dating relationship. The undergraduates said that dating benefits primarily had to do with having someone to be with and feeling special, as we saw earlier in the chapter. The benefits of hooking up were almost exclusively related to sexual gratification, enhanced by some of the excitement of having sex with a new partner. Guys also said the lack of commitment was a plus.[53]

As you might expect, the young men in this study were more likely to express a preference for hooking up than were the young women. But if you look at the study more closely, you find that only about a fourth of the guys said they'd prefer to hook up rather than to date; that's right—about 75 percent of guys said they'd choose dating over hooking up. Yet again, Casanova is in the minority.

Some teenage boys and young men explicitly cite the increased status they receive from their male peers as a reason to hook up.[54] As BD told me, "I think the big two factors when you're deciding if you're going to try and hook up with someone at a party is (a) if they're attainable and (b) what your friends think." Here, sex is not about connection or what's going on between the people sharing body fluids, it's about the guy and his friends. This gives peers a much bigger and very different role in hooking up than they have in dating.

At the extreme, this can lead to the kind of bad behavior that we saw from a group of relatively popular high school boys in California who called themselves the Spur Posse. They devised a fairly elaborate point system whereby each guy could earn points based on the extent of sexual activity and the girl's reputation. There were also bonus points for having sex with a virgin. In 1992, the guys were outed by a girl whom several of them had tried to seduce; she ultimately won a civil case of sexual harassment.

In the typical hookup, the risks are less dramatic than being arrested or sued, but they're just as important. Those risks include contracting a sexually transmitted infection (STI) or getting your partner pregnant. Guys also worry that a hookup partner will try to start a relationship after they've had sex,[55] something the real Casanova described in his memoirs—and avoided.[56]

If you're interested in hooking up, then the list of what you're looking for in a partner is a short one: someone who's willing, doesn't have an STI, and is also looking for no-commitment sex. If hooking up is also about peer status, then having a good-looking partner may be important—or not. As the crass expression goes, "Everyone's beautiful at 2AM."

One thing that becomes apparent when comparing dating relationships to hookups is that the criteria for what makes a good partner differs. This is sometimes called the Madonna-whore distinction; guys are reputed to want dates who are prim and proper and whom Mom would approve of, but they want to hook up with women who are wild sexual adventurers. I'll talk more about these kinds of double standards in Chapter Eleven.

Differences Between Friendship and Dating

Friendship requires many of the same skills and provides many of the same benefits as a romantic relationship. They're both about companionship, trust, emotional intimacy, and shared interests, among other things. Although friendship may include hugging or putting your arm around someone's shoulders, sexual contact is unusual and not expected.[57]

Because the vast majority of boys and men date and have sex with girls and women,[58] I'm going to focus on friendships with girls here. I'll talk about boys' friendships with other boys briefly in Chapter Five and at some length in Chapter Ten.

Researcher Jennifer Connolly explored the overlap between friendship and dating. Her research team asked fifth- through eighth-grade boys to provide a few words to describe a female friend and a girlfriend.[59] For friendship, companionship was the most common descriptor. The study's older participants, seventh- and eighth-graders, also mentioned emotional intimacy and trust with some regularity. For romantic relationships, companionship and emotional intimacy were again mentioned regularly. Adolescents also spoke about deep feelings of connection and physical intimacy.

As you can see, the primary components of an other-sex friendship were also present in dating relationships, but dating relationships added a level of passion and physical intimacy not seen in friendships.

If we shift from friendship in general to an individual's best friend, then we often find emotional intimacy that is as deep as romantic love, although quite different.[60] The research—and everyday experience—tells us that people who are good friends or who have good relationships with their parents and other family members also make good partners.[61]

Today, most boys have at least one friend who happens to be female—a "girl friend" but not a "girlfriend." That's remarkable. Forty years ago, this was incredibly rare; now it's so common that we don't really notice.[62] One 1986 adolescent development textbook devoted two full pages to adolescents' belief that having an other-sex friend would be difficult; it provided no discussion of actual other-sex friendships.[63] In the 1991 *Encyclopedia of Adolescence*, Willard Hartup and Susan Overhauser echoed this sentiment, reporting that "cross-sex friendships are relatively rare, accounting for only about 1 'best' friendship in 20."[64]

Other-sex friends play an important role in early dating experiences. During elementary school, children's friends tend to be of their same sex. This changes in middle school, in part due to the opportunity to and necessity of re-forming friendship networks due to the change in school buildings and classmates. Although a substantial fraction—about one-third or so—of early dating experiences are with someone who is a friend, first dating relationships are more likely to occur with someone who is a friend of a friend.[65] Stated differently, the majority of early relationships tend to be with someone who is either a first- or second-degree connection, a friend or a friend of a friend.

A guy's friends and his friend's friends also provide another important experience; these are the folks with whom he'll probably play kissing games like Spin the Bottle. Those games are a common but mostly unstudied phenomenon.[66] I don't have good statistics on them, but my impression is that these games often occur near the end of middle school, around ages thirteen through fifteen.

Changes from Early Adolescence into Early Adulthood

As boys move through adolescence, the odds that they'll date grow substantially.[67] Dating also means something different for younger as opposed to older adolescents. The differences seem to be the result of greater maturity, individual growth (including changes in thinking processes, as mentioned in Chapter Two), and more experience with relationships of all types: family, friendship, and dating.

When undergraduates are asked to recall those dating relationships during midadolescence and compare them to their current relationships, they report enjoyment, fun, and companionship for both ages. They also say that their adolescent relationships were more likely to be characterized by problems and were much less stable than their current relationships.[68]

––––––––––––

At the beginning of this chapter, I asked why boys start dating during high school if they're not planning to get married until their mid-twenties. The answers weren't all that surprising: companionship, support, and emotional intimacy were at the top of the list. Sure, many if not most guys hook up at least once in their life, but it's still only a small number of guys who do so regularly. Even though formal dating may be on the wane,[69] most guys clearly prefer dating to hooking up. That doesn't sound like the Casanova Complex at all.

Part II

Why We Believe in Casanova

4

Evolution, Biology, and Casanova

Human beings have inborn drives and behaviors. If you've spent time with an infant, you know this very well. Some of these inborn behaviors, such as reflexes, are obvious. If I hit you in just the right way below your kneecap, you'll kick your leg forward. It's called the patellar reflex, and even if you're putting all your effort into it, you won't be able to prevent that leg kick.

Sex, and especially Casanova-like behavior, are not as simple as the patellar reflex. After all, we know that if your family has a history of disease X, then you may—or may not—ever develop that disease. This might be a matter of genetics or diet or exercise or even just plain old luck; for many diseases, it's almost certainly an interaction of our genetic inheritance, the environments we live in, and the choices we make.

It's also important to remember that biology isn't destiny. Even when you're very hungry—"starving," we often say—you can still choose not to eat. You can also choose to eat at home, have food delivered, or eat in a restaurant; those choices might get food in your stomach right now, but they might also take half an hour or an hour. And, of course, you have a wide range of food choices, from pizza to paté.

Testosterone

In some ways, testosterone works as hunger does. We know that testosterone is related to an individual's level of sexual desire. Testosterone is a member of a class of hormones known as androgens; adrenaline, which contributes to our "fight or flight" reflex, is also an androgen. Everyone, male or female, produces androgens.

When a guy stops producing androgens, his level of sexual desire, his ability to achieve and maintain an erection, the size of that erection, and his ability to achieve orgasm can all suffer.[1] We also know that increasing someone's level of androgens, especially testosterone, can increase his level of sexual desire. Again, this is true for any guy or girl who's reached puberty.[2]

But read carefully. Yes, testosterone can increase sexual desire. But as far as we know, there's nothing about testosterone, or any of the androgens, that pushes us toward having many different partners or having just one partner, the same way that hunger doesn't really care what we eat just so long as we put food in our stomach. Testosterone doesn't really "care" about number of partners.

Debates about evolution's influence on human sexual behavior are relatively long-standing. Most of the debate focuses on very different conceptualizations of men's behavior—there's much less debate about women's sexual behavior—and comes down to the two theories described in the next sections.

Casanova as Men's Evolved State

There's an evolutionary explanation for sexual behavior that's been well known in scientific circles and in American culture for about thirty years. Sexual strategies theory (SST) relies on a physiological difference between men and women: a woman can produce only about one child per year, whereas a man could theoretically produce hundreds of children per year. SST's primary authors, David Buss and David Schmitt, claim that the theory is designed to help us understand the current-day differences in men's and women's sexual behavior.[3] According to SST, the goal of human mating is to produce children and thus to pass one's genes on to the next generation. Thus women should be very picky before having sex with a man; they need to find a man who has good genes and who is likely to provide for her while she's pregnant and nursing their child. By contrast, men should sleep around. The more sexual partners a guy has, the greater the chances that he'll conceive children with more than one woman and thus produce multiple children. SST also relies on the fact that a guy can never be 100 percent sure that a child is his. If he's having sex with lots of different women and one (or more) says she's pregnant, he may wonder whether the child is his or someone else's. Even if he's having sex with only one woman, there's always a chance she could be cheating on him, so even then, he can't be 100 percent sure.

SST isn't exactly a new theory. It's main principles were put forth in the 1970s as part of an approach called sociobiology; E. O. Wilson was the theory's biggest proponent. There was extensive criticism, perhaps most notably from Steven Jay Gould, and sociobiology was largely abandoned. In the 1990s, the theory was reconstructed and named evolutionary psychology.[4] At their centers, both sociobiology and evolutionary psychology are efforts to use biological theory—particularly Darwin's theory of evolution—to understand social behavior.

SST's authors extended the sociobiological description of mating by acknowledging that humans can choose to focus on finding short-term or long-term mates. Thus, some guys choose to be Casanovas and keep finding new partners, hoping they'll impregnate several of them. Other guys decide to be selective and choose a single partner. Because pregnancy happens within and to women's bodies, and birth leads to nursing a child, women are expected to be interested primarily, if not exclusively, in long-term relationships.[5]

We've long known that teenage boys, young men, and adult men report more partners, on average, than their female peers. On average, guys usually report a younger age of first sex, higher rates of "cheating" on their partner (extradyadic affairs), and greater willingness to have sex with someone they've just met (or don't know very well).[6] SST gives us a way to make sense of these patterns.

Desire for Short-Term Partners

SST's proponents have been very effective at collecting data from around the world in an effort to demonstrate that their findings truly represent a human phenomenon and not just something unique to the United States, English-speaking countries, or "the West." One project, known as the International Sexuality Description Project (ISDP), was led by Schmitt and included a team of 118 additional researchers. They surveyed folks in sixty-two nations, islands, and autonomous regions around the world. In each place, they recruited about one hundred male and one hundred female participants. Most participants were undergraduates, but some other adults were included. The participants completed surveys in their own language; this wasn't an English-only project.[7]

One survey question that SST's authors often focus on is this: "Ideally, how many different sex partners would you like to have . . ." across a series of eleven time frames, ranging from as short as one month to "your remaining lifetime." The question is open ended, so participants fill in whatever number they like. SST's proponents typically focus on the shortest time frame—one month—to demonstrate that men want more short-term partners than women. The focus is on desired partners, not actual partners, because desire is taken as a better indicator of our underlying evolutionary and biological tendencies than actual behavior.[8] That makes sense; just because you want to have sex with a new person, there are a variety of reasons why that might not happen.

In the worldwide study, the average for men was nearly two partners in the next month, whereas for women it was nearly one partner in the next month. This pattern—a higher average for men than for women—has been found in survey after survey.[9]

The researchers also point out that many more men than women say they want two or more partners; in that worldwide study, about one guy in four (25 percent) said he wanted two or more partners in the next month, whereas only about one woman in twenty (5 percent) said she wanted two or more partners in the next month. These values are also typical.[10]

Let's take a look at those numbers again. There's certainly a difference between men and women. But this is a book about men, and only 25 percent of guys say they want two or more partners in the next month. That means the majority—75 percent—want one or zero partners in the next month. Shouldn't we take that majority as telling us about the average or typical guy? If guys are biologically programmed to want multiple partners, why is it that these guys— undergraduate men who are at or near their physical and sexual peak, who are rarely married, who mostly live away from their parents in dormitories, and who are usually surrounded by lots of unmarried, healthy women—overwhelmingly say they're looking for only one partner when completing anonymous surveys?[11] As I've already pointed out in Chapter One, there are very few guys who actually have multiple partners in any given month.

Desire for New Partners

SST's authors have also demonstrated that the average guy is willing to have sex with a woman he's just met before the average woman is willing to have sex with a man.[12] In the worldwide study, guys were notably more likely than women to indicate that they'd be willing to have sex with a new partner less than one month after meeting her, just as the theory predicts.

An earlier study using American undergraduates went into more detail about that "when": for the average guy it was more than a day but less than a week before he was willing to have sex with someone he'd recently met; for the average girl, it was closer to a month.[13] But take another look at the time frame. Young men said they wanted more than a day but less than a week; that's not quite the random one-night stand or hookup we tend to imagine.

Desire for Attractive (Fertile) Partners

There's something else that we've all come to know from SST: guys are looking for attractive women, because attractiveness indicates fertility, and women are looking for guys who have lots of resources or status (because status often indicates resources). When SST's researchers survey undergraduates, their findings support this prediction: young men report greater emphasis on appearance than do women, and women give status higher priority than do men.[14]

In Chapter Three, I told you about one such study; it involved six rounds of surveying over fifty-seven years. Compared to young women, young men placed more importance on their (potential) partner's physical appearance. However, at best, young men ranked women's appearance as being only ninth most important among eighteen characteristics. Young men's top four characteristics in each round of surveying were dependable character, emotional stability (or maturity), pleasing disposition, and mutual attraction (or love).[15] Those things don't really fit with the idea that young men are looking for one-time-only partners.

By the way, that fifty-seven-year study was authored by Buss, one of SST's primary proponents.

Twin Studies

We've all heard those stories about identical twins who were separated at birth and then later found that both played baseball from ages six to eleven, both played third base, both wore number 7, both graduated in the top five of their high school class, and both married girls named Suzie when they were twenty-seven years old. Amazing—and, we're told, evidence of the importance of genes.

One innovative study suggests that our mate choices may not be guided by any kind of rule. This study included several hundred twins and the twins' spouses. Some of the twins were identical, some fraternal. There's a body of research which shows that people choose spouses or long-term partners who are similar to them in age, ethnicity, social class, political views, and religious beliefs. That's part of how dating Web sites like eharmony.com determine whom you're likely to hit it off with. If you've ever visited a site like that, you know that there may be hundreds, if not thousands, of people whose values are similar to yours and who live within fifty miles.

In the study of twins and their spouses, the researchers found that the really important similarities were primarily about a small set of socially and politically conservative beliefs.[16] As you probably expect, the identical twins were more similar to each other than the fraternal twins.

You'd also expect the spouses of identical twins to be more similar than the spouses of fraternal twins, because identical twins are so similar. After all, if identical twins separated at birth can end up playing the same position on their baseball teams and so on, then shouldn't they end up marrying partners who are similar?

It turns out they don't. The spouses of identical twins were no more similar than any pair of people picked randomly out of the entire survey. The spouses of fraternal twins weren't similar either. Not only were spouses dissimilar, only a small percentage of spouses said they "could have fallen for" the twin they didn't marry. About twice as many spouses said they really didn't like—or even hated—the twin they didn't marry, regardless of whether we're talking about identical or fraternal twins. The researchers concluded that even though we "tend to choose from among people like ourselves, another person who is remarkably like ourselves [an identical twin] is not likely to be drawn to the same choice we make."[17] In other words, your values may identify a group of acceptable spouses for you and your twin, but the odds that you and your twin will like the same person are pretty small.

Evolutionary History

Another important part of the story is our history as humans. SST says that evolution has programmed men to seek multiple partners in order to increase their chances of passing their genes on to the next generation. Darwin told us that the environment a species lives in "selects" the behaviors, and thus the genes, that provide an advantage. He illustrated this by showing how several species of finches adapted to different shapes of flowers.

Human history is dominated by what we might call male-female "pair-bonds" living together in a socially sanctioned manner.[18] "Socially sanctioned" can mean a marital relationship or living together, although living together was generally frowned on by Americans prior to the 1970s.

A couple's children would live with them, and other kin—the adults' parents or siblings—might also live with them. Although polygamy has been legal in more places than not, the vast majority of adults in those countries appear to have lived with a single partner.[19]

Logically, if you know that most men only have one wife at a time, then you'd probably expect only to have one wife. The people who make choices about couples, whether it's the man, the woman, his parents, or her parents, would expect a one man–one woman couple. And this pattern appears to be the norm for most humans who have ever lived, even in societies where having multiple spouses was legal.[20] From a Darwinian perspective, this represents an environmental pressure toward having one lifelong partner.[21] Just as the finches adapted to the environmental pressure of different flower shapes, human males would have adapted to this pressure toward having one lifelong partner. (And remember, until the twentieth century, most people didn't live beyond their forties.)

Human history also appears to favor children who are raised by their biological parents. Anthropologist Robert Quinlan reviewed a broad swath of studies that examined childrearing in a variety of human cultures: hunter-gatherers, agrarian cultures, and modern industrialized cultures. He also provided information from some non-human species. Quinlan found that when the biological father is not present, the child's likelihood of reaching puberty and adulthood drop notably, even when a stepfather or other adults—"alloparents"—provide for the child.[22] Quinlan also observed that the effects aren't limited to survival rates; on average, children raised by their biological parents were physically healthier and better adjusted than other children.

Quinlan's review also came to two other conclusions. First, children with alloparents typically do better than children with a single parent. Second, pair-bonds were most stable when males provided 40 to 60 percent of the couple's resources. This means that conceptions of primitive or modern cultures in which mothers tend the children but don't otherwise contribute resources to the "household" are not the evolutionary standard.

Children who don't survive long enough to reproduce don't pass their genes on to the next generation. From a Darwinian perspective, this means there would be a real evolutionary advantage to having a single mate and raising one's own children because it increases the odds of not only passing your genes on to the next generation but also seeing them passed on to the generation after that. Casanovas would be at a disadvantage because they don't stick around to raise their children. If there were a "Casanova gene," it might not be eliminated over time, but it would be expressed in only a minority of men.

Long-Term Pair-Bonding as Men's Evolved State

There is also a theory which suggests that long-term pair-bonding is the result of men's (and women's) evolutionary history. Called attachment theory, it was originally developed by John Bowlby in the 1960s. Bowlby drew from a variety of theoretical perspectives as well as research with nonhuman animals. He emphasized the importance of the relationship between child and parents. Consistent with the era and his own background, the focus was on the mother-child bond, although Bowlby acknowledged—and subsequent research has demonstrated—that the theory applies equally well to the father-child bond and, in fact, the bond of any individual who regularly cares for the child.[23]

Attachment begins with the relationships between a child and its primary caregivers during the first two years of the child's life. According to the theory, young children learn about relationships based on how they are treated during this time. This initial round of learning about relationships serves as the model for all relationships that an individual will ever form.

Because human infants are almost completely dependent on others for food, safety, and comfort during their first few years of life, they also learn about physical, emotional, and psychological safety. Thus, these early relationships are also of central importance for several other aspects of life.

Bowlby pointed out that this dependence on adults for food, comfort, and safety would be present throughout human history. He also pointed out that many other animals who give birth to live young (and some that produce eggs) also provide this kind of care for their infants, including our closest biological relatives. These factors suggest that attachment is biologically based and evolutionarily adaptive. Some researchers have reported evidence of a neurological circuit that facilitates attachment.[24]

Through the 1980s and 1990s, most attachment research focused on whether children were "securely" or "insecurely" attached and how that was related to other aspects of childhood, including school performance, delinquent behavior, and friendship patterns. Researchers also compared the characteristics of parents who had securely attached children with those of parents who had insecurely attached children.[25] If you work in the education, child-care, or health fields, you may be familiar with reactive attachment disorder; it refers to the same attachment.

Attachment is the result of experiences during infancy, but those early experiences aren't destiny. Research has demonstrated that although individuals usually retain the same attachment style throughout their life, change is possible. It may occur "naturally" after traumatic events or when an individual's immediate environment changes substantially, such as in cases of parental separation or death (for children), natural disasters, or war.[26] It can also change through the insight and effort that characterize effective psychotherapy.

From this theoretical and empirical database, theorists and researchers started to apply attachment theory to a broader set of human relationships. They argued that those early understandings of relationships should influence the relationships we create as adults, including one with a lifelong partner. Much of the theoretical work has been done by Cornell University psychologist Cindy Hazan.[27]

Children who demonstrate a secure or good attachment display four characteristics: they seek and maintain physical proximity with their attachment figure, they seek comfort or aid when they need it, they use the attachment figure as a secure base from which to explore new places, and they experience distress when there are prolonged or unexpected absences from their attachment figures.[28] This is the most common type of attachment worldwide; in American and Western studies, about two-thirds of children are found to be securely attached.[29]

These characteristics are also present in adult romantic relationships.[30] The physical proximity of childhood feeds into, or becomes, the touching, cuddling, and other forms of close physical contact we share with our romantic partners but not other good friends. The comfort seeking of childhood is replicated in adulthood when we turn to our romantic partners for solace or help. We often rely on our partners when trying new things; somehow, having our partner there tends to "make it better." And we become stressed when our partners are away, whether for a weekend, a weeklong business trip, or a military deployment that lasts for months or years. Given all these things that being with your partner means, is it any surprise that death of a spouse is often identified as the most stressful experience one can have, or why divorce or separation from a spouse ranks nearly as high?

Attachment theory also identifies the characteristics that caregivers of securely attached children are most likely to have. Adults who make good attachment figures for children tend to be kind, warm, responsive, and competent (caretakers), and it doesn't matter if they're female or male.[31] In Chapter Three, we saw that the characteristics guys value in a dating partner focus on companionship, love, emotional intimacy, and supportiveness. These lists—one for a child's caretaker, one for a long-term romantic partner—sound quite similar.

Overall, attachment theory helps us understand the behavior that most guys demonstrate. It tells us that men should develop deep connections with others, and that most will do this with only one romantic partner at a time.

Evolution and Evolution?

So far, I've presented two different evolutionary theories. They both have data that support their claims. In the research world, they're often positioned as competing theories, but I'm not convinced that they're really opposites; I think they just focus on different things. Attachment theory seems applicable to the majority of men, whereas SST applies to a minority. Attachment also describes behaviors that give children a better chance to live long enough to reproduce, an evolutionary goal.[32] But attachment theory doesn't explain the persistent and well-documented differences between males and females in actual and desired sexual behavior that SST does.[33]

Blending Attachment Theory and SST

Marco Del Giudice recently adapted attachment theory to accommodate for differences between males and females. Because most people are securely attached, Del Giudice's version retains the strengths of attachment theory that I noted in the previous section. Del Giudice also included relatively recent research demonstrating that boys with insecure attachment tend to have what's called the "avoidant" type, whereas girls with insecure attachment tend to have what's called the "anxious" or "resistant" type. People—primarily boys and men—with an avoidant attachment style tend to avoid becoming connected to other people; their relationships tend to be relatively shallow and don't last as long. Accordingly, they would be more likely to choose short-term sexual partners and rarely engage in long-term relationships.[34] In essence, these are the folks most likely to be Casanovas.

On the flip side, people—mostly girls and women—with an anxious or resistant attachment style tend to form relationships that may be described as "needy" or "clingy." The term "resistance" refers to separations. These folks strongly prefer long-term relationships, even if those relationships are not necessarily the best or healthiest.[35] It is possible that some of these folks would hook up if they thought they could turn those hookups into long-term relationships,[36] a situation the real-life Casanova actively avoided.

Neural Circuits

Research on neural "circuits" provides support for Del Giudice's synthesis. A circuit consists of a group of brain structures, the neural paths that connect them, and the neurotransmitters they use to communicate. Each circuit has a particular function. Like electrical circuits in a house, each circuit can be turned on (activated) and off (at rest). Each electrical circuit provides power to a specific part of your house or a specific appliance. When a circuit is activated, or turned on, then the appliances connected to that circuit can function; when a circuit is not activated, or turned off, the appliances don't work. Similarly, when a neural circuit is activated, the thoughts and behaviors controlled by that circuit become more likely to occur.

The existence of circuits within the brain allows the brain to divide up tasks instead of having to "figure out" which part of the brain will complete a task every single time that task needs to be done, which would slow things down considerably. We also know that, over time, circuits that are used frequently become better integrated and faster. In everyday life, practice enables things to happen more easily and more quickly, reflecting the increased integration of that neural circuit.

In her book *Why We Love*, Helen Fisher argues that the brain has distinct circuits for lust, love, and attachment.[37] This means that Casanova-like lust, as well as the connections to others propounded by Bowlby's original attachment theory and Del Giudice's updated version, both rely on neural circuitry that's evolved over millennia. So has a separate circuit for love, which plays a key role in young men's dating habits, as we saw in Chapter Three.

Genetic Explanations

This chapter has discussed a few different theories that tell stories about what happened millennia ago. Given all the difficulty we have predicting people's behavior today, I'm always somewhat skeptical when someone tells me how humans behaved millions of years ago. Whether you believe these stories or don't really buy into the theories I've described, we now have technologies like PET scanners, fMRIs, and genetic analysis that can help us figure out how our brains work today. From this research, it's clear that brain chemistry, brain structures, and genetics all play a role in understanding sexual behavior.

One explanation comes from the research on risk-taking, and positions Casanova-like behavior as a form of risk-taking. We know that sexual behavior is complex and multifaceted. (I hope that if I've done nothing else, I've convinced you of that by this point in the book.) We also know that many complex human behaviors are due to many different genes, not just a single gene. One recent study of biological factors associated with adolescent substance use examined six different aspects of brain function known to be related to risk-taking.[38] Working with children of alcoholics, the researchers found that males with relatively low levels of the neurotransmitter dopamine were more likely to use drugs. Others have also noted male-specific trends in brain functioning and risk-taking.[39]

We also know that some genetic conditions are more common among males than females because the relevant genes are transmitted on our so-called sex chromosomes. This is the twenty-third pair of chromosomes, and for most of the population it's either XX (female) or XY (male). The Y chromosome contains many fewer genes than the X it's matched with, so there are a fair number of gene pairs that are made up of only a single gene. Perhaps one—or several—of the genes that influence risk-taking are found in that area. If these risk-taking genes are recessive and some of them are transmitted along the X chromosome, males would be more risk-taking in general.

The evidence certainly supports the idea that guys are more inclined to take risks. Among adolescents, we see this in almost every "risk behavior" we look at: alcohol use, use of other substances, risky driving, delinquent behavior, and so on. These behaviors tend to cluster together; teenage boys and young men who engage in any one of these behaviors are more likely to engage in the others. And they're also more likely to start having sex at a younger age, to have more casual partners, and to have more total partners,[40] but the odds of engaging in these sexual behaviors don't increase nearly as much as the odds for those other behaviors. For example, adolescents who are drinking heavily are much more likely to also drive recklessly than they are to have multiple total sexual partners.

The evidence is clear: evolution and biology can help us understand young men's sexual behavior. But biology is complicated; there's a reason it's hard to get into med school. Biologically oriented theories can explain both connection and promiscuity, but they, too, demonstrate that promiscuity is enacted by only a minority of guys. For me, the more convincing case is made by theories that stress connections with others, because such connections provide the greatest chance that a guy's offspring will survive long enough to pass his genes on to yet another generation. It also jibes with the fact that most people who have ever lived have had a single life partner.

5

. . . .

Masculinity, Peers, and Identity

Beer companies these days are spending a lot of time and money talking about what it means to be a man. Miller Lite is now telling me to "man up," having already told me about "man law." It also has the "Liteguards" and other ways of pointing out unmanly behaviors. For Bud Light, it's the satiric Real Men of Genius. For Dos Equis, it's the Most Interesting Man in the World.

It's not just the beer companies though. One of the biggest-selling books of the 1980s was Bruce Feirstein's *Real Men Don't Eat Quiche*, published in 1982. In 2007, Conn and Hal Iggulden published *The Dangerous Book for Boys*. I'd guess there have been hundreds of titles of this sort in the twenty-five years between these books. There's even the *Good Men Project*, a book and Web site that "explore the world of men and manhood . . . , tackling the issues and questions that are most relevant to men's lives."[1]

If nothing else, the mere existence of all these different sources tells us one thing: there's a lot of discussion about what it means to "be a man."

Masculinity

Anthropologist David Gilmore examined definitions of masculinity across eleven different cultures. He concluded that there are three general ways a teenage boy can prove his masculinity, and called them the three P's:[2]

- Providing (for family or clan)

- Protecting (family or clan)

- Procreating

In the abstract, the three P's are all admirable and honorable goals. But if you're fifteen, living at home, attending high school, and lacking in superpowers that would let you save the world, these aren't really things that you can—or should—do. What's left? How can a teenage boy prove he's a man or, at least, "man enough"?

In some ways, the only one of these that young men can hope to achieve is procreation. But most fifteen- to eighteen-year-olds don't really want to be fathers quite yet; only about one young man in seven hopes to be a father by the time he's twenty-two.[3] There are certainly social prohibitions that discourage paternity at this age; it's not really what we do here in the United States at the beginning of the twenty-first century.

The description of current-day American masculinity that is probably most well known comes from Deborah David and Robert Brannon's *The Forty-Nine Percent Majority* (1976). They talked about four principles of masculinity:[4]

- Be a Big Wheel

- Be a Sturdy Oak

- No Sissy Stuff

- Give 'em Hell

In *Real Boys*, William Pollack called this "the Boy Code."[5] These directives tell guys what masculinity means and how to act in order to prove their masculinity in current-day America.

Like the three P's, this description gives young men a lot of leeway in their choices. For example, the Be a Big Wheel directive tells them to be a success, but it doesn't specify where that success should occur. Being the star quarterback and being the founder of a billion-dollar tech company are both ways to earn masculine "cred" (credentials).

It's important to know that the definition of masculinity or "being a man's man" has changed over the years. Mostly, this is slow, subtle change, visible over decades. Men have not undergone the kind of sudden change in roles that women experienced as a result of 1970s-era feminism.[6] Yes, there are recent constructions like "metrosexuals" or their 1970s predecessor, the "sensitive New Age guy," but these haven't exactly been big hits with the average guy or dramatically changed how most or all men view masculinity.[7]

Breadwinning

Despite recent changes in the economy and the workplace, we still expect adult men to be a breadwinner, which fulfills the providing criterion. We often talk about men's employment as being central to their sense of self,[8] and it's often the first thing we ask someone we've just met. Being the (primary) earner is one way that men care for their families.[9]

This definition of masculinity relies heavily on living in an industrialized (or postindustrialized) society where most people work for someone else. Two hundred years ago, most adults worked for themselves or in the family business and valued family and community standing over their job. In *Bowling Alone*, Robert Putnam argued that as recently as the 1960s, community standing was at least as important to men as their job.[10] That makes some sense; not everyone can—or should—be the boss, but everyone can be involved in his or her community. The "traditional" male qualities of hard work and dedication can get you pretty far in those volunteer-run community organizations.

Not Acting Feminine

Boys and men have long been warned about acting like girls or women. You can find writings about men's evolved superiority over women in American newspapers from the 1920s; men who acted womanly were considered inferior.[11] Child-rearing manuals from that era also talk about how to promote healthy masculine behavior and extinguish feminine behavior in young boys.[12]

When the Boy Scouts of America were created in the 1910s, its founders were concerned about boys becoming "feminized" due to the new trend of fathers' working outside the home. They were also worried about the new mandatory education law that would (1) expose boys to an array of teachers, almost all of whom were women and (2) require boys to be still and quiet, thus curbing their natural boisterousness.[13] If that sounds familiar, it's because it's being repeated a century later as people have lamented boys' school performance. *Newsweek* put this "Boy Crisis" on its cover in January 2006.[14]

Not Showing Emotion

The idea that men should not show emotion is fairly recent. In part, it comes from the idea that emotion is women's domain and one of the defining characteristics of femininity. This idea is endorsed by the general public and psychological researchers.[15]

During the Victorian era, which ended about one hundred years ago, men were expected to have "passions" and show their feelings. It was expected that men would develop deep friendships with other men and talk about their love for each other. They were also expected to think and use reason; those rational abilities helped distinguish men from women.[16]

Things changed for men as we moved into the modern era at the beginning of the twentieth century. Reason and clearheadedness shifted from being important to being central expectations for men; they were necessary for an age in which industry, large-scale production, and mass distribution would become common.[17]

Emotion was seen as unreasonable and a hindrance, so men were encouraged to stop being emotional. In this way, emotion and reason became opposites, and this idea remains with us today.[18] But emotion and reason seem like completely different things—not opposites—to me. Logically, or perhaps rationally, isn't being irrational the opposite of being rational? And isn't apathy the opposite of emotion? The whole idea of emotional intelligence[19] tells us that emotion and reason (aka intelligence) can and do exist together.

As we moved through the twentieth century, the idea that women could use reason and could be rational, effective problem solvers became increasingly accepted, largely due to women's presence in the workplace during and after World War II. As women's use of reason became more acceptable and expected, the tolerance for men's emotion decreased;[20] after all, men had to continue to be different from women.

Today, men are expected to display emotion only at major life events, such as births, weddings, and funerals. And after the big game, of course. But we expect these displays to be fairly short and expect men to be somewhat embarrassed by them. The only exception is anger, which men are allowed to express almost any time they feel it.[21]

This injunction against showing emotions can be problematic. Young men seem to need to get drunk in order to tell their male friends they care about them or that they love them.[22] It also means that young men have very few opportunities to talk about and explore their feelings with a trusted confidant, an issue I'll return to in Chapter Ten.

Some men have started challenging this injunction against showing emotion. When researchers talk to men who were born in the 1970s and 1980s and who are parenting young children, those men often describe their fathers as emotionally absent and sometimes as physically absent. Their dads followed a model of parenthood in which fathers were financial providers, disciplinarians, and perhaps someone you played catch with, but not someone you really "connected" with or told your secrets to. In response, these men are trying to "be there" for their kids by developing that kind of emotional connection they didn't have with their own fathers.[23]

Not Being Homosexual

Boys also know they're not supposed to be gay, even if it's not politically correct to say that. In *Dude, You're a Fag: Masculinity and Sexuality in High School*, CJ Pascoe describes a variety of way in which homosexuality serves as a foil boys use to demonstrate their masculinity, as well as their heterosexuality. She argues that "fag" has "both sexual and nonsexual meanings that always draw on notions of gender . . . [and] is a fluid identity that boys struggle to avoid, often by lobbing the insult at others."[24]

The idea that homosexuality is unmasculine relies on portrayals of gay men as effeminate and womanly. Concerns about the sexual aspect of homosexuality draw from descriptions of homosexuality as unnatural or perverted. Many of these claims regarding masculinity and sexuality date to the late 1800s and early 1900s.[25]

In real life, many gay men don't fit the effeminate stereotype. In the United States, retired professional athletes from Major League Baseball, the NFL, and the NBA have come out.[26] Gareth Thomas, a Welsh rugby player and former captain of his national team, recently came out; he appears to be the first athlete in a major team sport to come out while still playing.

Athletes are just the most extreme examples of men we think of as especially "manly" actually being gay. Most gay teens and gay men don't wear women's clothing or flounce or get highly emotional. Most are otherwise "normal" guys who also happen to be interested in dating and having sex with men, not women.[27]

I don't need to tell you all the ways in which the prohibition against homosexuality can cause problems for gay boys. The prohibition against homosexuality also diminishes the ability for any guy to be emotionally intimate with his male friends; openly expressing emotion and care for another man is one of the stereotypical components of male homosexuality.[28]

Being Promiscuous

We haven't always expected men to demonstrate the promiscuity associated with the Casanova Complex. During the eighteenth and nineteenth centuries, young men were understood to have powerful sexual urges that could be difficult to control. Although many a young couple was pregnant when the pair were married, male promiscuity was neither acceptable nor expected.[29]

We still expect men to have powerful sexual urges. And today, most teens and young adults view premarital sex as an acceptable behavior, not a reproachable one.[30] Today, being able to "score," and especially being able to score repeatedly, turns a boy into "the Man." Even though a fair number of guys I've interviewed have told me they don't really buy this, they're also clear that this is how things work. Showing Casanova-like promiscuity has moved from unacceptable behavior to *the*—or at least *a*—preferred behavior.

A guy who breaks these rules, by showing emotion, "acting gay," or not sleeping around—or not sounding as though he wants to sleep around—is likely to be called a sissy, a fag, or something of the sort. These names are all explicit challenges to a boy's masculinity. In many cases, just questioning why these are the expectations for guys will get you called those names. And once someone questions your masculinity, you have to prove it. Again.

Identity Formation

Adolescents are trying to figure out what their identity is, "who they are." The typical teenage boy may not know who he is or who he wants to be, but he's sure he doesn't want to be known as a "sissy," "fag," "girlie man," or any of those other emasculating words.[31] (And why do effeminate and emasculating mean almost the same thing?)

According to Erik Erikson, who coined the terms "identity" and "identity crisis," adolescents need to figure out what their values are and what's important to them.[32] They also need to identify their strengths and weaknesses. Teens doing "identity work" try to determine how they fit in to their family and how they fit in to society at large. In order to figure it out, adolescents might imagine or try out a variety of job titles (for example, teacher, engineer), job levels (worker, small business owner), hobbies (athlete, band member), or social roles (community organizer, criminal). Identity work also includes understanding what their past means and identifying the future they'd like to have (that is, setting goals). Many adolescents also need to integrate their ethnic heritage and sexual orientation into the mix.[33]

Sounds exhausting, huh? Jeffrey Arnett has argued that most people do not complete these tasks during the teen years. Instead, most folks continue this work into their early or mid-twenties. According to Arnett, the need for additional time is due to the fact that most adolescents now attend college and many defer marriage and their first child until several years after college graduation, which gives them more time to explore their options before committing to a particular identity (career, family, and so on). When Erikson developed his theory in the 1950s and 1960s, most people finished their schooling at age eighteen, and a substantial percentage were married or engaged by twenty-one.[34]

Needless to say, figuring all these things out requires a fair amount of exploration. Much of that exploration isn't directly visible to parents, although there are certainly conversations about the future during which it's quite obvious. It's also obvious when, for example, a teenager comes home, declares that he is now vegetarian, preaches the relevant gospel for a few days, then quietly returns to the land of the carnivores. Several decades of research tell us that the kids who have the opportunity to explore different options and then, eventually, commit to a particular set of values, goals, and behaviors tend to be relatively healthier and have better psychological functioning than other kids.[35]

Social Identity

This description of identity gives us a broad sense of what's going on, but it doesn't clue us in to the specific choices that adolescents make. For that, we need to talk about "social identity." This refers to the ways in which we identify with recognized social groups or categories, especially when we use those terms to describe ourselves or other people use those terms to describe us.[36]

Many social identities tap into stereotypes. When someone describes himself as a Casanova or player or Don Juan, he's invoking the stereotype as a form of shorthand to give you a sense of who he is. If you don't know the stereotype he's talking about, then the social identity isn't particularly useful in that situation.

A young man might also qualify his statement by saying he's "kind of" a Casanova, or only a Casanova at parties and not in other situations. It's a way of acknowledging that he sometimes conforms to the Casanova stereotype, but that it's not his primary mode of behavior.

In order for these identity claims to be effective, an individual has to be reasonably well described by that stereotype. Adolescents can tell who's "real" and who's a "poser." Fitting the stereotype too closely and barely fitting the stereotype will both lead to accusations of being fake.

Social identity theories remind us that individuals can have multiple identities and will shift from one to another as needed.[37] A teenage boy might describe himself as a "player," a "jock," and a "big brother." If you're reading this book at home and thinking as a parent about how you'll use this information, and then get interrupted by a phone call from a colleague, you can switch into your professional identity with little difficulty. Boys can also make those kinds of shifts.

Peers and Identity Groups

In addition to giving us a sense of who a teenage boy is, his social identity tells us something about his friends. As you'd expect, people with the same social identity tend to befriend each other.[38] Some researchers use the term "cliques,"[39] but I prefer to call them "identity groups." You know them by a set of different names: jocks, nerds, rebels, band-ies, and so on. If you're a fan of the TV show Glee, you know the characters as Gleeks, Cheerios, and to a lesser extent, members of the football team (who are rarely referred to as "jocks").

Identity groups typically become apparent when children move from elementary to middle school, especially when that middle school has more than about a hundred students per grade. These groups seem to be most obvious and most important around ninth and tenth grade, roughly ages fourteen through sixteen. Things usually loosen up during the junior and senior years of high school.[40]

Identity groups influence several aspects of adolescents' lives. One is friendship: adolescents typically befriend others who share their identity, because they have similar interests and have the opportunity to get to know those folks by spending time together in relevant activities, such as band practice. Another function has to do with social status; some groups have more status than others.[41] On Glee, for example, the Gleeks are at the bottom of the social ladder, and the Cheerios are at (or near) the top.

When identity group membership is at its peak levels of importance, adolescents find it difficult to move from one group to another; those who try to change groups run in to resistance from the group they're trying to leave and the group they're trying to enter. Adolescents who try to belong to two different groups are under pressure to choose one group over the other and to act in the expected ways. This pressure comes not only from the group members but from other adolescents. The first High School Musical (HSM) movie revolves around this facet of identity groups: can jock Troy and nerd Gabriella participate in the school's annual musical even though they're not friends with drama (club) queen Sharpay?

HSM also illustrates another aspect of group membership: it provides adolescents with a set of values, beliefs, and activities that are expected of them.[42] As I mentioned in Chapter One, players— modern slang for Casanovas—are expected to be well dressed, spend money freely, be socially adept, and believe in and engage in casual sex, among other things.[43] From the perspective of identity formation, this image can be helpful because it provides a set of readily available options to explore that are likely to be appealing or a "good fit."

At the same time, those ready-made options exclude other choices that may also be appealing. The exclusions may be direct, such as that players aren't expected to be interested in academics.[44] They may also be matters of omission; for example, being a player doesn't give you any information about being a vegetarian or an omnivore. The first ensemble song in HSM, "Stick to the Status Quo," gives voice to the characters' desire to break out of these predefined identities while experiencing the pressure to conform.

Peers, Identity, and Masculinities

Some researchers have drawn on the work of feminist theorists and applied the concept of hierarchy and privilege to the group known as "men."[45] Those men who show the greatest adherence to a culture's definition of masculinity—the Boy Code, for example—are those who also gain the greatest benefits from the system known as "patriarchy." Among adolescents, these benefits typically include high status, popularity, and possibly (sexual) access to girls. For young men, "hegemonic" displays of masculinity—those that closely fit the patriarchal system—often come from guys known as jocks or players.[46]

Groups of men who show only partial adherence to the culture's definition may be seen as complicit. Even though they may not be seen as highly masculine, they are "man enough." They don't challenge the status quo, and they may receive some of the cultural benefits described by the patriarchal system.[47] You might know these guys as "average Joes."[48]

Other versions of masculinity are "subordinated." They accept the cultural definitions of masculinity, but are generally unable to meet those standards. As a result, they have low status and receive few or no benefits from the patriarchal system. "Geeks," for example, are generally viewed as not-masculine and as having relatively low social status among adolescents. They definitely do not get the girls.[49] They may have access to other forms of recognition and social standing, but those benefits are the result of, and perhaps in spite of, not being "manly." Microsoft founder Bill Gates and Apple founder Steve Jobs probably don't strike you as stereotypically masculine, but they still have a lot of power and status.

Challenges are typically presented by yet other, "marginalized" forms of masculinity. They are quite different from the status quo and are often labeled as deviant; in some cases, they may be subject to persecution or discrimination.[50] Although being "gay" or "a homosexual" has become increasingly accepted in the United States, these men were and still are deprived of some legal protections, have been the subject of persecution, and are occasionally the targets of hate crimes, simply for being gay.[51]

Some researchers refer to these different types of masculinity—jock, average Joe, geek, homosexual, and so on—as "masculinities." The term is intended to highlight that there are a variety of ways to be masculine, not just one.[52]

Bernard Lefkowitz offers a detailed and graphic description of how these masculinities can work. In his book *Our Guys: The Glen Ridge Rape and the Secret Life of the Perfect Suburb*, he describes the events leading up to the rape of a sixteen-year-old cognitively impaired girl by several of the town's prominent teenage boys. This particular group of boys had grown up together and been best friends for years, and several were children of community leaders. The core of the football team, they "ruled" the school; everyone—adolescent and adult—knew they were at the top of the social ladder.[53]

Because of the boys' status and their parents' connections, some adults adopted a double standard, looking the other way when this group of boys misbehaved but enforcing the same rules for other boys. This is one of the benefits delivered to those who adopt the hegemonic form of masculinity.

Lefkowitz relates stories about how some of these boys would occasionally demand hand jobs or blow jobs (which they called "hoovering") from girls. At other times, the boys would get other boys, as well as some of the other girls, to encourage, embarrass, or otherwise coerce girls into "agreeing" to service the guys. Even in high school, sex can be a benefit of fitting the hegemonic mold.[54]

Although you may find this kind of behavior shocking for a group of teenage boys, there's nothing new about rich, famous, and powerful men trying to gain sexual favors from women they aren't interested in dating. Do you think Tiger Woods had to seduce his various mistresses or that Bill Clinton needed weeks or months to convince Monica Lewinski? Do rock stars need to convince their groupies to have sex?

In his description of the community, Lefkowitz identifies some other masculinities. They included the "Giggers, [who] got their label because they called their parties 'gigs.' . . . [They] were bound for artsy colleges." These teens accepted the system and their place on the social ladder, and had some social contact with the Jocks, including the rare boy who was both a Gigger and an athlete (but rarely a Jock). These adolescents had some popularity, but they weren't quite the "in" crowd, and adults rarely looked the other way when they broke the rules.[55] We might call the Giggers complicit.

The social ladder also included the "Achievers, whom less motivated students contemptuously labeled as 'nerds' or 'geeks.' . . . Their industry was recognized by a place on the honor roll" and entrance into elite universities. As in most places, these nerds had low status among their peers. They had occasional, but minimal, contact with the Jocks.[56] They could be categorized as subordinated.

And then there were the "Guidos, a disrespectful term . . . broadened to include youngsters who openly rejected the college-and-corporate-success ethic" of the town. Lefkowitz describes them as the town's "underclass" and observes that they had no real contact with the Jocks, outside of the necessity of being in the same school building. Because these teens were primarily in vocational classes, they were rarely in the same classes as the Jocks. The Guidos were effectively rejected and, according to Lefkowitz, not really considered part of the school's social ladder.[57] By rejecting the town's expected path of college and corporate success, they fit the definition of marginalized. They received no status, and you can probably imagine that the adults never looked the other way when one of these kids broke the rules.

Proving Your Masculinity

Even if we're not entirely sure what masculinity is, researchers and young men are clear about one thing: masculinity has to be proved, over and over; it is never a given.[58] Seventy-two-year-old Jack Palance knew this; when he received an Oscar for his role in *City Slickers* in 1992, he did a series of one-armed push-ups, on stage and wearing a tux, to prove that he was still an able man.

When anthropologists have explored manhood rituals or coming-of-age rituals in different cultures, they've found that they're administered by the adult males in the community. They're the ones who determine when a boy is ready, what he must do (if there is more than one variation), and what constitutes success.[59] In non- or preindustrialized cultures, you need all, or almost all, boys to successfully pass the test and be recognized as (adult) men. The rituals have as much to do with adulthood as with gender, if not more.[60]

In current-day America, we don't really have a group of men who perform this function or a distinct marker that separates boyhood from manhood.[61] According to sociologist Michael Kimmel, author of *Guyland*, the people who often stand in for these adults are groups of young men, typically as found in fraternities, athletic teams, or gangs. The full members often talk about the usefulness and necessity of going through an induction ritual, typically because it creates a shared experience. The rituals boys and young men design usually involve proving oneself in some way, often through physical risks, substance abuse, sexuality, criminality, or some combination of these.[62]

These themes were illustrated in one analysis of hazing practices by two British men's college sports teams in the early 2000s. Over the seven-year period they were observed, both teams favored drinking alcohol well beyond the point of intoxication as the preferred "method" of requiring the newbies to prove themselves. One team's hazing routine included semidrunken wrestling while partially (or fully) nude. The newcomers didn't seem concerned about the implicit homosexuality, which was often made explicit by the comments of the spectating full members, so it was eventually eliminated from the routine.[63]

These rituals are about proving that you're one of the guys. There's nothing in this team's ritual, or most rituals created by other teens or young adult men, that really helps a guy prove that he's an adult man.

You don't need an official organization to prove your masculinity. Teenage boys are very clear that sexual activity is one way to earn status in the eyes of other boys.[64] It's important that some of this be witnessed by those other boys. That can be kissing or making out or wandering off together to a bedroom or the bushes; guys don't have to watch their buddy having sex. This public component is necessary for establishing credibility.

In many ways, the connection between sex and status is really about status among boys; they're the ones who give other boys "props" for having sex and who are going to enhance a boy's reputation by telling others about the hot chick he scored with.[65] In Chapter Three, I pointed out that friends and peers played a minimal role when a young man is deciding whom to date, but were of higher importance when he chose a hookup partner.

These public displays also help "prove" one's heterosexuality. This may be especially important for young men who are accused of being gay, as well as for young man whose masculinity has been questioned in other ways.[66]

The idea that boys have sex with girls to impress other boys may seem odd, but that same logic is part of the reason why some guys will publicly propose sex with a complete stranger. You might think of stereotypical male construction workers ogling and yelling at the women who walk by (although they're hardly the only men who do it). I don't think the guy who yells "Hey baby, you're hot—wanna go get it on?" at a complete stranger has any belief that the woman he's yelling at is going to say yes and mean it. But his buddies may be impressed by how "ballsy" he is and the reactions he gets.

———————

What all this means is that we've created a system in which most boys and young men feel that they need to prove their masculinity but don't really have a meaningful way to do it. Most muddle through this during adolescence and young adulthood, periodically engaging in some relevant behavior in order to convince their friends and peers that they're man enough. Some guys choose to follow the dictates of the Casanova Complex and screw around.

6

. . . .

How the Media Promote Casanova

Over the years, you've probably gotten to know several guys who act out the Casanova Complex. They have names like Barney Stinson (Neil Patrick Harris) from *How I Met Your Mother*, Charlie Harper (Charlie Sheen) from *Two and a Half Men*, Joey Tribbiani (Matt LeBlanc) from *Friends*, Sam Malone (Ted Danson) from *Cheers*, and Jack Tripper (John Ritter) from *Three's Company*. And don't forget the Fonz (Henry Winkler) from *Happy Days* and Hawkeye Pierce (Alan Alda) from *MASH*, whom I mentioned in the Chapter One.

Every one of these TV shows aired for at least seven years, was regularly among the top twenty shows, and won at least one Emmy for Best Comedy. Every actor I listed won an Emmy as Best Male Lead in a Comedy for these roles; the only exception is Neil Patrick Harris, whose Emmy was for Best Male Supporting Actor in a Comedy.

The Casanova Complex doesn't just affect TV characters; you've also seen it in movies. *The Wedding Crashers*, a movie about a pair of Casanovas, was among the top ten grossing movies in 2005. And then there's James Bond, who's been seducing women around the globe since the 1970s.

The movies also give us a different expression of male sexuality, in the form of teenage boys who are desperate to lose their virginity and will do almost anything to make it happen. In the films, it seems as though the boys can think only about sex and that no risk is too great if it'll help them get laid; dating never seems to be an option. *Porky's* (1982) was the first of these movies; more recent films include *American Pie* (1999), *Superbad* (2007), and even *The 40 Year Old Virgin* (2005).

The latter set of movies are often categorized as sex comedies; the genre has been popular, and its big hits have been very profitable. *Porky's* spawned two sequels and, in some ways, created the genre. *American Pie*, produced at an estimated cost of $11 million, earned gross receipts of approximately $235 million and launched a franchise of seven movies. These guys may not quite be Casanovas, but they want to be.

I think this is incredibly important. Some researchers have begun talking about media as a "super-peer" because, like a friend, it's usually around, and it tells you a lot of things your parents don't.[1] Researcher Annika Suoninen argued that "talking about media and media contents is clearly the most important way in which media affect peer group relationships," but didn't dispute media's other potential effects.[2]

In this chapter, I'll talk about how mass media influence us and reinforce the Casanova Complex. If you think television doesn't influence us, then do you really think that all those major corporations spend billions of dollars per year on advertising and it doesn't work? If TV didn't occasionally inspire us to try new things, why would shows like MTV's *Jackass* tell us, "Don't try this at home?"

But before we go any further, a quick exercise. In the margin of the book or on a piece of scrap paper, jot down your answer to the following question: "How much do the media affect the average person in my age group?" using a 1–7 scale, where 1 means "not at all" and 7 means "very much." Got your score written down? Now I'd like you to answer another question: "How much do the media affect me?" using the same scale. When we ask research participants this pair of questions, and even when I ask it in my classrooms, most people say that media affect other people more than it affects them. Sometimes known as "the third person affect,"[3] this discrepancy also shows up when we ask people to rate other people's driving and their own driving.[4]

Even though this is a book about the sexual behavior of teenage boys and young men, I'm going to talk about media depictions of both men and women, and media that target both men and women. After all, guys who are interested in girls aren't just learning about their own sexuality through the media; they're learning about their potential partners as well. Likewise, girls and women form expectations about guys from the media. That said, I'll be looking in more detail at male-oriented images and sources than I will female-oriented images and sources.

How Pervasive Are Media Inputs?

According to the U.S. Census Bureau's 2006 figures, over 98 percent of households have at least one television; the average household has 2.6 television sets.[5] At the end of 2010, Nielsen estimated that just over 90 percent of households had cable or satellite.[6] One practical outcome of this is that most teenagers have a television set in their bedroom, often with cable; in fact, almost two-thirds of adolescents in one study said they had a TV in their room. Most American households also have at least one Internet-connected computer. In a very real way, the typical American teenage boy can watch anything he wants on TV, in his room, at any time.[7]

That television and cable content may or may not include pornography. Because pornography must be requested directly and is listed as a distinct charge on the cable or satellite bill, it's easy to exclude. Then again, HBO has its *Real Sex* series, and Cinemax has long had a reputation for showing "adult" movies, now labeled "after dark" and easily found on its Web site. Other networks reference this kind of content without showing it. The "basic cable" channel E! offers *The Girls Next Door*, which follows the lives of several Playboy Bunnies. Parents who know how to use the blocking restrictions can also prevent adolescents from seeing R-rated movies or movies with sexual content, but I suspect that very few parents of teens do that.

Music is even more accessible. In part that's because most cable and satellite companies provide several music-only channels, and there are a broad variety of radio stations and other music sources online. The majority of teens have at least a clock radio if not a stereo system. And then there are iPods and other portable devices, smart-phones, and so on. One pair of researchers suggested that "listening to popular music is properly seen as a natural and generally benign part of growing up in contemporary Western society."[8]

Documenting just how much time an individual spends with media is a bit challenging, but researchers have developed a variety of tech-niques to do so. Part of the problem arises from our ability to use media while doing something else. For example, many of us have the radio on while driving or while we're at the office, but does that really count as listening? Many adolescents and undergraduates play music or have the television on while studying; how should we count that? The portability of media, particularly music, makes this problem worse; obtaining an accurate estimate of music listening time for someone who "always" listens to music on his or her portable player (iPod, phone, mp3 player, and the like) can be challenging.

Still, the estimates are reasonably consistent. Adolescents and young adults typically report spending two to three hours per day watching television. Believe it or not, this may be an underestimate because researchers often ask about prime-time shows (8:00–10:00 PM) by name and focus on new episodes, thus ignoring times when pro-grams can be watched as reruns or on DVD.[9] This approach often omits sports programming, although one study reported an average of about two hours watching sports during the summer months.[10]

Teenage boys and young men also spend a fair amount of time watching music videos. The majority of eighth-grade boys watch music videos, typically for one-and-a-half to three hours per week. The amount seems to be the same for older adolescents and under-graduates, and again, music video time may increase during the summer months.[11]

According to a 2008 study, more than 90 percent of boys said they'd seen online pornography before they turned eighteen, and most said that it was intentional, not accidental. First exposure typically occurred during the high school years, ages fourteen through eighteen, although about one boy in three said he'd seen porn online before turning fourteen.[12]

Assessments of time spent listening to music also point to its potential for influence. In one study, 98 percent of eighth-grade boys reported listening to some audio music each week, with an average of nearly five hours per week. Music time appears to increase as individuals move through adolescence, with one study reporting an average of nearly seven hours of (audio) music per day during the summer.[13] Given the ability to have music playing in the background while doing other things, this figure seems entirely reasonable to me. In fact, I've been listening to music almost the entire time I've written this book.

Each month, about one guy in four reads what the British call "lad" magazines: *Maxim*, *FHM*, and the like; the average guy says he sees and reads a magazine of this sort a couple of times per year.[14] The *Sports Illustrated* swimsuit issue typically sells over four million copies, about one million more than any other week of the year.[15] Those numbers are just for the year's new issue; they don't include the calendars, online viewings, and other related products.

How Pervasive Is Sexual Content?

I don't think it's any surprise that teenage boys and young men spend a lot of time with media. Many people talk about current-day America as being media saturated because media are so pervasive. If we're going to talk about media's influence on boys' conceptions about sexuality, we need to know what sort of sexual content they're being exposed to.

On Screen

Dating, romantic relationships, and sexual behavior appear regularly on television, especially the shows that teens favor.[16] University of Michigan researcher Monique Ward illustrated the commonness of this sexual talk and some of the complexity of studying it. She analyzed the top ten shows for 2- to 11- and 12- to 17-year-olds during the 1992–1993 season; there were twelve shows overall because the top ten varied slightly for these age groups. Among teens, the top three were *The Fresh Prince of Bel Air*, *Blossom*, and *Roseanne*.[17]

Every one of the twelve shows included regular references to dating or sex. The research team talked about "interactions," not conversations, so that they could include occasions when a character interrupts a conversation to comment on somebody's appearance, for example, then returns to the conversational topic; that comment and the conversation were treated as separate interactions. Across all shows, approximately 30 percent of interactions between characters referred to sexuality in some way. *Full House* had the lowest frequency of sexual content, at about one interaction in seven, whereas sexuality was referenced in almost three of every five interactions on *Blossom* and about half the interactions on *Martin*. *Beverly Hills, 90210*, which you may remember as being all about sex and relationships, was in the middle of the list with about one interaction in four referencing sexuality.

Not all interactions were the same, though. Some were one-liners, like "she's hot"; others were extended conversations that included multiple comments about sexuality. *The Simpsons* and *The Fresh Prince of Bel Air* had the fewest interactions on average, primarily "sexual jokes, comments, and innuendoes." By contrast, *Roseanne* and *Martin* had the greatest number of sexual interactions and regularly featured "entire discussions about sexuality, competing for partners, and working through relationship conflict."[18]

Prime-time television is not the only video content. Music videos routinely feature sexualized content. One analysis of videos popular during December 2004 and January 2005 on MTV, VH1, BET, and CMT revealed that almost three of every four rap and R&B videos included sexual content; "only" one of every three rock or country videos included sexual content. Across all the videos analyzed, the average video had approximately eleven distinct sexual acts.[19]

Perhaps that shouldn't be surprising; there are a fair number of professionals—primarily directors and actresses—who started in the porn industry and have moved to music videos. Some musical performers have also crossed over. The most well known is probably rap performer Snoop Dogg; he produced and starred in his own pornographic film in 2001, *Doggstyle*.[20]

Pornography and its offshoots are ubiquitous in mainstream media. In the early adolescent movie *Diary of a Wimpy Kid*, *Playboy* magazine is important for establishing the conflict between Greg and his older brother, Rod. In the PG-13 *Charlie's Angels: Full Throttle*, the Angels go undercover at a strip club; on-screen, we see them performing in the "appropriate" attire. Porn even shows up in prime-time television shows like *How I Met Your Mother*. In one episode, Barney—our Casanova—records a "Save me from my relationship" message for his friend and roommate Ted on one of Barney's pornographic videotapes, believing that if he ever chooses to give away his porn collection, Ted will (1) watch it and (2) come to his rescue. (He does.) And, not surprisingly, Internet searches for information on sexuality and sexual health often return pornographic sites,[21] especially when there are no filters or blocking software. As the emcee of the 25th annual Porn Awards put it, the awards have moved from a "dark room in a [Las] Vegas shit hotel" to the "classiest hotel in Vegas."[22]

Even video games include sexual content. Nearly half of 2003's top twenty games for Xbox, PS2, and Nintendo's GameCube featured a character, usually a woman, wearing sexually revealing clothing. Nearly one in four games included a woman with voluptuous breasts. Men were rarely sexualized, although about one game in ten included men in sexually revealing clothing, and about one game in twenty showed a partially or totally nude male character.[23]

In Music

Although sexual content is less common in music, the number of songs that mention sex has been increasing since the 1980s. In an analysis of top fifty songs from each even-numbered year between 1960 and 2008 that I led, about 12 percent of all songs, or one in eight, talked about sex. By contrast, about 75 percent of songs talked about dating or romance, and that percentage didn't change much from one decade to the next.[24]

The increase in sexual lyrics was primarily due to rap songs.[25] Rap lyrics and music videos have been the subject of several analyses. An assessment of top-selling rap albums revealed that about one song in five was classed as misogynistic, primarily through sexual objectification, use of degrading or shaming names ("bitches," "hos" [whores], "gold diggers," and the like), or explicit statements of distrust of women in general.[26]

In Print

Lad magazines like Maxim, FHM, and Stuff average about two articles per issue that are explicitly focused on sex. These articles are almost always accompanied by a sexually suggestive picture of a woman, and are provided in addition to the provocative pictures related to the model, singer, or actress on the cover. About one-third of the photos that accompany these articles include pictures of multiple women. For those who don't read the articles, the visuals suggest that it's important to have multiple partners.[27]

Print media for women also routinely talk about dating and sexual relationships, and thus describe male sexuality. An analysis of several different teen's and women's magazines published in the mid-2000s revealed that just over one article in five talked about sexuality.[28] Girls and women also learn about men's sexuality from romance novels, the second most popular genre of books in the United States. Industry statistics suggest that nearly half of all women age thirteen or older read a romance novel in 2008.[29]

Media Messages About Sexuality

Given how common sexual content is, it's no surprise that boys and young adults report receiving a broad swath of lessons about dating and sexuality from media sources, and particularly lessons about sexual freedom.[30] When interviewed and surveyed, boys and young men tell us that sexual stereotypes about men (and women) are also fairly common.[31] Those messages tend to fit the Casanova Complex. At some point in their lives, but especially for preteens and younger teens, this content is new territory.

Male Sexuality on Screen

Prime-time television shows tend to present an image of male sexuality that looks and sounds a lot like the Casanova Complex. At least, that is the image of unmarried guys on situation comedies, the shows favored by teens and young adults. These TV guys are always willing to have sex. Boys and men watch girls and often comment on girls' appearance; males' appearance and bodies are occasionally praised and rarely the source of insults or putdowns. Guys get praised and their social status improves as a result of these comments and "scoring." Boys and young men are also expected to treat their buddies as a higher priority than their girlfriends—"bros before hos"; if they don't, they're considered "whipped."[32] Many of these themes also appear regularly in beer commercials,[33] which are often broadcast during sporting events, so that guys who watch only sports are given the message.

Music videos have been the focus of several analyses, with particular attention given to the storytelling "concept" videos; concert videos are typically not included in the research. Analysis after analysis tells us that music videos tend to follow a particular pattern: male performers are positioned as powerful, rich, and in control. They usually desire women they've just met, and they may desire several women; desire for just one woman occurs in less than half of videos with sexual content.[34]

Over the last twenty years or so, and especially among rap performers, male artists' bodies have become increasingly visible, well-built, and attractive. That said, men only occasionally dress in provocative clothing; most of the time, they're in "neutral" clothing.[35] I'll discuss men's appearance in the next chapter.

There are several themes that appear regularly in mainstream heterosexual porn, the largest segment of the porn industry. First and foremost are the ideas that men are always ready for sex and want sex with a variety of different partners. Male domination of women is very common and takes a variety of forms. One analysis revealed that about 80 percent of the most popular porn videos in 2005 included violence toward women, with physical violence occurring in over 80 percent of those films and verbal aggression in about half. Other forms of female maltreatment include offering to pay women for sex then reneging and leaving women naked on the side of the road and away from home after sex.[36]

Male Sexuality in Music

My analysis of music lyrics from 1960 to 2008 revealed an interesting trend for male performers. By "male performers," I mean solo artists like Elvis, Billy Joel, and Justin Timberlake, as well as all-male groups like the Beatles, the Rolling Stones, and the Backstreet Boys. From one decade to the next, male performers sang fewer songs that were just about dating or romance. At the same time, there was an increase in songs that talked about sex. During the 1970s and 1980s, most of these songs talked about both dating and sex. In the 1990s and 2000s, songs tended to talk about sex but not dating or relationships.[37] Although less detailed than video because the message has to come through the words without any visual information, the content parallels what we see on screen and contributes to our growing belief in the Casanova Complex as typical.

Male Sexuality in Print

In print, several themes about young men's sexuality stand out in both male-oriented and female-oriented publications. An analysis of Maxim, FHM, and Stuff magazines revealed that their major themes emphasized women's sexual preferences, "unorthodox" behaviors and sexual positions, and ways men can improve their sex lives. Although the focus on women's sexual preferences sounds egalitarian and perhaps even "liberated," these articles routinely emphasized that keeping a women sexually pleased would lead to more or better sex for the guy. The analysis also revealed that stories about sex with multiple women were fairly common. More than half the articles focused on sex with a dating partner, and about one in four discussed sex with strangers; less than 2 percent of the articles about sex involved a marital partner.[38] Although the magazines tended to highlight sex within dating relationships, the Casanova Complex appeared regularly.

In magazines for girls and women, boys and men are portrayed as being primarily interested in sex, and guys spend little time worrying about the negatives associated with sex (disease, pregnancy, or reputation).[39] This sounds a lot like the Casanova Complex.

The central male character in romance novels, call him the hero if you will, seems to be a Casanova. Laura Clawson analyzed sixty romance novels published between 1998 and 2000.[40] The hero is almost always employed, usually in a managerial or executive position. A substantial number of these guys—40 percent—are independently wealthy. He's also a "sexually magnetic, attractive man." The hero is almost always sexually experienced, the result of relationships with many different women over the years; the books are clear that he's not promiscuous, per se, and doesn't hook up. About one-third of these guys don't believe in love and believe that they'll never settle down and get married, but by the end of the book have fallen deeply in love with the heroine and actively choose to spend the rest of their lives with her. In essence, their Casanova-like behavior is "tamed" by the heroine.

Regardless of the medium, we are regularly presented with a Casanova-like image of male sexuality. It's no wonder that the authors of *Packaging Boyhood*, Lyn Mikel Brown, Sharon Lamb, and Mark Tappan, described the player as one of the most common images of masculinity;

he seems to be everywhere. From all these media, we learn that Casanova is the star, Casanova is the "real man," and Casanova rarely gets in trouble for his love 'em and leave 'em behavior.[41]

What the Media Tell Us About Female Sexuality

One of the primary messages that television provides about girls and women is that they should always appear attractive. Their appearance is fair game for comments and jokes by both male and female TV characters. More generally, women in the media regularly wear sexually provocative clothing, and their bodies are objectified in various forms of advertising, in music videos, in video games, and of course in pornography.[42] Although not officially pornographic, shows like BET's Un:Cut feature music videos that are more sexually explicit and provocative than "regular" videos.[43]

Although girls and women do refuse men's sexual advances at times, they say yes quite regularly in the prime-time comedies that teens prefer. In music videos, they're often shown as wanting men sexually and being willing to do almost anything for the opportunity to have sex with a man. They also touch themselves in a sexual or sexually provocative manner with some regularity. In mainstream pornography, women always want sex, all women are available for sex (that is, no one is off-limits), and women readily interrupt other activities to have sex with strangers. Women routinely submit to men's whims, requests, and commands, or are forced to do so and appear to enjoy it, even though the actresses talk about some of these behaviors as "gross"—or worse—when the filming stops. The idea that some women want sex, verbally refuse a man's advances, then have (fabulous) sex appears regularly in pornography.[44] This contradicts most boys' experience; they tend to believe that when a girl says no, then sex will not happen, but when a boy says no, he can be talked into having sex.[45]

Mass media acknowledge that bad things related to sex happen to girls and women, but this appears in a minority of storylines. On TV and in magazines, the negatives that occur most frequently have to do with girls' and women's reputations—concerns about being considered "easy" or a "slut." Teen girls' magazines regularly include stories of victimization and how to avoid being victimized. In one analysis of top ten TV shows from 2004 to 2006 that had storylines dealing with women's health, approximately one in every fourteen about female patients was related to her sexual life in some way.[46]

Taken as a whole, the media tell us that sex is a good thing. The most typical depiction of teenage boys and young men is one that includes a lot of interest in sex, always being ready for sex, desire for beautiful women, and either ambivalence toward or no interest in relationships. This portrayal is part and parcel of the Casanova Complex. Guys are often powerful, whether that's physical brawn or economic wealth. Girls and women are meant to be looked at and expected to be attractive. They're sexually willing, but they may play hard to get or be unwilling to say yes. Negatives are rare, and almost exclusively the province of women. Sut Jhally, a professor of communication, refers to this portrayal of sexuality, especially in music videos, as a "dreamworld."[47]

What the Media Don't Tell Us About Sexuality

So far, I've focused on the primary themes in various forms of media. These are the scripts we've all learned and the way we sometimes expect the world to work. But it's also important to talk about what gets left out. There are some facts, attitudes, and stories that rarely or never appear in the media.

Most media rarely talk about the importance of love before having sex or saving sex for married couples. The only real place where these topics appear regularly is in *Seventeen*, *CosmoGirl*, and other magazines for teenage girls. Over the last few decades, popular TV shows and movies have primarily told us that sex rarely occurs after marriage.[48]

Contraception is rarely discussed or shown on TV; it amounts to less than 5 percent of all sexual content. Similarly, commercials for condoms are rare, but commercials for Viagra, Cialis, and other products that facilitate or enhance sex are relatively common. Expert information on sexual health or sexual behavior is also rare; it occurs on only about one show in twenty, usually talk shows.[49]

Despite the apparent lack of contraception, unwanted pregnancy is rare in prime-time shows. The lack of protection doesn't lead to disease, either; sexually transmitted infections (STIs), including HIV/AIDS, are almost completely unheard of in prime time.[50]

If you look at the approximately 5 percent of shows that acknowledge downsides to sex, you'll find that the repercussions are almost entirely limited to the bad reputation that a female character might acquire: being called slut, home wrecker, and so on.[51] Concerns about reputation appear a little more often in magazines like *Seventeen* and *CosmoGirl*; they also talk about unwanted pregnancy and STIs at times. But even here, the negatives are almost always limited to girls.[52]

By contrast, boys and men in the media may receive social benefits, particularly status, from having sex. They are not encouraged to think preventively about pregnancy, disease, sexual health, or other negative potential outcomes of having sex. In one analysis of a year's worth of lad magazines, issues like HIV/AIDS, safe sex, and pregnancy were never the main theme of an article; at best, they got a substantial mention in 5 percent of the articles. But some topics—STIs, rape, and abortion—were never mentioned.[53]

As I noted earlier, about one in fourteen health-related story lines in prime time over a three-year period addressed a woman's sexual health in one way or another. In these same shows, no man's sexual health was ever part of a story, even indirectly through a topic such as testicular cancer.[54]

How We Learn from Media

Adolescents consistently tell us that media are one of their primary sources for information about dating and sexuality, along with parents and peers.[55] Researchers talk about several different ways in which television and other forms of media influence us. One of these is so obvious that we often fail to notice it: media provide us with information that we don't already have. Mostly we think about this in terms of news, sports scores, documentaries, or celebrity gossip. But comedies and dramas can also give us new information. More than half of boys say this is one of the reasons they view online porn, along with sexual excitation.[56]

When television sets were new, and again when the Internet became available to the general population, media's ability to educate us was highlighted. It was part of the original sales pitch for buying a TV or for getting on the Internet. It wasn't just about informing *you* about places you've never seen and things you hadn't previously heard of; it was also about informing and educating your children. There are entire cable networks—National Geographic, Discovery, and the History Channel, to name a few—for which this seems to be their primary programming goal. Sometimes we learn about something completely new, and sometimes we just add facts or fill in gaps in areas we already know something about.

We don't just learn about nature or science or history, though. We can learn about *any* topic. If you're just starting to be curious about dating or sex, you can learn about that. If you're twelve or fourteen and you've never dated someone, TV and other media sources can tell you—or show you—how to ask someone out, how to dress, what you should plan to do, and other aspects of how to behave. I'm pretty sure I learned how to put my arm around a girl's shoulder for the first time by watching Danny Zucko's feigned stretch during the drive-in scene of *Grease*. Yes, friends can and do help guys figure these things out, but TV and movies provide a level of detail and demonstration that can't be had through conversation. And in the privacy of your own room, you don't need to be embarrassed about asking your friends.

It's important to note that even when teens watch the same show, they may learn—or remember—different things from it. On the TV show *Friends*, Ross and Rachel got pregnant when they weren't planning to. That episode included a lot of discussion about condoms because the condom failed. Researchers who'd been tracking teens' media use and sexual behavior called teens who they knew were regular viewers of the series and asked if they'd seen it. Adolescents who correctly answered questions about the two different storylines in the episode were included in the study. Slightly more than half of them said the primary message about condoms was "lots of times, condoms don't prevent pregnancy."[57]

The episode specifically informed viewers that condoms are 95 to 100 percent effective when used correctly, repeating this information twice. Compared to teens who watched the show alone or with their friends, teens who watched the show with an adult were about twice as likely to recall this piece of information. They were also more likely to talk about sex or pregnancy or condoms with those adults.[58] This means that media can provide parents with opportunities to talk about sex with their kids using TV characters. These are "people" who parents and children know well but with whom they don't have a personal, emotional connection.

Part of what we can learn from media goes beyond factual knowledge. In some cases, beliefs come along with—or separate from—those facts. For example, the idea that it's okay for unmarried couples to have sex is an opinion or a belief or an "attitude," not a fact. On TV and in lad magazines, sex is almost always between unmarried people; married people rarely have sex.[59] I believe this is true for most media.

The knowledge and beliefs that media provide tend to be embedded in a story of some sort. When there's a script, the writers usually tell us one of a relatively small number of stories, but with a different set of details. On television and in movies, these are the stories that are repeated regularly, week after week, series after series, and movie after movie, not just once in a blue moon. If you have a favorite TV show or a favorite type of movie, you probably know its formula pretty well. When something happens that you "didn't see coming," it means the writers have left their regular script. In addition to learning some facts and some beliefs, we also learn these stories or scripts.[60]

On TV, we can see basically the same story with the same characters week after week. For example, on *Two and a Half Men*, most episodes showed Charlie and Alan in conflict. The conflict could be related to Jake's upbringing; their mother, Evelyn; or any of a thousand other things. In almost every episode, Charlie, our Casanova, ended up being right. It didn't matter whether things worked out in his favor because he was lucky, because he was able to seduce a woman involved or to pull strings, or because Alan finally relented; things just worked out in Charlie's favor. Not only that, housekeeper Berta almost always supported Charlie's perspective. So did the laugh track: Charlie's jokes and insults usually got bigger laughs than Alan's responses.

It's a little different in movies, where the basic story gets repeated with different characters. In movies like *Porky's*, *American Pie*, and *The 40 Year Old Virgin*, the story is the same. A group of guys makes a pact about getting laid; the pact may involve sex for every member of the group or just one guy. The pact is always about sex outside of a relationship. The group devises a number of strategies to find, identify, and ultimately seduce various girls or women, all of which fail hilariously. At the end, when the guys are ready to admit failure, the guy (or guys) get laid.

The problem isn't that we learn the stories; the problem is that the fictional world looks so much like the real world, and the people on screen act so similar to the people in our lives, that those of us who watch a lot of TV and movies start to expect that real-life events will play out in the same way that they do on screen.[61] In other words, we might expect real life to follow the same storylines that we've seen "a million times" on television and in movies.

The Effects of Media on Adolescent Sexuality

The research tells us that media are linked to adolescents' and young adults' beliefs about sexuality and their actual sexual behavior.[62] This means that media play a part in adolescents' sexuality, although they are just one piece among many. Still, mainstream media reach millions of teens, so the overall impact is rather substantial.

Up front, I'll acknowledge that people choose what to watch, listen to, and read. But if your choice is to channel surf until you find something acceptable, how much "choice" is that? Or if your choice is to listen to radio station X, are you really choosing each and every one of those songs? If you agree with me that there are a relatively small number of storylines with endless combinations of details, how much choice do we really have?

In laboratory settings, researchers have assessed adolescents' and young adults' beliefs, then exposed them to either sexual or neutral content (from TV shows or music videos), before asking them about their beliefs again. Time after time, we see clear, albeit small, changes in beliefs that are consistent with the video they've seen.[63] These studies tell us that TV and music videos cause a slight, short-term change in guys' sexual beliefs. Because it's unethical to lock people in a room and control what they see or hear for an extended period of time, we can never be certain that media *cause* a long-term change, but if a change occurs as a result of watching something for even ten minutes in the lab, I can't help but wonder what happens if you watch it for two hours per day, five days per week.

We do know that over the longer term, people who consume more media are more likely to hold the attitudes that the media typically display, regardless of the age group we're talking about. In nearly one hundred studies from the mid-1970s through the mid-1990s, researchers consistently found that people who watched more TV were more likely to endorse or believe in a set of themes that appear regularly on TV: the world is violent and crime ridden; the world is a "mean" and unhelpful place; and people tend to act in gender-stereotypical ways. These "heavy" viewers also estimated that diseases shown on TV were more common than they actually were. Before the divorce rate leveled off at about 50 percent of new marriages, these heavy viewers also provided higher than actual estimates of the divorce rate.[64]

One detailed example of the connections between media use, sexual beliefs, and sexual behaviors comes from a study of almost eight hundred undergraduate men. They were asked to report their prime-time viewing habits, music video consumption, movie viewing, and reading of men's magazines. They also answered a series of questions about their beliefs (sex is for marriage, men are sex driven, and non-relational sex is okay, for example), and they were asked to estimate the frequency of sexual behavior of their peers. Finally, they were asked about several aspects of their own sex lives.[65]

The results indicated that young men's media use was related to their beliefs. In particular, the researchers found that male youth who watched more movies per month or who read more men's magazines were more likely to believe that it was acceptable to have premarital sex and believed that their peers were having lots of sex. They were also more likely to say that it was acceptable to have hookup-type sex. At the same time, guys who spent more time watching music videos were more likely to believe that men are sex driven.

The researchers also demonstrated that several of those beliefs were also related to the men's sexual behavior. In particular, young men who believed that hookup-type sex was an acceptable behavior reported having more hookup partners and more total partners. Guys who believed that men were sex driven also reported less consistent use of protection.

The team also found direct connections between media use and sexual behaviors. Young men who watched more movies were younger at their first intercourse, and guys who read more men's magazines said they'd had more hookup partners and more partners in general. Altogether, these findings indicate that media have a direct impact on our behavior, as well as an indirect influence through our beliefs.

Other research, on magazines, revealed something I find especially concerning. When asked specific questions about sexual health, men averaged 24.1 correct answers out of 37, or 65 percent; young women did slightly better, with 25.1 correct answers, or 68 percent. These aren't exactly great scores. For men, reading magazines like *Maxim* and

FHM was not related to their sexual health knowledge, but it was related to greater confidence in their knowledge. So a guy might not be learning anything about sexual health or use of protection from these magazines, but he'll be confident about his sexual knowledge. Reading pornographic magazines wasn't related to either knowledge or confidence.[66]

A series of studies by Rebecca Collins and her colleagues at the RAND Institute indicate that consuming media with more sexual content may "speed up" an adolescent's progression from kissing to coitus. The research team conducted telephone interviews with 2,003 adolescents ages twelve through seventeen during spring 2001, then talked to those kids again in spring 2002 and spring 2004. They asked about extent of sexual behavior, including pregnancy, during each phone interview. During the first interview, they also asked about a variety of popular TV shows and musical performers, then analyzed those shows and song lyrics in order to assess how much sexual content adolescents were being exposed to.[67]

The RAND team focused on the adolescents who were virgins at the beginning of the study. They then examined how media use at the beginning of the study was related to sexual behavior one and three years later. In both cases, they controlled for other factors that we know are related to first sexual experience, such as age, parental education, number of parents in the house, GPA, and so on.

In their examination of TV, the research team found that the more sexual content adolescents watched, the faster they moved from kissing to oral sex and also the more likely they were to have had sex for the first time.[68] In their analysis of popular music, the researchers found a similar pattern of effects for degrading sexual lyrics; more of this content also seemed to accelerate an adolescent's progression from one sexual behavior to the next. Exposure to nondegrading lyrics did not serve as a counterbalance.[69]

To summarize, the research tells us that media consumption is related to many of our beliefs about men's sexuality, especially beliefs that are part of the Casanova Complex. Young men's media use is also connected to their sexual behavior. Some research indicates that certain types of video content can cause small, immediate changes in our beliefs, but there's no ethical way to conduct research that can definitely illustrate whether media impacts are long term. Other research demonstrates that after other factors are taken into account, being exposed to more sexual content leads to a faster progression through ever more intimate sexual behaviors. To me, this suggests that even though media aren't the biggest single force in a young man's sex life, they do have an effect on what he thinks, how he feels, and what he does.

Media messages about sexuality are common and tend to support the central tenets of the Casanova Complex. I don't think that media are the only influences on young men's sexual behavior, nor do I think that they're the most important. One review put the statistical impact of television at about the same level as the statistical impact of choice of neighborhood.[70] But mass media tell millions of boys and young men that the Casanova Complex is the way to be. In Chapter Eleven, I'll talk about ways to become media literate in order to combat these messages.

7

Appearance and the Casanova Complex

A common cultural stereotype of young men tells us that they're not particularly concerned about their clothing or their appearance. Generally, we think that boys don't worry about how clean they or their clothing are. But our personal experience doesn't entirely match the stereotype; how many guys do you know who don't shower (at least) once per day or who routinely choose to wear clothes that are visibly dirty?

The folks who make hygiene and grooming products think sex sells. If you've seen a commercial for Old Spice deodorant or any of the Axe products, then you know what I'm talking about. In the typical Axe ad, an unkempt teenage boy is literally attacked by a group of sexy women who apply the relevant products. In a few seconds, he's transformed into an attractive young man who can get the babes. When I was growing up, ads for Irish Spring soap showed me that if I used their product, I'd end up with a beautiful woman under each arm.

For boys who buy in to the Casanova Complex, appearance is a central part of the image.[1] Casanovas are supposed to look good. For current-day "players," it means a less dressy but just as carefully put together style that may include hundred-dollar sneakers that are worn for show, not sport.[2]

In the older or "traditional" sense of Casanova, it means being well dressed or "sharp," wearing "nice" or well-made clothing. And shoes, not sneakers. You might think back to men like Clark Gable or Cary Grant, but you might also think about recent stars like George Clooney or Denzel Washington.

For guys who want to look good, it's not just about clothing. Showing off your abs, chest, and arms also plays an important role. In recent years, children's Halloween costumes have started to include padding so that young boys can show off their biceps, in addition to the well-defined pecs and abs provided by plastic chestpieces.[3] For Andy in *The 40 Year Old Virgin*, it meant getting a makeover that included removing his chest hair. Even the Fox Sports football robot is feeling the pressure; already heavily shouldered and muscled in 2010, his shoulders became bigger and his waist narrower in 2011.

If you're old enough, you may remember claims that Ricardo Montalban received pectoral implants for his 1982 role in *Star Trek II: The Wrath of Khan*. The film's director, Nicholas Meyer, remembers the controversy well enough to have included it in his 2009 memoir. He says Montalban's chest was the result of working out, not surgery.[4]

Of course you've heard about the importance of looking good for girls. The media, other kids, various industries, and sometimes even parents have been telling girls for years that if they don't meet our culture's "thin ideal" beauty standard, then they're worthless.[5] Boys have been getting a parallel set of messages that emphasize being big and muscular. The research tells us that boys' efforts to achieve this image are associated with the same kinds of problems that girls experience.[6]

And, of course, a guy—and his body—need to be physically ready for sex at any time.

Bodies and Sex

Bodies are very important to boys. Adolescents who are more satisfied with their bodies tend to have higher self-esteem.[7] They also seem to be doing better in a variety of ways: in one study, they reported having multiple close friendships and better recovery after a romantic breakup; they were more egalitarian (or less sexist) and more willing to talk to their partners about sexual issues; and they expected to use condoms regularly.[8]

Although it seems obvious to say it, sex is a bodily experience. Young men who are more comfortable with their own bodies also tend to be more comfortable in sexual situations.[9]

Looking good presents something of a conundrum for guys who date girls. American culture positions fashion as a feminine concern and assumes that men who are fashion conscious are probably gay because gay men are incorrectly thought to be "gender inverted." If you're a so-called straight guy, this means you can't routinely ask your male friends to comment on your clothing, and you definitely can't ask them to go shopping with you. It also means that if you want to show off your ripped abs or comment on your buddy's chest, you need to say "no homo" before you do so.[10]

Sexual orientation does have some documented connections to body issues. Guys who date girls typically want to put on weight by becoming more muscular, although a smaller percentage are trying to lose weight. But guys who date other guys are more equally split. A fair number want to put on weight and have a better build; many others want to lose weight and have a more toned body.[11]

Regardless of whether they're dating girls or boys, guys tend to overestimate what their hypothetical partners want. Gay men tend to rate themselves as having about the right level of muscle but not being lean enough; straight men see themselves as being lean enough but not having enough muscle.[12]

Imagining the Body

Over the last five decades, the definition of "well built" has changed. Researchers Harrison Pope, Katharine Philips, and Roberto Olivardia have documented these changes in a series of research articles, and their book *The Adonis Complex* summarizes their work. They start with Steve Reeves, who dominated bodybuilding in the 1940s and 1950s.[13] As you might expect, pictures of him from back in the day show that beautiful body. By current standards, it's a good body, but it's not one you'd expect to win a bodybuilding competition.

Over time, the bodies of male actors and athletes have become better built and less fat. The increase in musculature, and the visibility of those muscles, are quite evident in films before and after 1970; imagine Clark Gable, Cary Grant, Errol Flynn, or John Wayne next to Sylvester Stallone, Arnold Schwarzenegger, or Dwayne "the Rock" Johnson. *Playgirl* centerfolds also show the same pattern.[14]

It's not just about a few well-known stars. An analysis of men in top-grossing action films between 1980 and 2006 assessed major and minor characters, heroes and villains. Just over three-fourths of male characters were muscular, and about two-thirds had low body fat. In other words, they were "cut." Although sex is relatively uncommon in action films, these characters were more likely to have a romantic partner and to have sex than their scrawny counterparts.[15]

The shift to ever more muscular and ever less fat male images can also be found in the action figures boys play with. In a provocative landmark study, Harrison Pope, Roberto Olivardia, and their colleagues examined the action figures sold to boys over the years. They highlighted GI Joe because he's been produced continuously since the 1960s and was marketed in several different variations during the 1990s. If the original GI Joe were a real man who stood 5'10" tall, he'd have had a 31.7" waist, a 44.4" chest, and 12.2" biceps. That's entirely reasonable. The 1974 update would have had the same waist and chest, but featured 15.2" biceps, also plausible. But the 1998 "Extreme" GI Joe would have had a 36.5" waist, a massive 54.8" chest, and incredible 26.8" biceps. According to the research team, that chest and those biceps are not physically possible. They also documented a substantial increase in muscularity for Luke Skywalker and Han Solo when their action figures were recast and rereleased as part of the twentieth anniversary of *Star Wars*.[16]

Barbie's not the only child's toy out there with an idealized and unrealistic body.

Supplements and Steroids

Over the past thirty years or so, we've become used to seeing men with particularly pronounced and developed upper bodies, particularly through the pectoral muscles ("pecs"), shoulders, and arms. Muscle mass in these areas can be increased by taking the dietary supplement creatine. And the desire for a bigger body can lead to more frequent weight training and steroid use.[17]

One survey of high school athletes in eleven different schools in Tennessee and Georgia found that nearly one boy in four had used oral creatine. Most boys took it for only a few months, primarily to increase their speed and build muscle mass.[18]

But creatine isn't the only way to get these effects. Anabolic-androgenic steroids (AAS), human growth hormone (HGH), and other drugs are widely used by young men who want to be bigger or better cut.[19] Many of these are explicitly banned by various professional sports associations.

Steroid use isn't exactly common, but it is widespread. According to the Youth Risk Behavior Survey (YRBS), the biannual survey of twelve thousand to fifteen thousand American high school students (which I also mentioned in Chapter One), somewhere between 3.6 and 6.9 percent of ninth-grade boys said they'd used steroid pills or shots without a doctor's prescription at least once in their life. Rates were at their lowest in 1993, peaked in 2001–2003, and appear to be hovering around 5 percent—or one boy in twenty—as we enter the 2010s.[20]

We have some idea of who is likely to use steroids, especially in larger doses or for longer periods of time. As you might expect, those young men tend to be more dissatisfied with their musculature and try to make sure they're sufficiently covered up when in public. They're also more distrustful of others, see themselves as ineffective, and see themselves as more masculine.[21]

Steroid use can have some serious consequences. It can cause extreme mood swings that may lead some guys to be violent (or more violent), colloquially known as "'roid rage." It can also lead to the development of female-like breasts, shrunken testicles, and decreased sperm production. And among teenage boys, steroid use can alter and ultimately short-circuit their natural growth.[22]

Plastic Surgery

Not everyone can look that cut by working out. It may be due to lack of time, lack of motivation, lack of dedication, or a desire for fast results. Whatever the cause, guys who want to look good don't have to spend all that time in the gym. They can have plastic surgery instead. Given the cost, surgical options may be more common among middle-aged men who wish to regain a "young and powerful" look.[23]

The American Society of Plastic Surgeons' 2010 annual report indicated that there were slightly more than two hundred thousand cosmetic surgeries performed on men and just over nine hundred thousand minimally invasive procedures. To be absolutely clear, these are classified as cosmetic procedures, not reconstructive surgery that occurs as a result of accidents. Although men represent only about 10 percent of the overall market, that's still a lot of work. The Society identifies cosmetic surgery for men as a source of growth.[24]

Among minimally invasive cosmetic procedures—work routinely done in a doctor's office—Botox injections were most popular; men received over 325,000 of them in 2010. Laser hair removal and micro-dermabrasion were also popular options for men; each of these was performed more than 150,000 times. And men received just over seventy-five thousand "soft tissue fillers," the category that includes lip augmentation and other slight adjustments.

The most popular surgical options were nose jobs, eyelid surgery, liposuction, (male) breast reduction, and hair transplants, each of which was performed more than thirteen thousand times. In notably smaller numbers, men also went for tummy tucks, pectoral implants, or buttocks implants.

Dressing the Body

Appearance is about more than the body. It's also about clothing, grooming, and having a style. Although they may not seem to be when they shop, boys are choosy about what they wear.[25] There's a reason that skateboarder Tony Hawk lent his name to a clothing line and Sean "Puffy" Combs developed his own line.

The emphasis on appearance comes at boys from different sources, each of which tends to promote its own styles.

Music is one of these sources. In 2011, Taio Cruz's song "Dynamite" talked about him "wearin' all his favorite brands." In 2004, Ludacris was late to the club because "our time and our clothes gotta coordinate" (in "Stand Up"). In 2002, Big Tymers wore "Gator boots, with the pimped out Gucci suit / Ain't got no job, but I stay sharp."

This theme isn't exactly new; in 1983, ZZ Top told us exactly what it meant to be a "sharp dressed man." However, it's become more common. In an analysis of lyrics of top fifty songs that I conducted, my research team found that references to men's appearance increased from 1960 through 2008, with a noticeable increase starting in the 1990s. That change was primarily driven by rap performers.[26]

Another source is the world of fashion. Although typically considered a feminine interest, a fair number of straight men pay attention to it. The magazines *Esquire*, published since 1932, and *GQ*, published since 1957, have long emphasized men's fashion. Some authors argue that sartorial consciousness and a certain amount of elegance are one defining characteristic of metrosexuality,[27] a term often applied to straight men who adopt some behaviors expected of gay men.

Fashion and style often reach the general public through advertising. Over the last four decades, marketers have consistently used male athletes as spokesmen and models. The use of athletes is particularly noteworthy because they are often seen as defining masculinity and are presumed to be heterosexual.[28] As a result, they send guys a message that being concerned with their appearance is OK and isn't gay.

The trend of using male athletes to sell what might otherwise be considered a feminine product had its greatest success a few decades ago. In an effort to sell diet beer, the Miller brewing company featured several retired NFL linemen in a series of commercials with the tag line "Tastes Great, Less Filling" starting in the early 1970s. After all, if a bunch of three-hundred-pound retired football players could drink "lite" beer, couldn't you? Today, the official beers of every major sports league are diet, or lite, beers. Even the "Round Mound of Rebound," Charles Barkley, is shilling for Weight Watchers for Men.

Less prominent companies also use this strategy. Alphanail, which sells nail polish and eyeliner for men, has a series of images of men who use their products. The images include football players and mixed martial artists. We see images of well-groomed men off the field and outside the arena, with hot women draped all over them.

In his book *The Metrosexual*, Garrett Coad provides a history of athletes as clothing models. He starts in the 1970s, when Baltimore Orioles pitcher Jim Palmer and New York Jets quarterback Joe Namath both became clothing models and spokesmen. Palmer took the lead in a series of underwear ads for Jockey, including ads featuring bikini-style underwear, often in a bright colors.[29] So long, tighty-whiteys. Namath was known for wearing a full-length fur coat on the sidelines, a practice adopted by several other players at the time and subsequently prohibited by the NFL.

Connections between men's fashion and sports have grown since then. There's an extensive "who's who" of premier athletes who were known for their play and their style. Most were perennial all-stars, and many have been or will be inducted into their respective Halls of Fame. The list includes "Dapper" Dan Marino, Magic Johnson, Isaiah Thomas, Dominique Wilkins, Akeem Olajuwon, Jerry Rice, Mike Piazza, Troy Aikman, Tiki Barber, Ozzie Smith, Andre Agassi, Alex Rodriguez, Carmelo Anthony, Kevin Garnett, and Pete Sampras. Several non-Americans are also on the list, including soccer players David Beckham and Ronaldo.[30]

NBA coaches Pat Riley and Phil Jackson have also been praised for their sartorial sense. I suspect that the coaches are particularly noteworthy because, unlike the players, they are much closer to average height and weight. During interviews, particularly with men's fashion magazines like GQ, the coaches and many of the athletes talk about the attention they give to various aspects of appearance and grooming.[31]

Even the media company ESPN emphasizes men's bodies on its cable television networks, radio shows, and magazine. The conversations routinely include discussion of abdominal, chest, and arm muscles, as might be expected. But they often include clothing and accessories. On some shows, and in some of the network's advertising, the appearance of the on-air hosts is often a focal point.[32]

For a guy who wants to get laid, being well-groomed sends a message about self-care. For some boys and young men, it's just about saying that he's not just some "dumb jock." But for would-be Casanovas, looking good is an important part of the image, and it's certainly one way to attract attention.

Sexualizing the Male Body

Just as sexual messages about the Casanova Complex are presented to boys from a variety of media sources, so are messages about the objectification of male bodies. Over the last three decades, images of male performers on the cover of *Rolling Stone* have become more sexualized. My own analysis of music lyrics from 1960 through 2008 reveals a similar trend, as do analyses of video games. In each case, the rate and degree of male objectification are less than they are for women, but in each case, they've increased over the last two decades or so.[33] So although objectification isn't as common for men as it is for women, it certainly exists.

Fashion and Sports

The increased focus on men's bodies and appearance is evident in a variety of media. An analysis of advertisements found in *Glamour* and *Cosmopolitan* magazines revealed that there's been a subtle increase in the number and percentage of partially or minimally clothed men since the magazines were first published in the 1950s. They were originally limited to advertisements where you'd expect to see them: underwear ads, vacation spots, resorts, and the like. Since the 1980s, they've started to appear in an ever broader range of ads.[34]

Although images of partially clad men have become increasingly common, they don't always highlight the sex appeal of the male body.[35] ESPN magazine publishes an annual "Body Issue" that features nearly nude images of male athletes;[36] those pictures tend to emphasize function and ability, not sexuality.

Yet sexualized images of male bodies do appear regularly. A lot of heads were turned when Joe Namath appeared in a 1973 commercial for Beauty Mist pantyhose. The ad starts with a long, slow pan up the body, starting with Namath's toes. Viewers don't know who the model is until about the middle of the ad; if the model were female, there would be little doubt that the commercial was sexualizing her body. Namath asks the viewer to contemplate how good his legs look and consider what the hose would do for a woman's body.

A current TV commercial has Mike Rupp pitching Lee jeans and telling viewers they make his butt look good. A commercial for Moen showerheads is more provocative. The ad starts with a male body wearing an indeterminate sports uniform getting into the shower. As the commercial progresses, the uniform washes off, showing the skin. The body changes repeatedly; most of the bodies shown are male, but some of the shots appear to be women's bodies, increasing the sexualization.

The best-known ad campaign with a sexualized male body may be a 1990s series of Calvin Klein underwear ads featuring "Marky" Mark Wahlberg. That ad campaign helped shift our cultural conception of men's underwear from a strictly utilitarian perspective to a view that men's undies can also be sexual. Coad concluded that this "radically new vision [of men's underwear] based on eroticizing the male genital area and men's buttocks is transforming the way men look at their bodies."[37] Calvin Klein, as well as newer companies like aussieBum (producer of the Wonderjock), C-IN2, and Hom, are among the sales leaders. Several of my friends refer to some of these products as "banana slings."

Getting Hard

According to the stereotype, guys—and especially Casanovas—need to be ready for sex at all times. And let's clarify: among heterosexuals, sex means an erect penis and intercourse.

For young men who are worried about their sexual ability, especially if they're expecting to have sex after a night of partying that includes alcohol and other substances that might decrease performance, there's an easy solution: take a pill. It might be Viagra, Cialis, Levitra, or something else of the sort. These drugs have become popular among young men.[38]

Part of the popularity is a result of how the drugs have been marketed. For most of the twentieth century, men who had difficulty achieving or maintaining an erection were classified as "impotent." They were understood to have psychological problems that somehow interfered with sexual activity, and were encouraged to see a therapist.[39]

Impotence has become "erectile dysfunction." The terminology started to change in the 1980s for researchers and in the 1990s for the rest of us. More important, erectile dysfunction became a physical problem that could be treated by a urologist or other medical specialist, not a psychological condition that required therapy. The first treatments were implants and injections, but these had a variety of limitations and never really caught on. The pills available today have fewer limitations, are simple to use, and are reasonably effective.[40]

Over the last ten years, erectile dysfunction has given way to "erectile quality." This has allowed the drug makers to shift from a relatively limited pool of middle-aged men who were suffering from a consistent physical problem that was often linked to other physical conditions (such as heart disease or obesity) to a nearly unlimited market of men who are worried about "not being able to perform." The advertising has also changed; instead of using seventy-something

Bob Dole, the companies are now using athletes and unnamed male models who appear to be in their thirties.[41] And although these medications require a prescription, there's no meaningful way a doctor can test for poor erectile quality.

The drugs have been hugely popular and successful. A decade after Viagra's release, Pfizer claimed that it was "one of the world's most recognized pharmaceutical brands." Viagra sales have exceeded over $1.5 billion worldwide for each of the last ten years. Introduced in the United States in 2003, Eli Lilly's Cialis broke the $1 billion worldwide sales mark in 2007. Levitra netted the Bayer Co. "only" about $576 million in 2010. Sales figures for all three drugs have increased almost every year they've been on the market. The increases are due to an increased number of prescriptions (demand) as well as price increases.[42]

Effects of an Emphasis on Appearance

We know that the cultural emphasis on women's appearance has a real impact on their lives. Some of that is simply a matter of the time, money, and effort spent to be considered thin and beautiful. Of more concern are the psychological effects, which include dislike of one's own body, poor self-esteem, depression, and a poor relationship with food. At a certain point, the latter can become severe enough to qualify as an eating disorder, most commonly anorexia nervosa or bulimia nervosa.[43]

There is little doubt that girls receive these messages about appearance from a variety of sources, each of which contributes to the overall problem. The sources include parents, peers, friends, and media.[44] This is also true for boys.

As it turns out, the factors that predispose some women to having body image problems and developing eating disorders are the same ones that predispose some men to these difficulties.[45] Only a fraction of men have appearance-related problems that are diagnosable. For men, it's usually not anorexia or bulimia; instead, their problem tends to be labeled as "body dysmorphic disorder," sometimes referred to as "bigorexia," and is centered around not being well built or "ripped."[46]

One of the most dramatic—and simplest—demonstrations of the importance of appearance comes from a study performed by Michelle Hebl, Eden King, and Jean Lin. They asked male and female undergraduate research participants to come to their laboratory. After the study was briefly described and students agreed to participate, they completed a short survey. Then a coin was tossed, and they were asked to change into either a swimsuit or a sweater provided by the research team (and washed after every use), complete a math test, and fill out the same survey again.[47]

You probably won't be surprised to learn that the young women felt worse about their bodies to begin with, or to learn that the young women who were asked to wear a swimsuit reported more body shame and lower self-esteem, and did worse on the math test than the young women who were asked to wear a sweater. You may be surprised to find out that the young men showed exactly the same pattern of results—more body shame, lower self-esteem, and poorer performance on the math test depending on the clothing they'd been assigned to wear. And not only was the pattern the same, but the amount of change was about the same for young men and young women.[48]

Advertising influences us in the same ways that mass media do. Guys who buy into the current cultural notion that men should be well built tend to pay more attention to the appearance of their own bodies. Similarly, boys who regularly compare their bodies to other boys' (or men's) bodies also tend to be less satisfied about their bodies. Together, these factors contribute to a young man's desire to build up his body.[49] From there, they may adjust their diet and exercise accordingly, although some go too far.

Young men who are focused on appearance are also more likely to feel worse about their bodies after seeing well-built male models. Researchers Duane Hargraves and Marika Tiggemann asked male undergraduates to watch a collection of fifteen commercials they'd recorded during popular television shows. Some men watched a set of commercials that highlighted well-built male models, and some men watched commercials that included more typical men's bodies and didn't focus on men's appearance. Young men who saw the commercials of well-built men felt much worse about their own bodies than young men who saw the "neutral" commercials.[50]

———

A persistent if low-level pressure to have a certain appearance and a well-cut body exists for young men, and it's an important part of being a Casanova. For some guys, this can lead to a reliance (or overreliance) on products used to treat erectile dysfunction. For others, it can lead to substantial insecurity, steroid use, and cosmetic surgery. If we don't think these are good for girls, then there's no reason to think they're good for boys either.

Part III

· ·

Challenging Casanova

8

Non-Casanova Approaches to Dating and Sexuality

Jeremy, a junior in college, had been interested in Julie for about a year. They were in the same major, and he'd seen her in some of his classes over the years, but they'd never had any contact outside of class. During junior year, they got invited to a few of the same parties and talked more. One night, they were dancing at a party, dancing close. And they'd been drinking heavily. They started kissing, then moved to making out, then went back to her place. They made out some more and eventually passed out without having sex.

Jeremy and Julie continued to spend time together. They had oral sex. Two weeks after that first kiss, they planned to go to a party. Without really talking about it, they intentionally drank very little. They left the party earlier than usual and went back to her place. They were making out, got undressed, and decided to have sex.

Jeremy told me that they did not talk about having sex beforehand, "but I knew it was going to [happen] eventually one of those weekends . . . Each time we hooked up, it progressively got more and more to that point of having sex." Jeremy made sure he had condoms with him that night; it was the first time since he'd started spending time with Julie that he brought condoms with him.

About a week later, Jeremy took Julie out to dinner. Although they'd spent a lot of time together, you might think of that as their first real date. After dinner, in the car on the way home, he asked if she wanted to be his girlfriend. She said yes.

I'm not entirely sure what you think of Jeremy at this point, but his story is becoming more common. It's part of the reason that social networking sites like Facebook include "It's complicated" as one of the preset options for a person's relationship status and contributes to the notion that we're in a "hookup culture."[1]

Jeremy was not a Casanova. He had sex for the first time during his freshman year at college, and could count his sexual partners—including Julie—on one hand.

Over the last twenty years or so, researchers have begun to make distinctions between Casanovas and other guys. It's clear that there are at least three distinct approaches to dating and sex that young men follow. One of those is to be a Casanova, but as I discussed in Chapter One, Casanovas represent only a small percentage of all guys. Being abstinent until marriage is another path, one taken by about 10 to 15 percent of male youth. That leaves all other guys, and they're the majority. They're not Casanovas, and they're not saving themselves for marriage either—they're like Jeremy, or Alan from *Two and a Half Men*, or Ted Mosby from *How I Met Your Mother*, or Ross from *Friends*. They're all examples of what I call "romantic men."

Our collective focus on the Casanova Complex as exemplifying what all guys want leads us to not really notice these other guys. Or perhaps we don't think of them as "typical" because they're not "the Man" or even particularly masculine; they're more like the geeks from *The Big Bang Theory* or *Revenge of the Nerds*. At best, boys who don't want to be Casanovas receive a mixed message about their choice. They may be lauded by some people—especially parents and other adults—while being insulted by others, particularly their peers and possibly the media.

Romantic Men

You may not believe me (yet), but most guys follow a reasonably traditional, romantic approach to dating.[2] Compared to other guys, romantic men have a moderate to low number of dating partners and even fewer sexual partners, certainly fewer than Casanovas. But what also makes these guys different from Casanovas is their hookups. For Casanovas, like Alex in Chapter One, a hookup is a one-time sexual experience with someone you've just met, don't know, and aren't interested in getting to know. Alcohol is typically involved. And the hookup is expected to include sex, not just making out. That Casanova-like description of a hookup doesn't describe Jeremy's experience with Julie. Their hookup, if you want to call it that, was very different. It wasn't just a one-time event, for starters. It wasn't between strangers either; Jeremy knew who Julie was, and he wanted to date her. And although their first night of making out was at least partially facilitated by alcohol, they intentionally did not get drunk before they had sex for the first time, two weeks later.

Romantic guys also tell more "traditional" stories about the beginning of their relationships. When I met Derek, for example, he'd been dating Sarah for about eight months. They'd met at a college party where his rock band was playing. She initially approached him, but he was busy setting up his drum kit and didn't really have the time to talk to her. She found him again when the band was on break and told him she was interested in getting to know him, but he was focused on playing and just got her phone number. Derek called Sarah a few days later, they went out, and had been a couple ever since.

Their first kiss occurred on their second "date," which consisted of hanging out. Although they progressed to oral sex fairly quickly—about the fourth time they were together, probably about a week-and-a-half after their first date—they didn't have sex for several weeks. The delay wasn't due to lack of interest or prudishness, and it wasn't because they were virgins. They waited because they decided to go for HIV testing at the local clinic. Derek told me, "The reason I waited and not just used a condom is because I developed a great affection for her that I knew I wanted to stick around and I knew I wanted to be there for a long time."

For Derek, sex within a relationship was closely tied to his "great affection" for Sarah. Not only that, but it included a longer-term focus and following the advice of sex educators everywhere to get tested for HIV.

When "Hooking Up" Isn't Exactly Hooking Up

What I've said so far doesn't mean that romantic men don't occasionally have those one-night-stand-style hookups. Some of them do. But unlike Casanovas, and going against our general conception of hooking up, these guys often hook up with people they know.

During high school, Derek dated Emily for a year or so. They broke up during senior year. They were still friends after the breakup (but not right after) and hung out some when they were both home from college on break. They were virgins when they dated, but they'd both lost their virginity after that.

Sophomore year of college, at a time when Derek wasn't dating anyone, Emily visited him, and they had sex. Derek told me, "It seemed like [hooking up] had more meaning to it because it was emotional although we both knew that at the same time it was just once and nothing to take too seriously." I asked Derek if they were a couple again after that visit, and he said no. But they didn't exactly remain friends either. Every time I tell this story, I can't help but wonder if part of the reason that Emily visited was because she thought they might get back together.

Jeremy, whose story I described at the start of this chapter, also had what he called a "random hookup." In fact, that was his first sexual experience. It happened at the beginning of his sophomore year when Jeremy was at a party and ran into Lindsay. Although it was her first year at college, they'd attended the same high school and knew each other a little, in the way that many of us kind of know some people in the class below us. According to Jeremy,

> We hung out one night and then the whole time, like she started . . . Have you ever gone to a frat party? She started making out with me and then she was like, let's go back to my dorm room. And then she was real aggressive and

everything like that. [P]retty much all she told me was like do you want to go to my place? I said sure.

Jeremy also told me that several of his friends who knew Lindsay teased him about hooking up with her.

Mike, a college senior, told me a story much like Jeremy's. He met Jenn during his first year at college, and they became good friends. Sophomore year, they started hooking up. They weren't dating or in a relationship or anything of the sort, just friends. He wasn't quite sure how it started, but they started making out one night. This happened a few times, until one night they were both drunk and "it just happened."

That was his first experience of intercourse. Mike regretted this because "your first time is supposed to be like really special or whatever but I just felt like it was just in a complete haze and like stupid decision making."

These hookup stories don't exactly fit our conception of a hookup as a one-time sexual experience with a stranger. Derek's emotional connection to Emily was what made the hookup possible. Jeremy and Mike each had sex outside of a dating relationship, but they didn't initiate it. Jeremy's clear that Lindsay hit on him; Mike's not really sure how any of that sexual contact with Jenn started, but he's clear that they moved from making out to sex over several weeks of hooking up. In *Hooking Up: Sex, Dating, and Relationships on Campus*, sociologist Kathleen Bogle tells us that this has become the new norm for starting relationships.[3]

Characteristics of Romantic Men

Romantic guys are the norm; most young men have sexual histories similar to those of Derek, Jeremy, and Mike. They date, typically starting around age sixteen or so. Many of them have (voluntarily) had sex before they graduated high school. But they don't date or have sex with a lot of different people.[4]

We know a little about how they're raised, but most of this knowledge is indirect and comes from contrasting them with Casanovas. Around the time they're entering puberty, their families tend to have relatively low levels of conflict. Their families are emotionally expressive; that doesn't mean they're "drama llamas" and would make for a good reality TV show. It just means that people in these families show their feelings at about an average level.[5]

As adolescents, these guys experience moderate levels of "parental monitoring"; that is, their parents are reasonably likely to know where they are and who they're with when they're not home.[6] As teens, they are also reasonably trusted by their parents.

They're not complete angels, though. These boys drink alcohol and use illicit drugs, but they do so at relatively low levels. In a similar vein, these boys may engage in a low to moderate level of "deviant" behavior—shoplifting, small-scale vandalism, being a public nuisance, and the like.[7] All of this occurs at a level parents might expect from their sons, and the behavior is appropriately punished by parents. At the same time, these are the kinds of things that parents who are involved in their adolescent's lives see no more than two or three times in a given year.

In one of the few studies to explicitly focus on this group, the researchers found that these young men were somewhat more likely to be married by age twenty-two than either the Casanovas or the religious guys I'll talk about later in this chapter.[8]

Risks for Romantics

Although guys like Derek try to be safe by rarely hooking up, using condoms, and getting tested for sexually transmitted infections (STIs), there are risks here. In Derek's relationship with Sarah, they got tested for HIV but nothing else. It's entirely possible that one or both of them had an STI that went undetected, but they both think they're "clean."

Another risk is implied. Derek said that he didn't want to use a condom prior to getting tested, and I suspect he didn't use one afterwards. In fact, many "committed" adolescent and young adult couples switch from condoms to chemical contraceptives (the pill, the ring) after they've been together for several months.[9] The most obvious problem here is that there may be an STI present that was untested for and thus undetected. There's also some risk of pregnancy, especially if oral contraceptives aren't taken properly (or at all), or if the dosage isn't correct.

For heterosexual guys, there's also a slight oddity here. We teach young men (and young women, for that matter) to be in charge of their lives and their futures. Yet when a guy chooses to let his girlfriend have sole responsibility for preventing pregnancy, he's giving up that control. Yes, it's a sign of trust in his partner, but I'm not sure it's a good way for a guy to show that he trusts his girl, especially if marriage, parenting, or "settling down" are not things he's planning to do any time soon.

Emo Men

Casanova isn't the only sexual stereotype that describes boys and men. Another refers to "emo guys."[10] According to the stereotype, they're sensitive, emotional guys who share their feelings—a lot, and possibly too much, according to several women I've met. When they tell me about these guys, they often tell me they were initially intrigued by them, but also couldn't quite figure them out. In general, they talked about those guys as nice, respectful, and generally interesting, but were concerned because the guys came off as passive and never quite asked them out or "made a move." I've conducted formal interviews with a few guys like this, and their stories were remarkably similar, so I'm going to introduce you only to Ben.

Emo guys describe themselves as having a moderate level of dating and sexual experience for their age. In practice, they have about as much relationship experience as the romantic men I described earlier, but they're more likely to hookup than the romantic guys. Unlike Casanovas, their hookups tend to consist of making out and not intercourse. It's entirely possible that these emo guys are really just an extreme, and somewhat "unsuccessful," version of romantic men like Derek.

Ben, age twenty-three, told me about his relationship with Katie, whom he knew a little. He told the story this way:

> We had been talking and she said—she was going to be singing in this concert that was going on and she said, "Hey, y'know, meet me after and maybe we can hang out." Well, here in my innocent mind I am thinking, well maybe we will go for coffee or something, y'know. Well, so she is like, yeah we are going to go to this party. I said, y'know, and I, y'know, get all nervous and I am going . . . I am going to be cool. This is going to be cool. So we went out to this party and just absolutely got ripped and that is not something I like to do in public a lot because it is not very safe, but, y'know, I did.
>
> That [first] night she basically was—she basically almost didn't want to give me a choice, y'know? And that is amazing to me and I was like, no I just don't think it is a good idea.
>
> But it was like, "already, you want to have sex?" And the funny thing is that we ended up dating for a while after that, 'cause I just sort of attributed that even to, well y'know, she was really drunk or whatever and so maybe that . . . But it turns out that had little to do with it and she was into sex, so . . .
>
> We did end up having sex quite a bit during the next . . . We were together for like three or four months, it wasn't very long or very worthwhile, but . . . In reality it wasn't much there, just that we had sex a lot. That was basically all that was driving the relationship, but we did end up having sex.

I guess she just kind of . . . Like I would think that maybe there be—you might wait until there is really some kind of connection between you before you have sex because otherwise, I don't know. It feels kind of meaningless. So . . . but I guess we ended up having sex, probably a few weeks into it. I don't know.

Emo young men seem to use hookups as a way to start relationships, but it doesn't seem to work out for them in the way in worked out for Jeremy with Julie. But what I found most striking about these guys is how passive they are. In Ben's story, he mostly responds to Katie: she invites him to the party, she makes the moves, and he complains that it's just about sex without any emotional connection. In fact, if you reread the story, you'll notice he rarely uses the word "I"; it's mostly "we" or "she."

These hookups are not what the Casanova Complex directs. They're not with strangers, and the men want the hookups to turn into relationships. In that way, the hookups of emo men are like the hookups of romantic men. Unlike those of romantic men, the hookup stories of emo men tend to be tinged with regret, as Ben's is, in regard to his lack of connection with Katie.

Are They Gay?

By this point, you might be thinking that Ben and guys like him are "confused" or "closeted" and that they're really gay. They're not. My "gaydar" is reasonably good, and I didn't sense anything of the sort. In their stories, they were genuinely interested in dating and having sex with women.

During interviews, I've asked Ben and guys like him if they'd ever be willing to have sex with a man. They don't seem to be interested, although they often leave open the possibility that they might be willing at some point in the future. Ben said, "I really wouldn't. I don't think. I mean 'would you ever consider,' y'know, leaves room for if you were to change your mind. So my current mind-set, 'no.'"

It's not unusual for gay men to date women and even have sex with them. When asked why, they usually explain it in one of a few ways. For some boys and young men, dating and having sex with women is a way to hide their sexual orientation. For others, it's curiosity; they want to know what it's like to have sex with a female body instead of a male body. For yet others, it's a way to prove to themselves that they really are gay; if you're on a date—or in bed—with a girl and it doesn't feel "right," then it's time to stop ignoring those attractions to boys and men.[11]

But these experiences tend to be fairly short lived, if not one time only. In twenty-first-century America, by the time they're in their early twenties, young men who are attracted to men are generally pretty clear about what's going on. Sure, they may be resisting their attractions and trying to convince themselves that they're really attracted to women, but the stories I've heard from emo guys sounded much more like those of men who were looking for some substance in their dating and sexual experiences with women, not guys who are trying to convince themselves they're straight.

Characteristics of Emo Men

As far as I can tell, there isn't research that specifically focuses on young men like this. It may also be an issue of labeling. I think some folks might incorrectly think that emo guys are gay. Others might label them metrosexuals or, in decades past, sensitive New Age guys.

I once asked about a hundred undergraduates to describe the characteristics of sensitive New Age guys as part of a survey. They told me that these guys were focused on their clothing, along the lines of what I talked about in Chapter Seven. Sensitive New Age guys were also routinely described as being "nice," "sensitive," "expressing their emotions," and "artsy." The undergraduates told me that these guys listened to a lot of music, but things like jazz and classical; nobody said they listened to mainstream music in the pop, rock, or rap categories. A few students said—or asked—if these guys were gay.[12]

I don't think emo men are particularly common; I'm guessing that they make up no more than 10 percent of boys and young men, probably less. But given their passivity, I wouldn't be surprised if they represent a much larger percentage of guys in their thirties who've never been married.

Risks for Emo Men

Emo men seem to run a moderate level of risk. Although they are hooking up with known partners, those events are occurring under the influence of alcohol and without effort to acquire their partner's sexual history or disease status, although this could be known from prior contact. The risks here are similar to the risks romantic men experience: potential for an STI and possibly pregnancy.

Given how passive Ben was and how he described his relationships, I have serious doubts about his ability to consistently use condoms. Can you imagine him standing up to Katie if she said "No condoms," "Don't worry about it," or "Just this once"?

Religious Men

There are also young men like John. As an undergraduate living away from home, he voluntarily attended church almost every Sunday. He didn't dream of becoming a member of the clergy and wasn't a youth pastor or anything like that, but his religion was very important to him. It provided a sense of comfort, and he became friends with other undergraduates, and some adults, who attended his church.[13]

About 10 to 15 percent of teens and young adults are like John. Their religion is a cornerstone of their lives. As such, it influences their approach to dating and sexuality.

John was a twenty-one-year-old college senior when I met him. He described his approach to dating (and sex) this way: "I'm trying to save myself for marriage and be, I guess you could say, kind of pure for my wife—my future wife. Whoever that may be." Chris, age twenty-three, told me almost the same thing:

I also chose to forgo all these things in knowing that God created us, intending us for marriage, not for, y'know, casual dating or casual sex or anything. I mean I guess those are good or those are fine for most people, but, from my perspective I feel like by having casual sex and by friends with benefits and all these things, you are giving a part of yourself away, and through that you are not saving yourself for your future wife or future husband.

When I interview young men about their dating and sexual histories, religious young men consistently connect dating (and sex) to marriage. Without prompting, they routinely mention their religious beliefs as well. In the next chapter, I'll talk more about the role values play in shaping a young man's dating and sexual behavior.

Religious men date in order to find a life partner, not because men are supposed to date in their early twenties or in order to have a companion that they might possibly marry in a few years. For them, the primary purpose of dating is to find a marital partner.

That's probably why surveys tell us that religious boys and young men are less likely than their age-mates to have ever dated. When they do start dating, it tends to be at a later age, and they seem to date fewer people. Some studies suggest that these guys also hit puberty later than their peers.[14]

It's unusual for these guys to have sex prior to marriage, and they don't hook up.[15] As John explained, "I see my perspective on this as changing to be even more like in line with what God wants. . . . I mean like before I might have joked around with my friends. Of course I'm not out having sex. . . . Now I can't even see myself really having that conversation [that is, joking] without saying like hey this [that is, sex within marriage] is what's right."

They're not all perfect, though. Religious young men who have had sex before marriage tend to have fewer partners (often just one) and tend to lose their virginity at a later age than other guys. And their sexual experiences are almost always with people they're dating.

Characteristics of Religious Men

Researchers have repeatedly profiled teenage boys and young men who are abstinent. On average, they're more religious than other young men their age. They're also more likely than their peers to live with two biological or adoptive parents, to have parents who are more educated, and to grow up in a household with a higher socioeconomic status. In other words, they're more likely to be upper-middle class, or at least middle class. There's a higher than average chance that these young men are of Asian descent, although there are certainly a fair number from every ethnic group. Their home lives tend to have good family relationships and relatively low levels of family conflict. They also have relatively low levels of emotional expression.[16]

Religious young men are better described as risk-avoidant than risk-taking. They tend to avoid alcohol, drugs, shoplifting, petty vandalism, and other similar behaviors that we sometimes expect of boys. And because they tend to befriend other kids who are like themselves as teenagers and young adults, their friends also have relatively low levels of these kinds of behavior.[17]

Among small-town and rural adolescents I surveyed, about 10 percent of the boys were highly religious; on a 1–5 scale, they scored 4 or higher. Using a college-style 4.0 scale, their average GPA was 3.35, notably better than the 3.09 for less religious boys. Other researchers have found that abstinent young men were more likely to attend college than their sexually experienced peers and that they might have higher IQs.[18]

Risks for Religious Men

I did meet one young man who was religious and who'd had sex. It's Chris, whom I quoted earlier explaining about his choice to forgo premarital sex. He grew up in a nominally Christian household, celebrating Christmas and Easter but not much else. At age eighteen, he had sex with his then-girlfriend. A year later, and after they'd been broken up for a while, he was Born Again and sought forgiveness for his actions.

Chris was twenty-five when I interviewed him. During most of the interview, he'd been articulate and pleasant, and had made good eye contact. But for the few minutes it took him to tell me about that sexual relationship, he gave shorter answers and studied the floor intently. It was clear to me that he was embarrassed and ashamed about what he'd done and that he'd only told me because I specifically asked. He also told me that none of his current friends—all observant Christians—knew about that experience. Although he believed that they would understand and would still be his friends, he also didn't want them to think less of him for having sinned in this fashion.

Chris's story isn't common, but it's not unheard of either. There are a number of religious guys who make out with their girlfriends, get caught up in the moment, and have sex. Some of them "suddenly" decide to get married and quickly have a child. There are also some religious young men who get seduced by someone who doesn't genuinely share their beliefs.

Regardless of the specifics, these guys (and girls) are unlikely to use condoms and thus are at a greater risk of getting someone pregnant. They are less likely to have sex with someone who has had other sexual partners, but if they do, they may also be at risk for catching an STI.

From Starting a Relationship to Starting a "Relationship"

There's another thing that I noticed while interviewing men: many guys don't quite seem to know how to start a relationship (or possibly a hookup). Some of that may be because guys are sensitive to rejection and don't want to risk being turned down. That's no small thing. If

you've ever tried out for a team or been turned down after a job interview, you can at least explain it to yourself as the result of having a
bad day and thus not being at your best during the tryout or interview.
Or maybe there really was someone else who was just flat out better.
But those rationalizations don't really cut it when you ask someone
out on a first date or for that first kiss. When you're turned down, it
means that the person just doesn't like you enough. It's usually not
about someone else's skill, and it's probably not about you having an
"off" day. It's just about you, and you're not good enough. For all his
bravery in the face of mortal danger, Harry Potter struggles mightily
to work up the courage to ask out Cho Chang.

This is less of an issue for religious men because they probably have
a friend who can quietly check to see if the woman is interested.
They're also following the "traditional" script in which you ask
someone out and get to know her through the process of dating. That's
not to say it's easy, just that he's less likely to have developed feelings
for her at this stage.

Nonverbal Communication

From our early dating experiences, as well as from TV, movies, and
other visual sources, most of us learn how to understand the body
language that goes along with dating and sexual scenarios. We learn
what it means when you're sitting on opposite sides of the restaurant
table and your date puts a hand in the middle of the table with no
apparent food-related purpose, what it means to have sustained eye
contact, how to lean in to suggest that first kiss, and so on. We also
learn how to "read between the lines" and understand the unspoken
messages that accompany the actual words. In one study of ninety-two
boys ages seventeen, eighteen, and nineteen, every boy generated a
very romantic and nonsexual story when presented with a picture of
a romantic couple.[19]

But not everyone learns to accurately interpret that nonverbal communication. Or maybe guys don't quite trust their nonverbal
comprehension. Perhaps it's because they've been repeatedly told that

"no means no" and that unless they hear an explicit, verbal yes, they don't initiate anything because it could be construed as sexual harassment. Or maybe it's just lack of practice with nonverbals: where else in life is so much said without words?

Starting a "Relationship"

As you've read, some romantic and emo men use hookups as one way to start their relationships. And their hookups tend to be with people they know, not strangers. Not that long ago, the only way for a guy to get to know someone was to go on a few dates with her. But that's not the case today.[20] As I mentioned in Chapter Three, most young people grow up with and have other-sex friends. Gay young men typically have other gay male friends, at least once they leave their parents' house.

In the days when other-sex friends were uncommon, it was much more difficult to have long periods of unsupervised and unscheduled time with those folks; "hanging out" was less common. There were fewer people in college—only about one-third of high school grads went to college in 1970, compared with almost half in 2009. And back in 1970, men outnumbered women about two to one on college campuses; now women outnumber men by a small margin.[21]

In addition to those changes, American culture has become more comfortable with sex before marriage. Not that everyone believes it's OK, but the percentage of adolescents and young adults who believe it's OK has risen steadily from the 1970s through the 1990s and is currently well over 50 percent.[22]

Today, approximately one-third of dating relationships among adolescents younger than fifteen are with people they already consider friends.[23] A substantial minority of dating relationships and hookups later in adolescence and during young adulthood also start off as friendships. After all, these people have already been "vetted" in some ways; friends are people you like and with whom you share some interests and values.

Taken together, all these factors allow a young man to spend a lot of time with someone and have a fair amount of sexual contact with that person before officially becoming that person's "boyfriend." In some ways, this leads us back to a question I asked in Chapter Two: "Why date?" When you can do all of the things that a dating couple would do, including having sex, why call it a dating relationship at all? That question becomes even more important for guys who think that dating means he's "whipped" or has a "ball and chain," and that marriage means the fun part of his life is over.[24]

After all, if a guy can have a regular partner by hanging out with someone whom he's not officially "dating," that would seem to be the best of both worlds. Strictly speaking, he's still single and thus not "tied down" or obligated to anyone else. Because he's not officially dating, he's not explicitly expected to be monogamous.

But those descriptions sell guys short. Most guys aren't interested in having more than one partner at the same time. Jeremy and Ben were interested in developing a longer-term relationship with their hookup partners. It worked for Jeremy, and it kind of worked for Ben; he dated Katie for several months. As we've seen at various places in this book, boys and men want relationships.

One of the problems with the Casanova Complex is that it tells us that the "only" or the "correct" way for boys and men to approach dating and sexuality is by being promiscuous. It thus encourages all of us to downplay or ignore men who don't fit this pattern, even though boys and young men are most likely to adopt a romantic approach. At the same time, there are at least as many religious men as Casanovas. I think it's time we started highlighting these approaches as desirable for young men, instead of ignoring them.

9

. . . .

Sexual Knowledge and Values

Ben remembers having "the Talk" with his father—or, more accurately, *not* having the Talk with his father. Ben and his brother were hanging out, watching TV in the family room, which happened to be in the basement of their house. His dad came downstairs, a fairly rare occurrence. Dad started to talk about sex, and the boys cut him off quickly. According to Ben, they said, "Dad, we already know that because of TV and the media." He thought that "it kind of blew [Dad's] mind because he didn't really think that. It was like a load off his shoulders." His father was relieved and promptly went back upstairs.

And then there's Jim. His parents were highly involved in his sex education. He told me, "In elementary school they were showing a video on the birds and the bees, the health video, and so my parents rented that exact video and said now we know. If you have any questions we want you to ask them to us first and then you could go to school." He also told me the video was boring.

When we look at how boys develop their beliefs about sex, there are several things we need to consider. One is that different boys learn different things from their parents,[1] as Ben and Jim's stories illustrate. In one recent study of young men, almost one in four said they did not remember learning anything from their parents about sex; by comparison, only about 5 percent said they didn't learn anything from the media.[2] In another study, almost 30 percent of adolescents said their parents did not talk to them about condoms,[3] even though condoms are the only form of contraception that is used by and readily accessible to young men.

Boys get sexual information from a variety of sources, but those sources typically talk about different aspects of sexuality and give different "do" and "don't" messages.[4] In one of the few direct comparisons across sources, University of Michigan researchers Marina Epstein and Monique Ward asked nearly three hundred undergraduates to indicate how much they'd learned from parents, from peers, and from the media on each of ten themes, including sexual intercourse, pregnancy, STDs, and birth control. Respondents used a 0–3 scale, where 0 was "nothing" and 3 was "a lot."[5]

Overall, undergraduates reported receiving the least information from parents and the most information from their peers. There were also substantial differences in what each source emphasized. The two most common parental messages, each of which was reported by 25 to 30 percent of young men, focused on contraceptive use and abstinence. Regardless of which method parents preferred, there's a clear parental focus on not getting someone pregnant. Friends tended to share personal stories (experiences) and sex-positive messages. Media messages tended to highlight the idea that sex is casual and illustrated how relationships work.

The mathematical middle of this scale is 1.5. According to the nearly three hundred young men who completed the survey, parents talked most about pregnancy and dating norms, with scores of 1.43 and 1.31. In fact, for almost every one of the ten topics assessed, parents provided less information than peers or the media.

In this chapter, I'll talk about some of the factors that influence how young men develop their beliefs and values. I'll focus mostly on parents and schools, although I'll also mention friends, religion, and other adults. I described the information and values typically presented by the media in Chapter Six.

Learning from Parents

When it comes to learning about the world and learning values, the people a child lives with are the first source.[6] It's parents who teach young children what things are called when they're first learning words, and parents who routinely explain to children how "we" do things. Parents are the people who decide what a child wears—or doesn't wear—when he's young. Until a child becomes mobile (by bicycle, car, or public transit), parents have nearly complete control over who a child's friends are. Or, at least, whom that child can spend time with face-to-face.

When it comes to sexual behavior, parents deliver a variety of messages. These messages start when a child is young and before he understands exactly what he's hearing or seeing. In fact, the earliest messages are nonverbal, and these are messages that teens may notice when they think back, but they're not the kinds of things that necessarily "jump out" of their memories. Do your kids ever see the two of you doing the "little" things—holding hands, kissing passionately, or snuggling?

In twenty-first-century America, the adults with whom children start their life with may not be the adults they're living with when they hit their eighteenth birthday. According to a 2011 Census Bureau report, about 62 percent of children were living with both of their biological parents, another 6 percent were living with stepparents, and 1 percent were living with adoptive parents. This means that about one-third of children were living with a single parent at the time the census asked about their living arrangements.[7]

Among that nearly 33 percent of kids, there's a small percentage of children who grow up living with neither their biological parents nor a couple that adopted them near birth. Most of these kids are raised by extended family members—grandparents, aunts and uncles, and so on—more or less from the time they are born. A smaller number shift from their parents to an extended family member, or sometimes a complete stranger, after they've started talking. Sometimes, that's because the parents have been killed. At other times, it's the result of child abuse.[8]

Regardless of who it is a child is living with, researchers typically call these folks "parents," and so will I.

Who Talks to Their Sons About Sex?

Before puberty, most children don't really hear much about sex from their parents. The only common exception is some form of answer to "Where do babies come from?" although parents may not talk about sex when they answer that question. Children overhear some conversations about who's having sex with whom, and they may be told things like "You're too young to have sex" or "Sex is something that adults do," but that's about it for most kids.

That changes around puberty. When we believe our child is about to hit puberty, or when we can no longer ignore that our child has already hit puberty (for the faint of heart), we have the Talk. Well, some of us have the Talk. Surveys of high school students and undergraduates tell us that only about half of American youth hear the Talk. It's entirely possible that the number is higher; parents are more likely than their children to report that the Talk occurred.[9] When the parents say it happened but the teenagers say it didn't, that's probably not a good sign.

And in survey after survey, girls are more likely to tell us they've had the Talk than boys. Not only that, but conversations with girls cover a broader variety of topics and last longer. That sex difference is paralleled by parents; mothers are more likely to have the Talk than fathers.[10]

Emory University researchers Colleen Dilorio, Erika Pluhar, and Lisa Belcher conducted an extensive review of the literature on parent-child communication about sex.[11] Using the databases favored by psychologists, medical researchers, and public health personnel, they found ninety-five studies about the Talk published between 1980 and 2002. About half of the studies included adolescents and their parents; the remainder were more likely to include adolescents than parents. About half of the studies included fathers, and only two focused exclusively on fathers (as opposed to twenty-nine that focused exclusively on mothers). The research team did not find any studies that focused on teenage boys, although sixteen included only teenage girls.

In studies that provided data from mothers and fathers (but not necessarily couples), the Emory team found that fathers were less likely to talk about sex with their kids than mothers and that fathers may talk about fewer topics than mothers. The team also found that parents reported spending more time and having more wide ranging conversations with their daughters than with their sons.

Parents often tell us they feel awkward talking to boys about the physical and sexual aspects of puberty. When the Talk happens, the boys are usually embarrassed, and so are their parents. There's very little eye contact, and the boys rarely ask any questions.[12]

Collectively, these results tell us that most parents are giving up their opportunity to serve as a more direct influence on their adolescent's sexual behavior. If we're not talking about it, our boys will have to guess what we think or infer it from what they've seen and perhaps what they've heard us say about other people.

What We Say

Then again, even the kids who remember having the Talk tell us, as Jim did, that there wasn't much to it. From the boys who remember it, we get a pretty bleak picture. As its name suggests, the Talk is typically a one-time event. It's almost always less than ten minutes, and it usually includes the three "don'ts": Don't have sex, Don't get a disease, and above all else, Don't get someone pregnant. Boys also tell us they usually get some vague biology about what's "in there" or "down there" and possibly some metaphors that don't really make any sense until they've had sex (or seen people having sex).[13]

Although the vast majority of parents—anywhere between 72 and 98 percent—said they had talked to their kids, the numbers get a lot smaller when researchers asked more specific questions. Among the topics researchers have asked about with some regularity, the only topic that more than half of parents routinely addressed was "reproduction, pregnancy, and birth"—the traditional birds-and-bees talk. Condoms, sexual values, and sexual abuse (including rape) were also things that more than half of parents said they talked about, but these topics have been assessed in only two or three studies.[14]

Yet adolescents don't remember a lot of what parents say they're talking about. Researchers have routinely asked adolescents what, if anything, they learned about menstruation, contraception and birth control, resisting pressure to have sex, abstinence, HIV/AIDS, condoms, and intercourse. Less than half of adolescents remember talking to parents about these things. In regard to topics researchers have assessed only two or three times, adolescents routinely recalled talking about friends' attitudes about sex, the risks of having multiple partners, and parenting.[15]

Clearly, these conversations leave a lot to be desired. There's little or no discussion of relationships, including what it means to be somebody's partner. There's also little or no discussion of those early bases—kissing, petting, or oral sex—and when you should (or shouldn't) do them. And these lacks occur despite parental knowledge that most teens date, often with some parental encouragement. This seems like quite a mixed message.

Most of us would be absolutely horrified at the thought of letting our children enter adolescence, let alone adulthood, without talking to them repeatedly about things like careers, time management, or money management. Yet most of us let our sons go through adolescence and young adulthood without really talking to them about sex and sexuality.

What We Do

As adults, we tend to hide sex—intercourse—from our children. Although many of us can tell embarrassing stories about the kids walking in on us or about when we walked in on our own parents, we don't think about some of the other sexual things we do (or don't do) with our partners in front of the kids. Teenage boys and young men are aware of whether or not their parents typically held each other's hands, snuggled on the couch, or kissed passionately. At least, they can tell you if that happened in the family home or in front of the kids.

When we're courting, these are the behaviors we do in public to affirm and announce our love for our partner. They're certainly the kinds of things married couples do in private.[16] And without making a big deal about it, these are also things that we might or might not do in front of our children. Before and after children hit puberty, have their first crushes, and gain the mental abilities of adults, they learn about sexuality by seeing what their parents do.

One thing that we can do for our kids is to stay with our marital partner and have a good relationship with our partner. Studies consistently indicate that adolescents whose parents are still together are less likely to have sex than adolescents whose parents have separated or divorced. The adolescents from those "intact" families are also older when they first have sex, on average, than kids whose parents are separated or divorced.[17]

In a unique analysis of families across three generations—adolescents, their parents, and their grandparents—the researchers saw this pattern in the two younger generations. Grandparents who lived together had daughters (mothers) who were older when they had sex for the first time. Those daughters (mothers), in turn, had children who were older when they had their first sexual experience.[18]

At the same time, it's not exactly clear *why* staying with your partner delays adolescents' first sex, and more general research on families suggests that "staying with your spouse for the kids' sake" doesn't work out particularly well for anyone. Adolescents from intact families with high levels of parental conflict are more likely to have sex, and do so at a younger age, than adolescents from intact families with little conflict.[19]

It's not just about the sex-related conversations we have with our kids; it's about the quality of our relationships with them. An analysis using the National Longitudinal Study of Adolescent Health (Add

Health), which involved more than fifteen thousand adolescents and their parents, provides more detail. The Add Health study assessed adolescents repeatedly over a six-year period as they moved into early adulthood. At the beginning of the study, adolescents were in grades 7 through 12 and had an average age of about sixteen. Parents also completed surveys at the beginning of the study.

One research team looked at how a variety of parental behaviors were connected to adolescents' condom use and likelihood of losing their virginity during the first year of the study. They found that adolescents who were more likely to use condoms or less likely to lose their virginity reported warmer (or closer) relationships with their parents.[20] These adolescents also reported relatively lower levels of independence, a desire for more years of education, and having parents who were more opposed to the adolescent's having sex.

Adolescents who were diagnosed with a sexually transmitted infection (STI) had the opposite pattern. They had poorer-quality relationships with their parents and were less likely to see college in their future. Overall, the authors concluded that a high-quality parent-adolescent relationship was the most important factor in the adolescents' sexual health.

Learning from School

Public opinion polls consistently show that 75 to 80 percent of American adults believe that schools should provide sex ed.[21] Yet sex education is a controversial topic in the United States, and has been for a long time. The primary concerns are related to beliefs about what is acceptable to teach, particularly where sex education runs into topics that are considered hot-button issues, such as contraception, teen pregnancy, abortion, and homosexuality.[22]

One result of this controversy is that only about half of American states require sex education in any form; and of those states, only about half require that the information be medically accurate.[23] The content varies from district to district, of course, as well as from one age group (or grade level) to another. In fifth grade, for example, the content may focus heavily on the external manifestations of puberty, such as growth spurt, change in voice, and the need to use deodorant, with minimal mention of sex; menstruation is usually discussed when girls are in the classroom, but rarely when the class is just for boys. For kids in the eighth and eleventh grades, the content shifts toward sex, pregnancy, and possibly disease.

Some people voice concern that if we teach children about sex, they'll go out and try it. (Personally, I don't think I've ever heard anyone say that about drug abuse prevention efforts.) I'll provide more detail in the next few paragraphs, but published studies of sex ed programs do not indicate that teaching kids about sex leads them to go out and try it. In general, the studies show that "ineffective" programs don't change adolescents' behavior at all; they don't reduce the amount of sex that teenagers are having, and they don't increase it. By contrast, effective programs typically lead to greater knowledge, less sex, and more consistent use of birth control.[24]

Similar evidence also comes to us from programs designed to reduce the risk of exposure to HIV; in a review of more than two hundred intervention studies, no program was found to increase the frequency with which participants—mostly age twenty-nine and younger—had sex.[25]

Abstinence-Only Education

Since 1995, the federal government has explicitly encouraged abstinence-only education. As funding for these programs has increased, funding for what's known as comprehensive sex education has decreased. The laws governing abstinence-only education aren't entirely clear, however, and the laws passed by state and federal government may define things differently.[26]

More important, those laws often use the term "abstinence" differently than how adolescents use it. For lawmakers, and adults in general, abstinence typically means voluntarily not having sex. These people often use "abstinence" interchangeably with words like "chastity" and "virginity" and intend it to have a moral or religious flavor.[27]

Many adolescents define abstinence as a naturally occurring period during which a teen begins to become interested in sex but is still a virgin. This period typically includes first experiences of dating, including kissing and groping. More important, most adolescents say that abstinence is part of a typical developmental progression from being not at all interested in sex to being interested in sex; for them, abstinence is about "not being ready" for sex.[28] A small percentage define abstinence as intentionally delaying sex until marriage, and these folks tend to be religiously observant.

Although abstinence-only education has been well funded—at least compared to other forms of sex ed—there have been few formal assessments of its effectiveness. Many of the assessments that have been conducted have the types of problems that undergraduates learn about when they take courses in research methods.[29] Because of the interest in the topic and the importance of understanding what federal dollars are paying for, many of the assessments are published despite their methodological shortcomings.

Collectively, abstinence-only education doesn't seem to be effective, at least not for the average adolescent. A minority of such programs change adolescents' behavior in the short term, but few appear to have an effect for as long as six months.[30] One review of twenty-six reasonably well designed studies found that in four abstinence-only programs, young men were *more* likely to get their partners pregnant after they'd completed their abstinence-only education; there was only one non-abstinence-only program where that was the case.[31]

There is one group for whom abstinence-only education works well: religious youth. The reason is simple. The programs tend to repeat and reinforce what these adolescents already believe, and thus may serve as a "booster shot."

Abstinence-only education is also flawed in ways that decrease its potential impact. In most abstinence-only curricula, male and female sexual behavior is presented in very stereotypical terms.[32] The male stereotype is the Casanova Complex, which, as we've seen, describes only a minority of boys. A teenage boy sitting in class who doesn't want to be a Casanova may very well see the material as irrelevant to his life.

Abstinence-only programs often contain inaccurate or misleading information, at least according to one governmental analysis. Eleven of thirteen programs were found to contain false, misleading, or distorted information about contraceptive effectiveness, abortion risks, or other issues.[33] When adolescents realize they're being misled, they may decide that the program is worthless and tune out everything else the instructors present.

These programs rarely include any discussion of gay men, lesbians, or other sexual minorities. When they are mentioned, these folks are typically portrayed as deviant, unnatural, or immoral.[34] When adolescents realize this, especially adolescents who are members of a sexual minority group or are good friends with an LGBTQ youth, they may ignore the curriculum or at least wonder what else is being left out. The absence of sexual minorities clearly isn't designed to help those adolescents achieve sexual health. At the extreme, some adolescents may take this omission as evidence that sexual minorities are deviant.

Reviewing abstinence-only policies, one research team concluded,

> Although health care is founded on ethical notions of informed consent and free choice, federal abstinence-only programs are inherently coercive, withholding information needed to make informed choices and promoting questionable and inaccurate opinions. Federal funding language promotes a specific moral viewpoint, not a public health approach. Abstinence-only programs are inconsistent with commonly accepted notions of human rights.[35]

Comprehensive Sex Education

Comprehensive sex education programs are typically broad in scope. They readily acknowledge that many high school students voluntarily have sex. These programs also address other "typical" behaviors, such as kissing and oral sex, and discuss a variety of methods of preventing pregnancy and disease. Comprehensive programs tend to be less stereotypical in their portrayals of boys and girls, and most, but not all, are LGBTQ-friendly. These programs, which were the typical form of sex ed from the mid-1970s through the mid-1990s, have become less common since the federal government started emphasizing abstinence-only programs.[36]

The effectiveness of these programs has also been evaluated. Collectively, they are only somewhat effective in preventing adolescents from having first sex, reducing pregnancy rates, or improving birth control use; some work and others don't.[37] A close look shows that about half of these programs led to adolescents' having sex less frequently, and about one-quarter of programs lead to older ages of first intercourse.[38]

Comprehensive programs talk about contraception, whereas abstinence-only programs don't. This educational component works: adolescents consistently report clear gains in their knowledge of how to prevent pregnancy. In most studies, they also report improved use of a variety of contraceptives, including but not limited to condoms.[39]

Comprehensive programs have their limits, though, and the primary challenge has to do with getting adolescents to incorporate the facts they learn into their everyday lives. Because comprehensive programs are designed to be relevant for a broad set of adolescent perspectives and values, they don't necessarily resonate with a particular subgroup in the way that religiously informed abstinence-only programs do. As a result, they have to rely on adolescents' desire to be or stay healthy. This is a notoriously difficult task, due in part to adolescents' general sense of invulnerability and omnipotence, and their belief that "it won't happen to me."[40]

One Prominent Example

In 2010, the research team of John Jemmott, Loretta Jemmott, and Geoffrey Fong made news when they revealed that their program was effective. Many news sources called it an abstinence-only program, even though it didn't fit the description I provided here. Teens who received this curriculum were less likely to have their first sexual experience in the next twenty-four months. For the researchers to really understand what worked and why, some adolescents received the abstinence curriculum, some received a comprehensive sex ed program, and some received a more general, "live a healthy lifestyle" program.[41]

The healthy lifestyle program described sexuality as a potentially risky behavior and encouraged adolescents to avoid having sex so as not to put themselves at risk of something bad happening. That's often how we describe alcohol and risky driving to teens—as things that can lead to problems and thus should not be done.

The research team designed the curriculum specifically for the community they were working with; that community had one of the highest pregnancy rates in the Philadelphia metro area. For all three versions of the program, the content was medically accurate; it encouraged adolescents to use condoms if they chose to have sex; and it did not talk about abstaining from sex until marriage.

The research team assumed that the sixth- and seventh-grade students in the program could make rational decisions about when and with whom to have sex, if they had it at all, so the programs encouraged adolescents to "delay sex until you're ready." This presentation is in line with adolescents' conceptions of abstinence as a naturally occurring period in which one is starting to be interested in sexual behaviors, but hasn't yet had sex.[42]

The abstinence and comprehensive sex ed programs were both effective in minimizing sexual behavior over a two-year period, although in different ways. Adolescents who received the abstinence program were less likely to have their first sexual experience (if virgins) or have sex with a new partner (if not virgins), and they had fewer partners than adolescents who received the general health promotion program. Boys and girls who received the comprehensive sex education program were also less likely to have sex and were more likely to use condoms when they did have sex than adolescents who received the general health promotion program.

Some adolescents also received "maintenance" sessions of their curriculum—booster shots, if you will. Compared to students who didn't get the maintenance sessions, those who did had fewer partners, on average, over the two-year period during which the researchers tracked them.

According to Jemmott et al., the healthy-lifestyle approach was less effective than either abstinence or comprehensive sex ed.

Learning from Peers and Siblings

Adolescents learn a lot about sex from their friends. That's hardly surprising; discussions of who's dating and who's having sex are common occurrences in school hallways.[43] Friends tend to be sex-positive and espouse the idea that there's no need to be abstinent. At the same time, they're also likely to express concerns about risks to one's reputation and encourage contraceptive use. In other words, friends tend to be more permissive than parents but less permissive than mass media.[44]

If you're thinking that these broad assessments of "friends" or "peers" sound a lot like the average for all adolescents, you're right. And that's part of the conundrum here. As I mentioned in Chapter Five, an adolescent's friends tend to share his values. As a group, they'll all tend to favor abstinence or promiscuity or sex within relationships.

But friends have an opportunity that isn't available to either parents or mass media. They can help a young man work through all the details of how to manage a relationship (emotional, sexual, or both), how far to go sexually, and so on as he's confronting those questions. Friends are willing to talk about these things, in depth, for long periods of time, and a guy is much less likely to be embarrassed talking to his friends about these kinds of issues than to his parents.[45]

Friends, and especially the broader group known as peers, have an impact. They create a standard of behavior, or a norm. When an adolescent thinks that most of his peer group has had sex, that increases the likelihood that he'll have sex. This also seems to be true for beliefs about being promiscuous, although to a lesser extent.[46]

As a researcher, I have a hard time conceptualizing friends' sexual knowledge. Some of that knowledge surely comes from their own experience, but a lot of it is just a secondhand version of the information presented by parents, media, schools, and other sources. When a guy's buddy tells him that condoms are better than 95 percent effective at preventing pregnancy and disease when they're used properly, that 95 percent figure probably came from some other source. This means that friends have the ability to amplify—or diminish—messages provided by their parents, the media, and so on. This also means that the sex education you provide to your son can influence his friends.

Siblings tend to provide the same kind of information that other teens provide—information from their own experiences and repetition of material from parents and media. But because siblings aren't usually in the adolescent's friendship group, they're likely to have a somewhat different perspective. Researchers have found that siblings have the greatest impact when they're relatively close in age and when they have a fairly close relationship; in these cases, siblings typically decrease the likelihood that an adolescent will have sex. This pattern appears to be true for all types of relationships—twins, biological siblings, half-siblings, and stepsiblings.[47]

Talking to Your Son About Sexuality

If—strike that—*when* you talk to your son about sex, there are some things you should definitely talk about and some things you can probably safely leave out. I'm going to start with what you can leave out: most of the biology, especially if you don't really understand it yourself.

That said, your son needs to know the biological basics of reproduction. He needs to know that sperm come out of the penis. And he needs to know that when sperm are ejected from the penis inside a vagina, there's a chance that pregnancy will occur. Your son also needs to know that sperm and urine come out through the same part of the penis. Even if you're absolutely certain that your son is gay, he still needs to hear about the vagina and egg. This is true because a substantial percentage of gay male youth have some kind of sexual contact with girls at some point.[48]

Don't use vague analogies. Your goal is to educate your son, so stick to what you know and be as clear as possible. If you're going to talk about birds and bees, then you and your child need to share some common knowledge about ornithology, insects, or botany. If your conversations with him don't teach your son what the *vas deferens* do or where exactly they are, that's OK. He'll probably get that in health class at some point.

Your son also needs to know that there are diseases that are specific to and transmitted during sex. Today, we mostly hear about HIV/ AIDS, although human papillomavirus (HPV) is also getting a fair amount of press these days. Things like syphilis, herpes, and gonorrhea still exist. And although they won't kill you in the short term, they can be plenty painful.

You may be surprised to hear it, but the most important thing to teach your son is *not* the mechanics of sex or the proverbial birds and bees. What your son needs to know are your values. The research consistently shows that parents who communicate their values and beliefs have adolescents who tend to be less sexually experienced, if they've had sex at all. This is true across the board; children tend to live up to—or down to—their parents expectations in a broad variety of areas. In one study, knowledge of parental values about sex at age twelve reduced the likelihood that an adolescent had lost his virginity at age fourteen.[49]

Sex educator Melanie Davis, creator of the Web site Honest Exchange, identifies nine different topics and issues that she suggests you talk about with your son. Of those, I think that these are the most important:

• Sex should be with a partner who clearly consents to it. (And "it" means using the word sex, not "doing it," "hooking up," or something else that doesn't have a clear definition.)

• If you can't talk about sex with your potential partner without being embarrassed, and if you're not comfortable having your partner see your naked body, you're not ready to have sex.

• Sex—whether it's oral, vaginal, or anal—always carries a certain risk of pregnancy, disease, or both, so it's not appropriate until [a parent-specified age].[50] (I think sixteen is OK for most kids, and as we saw in Chapter Two, that's a very common age for boys to have their first sexual experience, but it's important that you set an age that's in line with your values.)

I also recommend that you check out some of the resources on the Planned Parenthood of America (PPA) Web site, regardless of what you think about the organization's politics. PPA is the largest provider of sexual health and sex education material in the United States, and it covers a broad variety of topics. Its "resources for parents" Web page includes separate sections—and videos—on parent-teen relationships, talking to kids about sex and sexuality, keeping teens healthy by setting boundaries, helping teens delay having sex, parenting teens who may be sexually active, puberty 101 for parents, parenting LGBT and Questioning kids, and (general) resources for parents.[51]

I suggest that you talk explicitly about condoms. The research tells us that parents who talk to their children—male or female—about condoms are more likely to have adolescents who use condoms. Moreover, when parents talk to their son about condoms before he has sex for the first time, the odds that he will use condoms during first sex, and after that, increase dramatically. This is particularly important; adolescents who use condoms at their first sexual experience are almost twenty times more likely to use condoms for most of their subsequent sexual experiences, and are about ten times more likely to report having used a condom the last time they had sex.[52]

I know, I know. Condoms ruin the moment. Herpes does too, and the Centers for Disease Control and Prevention estimate that about one in six people ages fourteen to forty-nine has some form of herpes.[53] A crying infant isn't going to help the moment either.

Some guys say that condoms reduce the sensation. In response to this complaint, most condom companies now sell "sensitive" condoms designed to increase the feeling. If it takes a guy longer to achieve orgasm because there's less sensation, that means he's staying harder longer, something his partner may very well appreciate.

You should also know that the important thing is just talking to your kids about sex, not how comfortable you are while doing it. Any discomfort and concern parents have with talking to their children about sex does not increase the likelihood that their adolescent will have sex for the first time in the next year, influence their adolescent's likelihood of using condoms, or influence the likelihood that their child will have an unplanned pregnancy or contract an STI in the next five years.[54] This means that even if your conversations are awkward, the awkwardness isn't likely to influence your son's behavior.

The other thing you can do to decrease the likelihood that your son will have sex or the number of people he'll have sex with (in other words, no Casanova Complex) is to have a good relationship with him.[55] That's right: being a caring, reasonably involved parent who your son thinks is "all right" lowers the odds that he'll have sex and lowers the odds that he'll have multiple sexual partners.

Although having a good relationship with your son isn't just about sex, one way to do promote your relationship is to disclose more of your own dating and sexual history. That self-disclosure increases the likelihood that children will be more sexually conservative and less sexually experienced.[56]

All of these factors are true for both mothers and fathers. Yes, some boys express a specific preference for talking to their fathers about "guy things,"[57] but the research shows that mothers' involvement is important and effective.[58]

Generally speaking, boys trust their parents, and many boys want that trust to include shared confidences and not just trust in their parents as providers. They see parents who help with problems through intervention, listening, offering useful advice, and providing comfort as helpful and even trustworthy. Boys and young men see parents and adult mentors as role models and important shepherds on the path to adulthood.[59] This means that if you've talked about relationship dynamics with him before, there's a decent chance that he'll come back for another round when it's important, or that at least he'll be receptive if you start the conversation when it's about his relationships. Admittedly, boys and young men may have some preference for talking to their father or another man,[60] but they rarely rule out female adults just because they're female.

———

Whether you're raising the subject on your own or using TV as a springboard, I encourage you to start talking to your son about dating and sex before he starts doing those things. And keep talking to him about these topics. It probably took you weeks, if not months, to teach him to say please and thank you, and longer to understand what respect means. Getting him to understand dating and sexuality is going to take at least that long.

Intimacy

One of my favorite movie scenes is from *When Harry Met Sally*. No, it's not the restaurant scene. In my favorite, Harry (Billy Crystal) and his best friend, Jess (Bruno Kirby), are at a football game. Sitting side by side, they talk about their romantic relationships. During the conversation, they also stop to watch the game, comment on what's happening on the field, and even do the wave. After each interruption, they pick up the conversation where they left off, as if the conversation had never stopped.

For many of us, the idea of a couple of guys having a heartfelt conversation about an emotionally laden topic is hard to imagine, and that scene is one of the few ways to imagine it. Another variation is a guy telling his best (male) friends how important they are. But that usually requires the guy to be so drunk he can't walk without falling over. Then it's easy to picture him saying "I love you, man." You've seen this scene in dozens of films, including *The 40 Year Old Virgin*, *Superbad*, and *The Hangover*. Miller Lite spoofed this with a series of commercials in which a twenty-something man tells his father "I love you," and the father responds with "You can't have my beer."

Can you imagine a group of guys doing what the women of *Sex and the City* did: meeting at a restaurant and talking about this stuff while looking at each other and maintaining eye contact? The recently cancelled *Men of a Certain Age* received critical acclaim for its efforts to show guys having meaningful conversations, but couldn't attract enough viewers to get past its second season.

Although we know that those film and TV characters aren't real, we also accept those movies and shows as reasonably accurate reflections of reality; none of them would have been commercially successful if we didn't recognize those characters and couldn't identify with them.[1]

Part of what we know—or think we know—about boys' friendships comes from comparing them with girls' friendships. Yet one recent study of undergraduates revealed that young men spent as much time talking to their *close* friends as young women did. However, those same young men spent approximately 12 hours per week talking to their *best* friends, notably less than the almost 17.5 hours that young women spent talking to their best friends.[2] If you focus on comparing the sexes, girls spend much more time talking to their best friends.

Twelve hours a week is still a lot of time. For undergraduates, that's nearly as much time talking to friends as sitting in class. Of course, twelve hours is an average; some young men said they spent less than one hour per week in conversation with their best friends, and others said they spent more than twenty-five hours per week.[3]

Young men said they talked about a variety of things, including sports, sex, school, and work. They also talked about their friendships, romantic relationships, and personal feelings with their friends, but not as much as women did.[4]

In *Deep Secrets*, researcher Niobe Way explicitly tackles our understanding of boys' friendships. Drawing from her two decades of studying the topic, she details how important, meaningful, and intense these relationships are. She also mentions that many of her colleagues who should know better also buy into the stereotype that men don't have close relationships.[5]

Friendship is important for romantic relationships. Not because that's where most romantic relationships and sexual experiences come from—it's not; only about one-third of dating relationships occur with someone who's already a friend, and that's most common among younger teens.[6] Rather, friendship is important because many of the skills necessary for being a good friend are also necessary for being a good romantic partner. Both types of relationships require trust, honesty, maintaining confidences, and sharing. Friendship helps teenage boys and young men learn about and experience these qualities, while also gaining emotional maturity and a sense of their own wants, needs, and desires.[7] And, of course, having friends gives a guy people to talk to in order to understand what's going on in his romantic relationships.[8]

Friendship

Boys tell researchers that their friendships are very important. Young men are clear about their own goals for friendship: having someone to share confidences with and hang out with, and someone who's "got their back." Trust, intimacy, and connection are central to their "real" and "close" friendships.[9] As William Pollack put it:

> The boys spoke passionately about the importance of their relationship with girls and with other boys, about how much they cared about maintaining these friendships, and about the critical role their parents, grandparents, and, in some cases, older siblings played in mentoring them toward adulthood.[10]

This relational focus is at odds with our general conception of boys and their friendships as activity oriented. In boys' friendships with adults and mentors, there's also a clear desire for someone to serve as a model and provide advice.[11]

As a friendship gets stronger or deeper, so does the sharing. The increased intimacy includes sharing secrets, sharing money, and protecting from harm. It often includes knowing your friend's family and seeing your friend as part of your own family.[12] Some writers have suggested that the presence of one close, supportive relationship may be able to "protect" teenage boys from some of the negatives they'd otherwise experience.[13]

The research also tells us that adolescents have a clear preference for people they can hang out with and meet in person; relationships that are online-only are clearly a second choice. This is true even among adolescents who spend relatively large amounts of time online.[14]

Friendship and Masculinity

Relationships of all sorts, including friendship, are a central part of being human. They play a major role in theories that address development of self-concept as well as theories that address development of thinking.[15] Judith Rich Harris places an extreme emphasis on friends, arguing in *The Nurture Assumption* that parents have little or no impact on how their children turn out; she claims that children's friends and children's genes are almost entirely responsible.[16]

In *Real Boys*, Pollack pointed out a peculiar dilemma that boys face. He called it the "Boy Code" and said that it limited boys' ability to express their feelings. Borrowing from the work of authors Deborah David and Robert Brannon, Pollack talked about four principles that boys and men are expected to live up to. (I discuss them Chapter Five.) The No Sissy Stuff principle tells boys that they shouldn't show their emotions, because that's what girls do. The Be a Sturdy Oak principle tells boys that they should strive to be independent and not rely on anyone else. Taken together, these principles teach boys that close, intimate relationships are not necessary; they're not what "real" men do.[17]

This sounds bad for boys' development in general and their ability to function in relationships in particular. But like many other topics I've discussed, it's not that simple. Guys know that the expectations exist, but most don't blindly follow the Boy Code. Some reject it entirely, and others follow it selectively, choosing only certain aspects of the code or certain settings where it seems important.[18]

Tufts University researcher Renée Spencer shed some light on how teenage boys and young adult men "walk the tightrope" of relational connection and masculinity. She interviewed mentors and mentees in a program that paired teenage boys with adult role models. She focused on dyads who had a strong connection that had lasted for at least a year, and interviewed the boys and their mentors separately. Almost everyone talked a lot about the importance of his relationship with the mentor or mentee, including the emotional connections between them. And almost everyone she interviewed repeatedly told her that he wasn't effeminate, his mentor or mentee wasn't effeminate, and the relationship was masculine, not feminine.[19]

Friendship and Feelings

Boys value their close friendships. They tell us that those friendships, as well as good relationships with parents and adult mentors, are important sources of emotional support and a place where they can let their guard down and be vulnerable.[20] In Spencer's study of mentors and mentees, the mentors often talked about their first opportunity to provide emotional support, describing it as a milestone and turning point in the relationship.

Let me say it again: emotional sharing is an important part of boys' friendships. Feelings are part of the basic equipment of human beings; some evolutionary theorists even argue that emotions serve an important role because they help us choose between different evolutionarily adaptive behaviors.[21] There's even a specific part of the brain—the amygdala—that is devoted primarily to handling emotions.

In the 1990s, several books told us that boys had feelings, including Dan Kindlon and Michael Thompson's *Raising Cain* and Pollack's *Real Boys*. Michael Gurian's first books on boys came out around that time, and he's published several more since then, including *The Wonder of Boys* in 1996 and *The Purpose of Boys* in 2009. All these authors told us that boys often hid their feelings because that's what boys think they're supposed to do; feelings are for girls. In various ways, the authors describe what those boys felt and how they dealt with those feelings they weren't allowed to express.[22]

Over the last four decades, researchers have repeatedly asked teen-agers and young adults to rate their emotional expressiveness (or femininity) using 1–5 scales.[23] The boys consistently have lower average scores than the girls. But an interesting thing has happened since the 1970s: young men's emotional expression scores have slowly gone up. If you're worried that this means young men are becoming "wusses," don't sweat it. Young men's masculinity scores have also increased, so the averages have continually indicated that men were more masculine than feminine. And women's emotional expression scores have also increased, indicating that young men are still less expressive than young women.

Even though teenage boys and young men may view themselves as more emotional, kind, and caring than prior generations, that doesn't necessarily mean they're particularly good at expressing these feelings or are really encouraged to do it at length. Whereas many of us might encourage our teenage daughters to keep a diary and write out their feelings, I suspect there are a lot fewer of us who would encourage our sons to do the same. And we'd probably call it a journal instead of a diary.

The idea that boys and men should be stoic and unemotional is part of American culture, and it probably comes from our British heritage—stiff upper lip and all that, m'boy. Men from other ethnic groups, especially men of Spanish or Latino descent, challenge that unemotional stereotype. The stereotype doesn't really describe Italian men either. Or, at least, we have a different stereotype for Italian men. Would you describe the Corleone family or Tony Soprano as unemo-tional? Would you believe that the Corleones or Sopranos were realistic if they were as unemotional as Superman, James Bond, or Rambo? Or pretty much any action film character played by Robert Downey Jr., Tom Cruise, Liam Neeson, Nicholas Cage, Arnold Schwarzenegger, or Jean Claude Van Damme?

Although males are expected to "suck it up" and not cry, there are two clear exceptions, as I mentioned in Chapter Five. Tears are allowed after the big game, win or lose. We even show professional athletes crying on TV after the Super Bowl, World Series, NBA finals, and Stanley Cup playoffs. But only after the last game; reports of tears in the Miami Heat's locker room during the 2010–2011 season were generally met with scorn.[24]

Guys are allowed to shed a few tears at life-cycle events—births, weddings, and funerals—but out-and-out crying is not really acceptable. In *The Wedding Crashers*, those few tears helped our Casanovas get laid.

Anger is the other emotion that men can show. Men's angry displays are allowed more or less any time and any place. It doesn't really surprise us when a guy yells and uses foul language; if he's a boss, it might even be expected. If a woman does that, she's a bitch. In the same vein, if two guys get angry with each other and start fighting, we might be surprised that a fight actually started, but we're probably not surprised that it involved two males.

Yet expressing anger through violence—either verbally or physically—often gets boys in trouble. The mentees in Renée Spencer's study said that anger ultimately played an important part in their relationships with their mentors. More specifically, the boys were able to work with their mentors in order to find other, more acceptable ways to express their anger.[25]

As a culture, we're clear that it's hard for men to say "I love you" to a romantic partner, even though we know they do fall in love (see Chapter Three). Miller Lite recently had a series of ads in which guys were able to say they loved their car, their sports team, and of course their beer, but not their girlfriend. As those commercials pointed out, it's not a physical inability to form the words, but a reticence to say them.

Qualities of a Friend

In a detailed analysis, psychologist Jacob Vigil asked young men to rate themselves and their "ideal" same-sex friend on twelve different attributes. Men's self-descriptions highlighted their kindness, sense of humor, cooperativeness, and responsibility; these were the four highest-rated traits. These characteristics were also what they wanted in a best friend: kindness, cooperativeness, and sense of humor were in the top four, and responsibility "fell" to the sixth spot, but that's still in the top half. The list of less important traits included intelligence, athleticism, financial status, and appearance.[26] Generally speaking, teenage boys and young men want friends who are going to be nice to them and work with them, not people who are going to insult them or who are hypercompetitive.

This shouldn't be surprising. These qualities are exactly what a guy should be looking for if he believes that friendship is about trust, loyalty, and being there for your buddy.

Number of Friends

Research on friendship during adolescence gives some credence to our cultural notion about boys' friendships. On average, boys tend to have "chums" or "buddies" they hang out with and relatively few "real" or "best" friends with whom they share more intimate stories. But we often forget or ignore that "few" is different than "none" and that teenage boys and young men do have strong, deep connections to each other.[27]

Then again, the research also contradicts that general impression in some ways. Males typically report having larger social networks and more friends than females. In one study, undergraduate men reported an average of approximately ten close friends and four best friends; women had fewer in each category.[28] Young men also seem to be more tolerant of others than are young women; among first-year college students, young men reported less conflict with their roommates and were less likely to change rooms.[29]

During middle school, a guy's friends are usually limited to other people his age and grade,[30] even when those friendships start online.[31] In high school, and after that, his circle of friends expands to include others beyond his age and grade, eventually including people who are notably different in age and generation. Some of these may be strictly friends; others may also be considered mentors.

Romantic Relationships

If we think boys have trouble talking to their friends about their feelings and how important their friendships are, then it's no surprise that we think they're emotionally incompetent in romantic relationships. Here, "opening up" and telling your partner "what's going on" are the expectation, not the exception.

For boys who date girls, there are also some conflicting expectations to negotiate, or perhaps selectively ignore. Despite other cultural changes, many teenagers and young adults still expect the guy to "wear the pants" in the relationship and be in charge.[32] Yet girls are generally considered to be the relationship experts, which means that the non-expert is in charge. That doesn't sound like a good plan to me.

Talking about sex can be even more challenging than talking about relationships. Whether it's a hookup or relationship, motives for sex vary, as I discussed in Chapter Three. Although male youth typically view sex within a relationship as a way to get closer to their partner,[33] that's not always the purpose. In a relationship, a young man may see sex as method of strengthening a faltering relationship or as a way to please his partner (even though he's not really in the mood and may not enjoy sex very much in this particular moment). And, just as a small percentage of women attempt to get pregnant in order to hold on to a boyfriend, a small number of guys use pregnancy the same way.[34]

Cicely Marston and Eleanor King reviewed over two hundred studies in which adolescents and young adults were interviewed about their sexual practices. Among other things, the authors concluded that "young people often avoid speaking openly to partners about sex, instead using deliberate miscommunication and ambiguity."[35] The challenges to open communication ranged from being unable to explicitly ask about or consent to sex because it's not accepted within one's culture, to making sure a partner doesn't think you're too eager, to protecting your image, to outright lies.

Over the last forty years, American young men have become less sexist,[36] a topic I'll talk about in Chapter Eleven. However, several aspects of the double standard remain in place when it comes to sex. Boys who conform to the Casanova Complex get praised for their promiscuity; promiscuous girls are condemned as sluts.[37]

This double standard has some rather insidious components that make talking about sex difficult. At the more obvious level, a girl who seems eager for sex may be considered "easy" and a slut. This is the result of our inability to believe that girls (or adult women, for that matter) might be genuinely interested in sex. In *Dilemmas of Desire*, psychologist Deborah Tolman explored how this idea influences girls' sexual development.[38]

Between the double standard and our inability to grasp the idea that girls might genuinely desire and enjoy sex, girls' ability to protect themselves is impaired. A girl who tries to be responsible and carries condoms may be considered a slut. The same thing can happen if she tries to start a conversation about protection before she and her partner have had sex for the first time, or asks him to wear a condom.[39] As a result, girls need to present themselves as relatively naïve and unopinionated about contraception and disease prevention, even though that may mean putting themselves at risk of getting pregnant or contracting an STI.

It gets worse. Even when prospective partners do talk about sex, there's no guarantee of honesty. Remember David from Chapter One? He told me that many guys who follow the Casanova Complex may "spit game." That means a guy will say "whatever he has to say to the girl in order to get her to like him or to go home with him." He described these guys as cocky and said that he thought spitting game was kind of "vulgar."

Decisions about protection aren't just a one-time thing; they are made every time a couple has sex. Yet the couple will probably talk about contraception twice, at most. The first conversation typically happens around the time the couple has sex for the first time, although the conversation may occur after sex, not before it.

If one or both members of a couple are virgins, there's a reasonable chance that they'll talk about protection before they have sex the first time, although the odds aren't great. The odds go down substantially if sex is unplanned, if it's a hookup, or if one (or both) partners are drunk or otherwise impaired. The contraception conversation doesn't occur in couples where both, or even one, person is a member of a religion that views contraception as sinful and doesn't make allowances for disease prevention.

Researchers aren't clear how the odds change if both members of the couple have had sex before (but not with each other). University of Kansas professor Charlene Muehlenhard has studied "sexual consent" for about two decades. Her research consistently shows that college students usually provide consent nonverbally.[40] For example, a boy groping a girl's breast may move his hand from on top of her shirt to under her shirt, then stop and wait for a second or two to see if she moves his hand away or allows it to stay. It's important to note that in these nonverbal conversations, a lack of response—allowing the hand to stay in place—is generally understood to indicate consent.

The context in which this conversation happens is also important. According to Muehlenhard's research, asking about protection while making out carries an implicit indication of desire to have sex, in addition to the obvious meaning related to protection. Pulling a condom out of one's pocket, purse, bedside drawer, or other place also carries this pair of meanings.

That's not much of a conversation about protection.

The second time a couple is likely to talk about protection is a few months down the road. At that time, many adolescent and young adult couples switch from condoms to the pill (or the ring), so they might talk about protection again. The decision to switch is shaped by two factors: one is a tendency to emphasize pregnancy prevention and minimize disease prevention;[41] the other is trust.

If pregnancy prevention is the goal, then switching from condoms to chemicals doesn't change the odds very much; when used correctly, condoms, the pill, and the ring are all better than 90 percent effective. Many guys, especially guys who buy into the Casanova Complex and its image of masculinity, are willing to make the switch because they believe that pregnancy prevention is a female responsibility or otherwise not masculine.[42]

That's always struck me as odd. If a guy thinks he's supposed to be in charge, and he wants to be able to sleep around without making a commitment to one person, then why would he give the responsibility for preventing pregnancy to someone else? Young men certainly hear stories about getting "trapped" because she stopped using birth control, didn't tell him, and is now pregnant. Given that most guys start dating in their teens and don't get married until their mid- to late-twenties (see Chapter Two), why risk it?

Condom-free sex is also used as an indicator of trust in a relationship partner. In fact, young women often rely on their ability to determine whether or not a partner is trustworthy as a primary determinant of condom use.[43] Don't get me wrong: it's certainly important to trust your partner. But until a couple has been tested for every STI, repeatedly, and until they've committed to be together forever, why risk pregnancy or an infection?

From beginning to end, discussions regarding protection can be somewhat different for guys who date other guys. There's no risk of pregnancy, of course, and there's usually greater awareness of the risks of HIV/AIDS, if not other diseases. These boys and young men are somewhat more likely to endorse a policy of using condoms "no matter what."[44]

Gay youth who've come of age since AIDS became widespread are also aware that their partner may not truly—or accurately—know his HIV status; an individual can be infected for months before a test will return a positive result, meaning that they can't be sure about a partner's status for quite some time. Another part of this attitude comes from their awareness that their partner may be intentionally lying about his past, or even just shading his past in order to seem more appealing. Both of these factors diminish the emphasis on trust in male-male relationships.[45]

Teaching Boys About Friendships and Relationships

We can do a better job of teaching boys about relationships. We know—or at least believe—that girls will talk to adults about how friendship and romantic relationships work. We're quite certain they talk to their friends about it. And a fair number of them also read magazine articles on the topic.[46] As a result, girls acquire a better sense of relationship dynamics than boys.

Of course, there's no reason we can't talk to or teach boys about relationship dynamics. Admittedly, boys may be less likely to start or seek out these conversations, but it's pretty clear they're quite capable of understanding them. Just because they're less likely to show their feelings when a friend violates their trust, or to ask for our input about problems they're having with a friend, that doesn't mean we can't help them or give them some of the framework beforehand. In this case it's really up to us; there's no teen boy equivalent of *Seventeen* and its ilk, so we can't just gift a boy with a magazine subscription in order to enhance his knowledge and (we hope) start a conversation.

Our conversations about relationship dynamics can start early. Parents typically know who their children's friends are. If we're paying attention, we should notice when they become best friends with a new person or suddenly stop being friends with someone. The reasons for these changes tend to be the same for boys and girls. New friends are typically the result of shared interests, time already spent together, and similar values; friendships end because of a violation of trust, a friend's being "mean to me" (which may include hitting or ignoring for younger children), or a friend's turning his or her attention to someone else (in other words, dumping your child).[47]

All of these scenarios can be used to talk about relationship dynamics. Children in elementary school know you're not supposed to tell someone else's secret; this is the basis of trust. Adolescents certainly understand this. Teens' definitions of trust also include things like following through on promises and other agreements.

We can ask our sons about the limits of this kind of confidentiality. In later elementary school and much of middle school, it's not unusual to be told a "secret" about someone's crush. But it seems as though those secrets are intended to be shared, because that's how couples get formed at this age.[48] Does that mean it's really a secret? And how do you know what's a "real" secret and what's a secret that's supposed to be shared?

In these conversations, it's important to remember that adolescents define privacy somewhat differently than adults do. Their definitions tend to emphasize things kept private from parents; they're quite aware that things shared with friends are likely to be shared with a group of friends and possibly their entire social world, not just one person.[49]

Loyalty, which includes "having somebody's back," is also an important component of friendship. Boys are certainly aware of whom they've helped out and "been there for," and whether the support is reciprocal. They have some sense of which of their friends will support them no matter what, and whose support is more conditional. And although we don't often ask boys to think in those terms, it's a conversation worth having.

From loyalty, it's a small conversational step to commitment. In some ways, loyalty is simply following through on a commitment to someone. But when to commit? And what or how much do you commit? For guys who adhere to the Casanova Complex, committing to just one person can be a real challenge, but most guys don't really have trouble making that kind of promise.

If you listen to your son's music or watch his TV shows, you'll notice these kinds of themes. Bruno Mars's song "Grenade" is an example of extreme loyalty to a girlfriend. In the chorus, he sings, "I'd catch a grenade for ya / throw my hand on a blade for ya," among other forms of self-sacrifice, before lamenting "but you won't do the same / no no no no." You might ask your son what he thinks of Bruno's lyrics.

If you and your son both follow sports, you'll certainly find plenty of opportunities to talk about loyalty and commitment. LeBron James's departure from the Cleveland Cavaliers in 2011 was an intriguing example. Was James disloyal for leaving the team after seven years? Did the team expect too much of him, especially considering the other players they brought in? You can think of that last question as asking if the team committed enough support to helping James.

There are a host of similar questions that get played out every season: how loyal should a team be to an aging superstar who is past his prime and at the end of his contract? How much should a team stick with a promising young player who is struggling in his second or third year? Does a team "owe it" to the regular starter to put him back in the lineup when he's recovered from an injury, even though his replacement is doing very well? And what does the team "owe" to that replacement player?

Once you've had a conversation or two about relationship dynamics, you can shift to romantic relationships. You might start by asking about differences between friends and romantic partners. What does your son think about the expression "bros before hos"? Does choosing your romantic partner over your friends on a Friday night mean that you're "whipped"? Even if it's just once? Is choosing your sweetie over your friends necessarily a bad thing?

You can also ask your son what sexuality means in a romantic relationship. Do kissing, holding hands, and other public displays of affection (PDA) mean something different than sex?[50] In *Pretty Woman*, Vivian (Julia Roberts) initially refused to kiss Edward (Richard Gere) on the mouth because kissing was "too intimate." Does sex indicate a greater level of commitment by taking a relationship to "the next level"?

Conversations like this can also be prompted by advertisements for movies about getting laid, such as *American Pie*. It seems as though there are three or four of these movies every year, and the advertisements are rarely subtle, so you'll probably have plenty of opportunities. Ask the young men in your life about the loyalty and commitment displayed in these movies. In *Knocked Up*, we saw one possible answer to the question "What if a hookup leads to pregnancy?" It's probably worth adding that question to the conversation.

Discussions like these certainly get at the topics of loyalty, commitment, and mutual responsibility. Using athletes and fictional characters as jumping-off points for conversations gives you the opportunity to share your values without condemning your son (or his friends), and it's important that he knows what you think.

Challenging the Casanova Culture

So far, I've talked about things that you can do to help the boys in your life (and perhaps the girls) gain a more accurate perception of what most guys do and how to start some important conversations about dating, relationships, and sex. But I'm hoping that this book will be the start of something bigger. In this chapter, I'll talk about how we can start to push back against a culture which says that all boys and young men want to be Casanovas.

Thinking Differently

I believe we need to think about young men's sexuality differently. I think we need to conceptualize it as one part of growing up that's connected to the other parts of growing up, including changes in how boys think (Chapter Two) and how boys develop an identity and select friends (Chapter Six). I also think we should idealize and idolize some of the non-Casanova approaches to dating and sexuality I described in Chapter Eight.

When talking about how people think about bigger-picture stuff, the metaphor of a script can be helpful.[1] An actor learns his lines and is expected to deliver them in the right place and at the right time in order to create a credible character. Our culturally dominant script teaches all of us that boys and men are supposed to be Casanovas, and how to achieve that goal. You might prefer the metaphor of a frame (from framework) or even a role, but I'm going to stick with the script metaphor.

Scripts can be changed, of course. The director might ask for a rewrite, or an actor might ad-lib. Just like a script, our notions of sexuality and masculinity can also be changed. I've already talked about how the images of men's sexuality have changed in mainstream media (Chapter Six) and how our notions of masculinity have changed (Chapter Five), and in this chapter I'll talk about some ways that we can change it again.

One thing a script does is influence how we think about things; it tells us what's important, what to pay attention to, and what to expect. If the Casanova Complex is your script for the sexual behavior of boys and young men, then you assume that guys who fit the mold are the norm, that they're typical. And when we hear about Casanova-like behavior, it reaffirms our beliefs.

As I pointed out in Chapter One, only a small percentage of guys follow the Casanova Complex script. But because we understand young men's sexuality in terms of that script, we often fail to notice or emphasize the guys who aren't Casanovas. When we do notice them, we think they're exceptional and unusual, even though they are in fact the majority.

One way to start changing the script is to get accurate information on what's really happening. I've provided you with a lot of that information throughout the book. To get some additional numbers, including breakdowns by grade (9 through 12), race and ethnicity, and state, I recommend visiting the Web site of the Youth Risk Behavior Surveillance System, one component of which is the Youth Risk Behavior Survey I've cited elsewhere in this book.[2] There you can find twenty years' worth of survey data on the percentage of high school boys who've had sex, the number of partners they've had, their condom use, and several related behaviors. The interactive tables will let you examine the numbers in a variety of ways.

You can also try to change the script by getting the teenage boys you know to talk honestly about their sex lives, especially about the number of partners they've had or want to have. That may not be easy to do, especially in conversation, but it can be done by having a group of guys write down their number anonymously on a piece of paper and then throw it in a hat. In a minute or two, you can figure out the average and count how many guys have written zero or one partner. Then you can tell them what the average was, and how many guys had very few partners; they're likely to be surprised.

If you really want to drive the point home, you can also ask the guys to estimate the average in advance so that they get a sense of just how far off they were. Activities like this, combined with factual information, are known as "social norms" interventions and have helped change behaviors as diverse as alcohol consumption and home electricity use, as well as beliefs about masculinity.[3]

Sex Among Equal Partners

I've mostly focused on how we can talk to the boys and young men in our lives about sex. But it's also very important that they be able to talk openly to their partners about it. In order to do that, boys need to be clear about what they want to do and what they don't want to do. Helping your son think about the variety of sexual behaviors that exist, as well as the implications of those behaviors for a relationship, should help him. He also needs to know that he's allowed to say "No" or "Stop."

Boys and young men need to know something about relationship dynamics. In general, if you're not willing to do a lot of what your partner wants, that doesn't bode well for the relationship. Then again, if one person in a relationship is doing something he (or she) doesn't enjoy, but he (or she) is doing it because their partner wants to do it, that's likely to create resentment. And resentment is rarely good for a relationship over the long term.

The ability to negotiate with your partner when you disagree is an important skill to acquire, especially if you intend to have long-term relationships. And I mean negotiation, not one person (always) giving in to the other's desires. No twosome agrees with each other 100 percent of the time, and staying with someone over a long period of time involves a variety of tradeoffs. To use something of a stereotypical example, most guys enjoy receiving oral sex, but many fewer of them enjoy performing it (although more enjoy it than you might think). It seems obvious, but you shouldn't be asking for something if you're not willing to provide it. And if you're allowed to say no, so is your partner.

Yes Means Yes, No Means No, and the Silences in Between

Adolescents understand that yes means yes and no means no. Well, most of them do, anyway. As I discussed earlier, they typically interpret silence as yes.[4] Boys and young men understand that when a partner puts a boy's hand someplace, the partner is giving permission for the boy to have his hand there. Of course, the young man may feel pressured to keep his hand there even though he doesn't want to.

Adolescents should also connect these forms of permission giving to the idea of respecting their partner. After all, your son probably doesn't like it very much when he says he doesn't want to do something and then is forced to do it anyway, and that probably changes very little regardless of whether the request comes from his sweetie or his parents. If he tells you that his girlfriend—or his boyfriend, for that matter—doesn't know how to say yes, you can ask him how he knows that; I doubt that he's suddenly become telepathic without your knowledge. If you're willing to tread more deeply into his relationship, you might also ask him if there are other realms of his life where his sweetie has difficulty expressing her or his desires, or how much he likes being the one who gets to make all the (sexual) decisions.

Implications for Girls

For a guy to follow the Casanova Complex, at some level he has to see women—or at least, a substantial percentage of the women out there—as not worthy of his respect. In order to have sex with someone and then never talk to her again, especially if you've been lying to her or getting her drunk as part of the process, you can't really respect her. To a Casanova, a girl who sleeps with a guy she's just met does not deserve a guy's respect. To some guys, this logic is obvious and accepted, even though it's circular: she may not be a slut until after she's slept with you, and therefore you should respect her until that point.[5]

This isn't just about changing how we raise boys and talk to them about relationships and sexuality, it's also about changing girls. After all, if we continue to teach girls to be suspicious of boys' and young men's motives, then a guy who is honest about his sexual desires is going to run into problems.[6]

We need to get away from teaching girls a "defensive sexuality" based on stopping guys' advances, as Deborah Tolman called it in *Dilemmas of Desire*. Instead, we need to teach them to recognize, value, and express their own desires. Among other things, we need to stop assuming that girls are only interested in relationships, and acknowledge that some may be primarily (or exclusively) interested in sex. Allison Caruthers, a colleague of mine, had an undergraduate woman tell her that she planned to enter medical school immediately after receiving her BA and didn't see herself settling down until she was done, or nearly done, with medical school. But every now and again, she wanted to get laid. That's basically the same logic we heard from David in Chapter Three about not dating and only hooking up during his senior year of college.

Challenging the Double Standard

One obstacle to creating equal partnerships is that our culture tends to emphasize that boys and men are different from girls and women. As a result, we sometimes treat these groups differently, especially in the realm of dating and sexuality.

Following the Casanova Complex provides a young guy with status; we might call him a "stud" or simply "the Man" due to his sexual conquests.[7] But a woman who sleeps with a bunch of guys gets a different set of names, like "slut" or "easy," and she loses status and the respect of others.[8]

Most of the guys I've asked have told me the term "slut" really only applies to girls and women. David explained that the "double standard exists. I didn't create it; I just live it." He was sure that no matter how you cut it, any version of "girl player" was still going to come out as "slut" and therefore be bad. Matthew, a gay man, told me that the term slut only applied to women, that a slut has "no self-respect," and that her goal was "not to be sexually pleased but just like to get attention, y'know, from men."

If Matthew is right and sluts are just doing it to get attention from young men, what does that say about the guys who sleep with them? As we saw in Chapter Three, a guy's friends often play a substantial role in his hookup behavior. His choice of a partner is often influenced by what his friends will think; they're the people he'll brag to and who will give him "props" for getting laid. Doesn't that mean he's just trying to get attention too?

Perhaps if we're going to think poorly of a young woman who has sex with someone she's just met, then we should also think poorly of a young man who does that too. Isn't he just as "easy" or "attention seeking" as she is?

The double standard that says (male) Casanova = good, (female) slut = bad is part of a larger set of beliefs called sexism, of course. At its essence, sexism is about treating people differently based on whether they're male or female, and that's exactly what's going on here. The Casanova = good, slut = bad double standard draws a line between men and women so that one group (men) benefits from a behavior (sleeping around) while the other group (women) is punished for it.

This double standard persists despite the fact that, according to research, young men have become less sexist since the 1970s.[9] There are a variety of reasons for the decrease in sexism, including greater awareness of and access to successful women as role models. Having female friends throughout adolescence also plays a role, as does having girls compete with—and outperform—boys in many areas of schooling,[10] one of the few places where boys and girls compete directly against each other. And today, the idea that girls and boys are equally capable is one of the most common messages about gender that boys remember hearing from their parents.[11]

Sexual Power

In the typical relationship, girls may actually have more power than boys, at least when it comes to having sex. As adolescents explained it, if the girl says no to sex, then it's going to stay no. But if a guy says no, the girl may very well be able to talk him into it.[12]

But it's different with guys who are sexist. Guys who are sexist are more likely to agree with a set of statements known as "rape myths," including "In the majority of rapes, the victim is promiscuous or has a bad reputation," "When women go around braless or wearing short skirts and tight tops, they are just asking for trouble,"[13] "Many women secretly desire to be raped," and "Rape accusations are often used as a way of getting back at men."[14] In practice, these sexist guys are the ones who are least likely to accept that no means no and are most likely to use force, deceit, or intimidation to have sex with a woman.[15] They're also the guys who are most likely to see promiscuity as a good thing.

I want to be clear that I'm not saying that guys in general, or Casanovas in particular, usually or often rape women. What I am saying is that guys who are more sexist—and this includes many who subscribe to the Casanova Complex—are the guys who are the least likely to accept that "no" means no.

Men and Women as Partners, Not Enemies

I've been hearing about the battle of the sexes, and sometimes the war between the sexes, for my whole life. As far as I can tell, it's the only war in humanity's history where about 90 percent of the so-called combatants are dating or sleeping with each other.

We probably need to start talking and thinking about relations between men and women as something other than a competition or battle. In the battle and war metaphors, there's a winner and a loser, or perhaps a stalemate. But helping people become mature adults isn't a one-up, one-down competition; we need as many competent adults as possible. We need to start talking about "both-and," perhaps by focusing on the many things boys and girls, men and women have in common.

Don't get me wrong—I'm not saying there are no differences; but I am saying that if we focus primarily or exclusively on differences, then we're likely to think primarily in those terms, as though we were following a script. We're just as capable of focusing on the similarities.

We may never understand biology well enough to comprehend the complex interplay between nature and nurture that shapes how any given individual's genetic code is expressed,[16] and I don't think we need to wait for the answers to those types of questions. Over 150 years ago, Darwin pointed out that we are the result of both genetics and environment, nature and nurture,[17] so I'm not sure how much we gain by trying to pull the two apart. Instead, it seems that we might best be served by addressing human needs, such as the needs for safety, for companionship, and to be loved, and the desire to deal honestly with others and to live to one's potential.[18]

We also need to recognize that not everyone in the group called "male" acts the same way. Although boys are supposed to like sports, cars, and girls, you probably know some guys who only like one or two of those three, and you may very well know a male who doesn't like any of them. Instead of thinking less of them for not being "real" boys, you might ask why we're evaluating their realness and where that standard came from. Heck, in some cultures, there are more than two genders and different words to help delineate them.[19]

On the theme of "not all guys are the same," it's important to recognize that only a small percentage of boys and men genuinely have power or the opportunity to exercise it, even though most of the leaders we've had—be they political, religious, or economic—have been male. People who advocate for and study men have repeatedly made this point, whether it's coming from "masculist" Warren Farrell or feminist sociologist Raewyn Connell.[20]

In his *Myth of Male Power*, for example, Farrell acknowledges that the women's (or feminist) movement of the 1970 and 1980s was very good for helping women recognize the limits placed on them by the patriarchal system. He also argues that before we can reach true equality between the sexes, we'll need a men's movement to help men recognize the limits they face as a result of the patriarchal system.

Social psychologist Roy Baumeister takes a different approach and argues that male-female differences complement each other; he relied heavily on evidence that the group called men tends to favor having a small number of intimate relationships and a large network of acquaintances, but the group called women reverses the pattern and favors a greater number of intimate relationships and a smaller network of acquaintances. Baumeister suggests that men have used their networks to develop a variety of large groups, ranging from clans to nations, from IBM to the Indianapolis Colts. Regardless of size or purpose, the entities rely heavily on shallow networks of acquaintances in which any person is replaceable.[21]

Combating Media's Influence

On a larger scale, we need to change the images of boys, men, and masculinity we routinely present. We need to demand that mainstream media give us better models instead of continuing to emphasize Casanova as the primary way that teenage boys and young men can be happy or get the respect of other guys. For the last twenty years, most TV fathers have ranged from clueless to incompetent (yet somehow harmless), like Homer Simpson or Tim Taylor of *Home Improvement*. Worse, marriage means that guys will never have fun again; just ask Ray Barone from *Everybody Loves Raymond* or Al Bundy from *Married . . . With Children*. If being a Casanova looks like fun and being a grown-up means being a barely competent dad and never having any fun, then the choice to be a Casanova seems like a no-brainer.[22]

In the 1970s, women organized protests against the television networks because they wanted to see women on screen who were more than just eye candy or housewives. They wanted to see women who were capable of making a decision without first talking to a man, women who had careers instead of jobs, and women who could be role models for their daughters. They wrote letters, protested, and took action in a variety of ways, including turning off the shows that portrayed undesirable images. Forty years later, it's not unusual to see female detectives, doctors, lawyers, and CEOs on television, as well as in daily life. Yes, some disparities still exist—married women on TV are much more likely to be at home and without a specific career than are married men—but it's gotten better.[23]

If this strategy worked once for women, it can work again for men. We need to tell the companies that produce and air these programs that this content is insufficient. It's time to let our clickers do the talking.

Until the content changes, we need to learn how to think about media content and how to talk to our sons about dating and sexuality. You can start challenging the media messages your son receives about male sexuality by helping him become media literate—able to think critically about the media we're exposed to. It's a standard part of public education in most European nations, but not here in the United States.[24] That's unfortunate. In one study, 85 percent of teens ages twelve to seventeen said they found their peer-led media literacy sessions on sex to be "somewhat better" or "much better" than teacher-led sex education.[25]

There are a number of organizations and Web sites that promote and teach media literacy, and some offer curricula for use in schools. The National Association for Media Literacy Education is a fine place to start, as are the materials produced by the Media Education Foundation. The Resources section lists the Web sites of these organizations and others.

Media literacy teaches us to ask questions: "Who is the audience?" "What is being sold?" "What messages or themes are included as part of this story?" and others. You can promote literacy with children of almost any age by asking such questions as "Would that really happen?" "Would that really work?" or even "Would you do it that way?"[26]

"What's missing?" is also a good question, although it may not be very effective with children younger than eight or ten or when you're talking to someone who lacks the experience needed to answer the question. You can start by pointing out a number of things that happen in scripted shows that we never quite notice. You almost never hear a price when TV characters go shopping, and you rarely actually see them pay when they're a regular customer of a coffee shop or bar. TV characters rarely wear the same clothes twice, even characters who hate shopping and never seem to do it; the only exception is when that shirt (or whatever) is an explicit favorite, has other emotional value, or is a uniform.

Consider a show like Glee. Finn, the (original) male lead, hates shopping, but I'm pretty sure we've never seen him wear the same thing twice. The Gleeks rarely, if ever, practice together or with the musicians who play behind them. They routinely switch lead singers during a song, everybody always comes in on cue, nobody gets the words wrong (or forgets them), and their dance steps are choreographed. It all works perfectly almost every time we see it, even when they write their own song for a major competition the night before. If you've ever been part of a band or performed on stage, you know how long it takes to get it just right. But if you don't know better or you don't really think about these things, then you won't notice the discrepancies between the world on screen and real life.

On comedies, you may also notice that Casanova usually gets the best lines, is usually right about things, and typically has the support of the laugh track. Media literacy tells us to ask, "How come this character is the one who has all the answers?" "Why does he get the best lines?" and even "Why is the audience supporting this guy?" The last question works regardless of whether there's a live audience or a director who is controlling a prerecorded laugh track.

Watching TV with your son gives you the opportunity to talk about dating and sex without the conversation's being personal. In Chapter Six, I mentioned that adolescents who watched along with their parents the *Friends* episode in which Ross and Rachel got pregnant were more likely to talk to their parents about pregnancy and were more likely to remember that condoms are 95 to 100 percent effective.[27]

You can use TV and movie events to talk about sexual decision making, and possibly even as a foil to ask your son what he might do in the same situation. This approach is effective because you both "know" this character, but because he or she is fictional—and not your son or one of his friends—the conversation probably won't have the same emotional charge that it might have if you were talking about a real person.

When it comes to sexual behavior, questions about the values and the lifestyle portrayed are particularly important, as is the question regarding what's being omitted. Asking your son what he thinks when an unmarried couple has sex is an excellent question. It doesn't much matter if it's a hookup, friends with benefits, or an established monogamous couple. Asking your son if he thinks sex before marriage is OK in general or for this couple in particular, and why, creates an opportunity to challenge the media's portrayal of hookups and premarital sex as acceptable and typical. It also gives you an opportunity to talk about your own values.

Depending on the specifics, you can use the conversation to talk about how long someone needs to be in a relationship before having sex, having learned about a partner's sexual history (or not). The effect of sex on someone's reputation is also fair game. Discussions about pregnancy, birth control, sexually transmitted infections, and the like can also be worked into these conversations. These latter issues are particularly important because they are rarely discussed (or portrayed) on TV, as I mentioned in Chapter Six.

The focus on women's bodies is one topic that may generate different reactions from boys and girls. Regardless, both groups receive the same message from the media: the most important thing about a girl (or woman) is how attractive or sexy she is. Although it's not uncommon to teach our daughters that looks are not the most important thing, we rarely have the parallel conversation with boys: girls are more than their bodies.

Nor do we teach boys that they themselves are more than their sexual appeal, although given everything I discussed in Chapter Seven, I think that this message is more important for boys than it's ever been. After watching some of those commercials together, you can ask your son if he really wants to be with a partner—romantically or sexually—if that person wouldn't give him the time of day before he started using Product X and is now desperate to be with him.

And remember, you don't have to get it perfect, and you don't have to include every possible topic in the conversation. You can talk about the dating and sexual lives of TV characters over and over; it's certainly one of the writers' favorite topics.[28]

Starting and Maintaining the Conversation

Throughout the last few chapters, I've been encouraging you to talk to your son about what it means to be sexual and to be male. I don't think you should limit the conversation to your sons. Talk to your daughters too, and also your sweetie. If we want to change how we think about young men's sexuality, we're not going to get very far by working alone. It's also important to practice what we preach; adopting a hypocritical stance is a good way to lose your credibility.

You don't need to limit the conversation to young men's sexuality, either. We keep hearing that "men are in crisis" and that "it's the end of men." Political commentator Maureen Dowd even published a book called *Are Men Necessary?* and I suspect you can guess the answer. As I mentioned in Chapter Five, people have been talking about a masculinity crisis for nearly a century.[29]

Except for the Casanova Complex, mainstream media haven't given much thought to what it means to be male and sexual, but there are a small number of online magazines and Web sites that do. You might check out the Good Men Project (http://goodmenproject.com) or Role/Reboot (http://www.rolereboot.org), among others. Although

I find the language a little harsh and the rhetoric a little too anti-women, A Voice for Men (http://www.avoiceformen.com) will also give you plenty to think about.

We know that women's roles have changed since the 1970s, but somehow we tend to think that men's roles have stayed the same. They haven't. I think more and more people are starting to recognize this, in part due to the job losses sustained in the late 2000s—mostly in "traditional" male-dominated fields—and in part because they want something different for their children.

In the 1970s, feminists organized "consciousness-raising" meetings to help women see the ways in which their choices had been limited by society. I think we need to do the same thing regarding men's roles. In addition to thinking about young men's sexuality differently, we can also ask (adult) men what they wished they'd known about "being a man," how they deal with the ongoing pressure to "prove their masculinity," and what's hard about being a man.

Men's parallel to consciousness raising seems to have been to go into the woods, beat on drums around a campfire, and be "real" with each other without the presence of women. Sometimes called the mythopoetic movement because of the prominence of Robert Bly's *Iron John*, it provided a model of men's "being" and growth as something that happens away from everyday life, not as part of it. The ManKind Project started with that model, but subsequently revamped its programs so that participants receive support and encouragement to bring those changes into their everyday life.[30] Men's groups often provide that kind of insight and support as well.

As Mahatma Gandhi said, "You must be the change you want to see in the world." It's time to stop thinking about and treating all guys as though they subscribe to the Casanova Complex, and it's time to start highlighting and emphasizing that teenage boys and young men can be, and usually are, responsible human beings. It's time to start idealizing, idolizing, and respecting honorable, mature, responsible young men.

Resources

· ·

This resource list will help you find more information. It is not exhaustive; I have included organizations that are relatively large, have good reputations, and have more extensive Web sites. They're a good place to start. The listings are in alphabetical order within each section.

Easily Accessible Data on Young Men's Sexual Behavior

Centers for Disease Control and Prevention: Sexually Transmitted Disease Surveillance: http://www.cdc.gov/nchhstp/Default .htm

Monitoring the Future (MtF): http://monitoringthefuture.org/

National College Health Assessment, by American College Health Association (ACHA): http://www.achancha.org/

National Study of Family Growth (NSFG) key statistics: http:// www.cdc.gov/nchs/nsfg/abc_list.htm

Youth Risk Behavior Surveillance System (YRBSS) sexuality homepage: http://apps.nccd.cdc.gov/YouthOnline/App /QuestionsOrLocations.aspx?CategoryId=4

Sexuality

Advocates for Youth

Advocates for Youth (http://www.advocatesforyouth.org/index.php) champions efforts that help young people make informed and responsible decisions about their reproductive and sexual health.

> Contraception: http://www.advocatesforyouth.org/topics-issues /contraceptives?task=view
>
> Interventions: http://www.advocatesforyouth.org/for-professionals /programs-that-work
>
> Sex education: http://www.advocatesforyouth.org/for-professionals /sex-education-resource-center?task=view
>
> Sex ed for parents: http://www.advocatesforyouth.org/parents-sex -ed-center-home

Centers for Disease Control and Prevention (CDC)

The CDC is the U.S. government's official source for information regarding health, disease, and prevention on a wide range of topics.

> Pregnancy prevention: http://www.cdc.gov/reproductivehealth /UnintendedPregnancy/Contraception.htm
>
> STD Main Page: http://www.cdc.gov/std/default.htm
>
> STD Awareness Resource site: http://www.cdcnpin.org /stdawareness/
>
> Sexual Health: http://www.cdc.gov/sexualhealth/

Guttmacher Institute

The Guttmacher Institute (http://www.guttmacher.org/) works to advance sexual and reproductive health worldwide through research, policy analysis, and public education.

Contraception: http://www.guttmacher.org/sections
   /contraception.php

Men's sexuality: http://www.guttmacher.org/sections/men.php

Pregnancy: http://www.guttmacher.org/sections/pregnancy.php

Healthy Teen Network

Healthy Teen Network (http://www.healthyteennetwork.org/) is devoted to making a difference in the lives of teens and young families,
with an emphasis on teen pregnancy prevention, teen pregnancy, and
teen parenting.

Adolescent health: http://www.healthyteennetwork.org/index
   .asp?Type=B_BASIC&SEC={F8660EBE-1AF0-4231-AAAD
   -798689F83905}

Interventions: http://www.healthyteennetwork.org/index
   .asp?Type=B_LIST&SEC={84D38731-0591-41B6-90AF
   -03593EF836BA}

The National Campaign to Prevent Teen and
Unplanned Pregnancy

The National Campaign (http://www.thenationalcampaign.org
/default.aspx) seeks to improve the well-being of children, youth,
families, and the nation by preventing unplanned and unwanted
pregnancy.

Contraception: http://www.thenationalcampaign.org/resources
   /contraception.aspx

Interventions: http://www.thenationalcampaign.org/resources
   /programs.aspx

National data: http://www.thenationalcampaign.org/national
   -data/default.aspx

State data: http://www.thenationalcampaign.org/state-data/default.aspx

Planned Parenthood of America (PPA)

PPA (http://www.plannedparenthood.org/) promotes a commonsense approach to women's health and well-being, based on respect for each individual's right to make informed, independent decisions about health, sex, and family planning.

For teens: http://www.plannedparenthood.org/info-for-teens/

For parents: http://www.plannedparenthood.org/parents/

Men's sexual health: http://www.plannedparenthood.org/health-topics/men-4285.htm

Sex education: http://www.plannedparenthood.org/resources/

Sexuality Information and Education Council of the United States (SIECUS)

SIECUS (http://siecus.org/) provides information and education about sexuality and sexual and reproductive health.

Information and education: http://siecus.org/index.cfm?fuseaction=Page.viewPage&pageId=477

Sexual Advice for Teens

Go ask Alice (Columbia University): http://goaskalice.columbia.edu/

I wanna know (American Social Health Association): http://www.iwannaknow.org/teens/index.html

It's your sex life (MTV): http://www.itsyoursexlife.com/

Sex, etc. (Rutgers University): http://www.sexetc.org/

Stay Teen (The National Campaign): http://stayteen.org/

Teenwire (Planned Parenthood of America): http://www.teenwire .com

Young Men's Health Site: http://www.youngmenshealthsite.org/

Media Literacy Curricula

National Association for Media Literacy Education: http:// namle.net/

Center for Media Literacy: http://www.medialit.org/

Media Education Foundation: http://www.mediaed.org/cgi-bin /commerce.cgi?display=home

Media Literacy.com: http://www.medialiteracy.com/

Media Literacy Project (formerly the New Mexico Media Literacy Project): http://medialiteracyproject.org/

Other Organizations That Conduct or Support Research

General

Kaiser Family Foundation (primarily HIV/AIDS): http:// www.kff.org/

Society for Adolescent Health and Medicine (SAHM): http:// www.adolescenthealth.org//AM/Template.cfm?Section=Home

Society for Research in Child Development (SRCD): http:// srcd.org/

Society for Research on Adolescence (SRA): http://s-r-a.org/

Boys, Men, or Masculinity

American Men's Studies Association: http://mensstudies.org/

Society for the Psychological Study of Men and Masculinity (SPSMM): http://www.division51.org/

Sexuality

International Academy of Sex Research: http://iasr.org/

The Kinsey Institute: http://www.kinseyinstitute.org/about/index .html

Society for the Scientific Study of Sexuality (Quad-S): http:// sexscience.org/

Society for Sex Therapy and Research (SSTAR): http://www .sstarnet.org/

Notes

Introduction

1. Bay-Cheng, 2001; Santelli et al., 2006
2. Dilorio, Pluhar, & Belcher, 2003
3. Dilorio et al., 2003; Epstein & Ward, 2008
4. Kirby, 2002; Zimmer-Gembeck & Helfand, 2008
5. World Health Organization, 2004
6. Dariotis et al., 2008; Humblet et al., 2003
7. Regan, Durvasula, Howell, Ureño, & Rea, 2004; Smiler, Frankel, & Savin-Williams, 2011; Centers for Disease Control and Prevention, 2008
8. Kimmel, 2011; Marshall, 2010
9. Connolly, Craig, Goldberg, & Pepler, 1999
10. Buss & Schmitt, 1993
11. Schmitt & 118 members of the International Sexuality Description Project, 2003
12. Kimmel, 2008
13. Dilorio et al., 2003; Yates & Youniss, 1996
14. Kirby, 2002

Chapter 1

1. Brooks, 1995; Fein & Schneider, 1995; Levant, 1992; MacCorquodale, 1989; Mahalik et al., 2003; Pleck, Sonenstein, & Ku, 2004
2. Mikkelson, 2011; Fisher, Moore, & Pittenger, 2012
3. Trachtenberg, 1988
4. David & Brannon, 1976, p. 11
5. Ashmore, Del Boca, & Beebe, 2002; Edwards, 1992; Green & Ashmore, 1998
6. Smiler, 2003
7. Eckert, 1989
8. Kesten, 1955; Pizzamiglio, 2000
9. Smiler, 2006b
10. Unpublished data from Smiler, 2003

11. Oliver & Hyde, 1993; Wells & Twenge, 2005; see also Laumann, Gagnon, Michael, & Michaels, 1994; Bogle, 2008
12. Brooks & Marsh, 1999; McNeil, 1996
13. Brooks & Marsh, 1999; McNeil, 1996
14. Brooks & Marsh, 1999; McNeil, 1996
15. Thorn, 2012
16. Kesten, 1955; Pizzamiglio, 2000
17. Masters, 1969
18. Kesten, 1955; Pizzamiglio, 2000
19. Kesten, 1955; Pizzamiglio, 2000
20. Kesten, 1955; Masters, 1969; Pizzamiglio, 2000
21. Irvine, 2002; Levine, 2002; Welsh, Rostosky, & Kawaguchi, 2000
22. Chesson, Blandford, Gift, Tao, & Irwin, 2004; Deptula, Henry, & Schoeny, 2010; Guttmacher Institute, 2011; Sanfield, Kost, Gold, & Finer, 2011; Weinstock, Berman, & Cates, 2004
23. Dariotis, Pleck, Astone, & Sonenstein, 2011; Guttmacher Institute, 2011; Harrison, Gavin, & Hastings, 2012; Kaye, 2001
24. Deptula et al., 2010; Sanfield et al., 2011; Chesson et al., 2004; Weinstock et al., 2004
25. See reviews by Kirby, 2002; Zimmer-Gembeck & Helfand, 2008
26. For examples, see Lansford et al., 2010; Siebenbruner, Zimmer-Gembeck, & Egeland, 2007. See reviews by Kirby, 2002; Zimmer-Gembeck & Helfand, 2008. For discussion, see Tolman, 2002.
27. Kingsbury, 2008
28. Chandra et al., 2008; Kirby, 2002; Zimmer-Gembeck & Helfand, 2008
29. Kimmel, 2008
30. Smiler, 2003
31. Dariotis et al., 2008; Humblet, Paul, & Dickson, 2003; Pleck, Sonenstein, & Ku, 1993, 1994; Sinn, 1997
32. Chesson et al., 2004; Sanfield et al., 2011; Weinstock et al., 2004
33. Laumann et al., 1994
34. World Health Organization, 2004
35. Snow Jones, Astone, Keyl, Kim, & Alexander, 1999
36. Dariotis et al., 2011; for discussion of teenage boys vs. adult men who father children with teenage girls, see Kiselica, 2008; Marsiglio, 1988
37. Messner, 1992
38. Mahalik et al., 2003; Pleck et al., 1993, 1994; Smiler, 2006a; Tokar & Jome, 1998
39. Locke & Mahalik, 2005; Murnen, Wright, & Kaluzny, 2002
40. Twenge, 1997a
41. Tolman, 2002
42. Buss, 1995; Buss & Schmitt, 1993; Oliver & Hyde, 1993
43. Dariotis et al., 2008; Humblet et al., 2003
44. Rotundo, 1993
45. Herbert, 2002
46. Gutmann, 1997; Kimmel, 1997
47. Centers for Disease Control and Prevention, 2011a

48. Offer, Offer, & Ostrov, 2004
49. American College Health Association, 2007; Chandra et al., 2008; Humblet et al., 2003; Laumann et al., 1994
50. Humblet et al., 2003; Laumann et al., 1994; see also Offer et al., 2004
51. Humblet et al., 2003; Laumann et al., 1994; Dariotis et al., 2008
52. Offer et al., 2004
53. Dariotis et al., 2008; Humblet et al., 2003
54. Laumann et al., 1994, p. 214
55. Thorn, 2012
56. Dariotis et al., 2008; Humblet et al., 2003; Offer et al., 2004; see reviews by Smiler, 2011; Zimmer-Gembeck & Helfand, 2008
57. Fine, 1988; Fine & McClelland, 2006; Santelli et al., 2006

Chapter 2

1. U.S. Census Bureau, 2008b
2. Halpern, Waller, Spriggs, & Hallfors, 2006; Laumann, Gagnon, Michael, & Michaels, 1994
3. Buss, Shackelford, Kirkpatrick, & Larsen, 2001
4. Bogle, 2008; Feldman, Turner, & Araujo, 1999; Rosenthal & Smith, 1997
5. Feiring, 1996
6. Feiring, 1999; Shulman & Scharf, 2000
7. Feldman et al., 1999; Regan et al., 2004; Smiler, Frankel, & Savin-Williams, 2011
8. Smiler et al., 2011
9. Ott, Millstein, Ofner, & Halpern-Felsher, 2006; Welsh, Haugen, Widman, Darling, & Grello, 2005
10. Smiler et al., 2011
11. Smiler et al., 2011
12. Carpenter, 2001; Peterson & Muehlenhard, 2007; Remez, 2000
13. Chandra, Mosher, Copen, & Sionean, 2011; Laumann et al., 1994; Wells & Twenge, 2005
14. Carpenter, 2001; Hunt & Curtis, 2006; Peterson & Muehlenhard, 2007; Remez, 2000
15. Hunt & Curtis, 2006
16. Marston & King, 2006; Ott, Pfeiffer, & Fortbenberry, 2006
17. Centers for Disease Control and Prevention, 2011a
18. Centers for Disease Control and Prevention, 2011a
19. Feldman et al., 1999; Laumann et al., 1994; Regan et al., 2004; Smiler et al., 2011
20. Feldman et al., 1999; Regan et al., 2004; Smiler et al., 2011
21. Smiler et al., 2011
22. Smiler et al., 2011
23. Kirby, 2002; Zimmer-Gembeck & Helfand, 2008
24. Welsh et al., 2005
25. Crawford & Popp, 2003; David & Brannon, 1976; Kimmel, 2008; Oliver & Hyde, 1993

26. Lottes, 1993; Muehlenhard & Rodgers, 1998; Tolman, 2002
27. Chu, Porche, & Tolman, 2005; Pleck, Sonenstein, & Ku, 1993; Pleck, Sonenstein, & Ku, 1994; see review by Murnen, Wright, & Kaluzny, 2002
28. Carver, Joyner, & Udry, 2003; Feldman et al., 1999; Regan et al., 2004; Smiler et al., 2011; see also Halpern et al., 2006; Lam, Shi, Ho, Stewart, & Fan, 2002; Rosenthal & Smith, 1997; Shtarkshall, Carmel, Jaffe-Hirschfield, & Woloski-Wruble, 2009; Smith & Udry, 1985
29. Jakobsen, 1997; deGraaf, Vanwesenbeeck, Meijer, Woertman, & Meeus, 2009
30. Smiler et al., 2011
31. Guggino & Ponzetti, 1997; Smiler, Ward, Caruthers, & Merriwether, 2005; Sprecher, Barbee, & Schwartz, 1995
32. Guggino & Ponzetti, 1997; Smiler et al., 2005; Sprecher et al., 1995
33. Guggino & Ponzetti, 1997; Smiler et al., 2005
34. Centers for Disease Control and Prevention, 2011a
35. Smiler, 2003
36. Goldstein, 2011
37. Zimmer-Gembeck, Siebenbruner, & Collins, 2004
38. Lam et al., 2002; Halpern et al., 2006; Zimmer-Gembeck et al., 2004; see reviews by Crockett, Raffaelli, & Moilanen, 2003; Smith, Guthrie, & Oakley, 2005
39. Frankel, 2002; Stein & Reiser, 1994
40. Frankel, 2002; Stein & Reiser, 1994
41. Stein & Reiser, 1994
42. Frankel, 2002
43. Frankel, 2002; Stein & Reiser, 1994
44. Stein & Reiser, 1994
45. Giordano, Longmore, & Manning, 2006
46. Arnett, 2000, 2004, 2007; Erikson, 1968; Marcia, 1966; for a different perspective, see Kimmel, 2008
47. Perry, 1981; Piaget, 1970
48. Ott & Pfeiffer, 2008
49. Ott, Millstein et al., 2006
50. Ott, 2010; Ott, Millstein, et al., 2006
51. Forste & Haas, 2002
52. Ott, Millstein, et al., 2006; see also Rostosky, Wilcox, Comer Wright, & Randall, 2004
53. Kirby, 2002; Zimmer-Gembeck & Helfand, 2008
54. Regan et al., 2004
55. Carver et al., 2003; Regan et al., 2004
56. Feldman et al., 1999; Kim & Ward, 2007
57. Fuligni & Stevenson, 1995
58. Haffner, 1998; Russell, 2005; Tolman et al., 2003; Welsh et al., 2000; see also Smiler, 2007
59. Haffner, 1998; Ott, 2010; Russell, 2005; Tolman et al., 2003; Welsh et al., 2000
60. Hofstede, 1998; see also Marston & King, 2006

61. Forste & Haas, 2002; Miller, Norton, Fan, & Christopherson, 1998; reviews by Rostosky et al., 2004
62. See reviews by Kirby, 2002; Zimmer-Gembeck & Helfand, 2008
63. Laumann et al., 1994
64. William T. Grant Commission on Work, Family, and Citizenship, 1988; see also Bushaw & Lopez, 2010
65. French & Dishion, 2003; Lansford et al., 2010; Santelli et al., 2004; see review by Kirby, 2002
66. Savin-Williams, 2005
67. Pew Research Center, 2011
68. Worthington & Mohr, 2002
69. Savin-Williams, 1998, 2005
70. Eliason, 1995; for discussion of lack of research, see Frankel, 2004; Worthington & Mohr, 2002; Worthington, Navarro, Savoy, & Hampton, 2008
71. Diamond, 1998, 2003
72. Savin-Williams, 1998, 2005; Savin-Williams & Ream, 2006; Tejirian, 2000
73. Smiler et al., 2011
74. King & Hunter, 2004

Chapter 3

1. Collins, 2003; Graber, Britto, & Brooks-Gunn, 1999
2. Carver, Joyner, & Udry, 2003; Connolly, Craig, Goldberg, & Pepler, 2004; Feiring, 1999; Regan, Durvasula, Howell, Ureño, & Rea, 2004
3. Carver et al., 2003; Feiring, 1999; Giordano, Longmore, & Manning, 2006
4. Carver et al., 2003; Connolly et al., 2004; Feiring, 1999; Guggino & Ponzetti, 1997; Regan et al., 2004
5. Feiring, 1996
6. Connolly & Johnson, 1996; see also Carver et al., 2003
7. Carver et al., 2003; Regan et al., 2004; Smiler, 2008; Smiler, Frankel, & Savin-Williams, 2011
8. Carver et al., 2003; Giordano et al., 2006; Tolman, Spencer, Harmon, Rosen-Reynoso, & Striepe, 2004
9. Carver et al., 2003
10. Regan et al., 2004
11. Smiler et al., 2011
12. Smiler et al., 2011
13. Dariotis, Pleck, Astone, & Sonenstein, 2011
14. U.S. Census Bureau, 2008b
15. Feiring, 1996; Smiler, 2008
16. Bradshaw, Kahn, & Saville, 2010; Connolly et al., 1999, 2004; Connolly & Johnson, 1996; Feiring, 1996; Shulman & Kipnis, 2001; Smiler, 2008; Tolman et al., 2004
17. Smiler, 2008; Smiler & Ward, under review
18. Bradshaw et al., 2010; Connolly et al., 1999, 2004; Connolly & Johnson, 1996; Feiring, 1996; Shulman & Kipnis, 2001; Smiler, 2008

19. Feiring, 1996; see review by Cross & Madson, 1997
20. Connolly & Johnson, 1996
21. Bradshaw et al., 2010; Feiring, 1996
22. Shulman & Seiffge-Krenke, 2001
23. Welsh, Haugen, Widman, Darling, & Grello, 2005
24. Smiler, 2008
25. Feiring, 1996
26. Smiler, 2008
27. Little & Rankin, 2001; Maxwell, 2002; Santelli, et al., 2004; Ward, 2002; see reviews by Kirby, 2002; Miller & Benson, 1999; Zimmer-Gembeck & Helfand, 2008
28. Feiring, 1996
29. Bradshaw et al., 2010; see review by Marshall, 2010
30. Twenge, 1997a
31. Connolly, Craig, Goldberg, & Pepler, 1999; Feiring, 1996; Allen, 2007; Eaton & Rose, 2011
32. Ott, Adler, Millstein, Tschann, & Ellen, 2002
33. Feiring, 1996; Shulman & Kipnis, 2001
34. Feiring, 1996; Smiler & Kubotera, 2010
35. Feiring, 1996; Smiler & Kubotera, 2010
36. Carver et al., 2003; Laumann, Gagnon, Michael, & Michaels, 1994; Udry & Bearman, 1998
37. Buss, Shackelford, Kirkpatrick, & Larsen, 2001
38. Bogle, 2008
39. Giordano, Manning, & Longmore, 2010; Marston & King, 2006; Meston & Buss, 2007; Ott, Millstein, Ofner, & Halpern-Felsher, 2006; Smiler, 2008
40. Giordano et al., 2010; Meston & Buss, 2007; Ott, Millstein et al., 2006; Smiler, 2008
41. Marston & King, 2006
42. Ott, Millstein et al., 2006; see also Meston & Buss, 2007
43. Ott, Millstein et al., 2006; Smiler, 2008
44. Smiler, 2008
45. Meston & Buss, 2007; Ott, Millstein et al., 2006; Smiler, 2008
46. Bogle, 2008; Epstein, Calzo, Smiler, & Ward, 2009
47. Epstein et al., 2009
48. Epstein et al., 2009; see also Bogle, 2008
49. Smiler & Ward, under review
50. Bogle, 2008; Bradshaw et al., 2010
51. Manning, Longmore, & Giordano, 2005
52. Dariotis et al., 2008; Humblet, Paul, & Dickson, 2003
53. Bradshaw et al., 2010
54. Wight, 1994
55. Bogle, 2008; Bradshaw et al., 2010
56. Kesten, 1955; Pizzamiglio, 2000
57. Connolly & Johnson, 1996; see also Marshall, 2010; Way, 2011
58. Carver et al., 2003; Laumann et al., 1994

59. Connolly et al., 1999
60. Way, 2011
61. Connolly & Johnson, 1996
62. Kimmel, 2011
63. Newman & Newman, 1986
64. Hartup & Overhauser, 1991, p. 379
65. Feiring, 1999; Udry & Bearman, 1998; Giordano et al., 2006; Miller & Benson, 1999; Shulman & Seiffge-Krenke, 2001
66. Striepe & Tolman, 2003
67. Carver et al., 2003; Connolly & Johnson, 1996; Feiring, 1999; Giordano et al., 2006; Regan et al., 2004; Smiler et al., 2011
68. Shulman & Kipnis, 2001
69. Bogle, 2008

Chapter 4

1. Wibowo, Schellhammer, & Wassersug, 2011
2. Saad & Vongas, 2009; Wibowo et al., 2011
3. Buss, 1995; Buss & Schmitt, 1993
4. Tooby & Cosmides, 2005
5. Buss, 1995; Buss & Schmitt, 1993
6. Hyde & Oliver, 2000; Oliver & Hyde, 1993
7. Schmitt & 118 members of the International Sexuality Description Project, 2003; Schmitt et al., 2004; Schmitt, Realo, Voracek, & Allik, 2008
8. Buss, 1995; Buss & Schmitt, 1993
9. Buss & Schmitt, 1993; McBurney, Zapp, & Streeter, 2005; Miller & Fishkin, 1997; Schmitt & 118 members of the International Sexuality Description Project, 2003
10. Buss & Schmitt, 1993; McBurney et al., 2005; Miller & Fishkin, 1997; Schmitt & 118 members of the International Sexuality Description Project, 2003
11. Hazan & Diamond, 2000; Smiler, 2011
12. Buss & Schmitt, 1993; Schmitt & 118 members of the International Sexuality Description Project, 2003
13. Buss & Schmitt, 1993
14. Buss, Shackelford, Kirkpatrick, & Larsen, 2001
15. Buss et al., 2001
16. Lykken & Tellegen, 1993
17. Lykken & Tellegen, 1993, p. 66
18. Campbell & Ellis, 2005; Murdock, 1967
19. Campbell & Ellis, 2005; Murdock, 1967
20. Campbell & Ellis, 2005; Murdock, 1967; Quinlan, 2008
21. Smiler, 2011
22. Quinlan, 2008
23. Bowlby, 1969, 1982; for recent summaries, see Del Giudice, 2009; van Ijzendoorn & Sagi, 1999

24. Cacioppo, Bianchi-Demicheli, Frum, Pfaus, & Lewis, 2012; Diamond, 2004; Fisher, 1998; Fisher, Aron, Mashek, Li, & Brown, 2002
25. Del Giudice, 2009; van Ijzendoorn & Sagi, 1999
26. Bowlby, 1969, 1982; Del Giudice, 2009; van Ijzendoorn & Sagi, 1999
27. For example, see Hazan & Diamond, 2000; Hazan & Zeifman, 1999
28. Ainsworth & Wittig, 1969; Bowlby, 1969, 1982
29. Ainsworth & Wittig, 1969; van Ijzendoorn & Sagi, 1999; Schmitt et al., 2004
30. Diamond, 2004; Hazan & Diamond, 2000; Hazan & Zeifman, 1999
31. Del Giudice, 2009; Hazan & Diamond, 2000; Hazan & Zeifman, 1999
32. For example, see Hazan & Diamond, 2000; Hazan & Zeifman, 1999; Miller & Fishkin, 1997; Schmitt et al., 2004; Smiler, 2011
33. Oliver & Hyde, 1993; Buss, 1995; Buss & Schmitt, 1993
34. Del Giudice, 2009
35. Del Giudice, 2009
36. Bogle, 2008; Bradshaw, Kahn, & Saville, 2010
37. H. E. Fisher, 2004; see also Cacioppo et al., 2012; Diamond, 2004; Fisher, 1998; Fisher et al., 2002
38. Conner, Hellemann, Ritchie, & Noble, 2009
39. Dreber et al., 2009
40. Arnett, 2000, 2004; Crockett, Raffaelli, & Moilanen, 2003; Graber, Britto, & Brooks-Gunn, 1999

Chapter 5

1. Good Men Project, 2012
2. Gilmore, 1990
3. Dariotis, Pleck, Astone, & Sonenstein, 2011
4. David & Brannon, 1976
5. Pollack, 1998
6. Kimmel, 1996; Rotundo, 1993; Smiler, Kay, & Harris, 2008; Townsend, 1996; Faludi, 1999
7. Coad, 2008; Pompper, 2010
8. Pleck, 1987; Smiler et al., 2008
9. Deutsch & Saxon, 1998; Rotundo, 1993
10. Putnam, 2000
11. Smiler et al., 2008
12. Stearns, 1994
13. Hantover, 1978
14. Tyre et al., 2006
15. Bem, 1974; Spence & Helmreich, 1978, 1980; Tolman & Porche, 2000; Smiler, 2004
16. Rotundo, 1993; Townsend, 1996
17. Smiler et al., 2008; Rotundo, 1993; Townsend, 1996
18. Kimmel, 1996; Rotundo, 1993; Stearns, 1994; Townsend, 1996
19. Goleman, 1990; Mayer, Caruso, & Salovey, 1999
20. Smiler et al., 2008

21. Novack, 2011; Pollack, 1998; David & Brannon, 1976
22. Kimmel, 2008; Way, 2011
23. Rochlen, McKelley, & Whittaker, 2010; Rochlen, Suizzo, McKelley, & Scaringi, 2008; Pleck, 2007
24. Pascoe, 2007, p. 22.
25. Homosexuality as unmasculine: Madon, 1997; Pascoe, 2007; Vogel, Wester, Heesacker, & Madon, 2003. Homosexuality as unnatural: Connell, 1995; Irvine, 2002. Origins of these uses: Connell, 1995; Patterson, 1995.
26. See also Barry, 2011; Messner, 1992
27. Clarkson, 2006; Savin-Williams, 1998, 2005
28. Madon, 1997; Vogel et al., 2003
29. Rotundo, 1993; see also Kimmel, 1996
30. Buss, 1995; Oliver & Hyde, 1993; Wells & Twenge, 2005
31. Connell, 1995; Kimmel, 2008; Pascoe, 2007
32. Erikson, 1963
33. See also Arnett, 2004, 2007; Marcia, 1966
34. Arnett, 2000, 2004, 2007; for critique, see Hendry & Kloep, 2007; Kimmel, 2008
35. Marcia, 1966; Ashmore & Jussim, 1997; Clemans, DeRose, Graber, & Brooks-Gunn, 2010
36. McGarty, 2002; Thoits & Virshup, 1997; Turner, 1999
37. Thoits & Virshup, 1997; Turner, 1999
38. Stone, Barber, & Eccles, 2001
39. Brown & Huang, 1995
40. Barber, Eccles, & Stone, 2001; Brown & Huang, 1995; Eccles, Barber, Stone, & Hunt, 2003
41. Bogle, 2008; Eckert, 1989; Lefkowitz, 1997
42. Ashmore, Del Boca, & Beebe, 2002; Barber et al., 2001; Edwards, 1992; Green & Ashmore, 1998; Smiler, 2006b; Wade, 1998
43. Green & Ashmore, 1998; Smiler, 2006b
44. Ashmore et al., 2002
45. Connell, 1995; Connell & Messerschmidt, 2005
46. Smiler, 2006b
47. Connell, 1995; Farrell, 1993
48. Smiler, 2006b
49. Green & Ashmore, 1998; Smiler, 2006b
50. Connell, 1995; Eckert, 1989
51. Kimmel, 1996; Savin-Williams, 2005
52. Connell, 1995; Connell & Messerschmidt, 2005
53. Lefkowitz, 1997
54. Lefkowitz, 1997
55. Lefkowitz, 1997, p. 127
56. Lefkowitz, 1997, p. 127
57. Lefkowitz, 1997, p. 127
58. Gilmore, 1990; Kimmel, 1996, 2008; Rotundo, 1993
59. Gilmore, 1990; Mead, 1928/1973

60. Gilmore, 1990; Kimmel, 2008
61. Arnett, 2000, 2004; Kimmel, 2008
62. Kimmel, 2008; Anderson, McCormack, & Lee, in press
63. Anderson et al., in press
64. Fine, 1987; Kehily, 2001; Tolman, Spencer, Harmon, Rosen-Reynoso, & Striepe, 2004; Wight, 1994; see review by Marston & King, 2006
65. Brooks, 1997; Kehily, 2001; Wight, 1994
66. Rich, 1980; Tolman et al., 2004; Wight, 1994; See Messner, 1992

Chapter 6

1. Arnett, 1995; Brown, Halpern, & L'Engle, 2006; Suoninen, 2001
2. Suoninen, 2001, p. 209
3. Perloff, 1999
4. Lewis, Watson, & Tay, 2007
5. U.S. Census Bureau, 2008a
6. Nielsen, 2011
7. Juster, Ono, & Stafford, 2004; Kim et al., 2006
8. Roberts & Christenson, 2001, p. 398
9. Juster et al., 2004; Schooler, Sorsoli, Kim, & Tolman, 2009; Ward, 2002; Ward, Epstein, Caruthers, & Merriwether, 2011
10. Ward, Hansbrough, & Walker, 2005
11. Kistler, Rodgers, Power, Austin, & Hill, 2010; Ward, 2002; Ward et al., 2005, 2011
12. Sabina, Wolak, & Finkelhor, 2008
13. Kistler et al., 2010; see also LaFerle, Edwards, & Lee, 2000; Ward et al., 2005
14. Ward et al., 2011; Taylor, 2006; Walsh & Ward, 2010
15. Friedman, 2010; Spector & Bennett, 2011; Sports Illustrated Source, 2004; Association of Magazine Media, 2011
16. Kunkel, Cope, & Biely, 1999; Kunkel, Eyal, Finnerty, Biely, & Donnerstein, 2005; Ward, 1995
17. Ward, 1995
18. Ward, 1995, p. 603
19. Hurt, 2007; Jhally, 1994, 2007; Turner, 2011; Wallis, 2011
20. Picker & Sun, 2008
21. Lambiase, 2003; Smith, Gertz, Alvarez, & Lurie, 2000
22. Picker & Sun, 2008
23. Downs & Smith, 2010
24. Smiler & Hearon, under review
25. Smiler & Hearon, under review
26. Hurt, 2007; Turner, 2011; Weitzer & Kubrin, 2009
27. Taylor, 2005
28. Joshi, Peter, & Valkenburg, 2011; see also Carpenter, 1998
29. Romance Writers of America, 2011
30. Epstein & Ward, 2008
31. Epstein & Ward, 2008

32. Fouts & Burggraf, 2000; Fouts & Vaughan, 2002; Kunkel et al., 1999; Kunkel et al., 2005; Ward, 1995; Kimmel, 2008
33. Strate, 1992
34. For example, Hurt, 2007; Jhally, 1994, 2007; Turner, 2011; for critique, see Wallis, 2011
35. Hurt, 2007; Jhally, 1994, 2007; Turner, 2011; Wallis, 2011
36. Picker & Sun, 2008; see also Kimmel, 2008
37. Smiler & Hearon, under review
38. Smiler & Hearon, under review
39. Carpenter, 1998; Joshi et al., 2011
40. Clawson, 2005, p. 471
41. Brown, Lamb, & Tappan, 2009
42. Television: Fouts & Burggraf, 2000; Fouts & Vaughan, 2002; Kunkel et al., 1999; Kunkel et al., 2005; Ward, 1995. Advertising: Jhally, 2010; Kilbourne, 2000. Music videos: Hurt, 2007; Jhally, 1994, 2007; Turner, 2011; Wallis, 2011. Video games: Downs & Smith, 2010. Pornography: Picker & Sun, 2008. For overview and general comment, see American Psychological Association Task Force on the Sexualization of Girls, 2007.
43. Turner, 2011
44. Television: Ward, 1995. Music videos: Hurt, 2007; Jhally, 1994, 2007; Wallis, 2011. Pornography: Kimmel, 2008; Picker & Sun, 2008
45. Giordano, Longmore, & Manning, 2006
46. Carpenter, 1998; Joshi et al., 2011; Kunkel et al., 2005; Hether & Murphy, 2011
47. Jhally, 1994, 2007
48. Magazines: Carpenter, 1998; Joshi et al., 2011; Taylor, 2005. TV and movies: Kimmel, 2008; Ward, 1995. Media in general: Epstein & Ward, 2008.
49. Kunkel et al., 1999; Kunkel et al., 2005; Ward, 1995; Hust, Brown, & L'Engle, 2008
50. Kunkel et al., 1999; Kunkel et al., 2005
51. Kunkel et al., 2005
52. Carpenter, 1998; Joshi et al., 2011
53. Taylor, 2005
54. Hether & Murphy, 2011
55. Epstein & Ward, 2008; see reviews by Sutton, Brown, Wilson, & Klein, 2002; Ward, 2003
56. Brown & L'Engle, 2009; Sabina et al., 2008
57. Collins, Elliott, Berry, Kanouse, & Hunter, 2003, p. 1118
58. Collins et al., 2003
59. Kunkel et al., 1999; Kunkel et al., 2005; Ward, 1995; see review by Ward, 2003
60. Gerbner, Gross, Morgan, & Signorielli, 1994; Gerbner, Gross, Morgan, Signorielli, & Shanahan, 2002
61. Gerbner et al., 1994; Gerbner et al., 2002; Shanahan & Morgan, 1999
62. Arnett, 1991; Chandra et al., 2008; Collins et al., 2003; Kim et al., 2006; Kistler et al., 2010; Walsh & Ward, 2010; Ward et al., 2005, 2011; Ward & Friedman, 2006; Ward, Merriwether, & Caruthers, 2006

63. Ward, 2002; Ward et al., 2005
64. Gerbner et al., 1994; Gerbner et al., 2002; Shanahan & Morgan, 1999
65. Ward et al., 2011; for similar findings, see also Schooler, Impett, Hirschman, & Bonem, 2008; Schooler & Ward, 2006
66. Walsh & Ward, 2010
67. Collins et al., 2004; Martino et al., 2006
68. Collins et al., 2004; see also Brown & L'Engle, 2009
69. Martino et al., 2006
70. Impact of TV: Shanahan & Morgan, 1999; impact of choice of neighborhood: Leventhal & Brooks-Gunn, 2000

Chapter 7

1. Coad, 2008; David & Brannon, 1976; Green & Ashmore, 1998; Smiler, 2006b
2. Brown, Lamb, & Tappan, 2009
3. Turner, 2011; Brown et al., 2009
4. Meyer, 2010
5. American Psychological Association Task Force on the Sexualization of Girls, 2007
6. Brown et al., 2009; Pope et al., 2000; McCreary & Sasse, 2000
7. Cohane & Pope, 2001
8. Schooler, Impett, Hirschman, & Bonem, 2008
9. Schooler et al., 2008; Schooler & Ward, 2006
10. Griffin, 2011
11. Cohane & Pope, 2001; Davis, Karvinen, & McCreary, 2005; Duggan & McCreary, 2004; French, Story, Remafedi, Resnick, & Blum, 1996; McCreary & Sasse, 2000; McCreary, Saucier, & Courtenay, 2005; Pope et al., 2000; Calzo, Corliss, Blood, Field, & Austin, in press; Smith, Hawkeswood, Bodell, & Joiner, 2011
12. Smith et al., 2011
13. Pope et al., 2000
14. Katz & Earp, 1999; Pope et al., 2000
15. Morrison & Halton, 2009
16. Pope, Olivardia, Gruber, & Borowiecki, 1999
17. McCreary & Sasse, 2000; Parent & Moradi, 2011
18. Ray et al., 2001
19. Pope et al., 2000
20. Centers for Disease Control and Prevention, 2011b
21. Kanayama, Barry, Hudson, & Pope, 2006
22. Dickinson et al., 2005
23. Tamura, 2011
24. American Society of Plastic Surgeons, 2011
25. Brown et al., 2009
26. Smiler & Hearon, under review
27. Coad, 2008; see also Sandomir, 2007
28. Coad, 2008; Messner, 1992; see also Smiler, 2006b

29. Coad, 2008
30. Coad, 2008
31. Coad, 2008
32. Feiler, 2011
33. Hatton & Trautner, 2011
34. Pope, Olivardia, Borowiecki, & Cohane, 2001
35. Coad, 2008; Hatton & Trautner, 2011
36. Feiler, 2011
37. Coad, 2008, p. 107
38. Asberg & Johnson, 2009; "The New Young Face of Viagra Abuse," 2003; Wienke, 2005
39. Asberg & Johnson, 2009; Wienke, 2005
40. Asberg & Johnson, 2009; Wienke, 2005
41. Asberg & Johnson, 2009; Wienke, 2005
42. Pfizer, 2010, p. 27; Eli Lilly, 2010; Bayer AG, 2011
43. American Psychological Association Task Force on the Sexualization of Girls, 2007
44. American Psychological Association Task Force on the Sexualization of Girls, 2007; Cafri, Yamamiya, Brannick, & Thompson, 2005; Fredrickson & Roberts, 1997; Ward & Harrison, 2005
45. Davis et al., 2005; McCreary & Sasse, 2000; Pope et al., 2000
46. Pope et al., 2000
47. Hebl, King, & Lin, 2004
48. Hebl et al., 2004
49. Greenwood & Lippman, 2010; Parent & Moradi, 2011; Jones, 2001; Parent & Moradi, 2011
50. Hargreaves & Tiggemann, 2009; Leit, Gray, & Pope, 2002

Chapter 8

1. Bogle, 2008
2. Smiler & Ward, under review
3. Bogle, 2008
4. Lansford et al., 2010; Siebenbruner, Zimmer-Gembeck, & Egeland, 2007
5. Siebenbruner et al., 2007
6. Lansford et al., 2010
7. Forste & Haas, 2002; Lansford et al., 2010; Siebenbruner et al., 2007
8. Lansford et al., 2010
9. Woods et al., 2006
10. Smiler & Ward, under review
11. Savin-Williams, 1998, 2005; Savin-Williams & Ream, 2006; Smiler, Frankel, & Savin-Williams, 2011
12. Unpublished data from Smiler, 2003
13. Smiler & Ward, under review
14. Smiler & Ward, under review; Zimmer-Gembeck & Helfand, 2008; Siebenbruner et al., 2007

15. Rew & Wong, 2006; Rostosky, Regenerus, & Comer Wright, 2003
16. Rostosky et al., 2003; Siebenbruner et al., 2007; see reviews by Kirby, 2002; Zimmer-Gembeck & Helfand, 2008
17. Forste & Haas, 2002; Rostosky et al., 2003; Siebenbruner et al., 2007; see reviews by Kirby, 2002; Zimmer-Gembeck & Helfand, 2008
18. Lansford et al., 2010; Siebenbruner et al., 2007
19. Allen, 2007
20. Bogle, 2008
21. National Center for Education Statistics, 2010
22. Oliver & Hyde, 1993; Wells & Twenge, 2005
23. Carver, Joyner, & Udry, 2003; Feiring, 1996; Miller & Benson, 1999; Udry & Bearman, 1998
24. Kimmel, 2008

Chapter 9

1. T. D. Fisher, 2004
2. Epstein & Ward, 2008
3. K. S. Miller, Levin, Whitaker, & Xu, 1998
4. Sutton, Brown, Wilson, & Klein, 2002; Epstein & Ward, 2008
5. Epstein & Ward, 2008
6. Bandura, 1989; Bronfenbrenner, 1999; Epstein & Ward, 2008; T. D. Fisher, 2004; Halim & Ruble, 2010; Lytton & Romney, 1991; Pollack, 1998; Tenenbaum & Leaper, 2002
7. U.S. Census Bureau, 2011; see also Annie E. Casey Foundation, 2009
8. U.S. Census Bureau, 2011
9. Dilorio, Pluhar, & Belcher, 2003; T. D. Fisher, 2004
10. Dilorio et al., 2003; T. D. Fisher, 2004
11. Dilorio et al., 2003; T. D. Fisher, 2004
12. Frankel, 2002; Stein & Reiser, 1994; see also Dilorio et al., 2003; T. D. Fisher, 2004
13. Dilorio et al., 2003
14. Dilorio et al., 2003
15. Dilorio et al., 2003
16. Welsh, Haugen, Widman, Darling, & Grello, 2005; Ashdown, Hackathorn, & Clark, 2011
17. Amato & Gilbreth, 1999; T. D. Fisher, 2004; Johnson & Tyler, 2007
18. Johnson & Tyler, 2007
19. T. D. Fisher, 2004; Amato & Gilbreth, 1999
20. Deptula, Henry, & Schoeny, 2010; see also T. D. Fisher, 2004
21. Elam, 1990; see discussion by Englar-Carlson & Stevens, 2006; Levine, 2002; Santelli et al., 2006
22. Guttmacher Institute, 2012; Irvine, 2002; Levine, 2002
23. Guttmacher Institute, 2012
24. Bennett & Assefi, 2005; DiCenso, Guyatt, Willan, & Griffith, 2002
25. Smoak, Scott-Sheldon, Johnson, Carey, & Team, 2006
26. Santelli et al., 2006; see also Guttmacher Institute, 2012
27. Santelli et al., 2006

28. Ott & Pfeiffer, 2008
29. Bennett & Assefi, 2005; DiCenso et al., 2002
30. Bennett & Assefi, 2005; DiCenso et al., 2002; see also Santelli et al., 2006
31. DiCenso et al., 2002
32. Santelli et al., 2006
33. Santelli et al., 2006
34. Santelli et al., 2006
35. Santelli et al., 2006, p. 79
36. Santelli et al., 2006
37. Bennett & Assefi, 2005; DiCenso et al., 2002
38. Bennett & Assefi, 2005
39. Bennett & Assefi, 2005
40. Greene, Rubin, Hale, & Walters, 1996
41. Jemmott, Jemmott, & Fong, 2010; for a newspaper depiction of this program as abstinence education, see Lewin, 2010
42. Ott & Pfeiffer, 2008
43. Fine, 1988; Fine & McClelland, 2006
44. Epstein & Ward, 2008
45. Frankel, 2002; Stein & Reiser, 1994
46. Maxwell, 2002; Ward, Epstein, Caruthers, & Merriwether, 2011; Ward, 2002
47. McHale, Bissell, & Kim, 2009
48. Savin-Williams, 2005; Smiler, Frankel, & Savin-Williams, 2011
49. Parental values about sex: Halpern, Waller, Spriggs, & Hallfors, 2006; Miller, Norton, Fan, & Christopherson, 1998; Romo, Lefkowitz, Sigman, & Au, 2002; see review by T. D. Fisher, 2004. Parental expectations in general: Buchanan, 2003; Buchanan & Hughes, 2009; Rogers, Buchanan, & Winchell, 2003. Age twelve to fourteen effects: B. C. Miller et al., 1998.
50. Davis, 2011
51. Planned Parenthood, 2011
52. K. S. Miller et al., 1998
53. Centers for Disease Control and Prevention, 2012
54. Deptula et al., 2010
55. Killoren, Updegraff, & Christopher, 2011; B. C. Miller et al., 1998; see review by T. D. Fisher, 2004
56. Romo et al., 2002
57. Jeffries, 2004
58. Dilorio et al., 2003; T. D. Fisher, 2004
59. Jeffries, 2004; Pollack, 1998; Spencer, 2007
60. Jeffries, 2004

Chapter 10

1. Gerbner, Gross, Morgan, Signorielli, & Shanahan, 2002
2. Vigil, 2007
3. Vigil, 2007
4. Vigil, 2007; see also Way, 2011
5. Way, 2011
6. Carver, Joyner, & Udry, 2003; Feiring, 1996; Udry & Bearman, 1998

7. Miller & Benson, 1999; Zimmer-Gembeck, 2002
8. Kimmel, 2008; Vigil, 2007; Zimmer-Gembeck, 2002
9. Pollack, 1998; Spencer, 2007; Way, 2011; see also Cross & Madson, 1997; Marshall, 2010
10. Pollack, 2006, p. 194
11. Pollack, 1998; Spencer, 2007
12. Way, 2004
13. Chu, 2004
14. Gross, 2004; Wolak, Mitchell, & Finkelhor, 2002
15. Erikson, 1963, 1968; Gilligan, 1982; Raskin & Rogers, 2005; Ogbu, 1994; Piaget, 1970; Vygotsky, 1962
16. Harris, 1998
17. Pollack, 1998; see also David & Brannon, 1976
18. Chu, 2004; Kindlon & Thompson, 1999; Migliaccio, 2009; Pollack, 1998; Way, 2011; Connell, 1995; Mahalik et al., 2003; Messner, 1992; Smiler, 2006b; Wight, 1994
19. Spencer, 2007
20. Jeffries, 2004; Spencer, 2007; Way, 2011
21. Tooby & Cosmides, 2005
22. Kindlon & Thompson, 1999; Pollack, 1998; Gurian, 1996; Gurian & Stevens, 2005
23. Bem, 1974; Spence & Helmreich, 1978; for historical change, see Twenge, 1997b
24. Wallace, 2011
25. Spencer, 2007
26. Vigil, 2007
27. Cross & Madson, 1997; Marshall, 2010; Way, 2011; Wight, 1994
28. Vigil, 2007; for reviews, see Cross & Madson, 1997; Marshall, 2010
29. Benenson et al., 2009
30. Udry & Bearman, 1998
31. Wolak et al., 2002; Wolak, Mitchell, & Finkelhor, 2003
32. Allen, 2007; Chu, Porche, & Tolman, 2005; Lucke, 1998
33. Meston & Buss, 2007; Smiler, 2008
34. Marston & King, 2006
35. Marston & King, 2006, p. 1584
36. Twenge, 1997a
37. Bradshaw, Kahn, & Saville, 2010; Lucke, 1998; Marston & King, 2006; see review by Crawford & Popp, 2003
38. Tolman, 2002
39. See review by Marston & King, 2006
40. Muehlenhard, Andrews, & Beal, 1996; Muehlenhard & Rodgers, 1998; Hickman & Muehlenhard, 1999
41. MacPhail & Campbell, 2001; Ott, Adler, Millstein, Tschann, & Ellen, 2002; Woods et al., 2006; for rates of use of various prevention methods, see Harrison, Gavin, & Hastings, 2012
42. MacPhail & Campbell, 2001; Marston & King, 2006; Pleck et al., 1993, 1994

43. MacPhail & Campbell, 2001; Mutchler & McDavitt, 2011
44. Mutchler & McDavitt, 2011
45. Mutchler & McDavitt, 2011
46. Carpenter, 1998; Joshi, Peter, & Valkenburg, 2011; Kim & Ward, 2004; Prusank, 2007; Walsh & Ward, 2010; Ward & Harrison, 2005
47. Brown & Huang, 1995; Way, 2011
48. Bouchey & Furman, 2006; Zimmer-Gembeck, 2002
49. Boyd, 2009
50. Welsh, Haugen, Widman, Darling, & Grello, 2005

Chapter 11

1. Bem, 1997; Eagly, Wood, & Diekman, 2000; Gagnon & Simon, 1973; Pleck, 1981
2. Centers for Disease Control and Prevention, 2011a; for information from undergraduates, see American College Health Association, 2007
3. Agostinelli & Grube, 2005; Kilmartin et al., 2008; Schultz, Nolan, Cialdini, Goldstein, & Griskevicius, 2007
4. Hickman & Muehlenhard, 1999
5. Alden, 2011
6. Thorn, 2010
7. David & Brannon, 1976; Mahalik et al., 2003; Ward, 1995
8. Crawford & Popp, 2003; Hurt, 2007
9. Crawford & Popp, 2003; Eaton & Rose, 2011; Twenge, 1997a
10. Tyre et al., 2006
11. Epstein & Ward, 2011
12. Giordano, Manning, & Longmore, 2010
13. Burt, 1980
14. Payne, Lonsway, & Fitzgerald, 1999
15. Murnen, Wright, & Kaluzny, 2002; Mahalik et al., 2003; Parent & Moradi, 2009; Pleck et al., 1993, 1994; Smiler, 2006b
16. Bennett, 2008; Gottlieb, 1991; Scarr & McCartney, 1983
17. Darwin, 1853
18. Maslow, 1943
19. Herdt, 1994
20. Farrell, 1993; Connell, 1995
21. Baumeister, 2007; Baumeister & Sommer, 1997
22. Kimmel, 2008
23. Signorielli & Bacue, 1999
24. Potter, 2012
25. Pinkleton, Austin, Cohen, Chen, & Fitzgerald, 2008
26. National Association for Media Literacy Education, 2007
27. Collins, Elliott, Berry, Kanouse, & Hunter, 2003
28. Kunkel, Eyal, Finnerty, Biely, & Donnerstein, 2005; Ward, 1995
29. Hantover, 1978
30. ManKind Project, 2012

References

Agostinelli, G., & Grube, J. (2005). Effects of presenting heavy drinking norms on adolescents' prevalence estimates, evaluative judgments, and perceived standards. *Prevention Science, 6,* 89–99.

Ainsworth, M. D. S., & Wittig, B. A. (1969). Attachment and exploratory behavior of one-year-olds in a strange situation. In B. M. Foss (Ed.), *Determinants of infant behavior* (Vol. 4, pp. 111–136). London: Methuen.

Alden, S. (2011). If you'd sleep with her, you can't call her a slut. Good Men Project. Retrieved July 2, 2011, from http://goodmenproject.com/featured-content /if-youd-sleep-with-her-you-cant-call-her-a-slut/

Allen, L. (2007). "Sensitive and real macho all at the same time": Young heterosexual men and romance. *Men and Masculinities, 10,* 137–152.

Amato, P. R., & Gilbreth, J. G. (1999). Nonresident fathers and children's well-being: A meta-analysis. *Journal of Marriage and the Family, 61,* 557–573.

American College Health Association–National College Health Assessment. (2007). NCHA Web summary. Retrieved February 24, 2012, from http://www .acha-ncha.org/data/SEXF06.html.

American Psychological Association Task Force on the Sexualization of Girls. (2007). *Report of the APA task force on the sexualization of girls.* Washington, DC: American Psychological Association.

American Society of Plastic Surgeons. (2011). *Report of the 2010 plastic surgery statistics.* Arlington Heights, IL: Author.

Anderson, E., McCormack, M., & Lee, H. (in press). Male team sport hazing initiations in a culture of decreasing homohysteria. *Journal of Adolescent Research.*

Annie E. Casey Foundation. (2009). *KIDS COUNT indicator brief: Increasing the percentage of children living in two-parent families.* Baltimore: Author.

Arnett, J. J. (1991). Heavy metal music and reckless behavior among adolescents. *Journal of Youth and Adolescence, 20,* 573–592.

Arnett, J. J. (1995). Adolescents' uses of media for self-socialization. *Journal of Youth and Adolescence, 24,* 519–533.

Arnett, J. J. (2000). Emerging adulthood: A theory of development from the late teens through the twenties. *American Psychologist, 55,* 469–480.

Arnett, J. J. (2004). *Emerging adulthood: The winding road from the late teens through the twenties.* New York: Oxford University Press.

Arnett, J. J. (2007). Emerging adulthood: What is it and what is it good for? *Child Development Perspectives, 1,* 68–73.

Asberg, C., & Johnson, E. (2009). Viagra selfhood: Pharmaceutical advertising and the visual formation of Swedish masculinity. *Health Care Analysis, 17,* 144–157.

Ashdown, B., Hackathorn, J., & Clark, E. M. (2011). In and out of the bedroom: Sexual satisfaction in the marital relationship. *Journal of Integrated Social Sciences, 2,* 40–57.

Ashmore, R. D., Del Boca, F. K., & Beebe, M. (2002). "Alkie," "frat brother," and "jock": Perceived types of college students and stereotypes about drinking. *Journal of Applied Social Psychology, 32,* 885–907.

Ashmore, R. D., & Jussim, L. (1997). Toward a second century of the scientific analysis of self and identity. In R. D. Ashmore & L. Jussim (Eds.), *Self and identity* (pp. 3–22). New York: Oxford University Press.

Association of Magazine Media. (2011). Average total paid & verified circulation for top 100 ABC magazines. Retrieved July 7, 2011, from http://www.magazine.org /CONSUMER_MARKETING/CIRC_TRENDS/ABC2010TOTALrank.aspx.

Bandura, A. (1989). Social cognitive theory. In P. H. Mussen (Ed.), *Annals of child development* (Vol. 6, pp. 1–60). Greenwich, CT: JAI Press.

Barber, B. L., Eccles, J. S., & Stone, M. R. (2001). Whatever happened to the jock, the brain, and the princess? Young adult pathways linked to adolescent activity involvement and social identity. *Journal of Adolescent Research, 16,* 429–455.

Barry, D. (2011, May 15). A sports executive leaves the safety of his shadow life. *New York Times.* Retrieved April 20, 2012, from http://www.nytimes.com/2011 /05/16/sports/basketball/nba-executive-says-he-is-gay.html?pagewanted=all.

Baumeister, R. F. (2007). Is there anything good about men? Paper presented at the annual convention of the American Psychological Association. San Francisco, CA. Retrieved May 20, 2012, from http://www.psy.fsu.edu/~baumeistertice /goodaboutmen.htm.

Baumeister, R. F., & Sommer, K. L. (1997). What do men want? Gender differences and two spheres of belongingness: Comment on Cross and Madson (1997). *Psychological Bulletin, 122,* 38–44.

Bay-Cheng, L. Y. (2001). SexEd.com: Values and norms in web-based sexuality education. *Journal of Sex Research, 38,* 241–251.

Bayer, A. G. (2011). *Bayer AG Group annual report.* Leverkusen, Germany: Author.

Bem, S. L. (1974). The measurement of psychological androgyny. *Journal of Consulting and Clinical Psychology, 42,* 155–162.

Bem, S. L. (1997). Gender schema theory and its implications for child development. In T. Roberts (Ed.), *The Lanahan readings in the psychology of women* (pp. 539–552). Baltimore: Lanahan.

Benenson, J. F., Markovits, H., Fitzgerald, C., Geoffroy, D., Flemming, J., Kahlenberg, S. M., et al. (2009). Males' greater tolerance of same-sex peers. *Psychological Science, 20,* 184–190.

Bennett, A. J. (2008). Gene environment interplay: Nonhuman primate models in the study of resilience and vulnerability. *Developmental Psychobiology, 50,* 48–59.

Bennett, S. E., & Assefi, N. P. (2005). School-based teenage pregnancy prevention programs: A systematic review of randomized controlled trials. *Journal of Adolescent Health, 36,* 72–81.

Bly, R. (1990). *Iron John.* Reading, MA: Addison-Wesley.

Bogle, K. A. (2008). *Hooking up: Sex, dating, and relationships on campus.* New York: New York University Press.

Bouchey, H. A., & Furman, W. (2006). Dating and romantic experiences in adolescence. In G. R. Adams & M. D. Berzonsky (Eds.), *Blackwell handbook of adolescence* (pp. 313–329). Malden, MA: Blackwell.

Bowlby, J. (1969). *Attachment.* New York: Basic Books.

Bowlby, J. (1982). *Attachment* (2nd ed.). New York: Basic Books.

Boyd, D. (2009, October 27). Keynote address presented at the John Seely Brown Symposium on Technology and Society, Ann Arbor, MI.

Bradshaw, C., Kahn, A. S., & Saville, B. K. (2010). To hook up or date: Which gender benefits? *Sex Roles, 62,* 661–669.

Bronfenbrenner, U. (1999). Environments in developmental perspective: Theoretical and operational models. In S. L. Friedman & T. D. Wachs (Eds.), *Measuring environment across the life span: Emerging methods and concepts* (pp. 3–28). Washington, DC: American Psychological Associations.

Brooks, G. R. (1995). *The centerfold syndrome: How men can overcome objectification and achieve intimacy with women.* San Francisco: Jossey-Bass.

Brooks, G. R. (1997). The centerfold syndrome. In R. F. Levant & G. R. Brooks (Eds.), *Men and sex: New psychological perspectives* (pp. 28–57). Hoboken, NJ: Wiley.

Brooks, T., & Marsh, E. (1999). *The complete directory to prime time network and cable TV shows 1946–present.* New York: Ballantine.

Brown, B. B., & Huang, B.-H. (1995). Examining parenting practices in different peer contexts: Implications for adolescent trajectories. In L. C. Crockett & A. C. Crouter (Eds.), *Pathways through adolescence: Individual development in relation to social contexts* (pp. 151–174). Mahwah, NJ: Erlbaum.

Brown, J. D., Halpern, C. T., & L'Engle, K. L. (2006). Mass media as a sexual super peer for early maturing girls. *Journal of Adolescent Health, 36,* 420–427.

Brown, J. D., & L'Engle, K. L. (2009). X-rated: Sexual attitudes and behaviors associated with U.S. early adolescents' exposure to sexually explicit media. *Communication Research, 36,* 129–151.

Brown, L. M., Lamb, S., & Tappan, M. (2009). *Packaging boyhood: Saving our sons from superheroes, slackers, and other media stereotypes.* New York: St. Martin's Press.

Buchanan, C. M. (2003). Mothers' generalized beliefs about adolescents: Links to expectations for a specific child. *Journal of Early Adolescence, 23,* 29–50.

Buchanan, C. M., & Hughes, J. L. (2009). Construction of social reality during early adolescence: Can expecting storm and stress increase real or perceived storm and stress? *Journal of Research on Adolescence, 19,* 261–285.

Burt, M. R. (1980). Cultural myths and supports for rape. *Journal of Personality and Social Psychology, 38,* 217–230.

Bushaw, W. J., & Lopez, S. J. (2010). The 42nd annual Phi Delta Kappa/Gallup poll of the public's attitudes toward the public schools. *Phi Delta Kappan, 92,* 9–26.

Buss, D. M. (1995). Psychological sex differences: Origins through sexual selection. *American Psychologist, 50,* 164–168.

Buss, D. M., & Schmitt, D. P. (1993). Sexual strategies theory: An evolutionary perspective on human mating. *Psychological Review, 100,* 204–232.

Buss, D. M., Shackelford, T. K., Kirkpatrick, L. A., & Larsen, R. J. (2001). A half century of mate preferences: The cultural evolution of values. *Journal of Marriage and the Family, 63,* 491–503.

Cacioppo, S., Bianchi-Demicheli, F., Frum, C., Pfaus, J. G., & Lewis, J. W. (2012). The common neural bases between sexual desire and love: A multilevel kernel density fMRI analysis. *Journal of Sexual Medicine, 9,* 1048–1054.

Cafri, G., Yamamiya, Y., Brannick, M., & Thompson, J. K. (2005). The influence of sociocultural factors on body image: A meta-analysis. *Clinical Psychology: Science and Practice, 12,* 421–433.

Calzo, J. P., Corliss, H. L., Blood, E. A., Field, A. E., & Austin, S. B. (in press). Development of muscularity and thinness concerns in heterosexual and sexual minority males. *Health Psychology.*

Campbell, L., & Ellis, B. J. (2005). Commitment, love, and mate retention. In D. M. Buss (Ed.), *Handbook of evolutionary psychology* (pp. 419–442). Hoboken, NJ: Wiley.

Carpenter, L. M. (1998). From girls into women: Scripts for sexuality and romance in *Seventeen* magazine, 1974–1994. *Journal of Sex Research, 35,* 158–168.

Carpenter, L. M. (2001). The ambiguity of "having sex": The subjective experience of virginity loss in the United States. *Journal of Sex Research, 38,* 127–139.

Carver, K., Joyner, K., & Udry, J. R. (2003). National estimates of adolescent romantic relationships. In P. Florsheim (Ed.), *Adolescent romantic relations and sexual behavior: Theory, research, and practical implications* (pp. 23–56). Mahwah, NJ: Erlbaum.

Centers for Disease Control and Prevention. (2008). Youth risk behavior surveillance—United States, 2007. *Morbidity and Mortality Weekly Report, 57*(SS-4), 1–136.

Centers for Disease Control and Prevention. (2011a). *Youth online: Youth Risk Behavior Surveillance System sexual behaviors homepage.* Retrieved May 30, 2012, from http://apps.nccd.cdc.gov/youthonline/App/QuestionsOrLocations.aspx ?CategoryId=4.

Centers for Disease Control and Prevention. (2011b). *Youth online: Youth Risk Behavior Surveillance System substance use homepage.* Retrieved May 30, 2012, from http://apps.nccd.cdc.gov/youthonline/App/QuestionsOrLocations.aspx ?CategoryID=3.

Centers for Disease Control and Prevention. (2012). Genital herpes—CDC fact sheet. Retrieved March 1, 2012, from http://www.cdc.gov/std/herpes/stdfact -herpes.htm

Chandra, A., Martino, S. C., Collins, R. L., Elliott, M. N., Berry, S. H., Kanouse, D. E., et al. (2008). Does watching sex on television predict teen pregnancy? Findings from a national longitudinal survey of youth. *Pediatrics, 122,* 1047–1054.

Chandra, A., Mosher, W. D., Copen, C., & Sionean, C. (2011). *Sexual behavior, sexual attraction, and sexual identity in the United States: Data from the 2006–2008 National Survey of Family Growth.* Washington DC: U.S. Department of Health and Human Services.

Chesson, H. W., Blandford, J. M., Gift, T. L., Tao, G., & Irwin, K. L. (2004). The estimated direct medical cost of sexually transmitted diseases among American youth, 2000. *Perspectives on Sexual and Reproductive Health, 36,* 11–19.

Chu, J. Y. (2004). A relational perspective on adolescent boys' identity development. In N. Way & J. Y. Chu (Eds.), *Adolescent boys: Exploring diverse cultures of boyhood* (pp. 78–105). New York: New York University Press.

Chu, J. Y., Porche, M. V., & Tolman, D. L. (2005). The Adolescent Masculinity Ideology in Relationships Scale: Development and validation of a new measure for boys. *Men and Masculinities, 8,* 93–115.

Clarkson, J. (2006). "Everyday Joe" versus "pissy, bitchy queens": Gay masculinity on straightacting.com. *Journal of Men's Studies, 14,* 191–207.

Clawson, L. (2005). Cowboys and schoolteachers: Gender in romance novels, secular and Christian. *Sociological Perspectives, 48,* 461–479.

Clemans, K. H., DeRose, L. M., Graber, J. A., & Brooks-Gunn, J. (2010). Gender in adolescence: Applying a person-in-context approach to gender identity and roles. In J. C. Chrisler & D. R. McCreary (Eds.), *Handbook of gender research in psychology* (pp. 527–557). New York: Springer.

Coad, D. (2008). *The metrosexual: Gender, sexuality, and sport.* Albany: State University of New York Press.

Cohane, G. H., & Pope, H. G., Jr. (2001). Body image in boys: A review of the literature. *International Journal of Eating Disorders, 29,* 373–379.

Collins, R. L., Elliott, M. N., Berry, S. H., Kanouse, D. E., & Hunter, S. B. (2003). Entertainment television as a healthy sex educator: The impact of condom efficacy information in an episode of *Friends*. *Pediatrics, 112*, 1115–1121.

Collins, R. L., Elliott, M. N., Berry, S. H., Kanouse, D. E., Kunkel, D., Hunter, S. B., et al. (2004). Watching sex on television predicts adolescent initiation of sexual behavior. *Pediatrics, 114*, e280–e289.

Collins, W. A. (2003). More than myth: The developmental significance of romantic relationships during adolescence. *Journal of Research on Adolescence, 13*, 1–24.

Connell, R. W. (1995). *Masculinities*. Berkeley: University of California Press.

Connell, R. W., & Messerschmidt, J. W. (2005). Hegemonic masculinity: Rethinking the concept. *Gender & Society, 19*, 825–859.

Conner, B. T., Hellemann, G. S., Ritchie, T. L., & Noble, E. P. (2009). Genetic, personality, and environmental predictors of drug use in adolescents. *Journal of Substance Abuse Treatment, 38*, 178–190.

Connolly, J., Craig, W., Goldberg, A., & Pepler, D. (1999). Conceptions of cross-sex friendships and romantic relationships in early adolescence. *Journal of Youth and Adolescence, 28*, 481–494.

Connolly, J., Craig, W., Goldberg, A., & Pepler, D. (2004). Mixed-gender groups, dating, and romantic relationships in early adolescence. *Journal of Research on Adolescence, 14*, 185–207.

Connolly, J., & Johnson, A. M. (1996). Adolescents' romantic relationship and the structure and quality of their close interpersonal ties. *Personal Relationships, 3*, 185–195.

Crawford, M., & Popp, D. (2003). Sexual double standards: A review and methodological critique of two decades of research. *Journal of Sex Research, 40*, 13–26.

Crockett, L. J., Raffaelli, M., & Moilanen, K. L. (2003). Adolescent sexuality: Behavior and meaning. In G. R. Adams & M. B. Berzonsky (Eds.), *Blackwell handbook of adolescence* (pp. 371–392). Oxford, England: Blackwell.

Cross, S. E., & Madson, L. (1997). Models of the self: Self-construals and gender. *Psychological Bulletin, 122*, 5–37.

Dariotis, J. K., Pleck, J. L., Astone, N. M., & Sonenstein, F. L. (2011). Pathways of early fatherhood, marriage, and employment: A latent class growth analysis. *Demography, 48*, 593–623.

Dariotis, J. K., Sonenstein, F. L., Gates, G. J., Capps, R., Astone, N. M., Pleck, J. L., et al. (2008). Changes in sexual risk behavior as young men transition to adulthood. *Perspectives on Sexual and Reproductive Health, 40*, 225.

Darwin, C. (1853). *The origin of species: By means of natural selection or the preservation of favoured races in the struggle for life*. London: John Murray.

David, D., & Brannon, R. (1976). The male sex role: Our culture's blueprint for manhood and what it's done for us lately. In D. David & R. Brannon (Eds.), *The forty-nine percent majority: The male sex role* (pp. 1–48). Reading, MA: Addison-Wesley.

Davis, C., Karvinen, K., & McCreary, D. R. (2005). Personality correlates of a drive for muscularity in young men. *Personality and Individual Differences, 39,* 349–359.

Davis, M. (2011, April 21). The damaging impact of media consumption on girls. *Honest Exchange.* Retrieved November 27, 2011, from http://honestexchange.com /category/the-buzz/?PHPSESSID=9311fe7ea731fcc946c0139a372e374a.

deGraaf, H., Vanwesenbeeck, I., Meijer, S., Woertman, L., & Meeus, W. (2009). Sexual trajectories during adolescence: Relation to demographic characteristics and sexual risk. *Archives of Sexual Behavior, 38,* 276–282.

Del Giudice, M. (2009). Sex, attachment, and the development of reproductive strategies. *Behavioral and Brain Sciences, 32,* 1–67.

Denski, S., & Sholle, D. (1992). Metal men and glamour boys: Gender performance in heavy metal. In S. Craig (Ed.), *Men, masculinity and the media* (pp. 41–60). Thousand Oaks, CA: Sage.

Deptula, D. P., Henry, D. P., & Schoeny, M. E. (2010). How can parents make a difference? Longitudinal associations with adolescent sexual behavior. *Journal of Family Psychology, 24,* 731–739.

Deutsch, F. M., & Saxon, S. E. (1998). Traditional ideologies, nontraditional lives. *Sex Roles, 38,* 331–362.

Diamond, L. M. (1998). Development of sexual orientation among adolescent and young adult women. *Developmental Psychology, 34,* 1085–1095.

Diamond, L. M. (2003). Was it a phase? Young women's relinquishment of lesbian/ bisexual identities over a 5-year period. *Journal of Personality and Social Psychology, 84,* 352–364.

Diamond, L. M. (2004). Emerging perspectives on distinctions between romantic love and sexual desire. *Current Directions in Psychological Science, 13,* 116–119.

DiCenso, A., Guyatt, G., Willan, A., & Griffith, L. (2002). Interventions to reduce unintended pregnancies among adolescents: Systematic review of randomised controlled trials. *British Medical Journal, 324,* 1426–1430.

Dickinson, B., Goldberg, L., Elliot, D., Spratt, D., Rogol, A. D., & Fish, L. H. (2005). Hormone abuse in adolescents and adults: A review of current knowledge. *Endocrinologist, 15,* 115–125.

Dilorio, C., Pluhar, E., & Belcher, L. (2003). Parent-child communication about sexuality: A review of the literature from 1980–2002. *Journal of HIV/AIDS Prevention & Education for Adolescents & Children, 5,* 7–32.

Downs, E., & Smith, S. L. (2010). Keeping abreast of hypersexuality: A video game character content analysis. *Sex Roles, 62,* 721–733.

Dreber, A., Apicella, C. L., Eisenberg, D. T. A., Garcia, J. R., Zamore, R. S., Lum, J. K., et al. (2009). The 7R polymorphism in the dopamine receptor D4 gene

(DRD4) is associated with financial risk taking in men. *Evolution and Human Behavior, 30*, 85–92.

Duggan, S. J., & McCreary, D. R. (2004). Body image, eating disorders, and the drive for muscularity in gay and heterosexual men: The influence of media images. *Journal of Homosexuality, 47*, 45–58.

Eagly, A. H., Wood, W., & Diekman, A. B. (2000). Social role theory of sex differences and similarities: A current appraisal. In T. Eckes & H. M. Trautner (Eds.), *The developmental social psychology of gender* (pp. 123–174). Mahwah, NJ: Erlbaum.

Eaton, A. A., & Rose, S. (2011). Has dating become more egalitarian? A 35 year review using *Sex Roles. Sex Roles, 64*, 843–862.

Eccles, J. S., Barber, B. L., Stone, M., & Hunt, J. (2003). Extracurricular activities and adolescent development. *Journal of Social Issues, 59*, 865–889.

Eckert, P. (1989). *Jocks and burnouts: Social categories and identity in the high school.* New York: Teacher's College Press.

Edwards, G. H. (1992). The structure and content of the male gender role stereotype: An exploration of subtypes. *Sex Roles, 27*, 533–551.

Elam, S. M. (1990). The 22nd annual Gallup poll of the public's attitudes toward the public schools. *Phi Delta Kappan, 72*, 41–55.

Eli Lilly. (2010). *Annual financial report.* Indianapolis: Author.

Eliason, M. J. (1995). Accounts of sexual identity formation in heterosexual students. *Sex Roles, 32*, 821–834.

Englar-Carlson, M., & Stevens, M. (2006). *In the room with men: A casebook of therapeutic change.* Washington, DC: American Psychological Association.

Epstein, M., Calzo, J. P., Smiler, A. P., & Ward, L. M. (2009). "Anything from making out to having sex": Men's negotiations of hooking up and friends with benefits scripts. *Journal of Sex Research, 46*, 414–424.

Epstein, M., & Ward, L. M. (2008). "Always use protection": Communication boys receive about sex from parents, peers, and the media. *Journal of Youth and Adolescence, 37*, 113–126.

Epstein, M., & Ward, L. M. (2011). Exploring parent-adolescent communication about gender: Results from adolescent and emerging adult samples. *Sex Roles, 65*, 108–118.

Erikson, E. H. (1963). *Childhood and society* (2nd ed.). New York: Norton.

Erikson, E. H. (1968). *Identity: Youth and crisis.* New York: Norton.

Faludi, S. (1999). *Stiffed: The betrayal of the American man.* New York: Morrow.

Farrell, W. (1993). *The myth of male power.* New York: Berkley Books.

Feiler, B. (2011, February 3). Dominating the man cave. *New York Times.* Retrieved April 20, 2012, from http://www.nytimes.com/2011/02/06/fashion/06ThisLife.html?_r=1&scp=1&sq=dominating%20the%20man%20cave&st=cse.

Fein, E., & Schneider, S. (1995). *The rules: Time-tested secrets for capturing the heart of Mr. Right.* New York: Warner.

Feiring, C. (1996). Concepts of romance in 15-year-old adolescents. *Journal of Research on Adolescence, 6*, 181–200.

Feiring, C. (1999). Other-sex friendship networks and the development of romantic relationships in adolescence. *Journal of Youth and Adolescence, 28*, 495–512.

Feldman, S. S., Turner, R. A., & Araujo, K. (1999). Interpersonal context as an influence on sexual timetables of youths: Gender and ethnic effects. *Journal of Research on Adolescence, 9*, 25–52.

Fine, G. A. (1987). *With the boys: Little League baseball and preadolescent culture.* Chicago: University of Chicago Press.

Fine, M. (1988). Sexuality, schooling, and adolescent females: The missing discourse of desire. *Harvard Educational Review, 58*, 29–53.

Fine, M., & McClelland, S. I. (2006). Sexuality education and desire: Still missing after all these years. *Harvard Educational Review, 76*, 297–338.

Fisher, H. E. (1998). Lust, attraction, and attachment in mammalian reproduction. *Human Nature, 9*, 23–52.

Fisher, H. E. (2004). *Why we love: The nature and chemistry of romantic love.* New York: Holt.

Fisher, H. E., Aron, A., Mashek, D., Li, H., & Brown, L. L. (2002). Defining the brain systems of lust, romantic attraction, and attachment. *Archives of Sexual Behavior, 31*, 413–419.

Fisher, T. D. (2004). Family foundations of sexuality. In J. H. Harvey, A. Wenzel, & S. Sprecher (Eds.), *The handbook of sexuality in close relationships* (pp. 385–409). New York: Psychology Press.

Fisher, T. D., Moore, Z. T., & Pittenger, M.-J. (2012). Sex on the brain? An examination of frequency of sexual cognitions as a function of gender, erotophilia, and social desirability. *Journal of Sex Research, 49*, 69–77.

Forste, R., & Haas, D. W. (2002). The transition of adolescent males to first sexual intercourse: Anticipated or delayed? *Perspectives on Sexual and Reproductive Health, 34*, 184–190.

Fouts, G., & Burggraf, K. (2000). Television situation comedies: Female weight, male negative comments, and audience reactions. *Sex Roles, 42*, 925–932.

Fouts, G., & Vaughan, K. (2002). Television situation comedies: Male weight, negative references, and audience reactions. *Sex Roles, 46*, 439–442.

Frankel, L. (2002). "I've never thought about it": Contradictions and taboos surrounding American males' experiences of first ejaculation (semenarche). *Journal of Men's Studies, 11*, 37–54.

Frankel, L. (2004). An appeal for additional research about the development of heterosexual male sexual identity. *Journal of Psychology and Human Sexuality, 16*(4), 1–16.

Fredrickson, B., & Roberts, T. (1997). Objectification theory: Toward understanding women's lived experiences and mental health risks. *Psychology of Women Quarterly, 21*, 173–206.

French, D. C., & Dishion, T. J. (2003). Predictors of early initiation of sexual intercourse among high-risk adolescents. *Journal of Early Adolescence, 23,* 295–315.

French, S. A., Story, M., Remafedi, G., Resnick, M. D., & Blum, R. W. (1996). Sexual orientation and prevalence of body dissatisfaction and eating disordered behaviors: A population-based study of adolescents. *International Journal of Eating Disorders, 19,* 119–126.

Friedman, J. (2010, February 8). Tiny bikinis mean big money for SI. *MarketWatch.* Retrieved April 20, 2012, from http://articles.marketwatch.com/2010-02-08 /commentary/30813587_1_swimsuit-issue-si-swimsuit-sports-illustrated.

Fuligni, A. J., & Stevenson, H. W. (1995). Time use and mathematics achievement among American, Chinese and Japanese high school students. *Child Development, 66,* 830–842.

Gagnon, J. H., & Simon, W. (1973). *Sexual conduct: The social sources of human sexuality.* Chicago: Aldine.

Gerbner, G., Gross, L., Morgan, M., & Signorielli, N. (1994). Growing up with television: The cultivation perspective. In J. Bryant & D. Zillmann (Eds.), *Media effects: Advances in theory and research* (pp. 17–42). Mahwah, NJ: Erlbaum.

Gerbner, G., Gross, L., Morgan, M., Signorielli, N., & Shanahan, J. (2002). Growing up with television: Cultivation processes. In J. Bryant & D. Zillmann (Eds.), *Media effects: Advances in theory and research* (2nd ed., pp. 43–67). Mahwah, NJ: Erlbaum.

Gilligan, C. (1982). *In a different voice: Psychological theory and women's development.* Cambridge, MA: Harvard University Press.

Gilmore, D. D. (1990). *Manhood in the making: Cultural concepts of masculinity.* New Haven, CT: Yale University Press.

Giordano, P. C., Longmore, M. A., & Manning, W. D. (2006). Gender and the meanings of adolescent romantic relationships: A focus on boys. *American Sociological Review, 71,* 260–287.

Giordano, P. C., Manning, W. D., & Longmore, M. A. (2010). Affairs of the heart: Qualities of adolescent romantic relationships and sexual behavior. *Journal of Research on Adolescence, 20,* 983–1013.

Goldstein, J. R. (2011). A secular trend toward earlier male sexual maturity: Evidence from shifting ages of male young adult mortality. *PLoS ONE, 6,* e14826.

Goleman, D. (1990). *Emotional intelligence.* New York: Bantam Books.

Good Men Project. (2012). About us. Retrieved July 10, 2011, from http:// goodmenproject.com/about/.

Gottlieb, G. (1991). Experiential canalization of behavioral development: Theory. *American Psychologist, 27,* 4–13.

Graber, J. A., Britto, P. R., & Brooks-Gunn, J. (1999). What's love got to do with it? Adolescents' and young adults' beliefs about sexual and romantic relationships. In W. Furman, B. B. Brown, & C. Feiring (Eds.), *The development of romantic relationships in adolescence* (pp. 364–393). Cambridge, England: Cambridge University Press.

Green, R. J., & Ashmore, R. D. (1998). Taking and developing pictures in the head: Assessing the physical stereotypes of eight gender types. *Journal of Applied Social Psychology, 28,* 1609–1636.

Greene, K., Rubin, D. L., Hale, J. L., & Walters, L. H. (1996). The utility of understanding adolescent egocentrism in designing health promotion messages. *Health Communication, 8,* 131–152.

Greenwood, D. N., & Lippman, J. R. (2010). Gender and media: Content, uses, and impact. In J. C. Chrisler & D. R. McCreary (Eds.), *Handbook of gender research in psychology* (Vol. 2, pp. 643–669). New York: Springer.

Griffin, B. (2011, October 5). Man, he's got a nice body. Good Men Project. Retrieved April 20, 2012, from http://goodmenproject.com/featured-content/man-hes-got-a-nice-body/.

Gross, E. (2004). Adolescent Internet use: What we expect, what teens report. *Applied Developmental Psychology, 25,* 633–649.

Guggino, J. M., & Ponzetti, J. J., Jr. (1997). Gender differences in affective reactions to first coitus. *Journal of Adolescence, 20,* 189–200.

Gurian, M. (1996). *The wonder of boys: What parents, mentors and educators can do to shape boys into exceptional men.* New York: Putnam.

Gurian, M., & Stevens, K. (2005). *The minds of boys: Saving our sons from falling behind in school and life.* San Francisco: Jossey-Bass.

Gutmann, M. C. (1997). Trafficking in men: The anthropology of masculinity. *Annual Review of Anthropology, 26,* 385–409.

Guttmacher Institute. (2011). *New government data finds sharp decline in teen births: Increased contraceptive use and shifts to more effective contraceptive methods behind this encouraging trend.* New York: Author.

Guttmacher Institute. (2012). *State policies in brief: Sex and HIV education.* New York: Author.

Haffner, D. W. (1998). Facing facts: Sexual health for American adolescents. *Journal of Adolescent Health, 22,* 453–459.

Halim, M. L., & Ruble, D. (2010). Gender identity and stereotyping in early and middle childhood. In J. C. Chrisler & D. R. McCreary (Eds.), *Handbook of gender research in psychology* (pp. 495–525). New York: Springer.

Halpern, C. T., Waller, M. W., Spriggs, A., & Hallfors, D. D. (2006). Adolescent predictors of emerging adult sexual patterns. *Journal of Adolescent Health, 39,* e1–e10.

Hantover, J. P. (1978). The Boy Scouts and the validation of masculinity. *Journal of Social Issues, 34,* 184–195.

Hargreaves, D. A., & Tiggemann, M. (2009). Muscular ideal media images and men's body image: Social comparison processing and individual vulnerability. *Psychology of Men and Masculinity, 10,* 109–119.

Harris, J. R. (1998). *The nurture assumption: Why children turn out the way they do.* New York: Touchstone.

Harrison, A. T., Gavin, L., & Hastings, P. A. (2012). Pregnancy contraceptive use among teens with unintended pregnancies resulting in live births—pregnancy risk assessment monitoring system (PRAMS), 2004–2008. *Morbidity and Mortality Weekly Report, 61,* 25–29.

Hartup, W. W., & Overhauser, S. (1991). Friendships. In R. M. Lerner, A. C. Petersen, & J. Brooks-Gunn (Eds.), *Encyclopedia of adolescence* (pp. 378–384). New York: Garland.

Hatton, E., & Trautner, M. N. (2011). Equal opportunity objectification? The sexualization of men and women on the cover of *Rolling Stone. Sexuality & Culture, 15,* 256–278.

Hazan, C., & Diamond, L. M. (2000). The place of attachment in human mating. *Review of General Psychology, 4,* 186–204.

Hazan, C., & Zeifman, D. (1999). Pair bonds as attachments: Evaluating the evidence. In J. Cassidy & P. R. Shaver (Eds.), *Handbook of attachment: Theory, research, and clinical applications* (pp. 336–354). New York: Guildford Press.

Hebl, M. R., King, E. B., & Lin, J. (2004). The swimsuit becomes us all: Ethnicity, gender, and vulnerability to self-objectification. *Personality and Social Psychology Bulletin, 30,* 1322–1331.

Hendry, L. B., & Kloep, M. (2007). Conceptualizing emerging adulthood: Inspecting the emperor's new clothes? *Child Development Perspectives, 1,* 74–79.

Herbert, T. W. (2002). *Sexual violence and American manhood.* Cambridge, MA: Harvard University Press.

Herdt, G. (Ed.). (1994). *Third sex, third gender: Beyond sexual dimorphism in culture and history.* New York: Zone Books.

Hether, H. J., & Murphy, S. T. (2011). Sex roles in health storylines on prime time television: A content analysis. *Sex Roles, 62,* 810–821.

Hickman, S. E., & Muehlenhard, C. L. (1999). "By the semi-mystical appearance of a condom": How young women and men communicate sexual consent in heterosexual situations. *Journal of Sex Research, 36,* 258–272.

Hofstede, G. (1998). Comparative studies of sexual behavior: Sex as achievement or as relationship? In G. Hofstede (Ed.), *Masculinity and femininity: Taboo dimensions of national culture* (pp. 153–178). Thousand Oaks, CA: Sage.

Humblet, O., Paul, C., & Dickson, N. (2003). Core group evolution over time: High-risk sexual behavior in a birth cohort between sexual debut and age 26. *Sexually Transmitted Diseases, 30,* 818–824.

Hunt, A., & Curtis, B. (2006). A genealogy of the genital kiss: Oral sex in the twentieth century. *Canadian Journal of Human Sexuality, 15,* 69–84.

Hurt, B. (Writer and director). (2007). *Hip-hop: Beyond beats & rhymes* [DVD]. Northampton, MA: Media Education Foundation.

Hust, S. J. T., Brown, J. D., & L'Engle, K. L. (2008). Boys will be boys and girls better be prepared: An analysis of the rare sexual health messages in young adolescents' media. *Mass Communication & Society, 11*, 3–23.

Hyde, J. S., & Oliver, M. B. (2000). Gender differences in sexuality: Results from a meta-analysis. In C. B. Travis & J. W. White (Eds.), *Sexuality, society, and feminism* (pp. 57–78). Washington, DC: American Psychological Association.

Irvine, J. M. (2002). *Talk about sex: The battles over sex education in the United States.* Berkeley: University of California Press.

Jakobsen, R. (1997). Stages of progression in noncoital sexual interactions among young adolescents: An application of the Mokken Scale Analysis. *International Journal of Behavioral Development, 21*, 537–553.

Jeffries, E. D. (2004). Experience of trust with parents: A qualitative investigation of African American, Latino, and Asian American boys from low-income families. In N. Way & J. Y. Chu (Eds.), *Adolescent boys: Exploring diverse cultures of boyhood* (pp. 107–128). New York: New York University Press.

Jemmott, J. B., III, Jemmott, L. S., & Fong, G. T. (2010). Efficacy of a theory-based abstinence-only intervention over 24 months: A randomized controlled trial with young adolescents. *Archives of Pediatric Adolescent Medicine, 164*, 152–158.

Jhally, S. (Writer). (1994). *Dreamworlds 2: Desire, sex, & power in music video* [DVD]. Northampton, MA: Media Education Foundation.

Jhally, S. (Writer). (2007). *Dreamworlds 3: Desire, sex, & power in music video* [DVD]. Northampton, MA: Media Education Foundation.

Jhally, S. (Writer). (2010). *Killing us softly: Advertising's image of women* (4th ed.) [DVD]. Northampton, MA: Media Education Foundation.

Johnson, K., & Tyler, K. A. (2007). Adolescent sexual onset: An intergenerational analysis. *Journal of Youth and Adolescence, 36*, 939–949.

Jones, D. C. (2001). Social comparison and body image: Attractiveness comparisons to models and peers among adolescent girls and boys. *Sex Roles, 45*, 645–664.

Joshi, S. P., Peter, J., & Valkenburg, P. M. (2011). Scripts of sexual desire and danger in US and Dutch teen girl magazines: A cross-national content analysis. *Sex Roles, 64*, 463–474.

Juster, F. T., Ono, H., & Stafford, F. P. (2004). *Changing times of American youth: 1981–2003.* Retrieved December 1, 2004, from http://www.umich.edu/news /index.html?Releases/2004/Nov04/r111704a

Kanayama, G., Barry, S., Hudson, J. I., & Pope, H. G., Jr. (2006). Body image and attitudes toward male roles in anabolic-androgenic steroid users. *American Journal of Psychiatry, 163*, 697–703.

Katz, J. (Writer), Earp, J. (Writer), & Jhally, S. (Director). (1999). *Tough guise: Violence, media, and the crisis in masculinity* [DVD]. Northampton, MA: Media Education Foundation.

Kaye, H. E. (2001). *The affairs of men.* New York: Tom Doherty Associates.

Kehily, M. (2001). Bodies in school: Young men, embodiment, and heterosexual masculinities. *Men and Masculinities, 4,* 173–185.

Kesten, H. (1955). *Casanova.* New York: Harper & Brothers.

Kilbourne, J. (Creator), & Jhally, S. (Director). (2000). *Killing Us Softly 3: Advertising's Image of Women* [DVD]. Northampton, MA: Media Education Foundation.

Killoren, S. E., Updegraff, K. A., & Christopher, F. S. (2011). Family and cultural correlates of Mexican-origin youths' sexual intentions. *Journal of Youth and Adolescence, 40,* 707–718.

Kilmartin, C., Smith, T., Green, A., Heinzen, H., Kuchler, M., & Kolar, D. (2008). A real time social norms intervention to reduce male sexism. *Sex Roles, 59,* 264–273.

Kim, J. L., Collins, R. L., Kanouse, D. E., Elliott, M. N., Berry, S. H., Hunter, S. B., et al. (2006). Sexual readiness, household policies, and other predictors of adolescents' exposure to sexual content in mainstream entertainment televisions. *Media Psychology, 8,* 449–471.

Kim, J. L., & Ward, L. M. (2004). Pleasure reading: Associations between young women's sexual attitudes and their reading of contemporary women's magazines. *Psychology of Women Quarterly, 28,* 48–58.

Kim, J. L., & Ward, L. M. (2007). Silence speaks volumes: Parental sexual communication among Asian American emerging adults. *Journal of Adolescent Research, 22,* 3–31.

Kimmel, M. (1996). *Manhood in America: A cultural history.* New York: Free Press.

Kimmel, M. (1997). Masculinity as homophobia: Fear, shame and silence in the construction of gender identity. In M. M. Gergen & S. N. Davis (Eds.), *Toward a new psychology of gender* (pp. 223–242). New York: Routledge.

Kimmel, M. (2008). *Guyland: The perilous world where boys become men.* New York: Harper.

Kimmel, M. (2011, April 1). Keynote address presented at the annual conference of the American Men's Studies Association, Kansas City, MO.

Kindlon, D., & Thompson, M. (1999). *Raising Cain.* New York: Ballantine Books.

King, J. L., & Hunter, K. (2004). *On the down low: A journey into the lives of "straight" black men who sleep with men.* New York: Harlem Moon/Broadway Books.

Kingsbury, K. (2008, June 18). Pregnancy boom at Gloucester High. *Time.* Retrieved April 12, 2011, from http://www.time.com/time/world/article /0,8599,1815845,00.html.

Kirby, D. (2002). Antecedents of adolescent initiation of sex, contraceptive use, pregnancy. *American Journal of Health Behavior, 26,* 473–485.

Kiselica, M. S. (2008). *When boys become parents: Adolescent fatherhood in America.* New Brunswick, NJ: Rutgers University Press.

Kistler, M., Rodgers, K. B., Power, T., Austin, E. W., & Hill, L. G. (2010). Adolescents and music media: Toward an involvement-mediational model of consumption and self-concept. *Journal of Research on Adolescence, 20,* 616–630.

Kunkel, D., Cope, K. M., & Biely, E. (1999). Sexual messages on television: Comparing findings from three studies. *Journal of Sex Research, 36*, 230–236.

Kunkel, D., Eyal, K., Finnerty, K., Biely, E., & Donnerstein, E. (2005). *Sex on TV 4*. Menlo Park, CA: Henry J. Kaiser Family Foundation.

LaFerle, C., Edwards, S. M., & Lee, W.-N. (2000). Teens' use of traditional media and the Internet. *Journal of Advertising Research, 40*, 55–65.

Lam, T. H., Shi, H. J., Ho, L. M., Stewart, S. M., & Fan, S. (2002). Timing of pubertal maturation and heterosexual behavior among Hong Kong Chinese adolescents. *Archives of Sexual Behavior, 31*, 359–366.

Lambiase, J. (2003). Codes of online sexuality: Celebrity, gender and marketing on the web. *Sexuality & Culture, 7*, 57–78.

Lansford, J. E., Yu, T., Erath, S. A., Pettit, G. S., Bates, J. E., & Dodge, K. A. (2010). Developmental precursors of number of sexual partners from ages 16 to 22. *Journal of Research on Adolescence, 20*, 651–677.

Laumann, E. O., Gagnon, J. H., Michael, R. T., & Michaels, S. (1994). *The social organization of sexuality: Sexual practices in the United States*. Chicago: University of Chicago Press.

Lefkowitz, B. (1997). *Our guys: The Glen Ridge rape and the secret life of the perfect suburb*. New York: Vintage.

Leit, R. A., Gray, J. J., & Pope, H. G., Jr. (2002). The media's representation of the ideal male body: A cause for muscle dysmorphia? *International Journal of Eating Disorders, 31*, 334–338.

Levant, R. F. (1992). Toward the reconstruction of masculinity. *Journal of Family Psychology, 5*, 379–402.

Leventhal, T., & Brooks-Gunn, J. (2000). The neighborhoods they live in: The effects of neighborhood residence on child and adolescent outcomes. *Psychological Bulletin, 126*, 309–337.

Levine, J. (2002). *Harmful to minors: The perils of protecting children from sex*. Minneapolis: University of Minnesota Press.

Lewin, T. (2010, February 2). Quick response to study of abstinence education. *New York Times*. Retrieved April 20, 2012, from http://www.nytimes.com/2010/02/03/education/03abstinence.html.

Lewis, I., Watson, B., & Tay, R. (2007). Examining the effectiveness of physical threats in road safety advertising: the role of the third-person effect, gender, and age. *Transportation Research Part F, 10*, 48–60.

Little, C. B., & Rankin, A. (2001). Why do they start it? Explaining reported early-teen sexual activity. *Sociological Forum, 16*, 703–729.

Locke, B. D., & Mahalik, J. R. (2005). Examining masculinity norms, problem drinking, and athletic involvement as predictors of sexual aggression in college men. *Journal of Counseling Psychology, 52*, 279–283.

Lottes, I. L. (1993). Nontraditional gender roles and the sexual experiences of heterosexual college students. *Sex Roles, 29*, 645–669.

Lucke, J. C. (1998). Gender roles and sexual behavior among young women. *Sex Roles, 39,* 273–297.

Lykken, D. T., & Tellegen, A. (1993). Is human mating adventitious or the result of lawful choice? A twin study of mate selection. *Journal of Personality and Social Psychology, 65,* 56–68.

Lytton, H., & Romney, D. M. (1991). Parents' differential socialization of boys and girls: A meta-analysis. *Psychological Bulletin, 109,* 267–296.

MacCorquodale, P. (1989). Gender and sexual behavior. In K. McKinney & S. Sprecher (Eds.), *Human sexuality: The societal and interpersonal context* (pp. 91–112). Norwood, NJ: Ablex.

MacPhail, C., & Campbell, C. (2001). "I think condoms are good but, aai, I hate those things": Condom use among adolescents and young people in a Southern African township. *Social Science & Medicine, 52,* 1613–1627.

Madon, S. (1997). What do people believe about gay males? A study of stereotype content and strength. *Sex Roles, 37,* 663–685.

Mahalik, J. R., Locke, B. D., Ludlow, L. H., Diemer, M. A., Scott, R. P. J., Gottfried, M., et al. (2003). Development of the Conformity to Masculine Norms Inventory. *Journal of Men and Masculinity, 4,* 3–25.

ManKind Project (2012). About the ManKind Project. Retrieved March 1, 2012, from http://mankindproject.org/about-mankind-project.

Manning, W. D., Longmore, M. A., & Giordano, P. C. (2005). Adolescents' involvement in non-romantic sexual activity. *Social Science Research, 34,* 384–407.

Marcia, J. E. (1966). Development and validation of ego-identity status. *Journal of Personality and Social Psychology, 3,* 551–558.

Marshall, T. C. (2010). Gender, peer relations, and intimate romantic relationships. In J. C. Chrisler & D. R. McCreary (Eds.), *Handbook of gender research in psychology* (Vol. 2, pp. 281–310). New York: Springer.

Marsiglio, W. (1988). Adolescent male sexuality and heterosexual masculinity: A conceptual model and review. *Journal of Adolescent Review, 3,* 285–303.

Marston, C., & King, E. (2006). Factors that shape young people's sexual behaviour: A systematic review. *Lancet, 368,* 1581–1586.

Martino, S. C., Collins, R. L., Elliott, M. N., Strachman, A., Kanouse, D. E., & Berry, S. H. (2006). Exposure to degrading versus nondegrading music lyrics and sexual behavior among youth. *Pediatrics, 118,* 430–441.

Maslow, A. H. (1943). A theory of human motivation. *Psychological Review, 50,* 370–396.

Masters, J. (1969). *Casanova.* New York: Bernard Geis Associates.

Maxwell, K. A. (2002). Friends: The role of peer influence across adolescent risk behaviors. *Journal of Youth and Adolescence, 31,* 267–277.

Mayer, J. D., Caruso, D. R., & Salovey, P. (1999). Emotional intelligence meets traditional standards for an intelligence. *Intelligence, 27,* 267–298.

McBurney, D. H., Zapp, D. J., & Streeter, S. A. (2005). Preferred number of sexual partners: Tails of distributions and tales of mating systems. *Evolution and Human Behavior, 26,* 271–278.

McCreary, D. R., & Sasse, D. K. (2000). An exploration of the Drive for Muscularity in adolescent boys and girls. *Journal of American College Health, 48,* 297–304.

McCreary, D. R., Saucier, D. M., & Courtenay, W. H. (2005). The Drive for Muscularity and masculinity: Testing the associations among gender-role traits, behaviors, attitudes, and conflict. *Psychology of Men and Masculinity, 6,* 83–94.

McGarty, C. (2002). Stereotype formation as category formation. In C. McGarty, V. Yzerbyt, & R. Spears (Eds.), *Stereotypes as explanations: The formation of meaningful beliefs about social groups* (pp. 16–37). Cambridge, England: Cambridge University Press.

McHale, S. M., Bissell, J., & Kim, J.-Y. (Eds.). (2009). Sibling relationship, family, and genetic factors in sibling similarity in sexual risk. *Journal of Family Psychology, 23,* 562–572.

McNeil, A. (1996). *Total television.* New York: Penguin Books.

Mead, M. (1973). *Coming of age in Samoa.* New York: Morrow Quill Paperbacks. (Original work published 1928)

Messner, M. A. (1992). *Power at play: Sports and the problem of masculinity.* Boston: Beacon Press.

Meston, C. M., & Buss, D. M. (2007). Why humans have sex. *Archives of Sexual Behavior, 36,* 477–507.

Meyer, N. (2010). *The view from the bridge: Memories of Star Trek and a life in Hollywood.* New York: Plume.

Migliaccio, T. (2009). Men's friendships: Performances of masculinity. *Journal of Men's Studies, 17,* 226–241.

Mikkelson, L. (2011). *Daydream deceiver.* Retrieved January 4, 2012, from http://www.snopes.com/science/stats/thinksex.asp.

Miller, B. C., & Benson, B. (1999). Romantic and sexual relationship development during adolescence. In W. Furman, B. B. Brown, & C. Feiring (Eds.), *The development of romantic relationships in adolescence* (pp. 99–124). Cambridge, England: Cambridge University Press.

Miller, B. C., Norton, M. C., Fan, X., & Christopherson, C. R. (1998). Pubertal development, parental communication and sexual values in relation to adolescent sexual behaviors. *Journal of Early Adolescence, 18,* 27–52.

Miller, K. S., Levin, M. L., Whitaker, D. J., & Xu, X. (1998). Patterns of condom use among adolescents: The impact of mother-adolescent communication. *American Journal of Public Health, 88,* 1542–1544.

Miller, L. C., & Fishkin, S. A. (1997). On the dynamics of human bonding and reproductive success: Seeking windows on the adapted-for-human–environmental interface. In J. A. Simpson & D. T. Kenrick (Eds.), *Evolutionary social psychology* (pp. 197–236). Mahwah, NJ: Erlbaum.

Morrison, T. G., & Halton, M. (2009). Buff, tough, and rough: Representations of muscularity in action motion pictures. *Journal of Men's Studies, 17,* 57–74.

Muehlenhard, C. L., Andrews, S. L., & Beal, G. K. (1996). Beyond "just saying no": Dealing with men's unwanted sexual advances in heterosexual dating contexts. *Journal of Human Sexuality, 8,* 141–168.

Muehlenhard, C. L., & Rodgers, C. S. (1998). Token resistance to sex: New perspectives on an old stereotype. *Psychology of Women Quarterly, 22,* 443–463.

Murdock, G. P. (1967). *Ethnographic atlas.* Pittsburgh: University of Pittsburgh.

Murnen, S. K., Wright, C., & Kaluzny, G. (2002). If "boys will be boys," then girls will be victims? A meta-analytic review of the research that relates masculine ideology to sexual aggression. *Sex Roles, 46,* 359–375.

Mutchler, M. G., & McDavitt, B. (2011). "Gay boy talk" meets "girl talk": HIV risk assessment assumptions in young gay men's sexual health communication with best friends. *Health Education Research, 26,* 489–505.

National Association for Media Literacy Education. (2007, November). *Core principles of media literacy education in the United States.* Retrieved February 15, 2012, from http://namle.net/publications/core-principles/.

National Center for Education Statistics. (2010). Table 212. Enrollment rates of 17- to 24-year-olds in degree-granting institutions, by type of institution and sex and race/ethnicity of student: 1967 through 2009. Retrieved December 21, 2011, from http://nces.ed.gov/programs/digest/d10/tables/dt10_212.asp?referrer=list.

The new young face of Viagra abuse. (2003, December 23). *Chicago Tribune.* Retrieved April 20, 2012, from http://www.azcentral.com/health/men/articles /1226viagra-abuse-ON.html.

Newman, B. M., & Newman, P. R. (1986). *Adolescent development.* Columbus, OH: Merrill.

Nielsen Company. (2011). *The cross-platform report Q1, 2011.* New York: Author.

Novack, J. (2011). Crying and being a man. Good Men Project. Retrieved July 27, 2011, from http://goodmenproject.com/featured-content/crying-and-being-a-man/.

Offer, D., Offer, M. K., & Ostrov, E. (2004). *Regular guys: 34 years beyond adolescence.* New York: Kluwer.

Ogbu, J. U. (1994). From cultural differences to differences in cultural frames of reference. In P. M. Greenfield & R. R. Cocking (Eds.), *Cross-cultural roots of minority child development* (pp. 365–391). Mahwah, NJ: Erlbaum.

Oliver, M. B., & Hyde, J. S. (1993). Gender differences in sexuality: A meta-analysis. *Psychological Bulletin, 114,* 29–51.

Ott, M. A. (2010). Examining the development and sexual behavior of adolescent males. *Journal of Adolescent Health, 46,* S3–S11.

Ott, M. A., Adler, N. E., Millstein, S. G., Tschann, J. M., & Ellen, J. M. (2002). The trade-off between hormonal contraceptives and condoms among adolescents. *Perspectives on Sexual and Reproductive Health, 34,* 6–14.

Ott, M. A., Millstein, S. G., Ofner, S., & Halpern-Felsher, B. L. (2006). Greater expectations: Adolescents' positive motivations for sex. *Perspectives on Sexual and Reproductive Health, 38,* 84–89.

Ott, M. A., & Pfeiffer, E. J. (2008). "That's nasty" to curiosity: Early adolescent cognitions about sexual abstinence. *Journal of Adolescent Health, 44,* 575–581.

Ott, M. A., Pfeiffer, E. J., & Fortbenberry, J. D. (2006). Perceptions of sexual abstinence among high-risk early and middle adolescents. *Journal of Adolescent Health, 39,* 192–198.

Parent, M. C., & Moradi, B. (2009). Confirmatory factor analysis of the Conformity to Masculine Norms Inventory and development of the CMNI-46. *Psychology of Men and Masculinity, 10,* 175–189.

Parent, M. C., & Moradi, B. (2011). His biceps become him: A test of objectification theory's application to drive for muscularity and propensity for steroid use in college men. *Journal of Counseling Psychology, 58,* 246–256.

Pascoe, C. J. (2007). *Dude, you're a fag: Masculinity and sexuality in high school.* Berkeley: University of California Press.

Patterson, C. J. (1995). Sexual orientation and human development: An overview. *Developmental Psychology, 31,* 3–11.

Payne, D. L., Lonsway, K. A., & Fitzgerald, L. F. (1999). Rape myth acceptance: Exploration of its structure and its measurement using the Illinois Rape Myth Acceptance Scale. *Journal of Research in Personality, 33,* 27–68.

Perloff, R. M. (1999). The third-person effect: A critical review and synthesis. *Media Psychology, 1,* 353–378.

Perry, W. G., Jr. (1981). Cognitive and ethical growth: The making of meaning. In A. W. Chickering & Associates, *The modern American college* (pp. 76–116). San Francisco: Jossey-Bass.

Peterson, Z. D., & Muehlenhard, C. L. (2007). What is sex and why does it matter? A motivational approach to exploring individuals' definitions of sex. *Journal of Sex Research, 44,* 256–268.

Pew Research Center. (2011). *Most say homosexuality should be accepted by society.* Pew Research Center. Retrieved April 20, 2012, from http://pewresearch.org /pubs/1994/poll-support-for-acceptance-of-homosexuality-gay-parenting-marriage.

Pfizer. (2010). *Annual financial report.* New York: Author.

Piaget, J. (1970). Piaget's theory. In P. H. Mussen (Ed.), *Carmichael's manual of child psychology* (Vol. 1, pp. 703–752). Hoboken, NJ: Wiley.

Picker, M. (Director), & Sun, C. (Writer and director). (2008). *The price of pleasure: Pornography, sexuality, and relationships* [DVD]. Northampton, MA: Media Education Foundation.

Pinkleton, B. E., Austin, E. W., Cohen, M., Chen, Y.-C., & Fitzgerald, E. (2008). Effects of a peer-led media literacy curriculum on adolescents' knowledge and attitudes toward sexual behavior and media portrayals of sex. *Health Communication, 23*, 462–472.

Pizzamiglio, G. (2000). Introduction (S. Sartarelli & S. Hawkes, Trans.). In S. Sartarelli & S. Hawkes (Eds.), *Giacomo Casanova: The story of my life* (pp. i–xxii). New York: Marsilio Publishers.

Planned Parenthood. (2011). *Tools for parents.* Retrieved November 27, 2011, from http://www.plannedparenthood.org/parents/.

Pleck, J. H. (1981). *The myth of masculinity.* Cambridge, MA: MIT Press.

Pleck, J. H. (1987). The theory of male sex-role identity: Its rise and fall, 1936 to the present. In H. Brod (Ed.), *The making of masculinities: The new men's studies* (pp. 21–38). Boston: Allen & Unwin.

Pleck, J. H. (2007). Why could father involvement benefit children? Theoretical perspectives. *Applied Developmental Science, 11*, 196–202.

Pleck, J. H., Sonenstein, F. L., & Ku, L. C. (1993). Masculinity ideology: Its impact on adolescent males' heterosexual relationships. *Journal of Social Issues, 49*, 11–29.

Pleck, J. H., Sonenstein, F. L., & Ku, L. C. (1994). Attitudes toward male roles: A discriminant validity analysis. *Sex Roles, 30*, 481–501.

Pleck, J. H., Sonenstein, F. L., & Ku, L. (2004). Adolescent boys' heterosexual behavior. In N. Way & J. Y. Chu (Eds.), *Adolescent boys: Exploring diverse cultures of boyhood* (pp. 256–270). New York: New York University Press.

Pollack, W. (1998). *Real boys: Rescuing our sons from the myths of boyhood.* New York: Holt & Co.

Pollack, W. (2006). The "war" for boys: Hearing "real boys" voices, healing their pain. *Professional Psychology: Research and Practice, 37*, 190–195.

Pompper, D. (2010). Masculinities, the metrosexual, and media images: Across dimensions of age and ethnicity. *Sex Roles, 63*, 682–696.

Pope, H. G., Jr., Olivardia, R., Borowiecki, J. J., III, & Cohane, G. H. (2001). The growing commercial value of the male body: A longitudinal survey of advertising in women's magazines. *Psychotherapy and Psychosomatics, 70*, 189–192.

Pope, H. G., Jr., Olivardia, R., Gruber, A., & Borowiecki, J. (1999). Evolving ideals of male body image as seen through action toys. *Eating Disorders, 26*, 65–72.

Pope, H. G., Jr., Phillips, K. A., & Olivardia, R. (2000). *The Adonis complex: The secret crisis of male body obsessions.* New York: Free Press.

Potter, W. J. (2012). The state of media literacy. *Journal of Broadcasting and Electronic Media, 54*, 675–696.

Prusank, D. T. (2007). Masculinities in teen magazines: The good, the bad, and the ugly. *Journal of Men's Studies, 15*, 160–177.

Putnam, R. (2000). *Bowling alone: The collapse and revival of American community.* New York: Touchstone.

Quinlan, R. J. (2008). Human pair-bonds: Evolutionary functions, ecological variation, and adaptive development. *Evolutionary Anthropology, 17,* 227–238.

Raskin, N. J., & Rogers, C. R. (2005). Person-centered therapy. In R. J. Corsini & D. Wedding (Eds.), *Current psychotherapies* (7th ed., pp. 130–165). Belmont, CA: Thomson Brooks/Cole.

Ray, T. R., Eck, J. C., Covington, L. A., Murphy, R. B., Williams, R., & Knudston, J. (2001). Use of oral creatine as an ergogenic aid for increased sports performance: Perceptions of adolescent athletes. *Southern Medical Journal, 94,* 608–612.

Regan, P. C., Durvasula, R., Howell, L., Ureño, O., & Rea, M. (2004). Gender, ethnicity, and the developmental timing of first sexual and romantic experiences. *Social Behavior and Personality, 32,* 667–676.

Remez, L. (2000, November/December). Oral sex among adolescents: Is it sex or is it abstinence? *Family Planning Perspectives, 32.* Retrieved May 19, 2012, from http://www.guttmacher.org/pubs/journals/3229800.html.

Rew, L., & Wong, Y. J. (2006). A systematic review of associations among religiosity/spirituality and adolescent health attitudes and behaviors. *Journal of Adolescent Health, 38,* 433–442.

Rich, A. (1980). Compulsory heterosexuality and lesbian existence. *Signs: Journal of Women in Culture and Society, 5,* 631–660.

Roberts, D. F., & Christenson, D. G. (2001). Popular music in childhood and adolescence. In D. G. Singer & J. L. Singer (Eds.), *Handbook of children and the media* (pp. 395–413). Thousand Oaks, CA: Sage.

Rochlen, A. B., McKelley, R. A., & Whittaker, T. A. (2010). Stay-at-home fathers' reasons for entering the role and stigma experiences: A preliminary report. *Psychology of Men and Masculinity, 11,* 279–285.

Rochlen, A. B., Suizzo, M.-A., McKelley, R. A., & Scaringi, V. (2008). "I'm just providing for my family": A qualitative study of stay-at-home fathers. *Psychology of Men and Masculinity, 9,* 193–206.

Rogers, K. N., Buchanan, C. M., & Winchell, M. E. (2003). Psychological control during early adolescence: Links to adjustment in differing parent/adolescent dyads. *Journal of Early Adolescence, 23,* 349–383.

Romance Writers of America. (2011). Romance literature statistics: Readership statistics. Retrieved June 30, 2011, from http://www.rwa.org/cs/readership_stats.

Romo, L. F., Lefkowitz, E. S., Sigman, M., & Au, T. K. (2002). A longitudinal study of maternal messages about dating and sexuality and their influence on Latino adolescents. *Journal of Adolescent Health, 31,* 59–69.

Rosenthal, D. A., & Smith, A. M. A. (1997). Adolescent sexual timetables. *Journal of Youth and Adolescence, 26,* 619–636.

Rostosky, S. S., Regenerus, M. D., & Comer Wright, M. L. (2003). Coital debut: The role of religiosity and sex attitudes in the Add Health survey. *Journal of Sex Research, 40,* 358–367.

Rostosky, S. S., Wilcox, B. L., Comer Wright, M. L., & Randall, B. A. (2004). The impact of religiosity on adolescent sexual behavior: A review of the evidence. *Journal of Adolescent Research, 19*, 677–697.

Rotundo, E. A. (1993). *American manhood: Transformations in masculinity from the revolution to the modern era.* New York: Basic Books.

Russell, S. T. (2005). Conceptualizing positive adolescent sexuality development. *Sexual Research and Social Policy, 2*(3), 4–12.

Saad, G., & Vongas, J. G. (2009). The effect of conspicuous consumption on men's testosterone levels. *Organizational Behavior and Human Decision Processes, 110,* 80–92.

Sabina, C., Wolak, J., & Finkelhor, D. (2008). The nature and dynamics of Internet pornography exposure for youth. *CyberPsychology and Behavior, 11,* 691–693.

Sandomir, R. (2007, May 23). For ESPN morning team, opposites attract ratings. *New York Times.* Retrieved April 20, 2012, from http://query.nytimes.com/gst /fullpage.html?res=9C03E5D71F31F930A15756C0A9619C8B63&pagewanted=all.

Sanfield, A., Kost, K., Gold, R. B., & Finer, L. B. (2011). The public costs of births resulting from unintended pregnancies: National and state-level estimates. *Perspectives on Sexual and Reproductive Health, 43*, 94–102.

Santelli, J., Kaiser, J., Hirsch, L., Radosh, A., Simkin, L., & Middlestadt, S. (2004). Initiation of sexual intercourse among middle school adolescents: The influence of psychosocial factors. *Journal of Adolescent Health, 34,* 200–208.

Santelli, J., Ott, M. A., Lyon, M., Rogers, J., Summers, D., & Schleifer, R. (2006). Abstinence and abstinence-only education: A review of US policies and programs. *Journal of Adolescent Health, 38,* 72–81.

Savin-Williams, R. C. (1998). *". . . and then I became gay."* New York: Routledge.

Savin-Williams, R. C. (2005). *The new gay teenager.* Cambridge, MA: Harvard University Press.

Savin-Williams, R. C., & Ream, G. L. (2006). Pubertal onset and sexual orientation in an adolescent national probability sample. *Archives of Sexual Behavior, 35,* 279–286.

Scarr, S., & McCartney, K. (1983). How people make their own environments: A theory of genotype greater than environment effects. *Child Development, 68,* 69–79.

Schmitt, D. P., & 118 members of the International Sexuality Description Project. (2003). Universal sex differences in the desire for sexual variety: Tests from 52 nations, 6 continents, and 13 islands. *Journal of Personality and Social Psychology, 85,* 85–104.

Schmitt, D. P., Alcalay, L., Allensworth, M., Allik, J., Ault, L., Autsters, I., et al. (2004). Patterns and universals of adult romantic attachment across 62 cultural regions: Are models of self and of other pancultural constructs? *Journal of Cross-Cultural Psychology, 35,* 367–402.

Schmitt, D. P., Realo, A., Voracek, M., & Allik, J. (2008). Why can't a man be more like a woman? Sex differences in big five personality traits across 55 cultures. *Journal of Personality and Social Psychology, 94*, 168–182.

Schooler, D., Impett, E. A., Hirschman, C., & Bonem, L. (2008, December). A mixed-method exploration of body image and sexual health among adolescent boys. *American Journal of Men's Health, 2*, 322–339.

Schooler, D., Sorsoli, C. L., Kim, J. L., & Tolman, D. L. (2009). Beyond exposure: A person-oriented approach to adolescent media diets. *Journal of Research on Adolescence, 19*, 484–508.

Schooler, D., & Ward, L. M. (2006). Average Joes: Men's relationships with media, real bodies, and sexuality. *Psychology of Men and Masculinity, 7*, 27–41.

Schultz, P. W., Nolan, J. M., Cialdini, R. B., Goldstein, N. J., & Griskevicius, V. (2007). The constructive, destructive, and reconstructive power of social norms. *Psychological Science, 18*, 429–434.

Shanahan, J., & Morgan, M. (1999). *Television and its viewers: Cultivation theory and research.* Cambridge, England: Cambridge University Press.

Shtarkshall, R. A., Carmel, S., Jaffe-Hirschfield, D., & Woloski-Wruble, A. (2009). Sexual milestones and factors associated with coitus initiation among Israeli high school students. *Archives of Sexual Behavior, 38*, 591–604.

Shulman, S., & Kipnis, O. (2001). Adolescent romantic relationships: A look from the future. *Journal of Adolescence, 24*, 337–351.

Shulman, S., & Scharf, M. (2000). Adolescent romantic behaviors and perceptions: Age- and gender-related differences, and links with family and peer relationships. *Journal of Research on Adolescence, 10*, 99–118.

Shulman, S., & Seiffge-Krenke, I. (2001). Adolescent romance: Between experience and relationships. *Journal of Adolescence, 24*, 417–428.

Siebenbruner, J., Zimmer-Gembeck, M. J., & Egeland, B. (2007). Sexual partners and contraceptive use: A 16-year prospective study predicting abstinence and risk behavior. *Journal of Research on Adolescence, 17*, 179–206.

Signorielli, N., & Bacue, A. (1999). Recognition and respect: A content analysis of prime-time television characters across three decades. *Sex Roles, 40*, 527–544.

Sinn, J. S. (1997). The predictive and discriminant validity of masculinity ideology. *Journal of Research in Personality, 31*, 117–135.

Smiler, A. P. (2003). *Living the stereotype: Connections between male behavior and male images.* Doctoral dissertation, University of New Hampshire, Durham.

Smiler, A. P. (2004). Thirty years after gender: Concepts and measures of masculinity. *Sex Roles, 50*, 15–26.

Smiler, A. P. (2006a). Conforming to masculine norms: Evidence for validity among adult men and women. *Sex Roles, 54*, 767–775.

Smiler, A. P. (2006b). Living the image: A quantitative approach to masculinities. *Sex Roles, 55*, 621–632.

Smiler, A. P. (2007). Sexuality. In M. Flood, J. K. Gardiner, B. Pease, & K. Pringle (Eds.), *International encyclopedia of men and masculinities* (pp. 561–565). London: Routledge.

Smiler, A. P. (2008). "I wanted to get to know her better": Adolescent boys' dating motives, masculinity ideology, and sexual behavior. *Journal of Adolescence, 31,* 17–32.

Smiler, A. P. (2011). Sexual strategies theory: Built for the short term or the long term? *Sex Roles, 64,* 603–612.

Smiler, A. P., Frankel, L., & Savin-Williams, R. C. (2011). From kissing to coitus? Sex-of-partner differences in the sexual milestone achievement of young men. *Journal of Adolescence, 34,* 727–735.

Smiler, A. P., & Hearon, B. (under review). From "I Wanna Hold Your Hand" to "Promiscuous": Sexuality in popular music lyrics, 1960–2000. *Journal of Adolescence.*

Smiler, A. P., Kay, G., & Harris, B. (2008). Tightening and loosening masculinity's (k)nots: Masculinity in the Hearst press during the interwar period. *Journal of Men's Studies, 16,* 266–279.

Smiler, A. P., & Kubotera, N. (2010). Instrumental or expressive? Heterosexual men's expectations of women in two contexts. *Men and Masculinities, 12,* 565–574.

Smiler, A. P., & Ward, L. M. (under review). Dating relationships and hookups: Evidence for three trajectories among young men. *Journal of Research in Adolescence.*

Smiler, A. P., Ward, L. M., Caruthers, A., & Merriwether, A. (2005). Pleasure, empowerment, and love: Factors associated with a positive first coitus. *Sexual Research and Social Policy, 2*(3), 41–55.

Smith, A. R., Hawkeswood, S. E., Bodell, L. P., & Joiner, T. E. (2011). Muscularity versus leanness: An examination of body ideals and predictors of disordered eating in heterosexual and gay college students. *Body Image, 8,* 232–236.

Smith, E. A., & Udry, J. R. (1985). Coital and noncoital sexual behaviors of white and black adolescents. *American Journal of Public Health, 75,* 1200–1203.

Smith, L. H., Guthrie, B. J., & Oakley, D. J. (2005). Studying adolescent male sexuality: Where are we? *Journal of Youth and Adolescence, 34,* 361–377.

Smith, M., Gertz, E., Alvarez, S., & Lurie, P. (2000). The content and accessibility of sex education information on the Internet. *Health Education & Behavior, 27,* 684–694.

Smoak, N. D., Scott-Sheldon, L. A. J., Johnson, B. T., Carey, M. P., & Team, S. R. (2006). Sexual risk reduction interventions do not inadvertently increase the overall frequency of sexual behavior: A meta-analysis of 174 studies with 116,735 participants. *Journal of Acquired Immune Deficit Syndrome, 41,* 374–384.

Snow Jones, A., Astone, N. M., Keyl, P. M., Kim, Y. J., & Alexander, C. S. (1999). Teen childbearing and educational attainment: A comparison of methods. *Journal of Family and Economic Issues, 20,* 387–418.

Spector, D., & Bennett, D. (2011, February 15). How the swimsuit issue became *Sports Illustrated*'s biggest cash cow. *Business Insider*. Retrieved April 20, 2012, from http://www.businessinsider.com/facts-about-the-si-swimsuit-edition-2011-2?op=1.

Spence, J. T., & Helmreich, R. L. (1978). *Masculinity and femininity: Their psychological dimensions, correlates and antecedents*. Austin: University of Texas Press.

Spence, J. T., & Helmreich, R. L. (1980). Masculine instrumentality and feminine expressiveness: Their relationships with sex role attitudes and behaviors. *Psychology of Women Quarterly, 5*, 147–163.

Spencer, R. (2007). "I just feel safe with him": Emotional closeness in male youth mentoring relationships. *Psychology of Men and Masculinity, 8*, 185–198.

Sports Illustrated Source, Sales & Marketing Information Center. (2004). *Rate card #62*. Retrieved July 8, 2011, from http://sportsillustrated.cnn.com/adinfo/si/ratecardframe.html.

Sprecher, S., Barbee, A., & Schwartz, P. (1995). "Was it good for you, too?" Gender differences in first sexual intercourse experiences. *Journal of Sex Research, 32*, 3–15.

Stearns, P. N. (1994). *American cool: Constructing a twentieth-century emotional style*. New York: New York University Press.

Steele, J. R. (1999). Teenage sexuality and media practice: Factoring in the influences of family, friends, and school. *Journal of Sex Research, 36*, 331–341.

Stein, J. H., & Reiser, L. W. (1994). A study of white middle-class adolescent boys' responses to "semenarche" (the first ejaculation). *Journal of Youth and Adolescence, 23*, 373–384.

Stone, M. R., Barber, B. L., & Eccles, J. S. (2001, April). *Adolescent "crowd" clusters: An adolescent perspective on persons and patterns*. Paper presented at the Society for Research on Child Development, Minneapolis, MN.

Strate, N. (1992). Beer commercials. In S. Craig (Ed.), *Men, masculinity and the media* (pp. 78–92). Thousand Oaks, CA: Sage.

Striepe, M. I., & Tolman, D. L. (2003). Mom, dad, I'm straight: The coming out of gender ideologies in adolescent sexual-identity development. *Journal of Clinical Child and Adolescent Psychology, 32*, 523–530.

Suoninen, A. (2001). The role of media in peer group relations. In S. Livingstone & M. Bovill (Eds.), *Children and their changing media environment: A European comparative study* (pp. 201–219). Mahwah, NJ: Erlbaum.

Sutton, M. J., Brown, J. D., Wilson, K. M., & Klein, J. D. (2002). Shaking the tree of knowledge for forbidden fruit: Where adolescents learn about sexuality and contraception. In J. D. Brown, J. R. Steele, & K. Walsh-Childers (Eds.), *Sexual teens, sexual media: Investigating media's influence on adolescent sexuality* (pp. 25–55). Mahwah, NJ: Erlbaum.

Tamura, L. (2011, June 20). Why are more men opting for cosmetic surgery? *Washington Post*. Retrieved April 10, 2012, from http://www.washingtonpost.com

/national/why-are-more-men-going-opting-for-cosmetic-surgery/2011/03/25
/AGALTKdH_story.html.

Taylor, L. D. (2005). All for him: Articles about sex in American lad magazines. *Sex Roles, 52,* 153–163.

Taylor, L. D. (2006). College men, their magazines, and sex. *Sex Roles, 55,* 693–702.

Tejirian, E. J. (2000). *Male to male: Sexual feeling across the boundaries of identity.* New York: Routledge.

Tenenbaum, H. R., & Leaper, C. (2002). Are parents' gender schemas related to their children's gender-related cognitions? A meta-analysis. *Child Development, 38,* 615–630.

Thoits, P. A., & Virshup, L. K. (1997). Me's and we's: Forms and functions of social identities. In R. D. Ashmore & L. Jussim (Eds.), *Self and identity: Fundamental issues* (pp. 106–133). New York: Oxford University Press.

Thorn, C. (2010). Why do we demonize men who are honest about their sexual needs? Good Men Project. Retrieved December 20, 2011, from http://goodmenproject.com/sex-relationships/why-do-we-demonize-men-who-are-honest-about-their-sexual-needs/.

Thorn, C. (2012). *Confessions of a pickup artist chaser: Long interviews with hideous men.* Author.

Tokar, D. M., & Jome, L. M. (1998). Masculinity, vocational interests, and career choice traditionality: Evidence for a fully mediated model. *Journal of Counseling Psychology, 45,* 424–435.

Tolman, D. L. (2002). *Dilemmas of desire: Teenage girls talk about sexuality.* Cambridge, MA: Harvard University Press.

Tolman, D. L., & Porche, M. V. (2000). The Adolescent Femininity Ideology Scale: Development and validation of a new measure for girls. *Psychology of Women Quarterly, 24,* 365–376.

Tolman, D. L., Spencer, R., Harmon, T., Rosen-Reynoso, M., & Striepe, M. (2004). Getting close, staying cool: Early adolescent boys' experiences with romantic relationships. In N. Way & J. Chu (Eds.), *Adolescent boys: Exploring diverse cultures of boyhood* (pp. 235–255). New York: New York University Press.

Tolman, D. L., Striepe, M. I., & Harmon, T. (2003). Gender matters: Constructing a model of adolescent sexual health. *Journal of Sex Research, 40,* 4–12.

Tooby, J., & Cosmides, L. (2005). Conceptual foundations of evolutionary psychology. In D. M. Buss (Ed.), *Handbook of evolutionary psychology* (pp. 5–67). Hoboken, NJ: Wiley.

Townsend, K. (1996). *Manhood at Harvard: William James and others.* Cambridge, MA: Harvard University Press.

Trachtenberg, P. (1988). *The Casanova complex: Compulsive lovers and their women.* New York: Simon & Schuster.

Turner, J. C. (1999). Some current issues in research on social identity and self-categorization theories. In N. Ellemers, R. Spears, & B. Doosje (Eds.), *Social identity: Context, commitment, content* (pp. 6–34). Oxford, England: Blackwell.

Turner, J. S. (2011). Sex and the spectacle of music videos: An examination of the portrayal of race and sexuality in music videos. *Sex Roles, 64*, 173–191.

Twenge, J. M. (1997a). Attitudes toward women, 1970–1995. *Psychology of Women Quarterly, 21*, 35–51.

Twenge, J. M. (1997b). Changes in masculine and feminine traits over time: A meta-analysis. *Sex Roles, 36*, 305–325.

Tyre, P., Murr, A., Juarez, V., Underwood, A., Springen, K., & Wingert, P. (2006, January 30). The trouble with boys: They're kinetic, maddening, and failing at school. *Newsweek.* Retrieved April 10, 2012, from http://www.thedailybeast.com/newsweek/2006/01/29/the-trouble-with-boys.html.

Udry, J. R., & Bearman, P. S. (1998). New methods for new research on adolescent sexual behavior. In R. Jessor (Ed.), *New perspectives on adolescent risk behavior* (pp. 241–269). Cambridge, England: Cambridge University Press.

U.S. Census Bureau. (2008a). *Conversion from analog to digital-TV.* Washington, DC: Author.

U.S. Census Bureau. (2008b). *Estimated median age at first marriage, by sex: 1890 to the present.* Washington, DC: Author.

U.S. Census Bureau. (2011). Children/1 by presence and type of parent(s), race, and Hispanic origin/2: 2011. Washington, DC: Author.

van Ijzendoorn, M. H., & Sagi, A. (1999). Cross-cultural patterns of attachment: Universal and contextual dimensions. In J. Cassidy & P. R. Shaver (Eds.), *Handbook of attachment* (pp. 713–734). New York: Guilford Press.

Vigil, J. M. (2007). Asymmetries in the friendship preferences and social styles of men and women. *Human Nature, 18*, 143–161.

Vogel, D. L., Wester, S. R., Heesacker, M., & Madon, S. (2003). Confirming gender stereotypes: A social role perspective. *Sex Roles, 48*, 519–528.

Vygotsky, L. (1962). *Thought and language.* New York: MIT Press & Wiley.

Wade, J. C. (1998). Male reference group identity dependence: A theory of male identity. *Counseling Psychologist, 26*, 349–383.

Wallace, M. (2011). Miami Heat address crying comments. ESPN.com. Retrieved December 19, 2011, from http://espn.go.com/espn/print?id=6191031&type=story.

Wallis, C. (2011). Performing gender: A content analysis of gender display in music videos. *Sex Roles, 64*, 160–172.

Walsh, J., & Ward, L. M. (2010). Magazine reading and involvement and young adults' sexual health knowledge, efficacy, and behaviors. *Journal of Sex Research, 47*, 285–300.

Ward, L. M. (1995). Talking about sex: Common themes about sexuality in the prime-time television programs children and adolescents view most. *Journal of Youth and Adolescence, 24*, 595–615.

Ward, L. M. (2002). Does television exposure affect emerging adults' attitudes and assumptions about sexual relationships? Correlational and experimental confirmation. *Journal of Youth and Adolescence, 31*, 1–15.

Ward, L. M. (2003). Understanding the role of entertainment media in the sexual socialization of American youth: A review of empirical research. *Developmental Review, 23*, 347–388.

Ward, L. M., Epstein, M., Caruthers, A., & Merriwether, A. (2011). Men's media use, sexual cognitions, and sexual risk behavior: Testing a mediational model. *Developmental Psychology, 47*, 592–602.

Ward, L. M., & Friedman, K. (2006). Using TV as a guide: Associations between television viewing and adolescents' sexual attitudes and behavior. *Journal of Research on Adolescence, 16*, 133–156.

Ward, L. M., Hansbrough, E., & Walker, E. (2005). Contributions of music video exposure to black adolescents' gender and sexual schemas. *Journal of Adolescent Research, 20*, 143–166.

Ward, L. M., & Harrison, K. (2005). The impact of media use on girls' beliefs about gender roles, their bodies, and sexual relationships: A research synthesis. In E. Cole & J. H. Daniels (Eds.), *Featuring females: Feminist analyses of media* (pp. 3–23). Washington, DC: American Psychological Association.

Ward, L. M., Merriwether, A., & Caruthers, A. (2006). Breasts are for men: Media, masculinity ideologies, and men's beliefs about women's bodies. *Sex Roles, 55*, 703–714.

Way, N. (2004). Intimacy, desire, and distrust in the friendships of adolescent boys. In N. Way & J. Y. Chu (Eds.), *Adolescent boys: Exploring diverse cultures of boyhood* (pp. 167–196). New York: New York University Press.

Way, N. (2011). *Deep secrets: Boys' friendships and the crisis of connection.* Cambridge, MA: Harvard University Press.

Weinstock, H., Berman, S., & Cates, W., Jr. (2004). Sexually transmitted diseases among American youth: Incidence and prevalence estimates, 2000. *Perspectives on Sexual and Reproductive Health, 36*, 6–10.

Weitzer, R., & Kubrin, C. E. (2009). Misogyny in rap music: A content analysis of prevalence and meanings. *Men and Masculinities, 12*, 3–29.

Wells, B. E., & Twenge, J. M. (2005). Changes in young people's sexual behavior and attitudes, 1943–1999: A cross-temporal meta-analysis. *Review of General Psychology, 9*, 249–261.

Welsh, D. P., Haugen, P. T., Widman, L., Darling, N., & Grello, C. M. (2005). Kissing is good: A developmental investigation of sexuality in adolescent romantic couples. *Sexuality Research and Social Policy, 2*(4), 32–41.

Welsh, D. P., Rostosky, S. S., & Kawaguchi, M. C. (2000). A normative perspective of adolescent girls' developing sexuality. In C. B. Travis & J. W. White (Eds.), *Sexuality, society, and feminism* (pp. 111–140). Washington, DC: American Psychological Association.

Wibowo, E., Schellhammer, P., & Wassersug, R. J. (2011). Role of estrogen in normal male function: Clinical implications for patients with prostate cancer on androgen deprivation therapy. *Journal of Urology, 185,* 17–23.

Wienke, C. (2005). Male sexuality, medicalization, and the marketing of Cialis and Levitra. *Sexuality & Culture, 9,* 29–57.

Wight, D. (1994). Boys' thoughts and talk about sex in a working class locality of Glasgow. *Sociological Review, 42,* 703–737.

William T. Grant Commission on Work, Family and Citizenship. (1988). *The forgotten half: Pathways to success for America's youth and young families.* Washington, DC: Author.

Wolak, J., Mitchell, K. J., & Finkelhor, D. (2002). Close online relationships in a national sample of adolescents. *Adolescence, 37,* 441–455.

Wolak, J., Mitchell, K. J., & Finkelhor, D. (2003). Escaping or connecting? Characteristics of youth who form close online relationships. *Journal of Adolescence, 26,* 105–119.

Woods, J. L., Shew, M. L., Tu, W., Ofner, S., Ott, M. A., & Fortbenberry, J. D. (2006). Patterns of oral contraceptive pill-taking and condom use among adolescent contraceptive pill users. *Journal of Adolescent Health, 39,* 381–387.

World Health Organization. (2004). *Adolescent pregnancy: Issues in adolescent health and development.* Geneva: Author.

Worthington, R. L., & Mohr, J. J. (2002). Theorizing heterosexual identity development. *Counseling Psychologist, 30,* 491–495.

Worthington, R. L., Navarro, R. L., Savoy, H. B., & Hampton, D. (2008). Development, reliability, and validity of the Measure of Sexual Identity Exploration and Commitment (MOSIEC). *Developmental Psychobiology, 44,* 22–33.

Yates, M., & Youniss, J. (1996). A developmental perspective on community service in adolescence. *Social Development, 5,* 85–111.

Zimmer-Gembeck, M. J. (2002). The development of romantic relationships and adaptations in the system of peer relationships. *Journal of Adolescent Health, 31,* 216–225.

Zimmer-Gembeck, M. J., & Helfand, M. (2008). Ten years of longitudinal research on U.S. adolescent sexual behavior: Developmental correlates of sexual intercourse, and the importance of age, gender and ethnic background. *Developmental Review, 28,* 153–224.

Zimmer-Gembeck, M. J., Siebenbruner, J., & Collins, W. A. (2004). A prospective study of intraindividual and peer influences on adolescents' heterosexual romantic and sexual behavior. *Archives of Sexual Behavior, 33,* 381–394.

About the Author

. . . .

Andrew Smiler's research examines masculinity and sexuality. His sexuality research, which he conducts primarily with fifteen- to twenty-five-year-olds, focuses on normative aspects of sexual development, such as age and perception of first kiss, first "serious" relationship, and first intercourse. His research also examines definitions of masculinity, including such terms as "jock," "nerd," and "rebel," as well as the connections to preferred media. This research includes males and females, from teens through older adults. Smiler also examines the ways that researchers have defined and approached masculinity and gender.

Smiler obtained BA degrees in psychology and mathematics from Virginia Tech, followed by an MA in clinical psychology from Towson University. After five years as a family therapist, he returned to school and earned a PhD in developmental psychology from the University of New Hampshire.

For more information, please visit Smiler's Web site: http://andrewsmiler.com/.

Follow him on Twitter: @andrewsmiler.

Index

DETERMINED FICTIONS

LEE CLARK MITCHELL

Determined Fictions

American Literary Naturalism

Columbia University Press
New York

Taking Determinism Seriously

LITERARY NATURALISM has never enjoyed an easy time with the critics, perhaps because even admirers have felt compelled to concede two crippling points: that naturalism offers a behavioral model encountered nowhere in life, and that its style falls woefully short of the standards deemed appropriate for art. Ever since 1868, when Émile Zola heralded a new fiction of determinism—of characters "completely dominated by their nerves and blood, without free will"[1]— readers have taken a perverse delight in naturalism's fateful plots. Yet narratives of victims beleaguered by events have rarely inclined those same readers to praise the dislocated styles that seem so characteristic of the mode. Only occasionally has the "power" often attributed to literary naturalism seemed anything like a just compensation for its apparent lack of craft. Among more discriminating readers, in fact, the less said about craft, the better.

For a variety of reasons, the naturalist "movement" attracted less

interest abroad than it did in America, which has had the effect of
making the debate on its literary status more pressing here than
elsewhere. The basic terms of that debate, however, have altered
little in more than a century—and this despite changing tastes and
theories that have dramatically reshaped the literary canon. The critical bench mark applied to naturalism remains for most the same as
ever, accepted by advocates and detractors alike because it is based
on a common judgment: that the naturalists devised forceful plots
for what otherwise seems rather thin as philosophy, and yet that
their writing rattles and creaks. Some have simply attributed these
flaws to the very premise of naturalism, assuming that only incompetent writers could be drawn to so limited a vision of human
behavior. Whatever their views of determinism, however, few would
deny Zola's identification of the philosophy with naturalism.

Despite an astonishing variety in writers as different as Stephen
Crane and Theodore Dreiser; despite the refusal of Crane and Jack
London ever to accept the naturalist label; despite the failure of all
but Dreiser to persist in the mode throughout a career, or of any
writer to acknowledge a common thread to their collective efforts:
despite all this, a consensus on American naturalism has emerged.
The alleged movement's "classic" phase occurred near the turn of
the century, so all concede, and further agree that it consists primarily of works by a central quartet of writers: Crane, Dreiser, London,
and Frank Norris. Sometimes included as well are novels by Harold
Frederic and Hamlin Garland, Edith Wharton, David Graham Phillips, and Upton Sinclair. The usual reason for including these texts,
notwithstanding their notable differences, is that each depicts the
range of human activity as if determined, not free. Each one as well
supposedly offers a Darwinian version of literary realism that elabo-
rates the ever fuller, ever more oppressive constraints of heredity and
environment.[2]

Darwin's theory formed only part of a larger intellectual upheaval
that supposedly cleared the ground of religious myths and humanis-
tic sentiments. Science had confidently taken the field, as announced
at the time by one of its most prominent spokesman, Ernst Haeckel:

> The great struggle between the determinist and the indeterminist,
> between the opponent and the sustainer of the freedom of the will,
> has ended to-day, after more than two thousand years, completely
> in favor of the determinist. The human will has no more freedom

than that of the higher animals, from which it differs only in degree, not in kind . . . We now know that each act of the will is as fatally determined by the organization of the individual and as dependent on the momentary condition of his environment as every other psychic activity.[3]

Accompanying this pride in the newly discovered laws of human behavior was a corresponding assurance in a new literary aesthetic, expressed some years earlier by the very man responsible for popularizing Social Darwinism. "In a good modern work of imagination," pronounced Herbert Spencer, echoing Zola, "the events are the proper products of the characters living under given conditions, and cannot at will be changed in their order or kind."[4] All that naturalist authors now needed to consider in their art were "given conditions"—a proposition so self-evident to Spencer's contemporaries that subsequent definitions of naturalism have focused on the characteristic conditions favored by its authors.

It will become clear in the opening chapter why this line of reasoning seems misguided to me—why naturalism refuses to be reduced to a "distinctive array of features," whether of particular scenes, or special themes, or characters and kinds of activities.[5] Still, the logic of adducing such features continues to seem attractive to critics, perhaps because many assume that determinism in fiction must mean "pessimistic realism"—a low-rent version, as it were, of efforts by George Eliot and William Dean Howells. Even those who rightly reject so reductive an equation rarely go on to envision the more profound implications of determinism for narrative.[6] Instead, they too have turned to supposedly appropriate themes and materials, or put the issue aside entirely in favor of other literary models. Philip Fisher, for instance, argues that naturalism consists of "the plot of decline," while June Howard more broadly identifies the "genre" with "documentary organization, the plot of decline, [and] the incorporation of melodramatic and sentimental formulas"; Eric Sundquist asserts that in naturalism "the abnormal becomes the barely submerged norm," resulting in a "Gothic *intensification of detail* that approaches the allegorical"; Alfred Habegger announces instead that the greatest triumph of naturalism is its defense of "American masculinity," while for Mark Seltzer, "an autonomous and masturbatory economy of production characterizes the discourse of naturalism generally"; Walter Benn Michaels identifies that discourse with "the

working-out of a set of conflicts between pretty things and curious ones, material and representation, hard money and soft, beast and soul."[7] These, among the best younger critics, persuade us to reconsider naturalism through inventive, sometimes trenchant readings of individual texts. But they do so all by giving short shrift to the very determinism they grant as its premise.

Perhaps this neglect has occurred because of the kinds of difficult issues raised by a necessitarian vision, which in any case seem to lie in the province of philosophy rather than that of literary criticism. Still, current work in narratology encourages us to turn our attention to questions like, How can an action be shown to be impersonally caused rather than motivated? or, When does fiction dissociate an agent's will from a world of events? or, What does lack of responsibility entail in terms of narrative perspective, or plot sequence, or even syntax itself? To treat such questions with philosophical rigor is necessarily to confront head-on the "problem" of naturalist style. Its irritating repetitions and dislocations, its grammatical excesses and wrenching maneuvers cannot any longer be curtly dismissed as the irrelevant lapses of incompetent writers; nor can we simply assume it is enough to know Theodore Dreiser is not Henry James. We need, if only for the moment, to relax the stranglehold of literary "standards" in order to appreciate how fully any enacted philosophy depends on its style—or rather, to recall that the two are one and the same, and that an extreme philosophy can only be realized in correspondingly extreme styles. Inquiring thus into the sometimes awkward, invariably disruptive styles of determinism may well compel us into a larger reconsideration of narrative standards themselves. In any event, we will discover how much a larger pattern to grammatical improprieties can alter some of the deepest assumptions we bring to bear on the world around us.

Nearly forty years ago, Saul Bellow commented on Dreiser's reception by wondering why "no one has thought to ask just what the 'bad writing' of a powerful novelist signifies."[8] Now we can venture an answer: "bad writing" (at least in the hands of the naturalists) signifies determinism, and it may well be that our scorn for the former is linked to our general aversion to the latter. Critics of naturalism have for far too long avoided its problematic style, and have done so (I would assert) because they inadequately acknowledge its philosophical terms. My approach can most simply be distinguished from other studies of naturalism, then, in the seriousness

with which I explore the narrative effects of determinism.[9] That is my reason for turning first to recent work in moral philosophy, which differs from that of the naturalists' contemporaries (William James, say, or Charles Peirce) in striving to clarify the distinctly narrative implications of any such premise.[10] Peter Strawson, for instance, has observed that the traditional opposition of free will and determinism corresponds to an ongoing conflict in our most basic human attitudes, and in particular those attitudes we cannot help but maintain toward each other. Understanding that conflict helps us to see that the problem for naturalism is one of encouraging readers to adopt a set of attitudes associated with a necessitarian view.

Even more radically, Thomas Nagel claims that our accounts of behavior stand always at odds with themselves, and that therefore the assumptions we project on each other immerse us in a realm of "moral luck"—a realm in which little we do seems to lie within our control. Not only does Nagel's suggestion alter our understanding of naturalist plots, but it helps to clarify as well why their textual rhythms are so disruptive. And to begin to think in this way about the effects of sometimes perturbing prose styles is to realize how a new angle of vision can alter literary flaws into narrative strengths. Closer attention to the texture of naturalism—from its selection of words to its structure of scenes—reveals that the "lapses" most critics feel compelled to excuse are in direct support of its premise. Resist and even resent as we do the misplaced phrases and unseemly repetitions, the "power" of naturalism is established through a perspective that thoroughly unsettles our views. In short, a concession to standards of style obscures an understanding of what the naturalists achieved.

The naturalists, contrary to the central claim advanced by proponents ever since Zola, did not simply substitute a mechanistic determinism for the assumed agency by the realist novel. In far more searching endeavors, they depicted the ways in which "agency" itself is constructed only after the fact, made up as we go along in the stories we tell about the moments of our lives. The imposition of causality and motive on a series of past events is, as recent theoreticians have observed, the inevitable consequence of narration itself. What distinguishes the naturalists, however, is their sensitivity to the logic that informs such rationalization, not just at the level of narrative plot but at those of syntax and verbal style. The collective agenda behind their efforts was nothing less than to expose that

logic, thereby to compel a larger reconsideration of the assumptions we hold about the coherent self.

These rather large claims have implications that can only be addressed in local terms, which is why four of the chapters that follow offer readings of individual texts—one apiece by each of the major naturalists. Before turning to particulars, however, we need to examine the overall process by which characters are created who remain determined by forces beyond themselves. An extended introduction initially does this by considering the kind of moral vision the naturalists repudiated—a vision exemplified in the work of William Dean Howells, Henry James, and Mark Twain. Idiosyncratic as was each of these realists, they all presented characters as "subjective selves" who possessed clear capacities for restraint and responsibility. By contrast, Crane, Dreiser, London, and Norris rejected the very category of the "self," creating characters who seem little more than occasions for passing events—who merely mark the bodily intersections of outer force and inner desire. Realist authors enforced a moral perspective on narrative action, a perspective involving the same considerations of intention and responsibility we habitually project on each other (and onto fictional characters as well). Those seemingly "natural" projective impulses are precisely what naturalists seek to subvert, and they do so in two major ways: through distinctive means of presenting plot crisis; and through stylistic strategies that serve to defamiliarize our sense of the "self."

Realist crises, first of all, occur typically in scenes of deliberation, which means that individuals are defined through an elaborate process of responsible choice; they seem to possess moral selves that are greater than the sum of forces that go into making them. Naturalist characters, on the contrary, are ever unable to forestall their own actions when a combination of inner and outer forces otherwise impels them. They may respond to experience out of a similar constellation of yearnings and motives, but they lack in addition the wills that would enable them to resist desire or alter behavior. Yet the premise of agency is subverted in naturalism through means more subtle than plot or motive, including most importantly prose style. Its repetitions, for instance, expose the absence of a controlling will, and do so altogether variously—whether through reiterated scenes, or stuttering syntax, or characters psychologically doubling each other. Contrary to conventional wisdom, in other words, this opening chapter argues that naturalism forms as complex a mode as

realism, with as extensive a repertoire of characters, events, plots, settings, and styles. The sole handicap under which naturalism works is the requirement (introduced by its very premise) to disrupt the habitual and powerful process by which we create not only ourselves but each other as responsible agents.

In shifting from theoretical speculation to the specifics of naturalist texts, chapter 2 turns to London's "To Build a Fire" (1906) for two reasons: because London has rarely been read for his style, and because the story is so frequently interpreted as an account of irresponsible negligence. On the contrary, the narrative presents an unnamed man's fatal incompetence so as to emphasize the importance of circumstance, not character. Negating through verbal and scenic repetitions our customary categories of selfhood, the text succeeds at last in discrediting any ascription of responsibility. And by denying all but entirely the importance of contingency in events, it not only derails assumptions of human autonomy but elegantly stops narrative time altogether. Still, the story also reveals how essential the notion of agency is to narrative, even when that capacity has been clearly excluded. Blame is as misplaced a response in this world as either regret or guilt, and yet the character, the narrator, and the reader as well are all impelled to reintroduce the categories. The story becomes, therefore, as much an account of that recalcitrant narrativizing impulse as it is of a man's death.

Just as "story-telling" forms the general problem in London's text, the more complicated process of constructing a "self" haunts Dreiser's *American Tragedy* (1925). In chapter 3, I show that narrative repetition, relentless foreshadowing, and psychic doubling all work to deny an autonomous selfhood to Clyde Griffiths. His actions, in fact, are little more than the sum of circumstances beyond his control. Raised to success by the same plot motion that plunges him gradually downward toward failure, he endures the paradox of being lifted socially through events that coerce him toward death. Throughout the novel, moreover, a process of psychic doubling highlights the central repetition of Clyde in his lover, and renders his "murder" of Roberta Alden a death of the double that confirms the narrative's psychological determinism. The supposed agency of a coherent subject is again no more than a fiction that has been pieced together retrospectively, in the lengthy trial of Clyde for Roberta's murder. It is useless to complain about the "repetitious" plot, or Clyde's "failure to learn," or his "undeveloped" character, since

these are part of the very problem the novel works to illuminate. From this perspective, *An American Tragedy* interests us less for its relentless determinism than for its revelation of the disparity between Clyde's apparent "self" and the circumstances that define him.

What allows this contradiction to be accepted, even perpetuated, by readers is language itself—the primary deterministic force in my reading of naturalism. That is the reason for turning next to Norris' *Vandover and the Brute* (1914), in order to focus attention on the moral suasions of narrative discourse in a novel commonly read as a textbook illustration of mechanistic determinism. More narrowly than Dreiser, Norris defines his hero as accommodating to circumstance, so much so that in the alliance of inner and outer experience he comes to seem indistinguishable from his surroundings. Even so, and despite his affliction with a disease that reduces him to animal howls and yelps, Vandover is destroyed less by natural forces than by the dictates of social convention. Like Crane's Bowery heroine, Maggie (who undergoes a similar decline and fall), he is blind to the self-destroying morality by which his actions are judged. What makes that morality possible, moreover, is the structure of conventional language itself—not only in Vandover's society but our own; not only in the world represented by the novel but in the readerly premises quietly but firmly reinforced by that representation. The very medium of naturalism is exposed as replete with assumptions about action and intention that encourage us, like Vandover, to accept moral labels for otherwise unaccountable events.

It is only a step from this verbal determinism to the specular absorption of Henry Fleming in Crane's *Red Badge of Courage* (1895). The conventional morality of ordinary language in Norris assumes visual form in Crane, as Henry actively learns to *see* the rationalizing narrative by which his culture ascribes responsibility to individuals. He can thus come to imagine that he is a "hero" by the end of the novel, even though the actions that change him emerge from nothing but a series of unaccountable desires. From our perspective, in fact, he appears fragmented by the very syntax of his presentation, leaving his emotions, thoughts, and behavior profoundly unaligned. Crane was aware of the powerful impulse (of readers as well as characters) to transform those contradictory impulses called "Henry Fleming" into a moral agent. At every point, he unsettles his narrative's tendency to become a coherent "story," the story in particular of Henry's "education" into heroic behavior. He dramatizes the propensity

of characters to interpret circumstances as warrants of identity, even as he establishes an ironic distance from his narrative through repetition and syntactic disruption. In the process, he leaves the reader with two rather clear alternatives: either to reproduce the moral "heroism" of Henry (and thus be duped by the text) or to deconstruct the illusion of "Henry Fleming" as a coherent personality.

Clearly, the "mechanisms" of literary naturalism belong less to some physical "universe of force" than to the grammatical pressures of distinctively verbal realms. Yet in shifting attention away from scientific to linguistic forms of determinism, I have been intent on developing a further argument based on my selected texts: that each one defines a contradiction in its central character, between a self-image as an autonomous, integrated, freely willing agent, and the narrative's revelation of him as no more than a set of conflicting desires. That is the reason my sequence of chapters defies the customary chronology that opens with Crane and ends with Dreiser (usually because of their published dates), in order to establish a larger logic in my treatment of linguistic determinism. One formulation of that logic is as the passage of a misplaced morality gradually into the text, as it were, from an omniscient narrator to characters who seem increasingly benighted: from London's inculpating narrative voice; to the retrospective judgment of Clyde's peers; to Vandover's thoughtful adoption of an irrelevant social code; finally, to Henry's incoherent self-definition. As well, however, my sequence of chapters is informed by an obverse logic, as a transition in the kinds of constraints that determine a person's behavior: from London's intense physical world of intractable circumstance, to Dreiser's fraught psychological realm of uncontrollable desire, to Norris' social domain of ineluctable convention, to Crane's integration of all three. I hasten to add that the hierarchy implied by this sequence from material to cultural spheres reveals nothing special about each author's particular accomplishment. What my readings *do* reveal is how fully each context requires the other, if sometimes only implicitly, and how much the differences between them emerge through verbal stresses and narrative slants.

For too long, critics have simply avoided the disturbing language of naturalism, turning instead to the historical conditions that drew a generation to so singular a philosophy, or focusing on the naturalists' shaping interests in biology and psychology, or even adducing biographical sources for fictional materials. More recently, New Histo-

ricists have shifted our attention to contemporary texts in economics, sociology, and philosophy in order to reveal the structural correspondences they share with naturalist fiction. Each of these perspectives helps inform our understanding of that curious body of work, and each is valuable enough in its own right to warrant further critical efforts. Indeed, I myself have elsewhere read naturalist texts as the products of socioeconomic conditions, and those interested in such questions should turn to studies devoted to them.[11] My argument here, however, is a formalist one, based on the assumption that naturalism's strengths are apparent not through cultural influences nor through authorial motives inferred from other sources (Dreiser's editorial pronouncements, say, or Norris' essays, or London's letters). What draws us to naturalism is not what lies *behind* its narrative structures but what exists *in* the conflicts and disruptions we feel as we read it even today.[12]

The reason we continue to experience this sense of disruption is because we project a series of expectations that go unfulfilled—expectations instilled in us by a tradition of literary realism. Other critics have generally seen naturalism as an extension of realism, as if in a kind of ongoing dialogue with that earlier, more comforting mode. My argument is, on the contrary, that naturalism poses an attack on the reader by undermining narrative assumptions that realist authors invoked in their fiction, assumptions by which we otherwise more generally author our own selves into life. The naturalists assaulted the reader by writing iconoclastically, inverting the strategies implicit in any structuring of a moral self. It hardly matters that this description of their efforts would have been incomprehensible to them, except as a way of reminding ourselves of their lack of interest in abstract philosophy and, more particularly, in any sustained or systematic analysis of determinism. The important point is that they constructed an assortment of convincing determinist models by rejecting the premise essential to realism.

To reiterate, the naturalists' most radical innovation was in their perspective, not their material, and thereby entailed far more than a simple embrace of stupider characters, or more squalid subjects, or less optimistic plots than had been found before in fiction. Such commonplaces of literary history ignore the extreme reversals of a determinist logic, suggesting that naturalism was little more than a tedious (and awkward) rehearsal of possibilities already mapped out by realist authors. Nothing could be less true of the remarkable

variety evinced by naturalist writers from their unusual premise—a variety that belies any single set of principles, thematic, structural, or stylistic. And that is part of the problem, since supposedly representative claims gloss over the idiosyncracies that make particular narratives naturalistic.

Still, it should already be clear why the usual criticisms seem to me misguided—those attacking mechanical characters, say, or excessive repetition, or disjunctive syntax. Instead of liabilities, these elements actively generate the narrative power of naturalism, which unsettles our most cherished conceptions of agency precisely through distortions of usage. To take naturalism seriously is to recognize how deeply we resist a determinist vision, how predisposed we are to assume capacities we cannot prove we possess. Conversely, to accept (if only for the moment) the prospect that determinism may actually be true is to recognize how fully our assumptions about character and event, like those of prose style, may be based on nothing other than convention.

I began thinking about this book in 1981–82, at the Institute for Research in the Humanities, Madison, Wisconsin, and completed writing it in 1986–87, at the National Humanities Center, Research Triangle Park, North Carolina. For generous assistance from both institutions, as well as from the Henry Huntington Library, I am sincerely grateful. Over this period, friends, colleagues, and students have helped me to sharpen ideas, sometimes unaware of the transformations they prompted in my thinking. Terse acknowledgment hardly expresses the depth of my gratitude to Carolyn Abbate, Wye Allanbrook, Martha Banta, Montgomery Furth, William Howarth, Howard Horsford, Kathryn Humphreys, Jules Law, Marta Petrusewicz, Thomas Strychacz, David Van Leer, and David Wyatt. A few gave generously of their time in reading the entire manuscript, and although I have not always followed advice, theirs has been always encouraging: Frank Bergon, Douglas Gordon, Linda Kauffman, David Leverenz, John Carlos Rowe, and Garrett Stewart. For opportunities to try out ideas in lectures, I want to thank Davidson College, Emory University, North Carolina State University, the University of Rochester, and the University of Wisconsin. Likewise, I wish to thank the editors of the following journals for allowing me to include revised versions of essays that originally appeared in their pages: chapter 2 in *Journal of Modern Literature*, chapter 3 in *Novel*, and chapter 4 in *Papers in Language and Literature*.

DETERMINED FICTIONS

I.

Naturalism and the Excluded Self

MOST OF us take for granted an ability to decide what we are going to do: whether to go to work or to the dogs, to join the Marines or the Communist Party, to continue this sentence or fly off to Hong Kong. We tend to assume not only that we are the kind of beings who act in the world, but that our actions (at least the important ones) result from choices we have consciously made. And we treat others similarly, judging them by the choices we can infer from the actions they perform. Yet the more we reflect on this assumption, the less coherent it comes to seem, as we grow to appreciate how fully we are all a part of the world beyond our control. We begin to wonder how to distinguish our actions from other events in that world, which leads in turn to a consideration of what it would mean for us to be somehow determined. Would we possess a sense of ourselves akin to the one we presently have and, if so, would we extend that sense of the self's capacities to others? Would we deliber-

ate about matters of choice, or instead give up the process? And would our conception of responsibility come to seem as irrelevant as it in fact now was? These questions all emerge from a classic philosophical crux about freedom and action—one that reveals how sharply opposed are our deepest beliefs about ourselves. On the one hand, we are part of a world that appears to be structured by laws of causality; on the other, when our actions are reduced to those laws, we seem to disappear as responsible agents. Determinism appears to fit our normal conception of the physical world and yet at the same time it leaves us feeling, in the words of one philosopher, that "there is no elbow room left for our own selves."[1]

From the beginning, this paradox has inspired masterworks of Western literature: Oedipus resisting the oracle's truth, Job bowing to an implacable God, and countless tragedies since in which noble characters confront untoward events. Artists would not extend this conception to depictions of lower-class life, however, until well into the nineteenth century, by which time innovations in fictional realism had so altered mimetic conventions as to lend the illusion that characters were fully immersed in a world of recalcitrant things. Realism bound characters ever more firmly to the demands and contingencies of everyday life, and yet it significantly continued to treat individuals as moral agents. No matter that they were coerced more than ever before by the bonds of class and gender, characters were still expected to take responsibility for the course of their lives —no less so than when the sole constraints had been circumstance and temperament. Readers, that is, were expected to judge them no less by a notion of moral worth.[2]

A generation after the realists, the naturalists sharply rejected this view, exploring instead the prospect that ethics might be irrelevant to the lives we live. Or as Jacques Loeb pointedly asked in *The Mechanistic Conception of Life* (1912): "If our existence is based on the play of blind forces and only a matter of chance; if we ourselves are only chemical mechanisms—how can there be an ethics for us? The answer is, that our instincts are the root of our ethics and that the instincts are just as hereditary as is the form of our body." We end up, in other words, approving simply "what instinct compels us 'machine-like' to do."[3] So strict a causal logic would have inspired the realists with genuine horror, not only at its stark amorality but at the evident thinness of its narrative claims. The naturalists, on the contrary, felt at once a release from outmoded Victorian ethics and a rekindled hope in the possibilities now available to fiction.

Despite the sharp philosophical break of the naturalists with their predecessors, few critics have agreed on what distinguishes their efforts from literary realism.[4] Consistently, the debate bogs down into a discussion of aspects of either mode, with everyone simply assuming the problem is a matter of identifying salient features. The difficulty in this approach is that both categories come to seem too restrictive, as problematic texts are excluded on the basis simply of character or plot. To take the obvious example: if middle-class life as delineated by William Dean Howells is assumed to represent the realist range, then naturalism will by default consist (in the words of one offended critic) of the "sordid, squalid, dirty, slimy, repulsive, brutal, and pathetic."[5] And by that same logic, a narrative as restrained as London's *Martin Eden* (1908) will seem to share little with such graphic texts as Upton Sinclair's *Jungle* (1906) or Norris' *McTeague* (1899).

Yet nothing requires us to adopt this method of contrasting naturalism with realism—of adducing distinctive features of scenic structure or narrative detail, of character type or patterns of plot—especially since a more flexible approach exists in their alternative conceptions of a person. Simply put, realism assumes that individuals are responsible for their lives, while naturalism offers up characters who are no more than events in the world. Or as Richard Chase observed years ago, the naturalist character "seems to *have* no self."[6] Realist characters, by contrast, were provided with as full an illusion of selfhood as possible, having been granted the powers to choose and to act in contexts readily familiar to readers. When naturalists occasionally placed their characters in contexts similarly familiar, it was always to deny them recognizable capacities, with the effect of making their circumstances seem themselves somehow alien.

Later, this chapter develops the claim that naturalism fictionalizes the kind of character who might exist in a determined world. For the moment, however, we need to articulate a clearer conception of certain terms, including most prominently "self" and "character." And the best way to appreciate how thoroughly the naturalists redefined those terms is to see what the realists meant by them, perhaps especially as reflected in their narrative enactments of responsible choice. After all, the naturalists repudiated ethics not primarily as a matter of philosophical principal, but out of frustration with the inadequacies they found in narrative forms of representation.

Choice, or Restraint?

SCHOLARS GENERALLY agree that the major American realists are Mark Twain, William Dean Howells, and Henry James, and agree further that their most representative "realist" novels are *Adventures of Huckleberry Finn* (1885), *The Rise of Silas Lapham* (1885), and *The Portrait of a Lady* (1881). Despite the diversity of these texts, moreover, few readers would hesitate to identify the single most powerful scene in each—each one a scene of moral crisis. Huck's ongoing bout between "a sound heart and a deformed conscience" climaxes in chapter 31, when he must decide between helping Jim escape or informing the runaway slave's owner. Should he send a letter to Miss Watson revealing Jim's whereabouts, or not?

> It was a close place. I took it [the letter] up, and held it in my hand. I was a trembling, because I'd got to decide, forever, betwixt two things, and I knowed it. I studied a minute, sort of holding my breath, and then says to myself:
> "All right, then, I'll *go* to hell"—and tore it up.[7]

The prospect of a similar hell faces Silas Lapham near the end of Howells' novel. Confronted by the humiliating prospect of bankruptcy, he is tempted to unload a worthless investment into the hands of gullible English investors:

> Every selfish interest of his nature joined with many obvious duties to urge him to consent. He did not see why he should refuse. There was no longer a reason. He was standing out alone for nothing, anyone else would say . . . He went in and shut the door, and by and by his wife heard him begin walking up and down; and then the rest of the night she lay awake and listened to him walking up and down.[8]

Much like Silas Lapham's ambulatory "rise" above self-interest, Isabel Archer's sedentary self-confrontation lasts through the night. Her crisis, however, is offered from her own tormented perspective in what James himself claimed was the finest sequence in the novel, chapter 42:

> After [Osmond] had gone she leaned back in her chair and closed her eyes; and for a long time, far into the night and still further, she sat in the still drawing-room, given up to her meditation. . . . What was coming—what was before them? That was her constant question. What would he do—what ought *she* to do? When a man hated his wife what did it lead to?[9]

By morning, Isabel will have moved beyond self-pity to recognize her responsibility for creating an unhappy marriage.

Huck, Silas, and Isabel are each presented through distinctive narrative voices: Twain's direct first-person vernacular, Howells' meditative third-person, and James' quietly mediatory free indirect discourse. Moreover, each character's experience is thoroughly unlike those of the other two. Yet the important link connecting the three is that each faces a crucial turning point in his or her life, and each decides how best to act by accepting responsibility for circumstances. Divided between clear alternatives—whether to re-enslave Jim or help him go free; to defraud investors or bankrupt oneself; to honor a marital pledge or not—each character makes a difficult choice that involves substantial psychic discomfort. By doing so, each triumphs over self-serving considerations to redeem a belief in their moral integrity, defining a self that exists beyond the pressures of temptation and desire.

Notwithstanding considerable differences in setting, perspective, and tone, then, the three scenes reinforce a set of clear assumptions about the "self," assumptions intimated in the kinds of abstractions I have been using all along: "responsibility," "choice," "morality," "integrity." Twain, Howells, and James (and by extension, all American realists) conceived of the "self" as the "responsible self" out of the belief that individuals were to be known and judged from a moral perspective. The novelist was therefore, as Howells put it, "bound to distinguish so clearly that no reader of his may be misled, between what is right and what is wrong, what is noble and what is base, what is health and what is perdition, in the actions and characters he portrays."[10] Or as James more succinctly observed: "Every out-and-out realist . . . is a moralist." Little as they held in common, these writers cherished a belief in a moral universe (at least in this part of their careers).[11] Which means that their characters define themselves not by actions they *happen* to perform but by the very capacity for *choosing* certain actions over others.

Naturalism sometimes resembles realism in subject matter and plot development (even occasionally in its use of language), but their different conceptions of a person are revealed in the way they present moral quandaries. No naturalist character stands accountable for having acted out of desire, whether Sister Carrie beds her way to success or Susan Lennox her way to failure. Neither one is given alternatives or allowed to feel regret, nor is marriage and adultery viewed in either novel from the perspective established in *A Modern Instance* (1885), say, or *The Golden Bowl* (1908). Strictly speaking, determinism means that no one has any freedom of will, since everyone possesses more or less similar powers of agency in a self-consistent universe. If options exist that allow one person to act rather differently than he or she does, options must exist for others as well, making anyone's special inability in such a world (either real or fictional) a problem for psychopathology, not metaphysics. Of course, not everyone acts with equal responsibility in realist fiction, even though we apply the same standard in treating everyone as equally a responsible agent. By the same token, no one can escape being fully determined in naturalism, precluding anyone from being held accountable.[12]

This contrast in two sets of novels has led to surprising judgments, however, including the belief that naturalist characters are somehow unable to choose. Even a brief review controverts this belief, and does so despite the compulsions and circumstances that guarantee naturalist characters will always act as they do. The George Hurstwoods and Maggie Johnsons imagined by Dreiser and Crane, the Vandovers and Wolf Larsens of Norris and London: all appear troublingly diminished beings because they act over and over as they must. Yet however diminished, they still are able to choose the actions by which they are known.[13] Sister Carrie deliberately chooses to leave her family's care for Drouet, then chooses to leave Drouet for Hurstwood and in turn Hurstwood for the stage—along the way making countless other choices as well. The Swede in Crane's "The Blue Hotel" (1898) chooses (albeit drunkenly) to leave the hotel and enter a saloon, and then in a fit of rage to accost a gambler in what turns out to be a fatal mistake. Norris' hulk of a dentist, McTeague, and London's thoughtful Martin Eden make choices for fully different careers, but choices nonetheless. The point is that naturalist characters resemble their realist counterparts in nothing so much as being able to choose—in deliberating carefully before they act, after having considered among a full array of motives and desires.[14]

How then do these ostensibly different narrative modes actually differ? The question may not be easy but it is also happily not philosophical, since we need not distinguish the abstract claims of agency from necessity, say, or of motive from cause, nor do our criteria need to be otherwise philosophically watertight. Instead of testing the philosophical logic of the two positions, all we must do is identify the textual strategies associated with either mode, and the best place to begin is with the classic realist crises described above. Each of those scenes enacts a lengthy process of deliberation, a weighing of alternative actions through a thoughtful consideration of consequences. Yet notably, choice in each scene leads at first not to action but inaction. Huck, in the event, decides at last *not* to send his letter to Miss Watson; Silas *fails* to draw a conclusion (as he admits to his wife the next morning), thus allowing the crooked deal to collapse; and Isabel ends her long night by choosing *not* to leave Osmond. Later, of course, the three will act in accord with the decisions they have made here, but for the moment those decisions lead to restraint from obvious actions. And such instances of restraint only confirm a more general pattern by which realist characters appear to refuse easy options.[15]

Variously as the naturalists presented choice, they never did so in this way, having tacitly understood that when everything required for an action is present, determined characters cannot refrain. Because they always choose to act as their strongest desires dictate, their choices always seem predictable and outside their control. Carrie can refrain from impulse no better than Cowperwood or Henry Fleming, and McTeague hovering over Trina in the dentist's chair or Hurstwood fumbling at the safe door exemplify this inability to deflect desire. Naturalism illustrates the principle that the compulsion to act in a predictable fashion undermines our assumption of human agency. Gradually, we withdraw that assumption, since all we now need to explain any action are a set of conditions, not a responsible self.

Yet much as this view of compulsion contributes to an understanding of naturalism, it also fails to withstand scrutiny as a philosophical premise—exemplified in the realist scenes that have been adduced above. Despite my assertion that Huck refrains from action, for instance, the issue is more confused: Is "not-sending" the letter to Miss Watson truly a non-action or an action itself? The phrasing's very awkwardness attests to the awkwardness of the issue, but no philosopher would venture a conclusion on the evidence of the scene. Or again, since Huck follows his inclination in defiance of what he

"knows" is his duty, the scene would seem to refute Kant's twin requirements for both a good and freely willed action. It is as if Twain were shrewdly dismissing the Kantian conditions for praise and blame, exposing thereby the vacuousness of any strict moral logic. Further problems exist with this scene (as they do with crises in Howells and James), but our readerly response is unambiguous. Huck seems to us morally triumphant because he at last decides not to do what we had expected he would—or even thought he might do (and the simple tendency is enough). The "freight of expectations" we bring to the narrative has been effectively derailed.

The larger point at issue here is that a pair of literary strategies have evolved from the ongoing deadlock between free will and determinism, a deadlock nothing seems able to break short of Dr. Johnson's conversation-stopper: "Sir, we *know* our will is free, and *there's* an end on't."[16] Yet for skeptics unwilling to "end on't," the question consists not in which view to take but in how to take either one. For whatever else is true of both views, they involve a set of expectations placed willy-nilly on behavior. We need therefore to examine the hidden assumptions that structure the accounts we give in order to assess how those accounts reinforce either agency or determinism.

The recurrent solution devised by the realists as the best means of depicting agency was not to show characters freely acting but to show them freely *not* acting. Paradoxical as it sounds, the "will to will" meant to them the choice not to do, a distinction that clarifies the naturalists' preference for scenes of unrestrained action rather than those of choice forestalled. Nothing about choice itself denies determinism, after all, since characters opting for an alternative may still be determined to make that choice (indeed, this is precisely why naturalists did not shrink from portraying choice, as we have seen). Determinism simply implies an absolute responsiveness to forces that seem to have nothing to do with the character's "self." A.J. Ayer seems to have had this in mind in observing of the kleptomaniac that his deliberations are "irrelevant to his behavior. Whatever he resolved to do, he would steal all the same. And it is this that distinguishes him from the ordinary thief."[17] Naturalism regularly exploits this disjunction between resolution and action, anticipation and consequence, in order to let us imagine what determinism means. Realist characters withstand the forces that pressure them into action and announce their wills by not giving way once they have resolved

to restrain themselves—by standing firm in battle when momentarily overcome by fear, or refusing to submit to extortion although threatened by public exposure, or simply not raiding the refrigerator when on a diet. Naturalist characters, by contrast, will always accede to their strongest desire whatever it is they resolve to do.[18]

Will and desire are often conflated in discussions of literary naturalism and we need to recall that strong desires are not equivalent to a moral "will," any more than weak desires imply that one is somehow determined. The issue, again, is one not of logical proof but a reader's projective assumptions about the moral self caught in a world of constraints.[19] More than other realists, Henry James refined the issue by limiting his fiction to certain characteristic emphases, generic as well as economic. He turned most often to the supposedly weaker sex of an enervated class in the belief that well-born women were doubly insulated from the hurly-burly of a new finance capitalism. The limits of responsibility, he thought, could best be illustrated in the narrow contexts within which Victorian women moved. Since they were meant not to do but to be, the world came to them, not they to it, and Isabel Archer and her sisters define themselves by refusing what others assume they can only accept. Or as Ralph Touchett enthusiastically exclaims to Isabel: "What I mean is that I shall have the thrill of seeing what a young lady does who won't marry Lord Warburton" (133). By resisting social pressure and effectively deferring their own desires, James' women are able to achieve a series of distinctive moral triumphs.

Only gradually over the course of a long career, however, did James come to appreciate the full effect of various forms of restraint, and it is instructive to observe the shift in the kinds of resistance he imagined for his characters. At the end of his early novel, *The American* (1877), for instance, Christopher Newman confirms his final release from the grip of revenge by burning a letter which is all that incriminates the family that has wronged him. A year later, Daisy Miller asserts her youthful independence by flouting social decorum, as in turn does an older Isabel Archer in a rather more thoughtful if tormented fashion. Increasingly, James' characters learn the power of restraint in a line of development that culminates two decades later with *The Golden Bowl*, when Maggie Verver discovers her silent ability to break the "chain of causes and consequences." In the process of discovering how to mend her troubled marriage, she allows herself to do nothing more than resist her husband's willful

embrace: "Whatever he might do she mustn't be irresponsible. Yes, she was in his exerted grasp, and she knew what that was; but she was at the same time in the grasp of her conceived responsibility, and . . . of the two intensities, the second was presently to become the sharper."[20] The moment is crucial, initiating what will become a ruthless habit of self-restraint by which Maggie succeeds in compelling others to act on not only her own behalf but on that of an encompassing moral order as well. Her brilliant behavior, moreover, culminates three decades of Jamesian inquiry into the problem of responsible action and, more importantly, its effective dramatization. At times, James' ongoing fascination with renunciation in all its forms has been ascribed to his "negative imagination," but that does nothing to diminish the effect of that narrative pattern in revealing a character's moral autonomy.[21]

To reiterate, a basic realist strategy is to give at least the illusion of autonomy by having characters *not* act as one would have expected they would at moments of moral crisis. Because their "selves" depend upon neither the world outside nor their inner desires, they seem to have wills that allow them to act independently of each. And the greater the gap between impulse and act, the greater the moral capacity we seem willing to attribute to them. Part of the reason we do so is that we automatically imagine a narrative process, inferring for that temporal gap a progression in conscious thought: from hesitation through deliberation, and finally to a decision. We see these characters, as it were, narrating their way out of impulsive behavior. By contrast, naturalist characters are only rarely given to hesitation, and when they are—as is Hurstwood before the safe, or Clyde Griffiths in the boat, or Henry Fleming in battle—their hesitation leads not to a willed instance of restraint but merely to a postponement of the inevitable.

Since naturalist characters cannot defer or displace their insistent desires, they appear themselves displaced by the force of desire into a world of things. They gradually lose whatever distinctiveness they may have had from other objects, and come to seem appropriately measured by a straightforward, objective standard. The difference between such figures as Carrie Meeber and Isabel Archer, then, or between Clyde Griffiths and Huck Finn, lies most significantly in what Ellen Moers called the "thinness" of the former characters' consciousnesses.[22] Unable to define themselves independently of whatever it is to which they are drawn, naturalist characters appear

little more than windows on the world. In short, naturalism depicts the power of events to absorb such characters *into* the world, while realism celebrates instead a moral awareness *of* the kind of world in which teen-aged river-rats, rising businessmen, and self-preoccupied young women can test their growing capacities for ethical distinction.[23]

Two qualifications are in order: the first, philosophical; the second, literary. It should be clear by now that restraint itself forms no criterion of agency, since it can be induced as readily as any other kind of behavior.[24] Temperateness, that is, hardly constitutes philosophical proof of an autonomous will. We nonetheless respond to such situations before we pause to consider them logically and assume (at least initially) that such characters are not determined. This leads to the second qualification: that restraint in itself does not always serve to distinguish realist from naturalist actions, any more than does deliberation or choice. Its weakness as a category results in part from the way in which restraint is necessarily presented, not through clear-cut turns of plot but as a matter of narrative emphases —of more or less typical aspects of character that lend one the appearance of having a will. Even when restraint is made to seem in this fashion all but self-evident, representative instances of both modes are not always clear.

Consider a pair of classic texts: one a novel by Edith Wharton often cited as naturalist; the other a supposedly realist novel by Howells. Wharton's *House of Mirth* (1905) portrays Lily Bart as a vital, attractive, unmarried woman who knows she must win a rich husband to live in the manner to which she has long since grown accustomed. Bound by Victorian upper-class constraints, where unattached women are "brought up to be ornamental," she cannot escape a sense "of being something rootless and ephemeral, mere spin-drift of the whirling surface of existence, without anything to which the poor little tentacles of self could cling before the awful flood submerged them."[25] The novel bears out this impression in charting her long, impulsive, drifting decline from elegant houseguest of the rich to impoverished tenement dweller. The seemingly determinist pattern that culminates in Lily's suicide only confirms for many the novel's status as "pessimistic realism." Nonetheless, she does seem to have at least one moment of moral discrimination when she refuses to stoop to extortion to regain her lost social position. Like Christopher Newman similarly tempted, she burns the very

evidence that might save her: a packet of embarrassing letters that has fallen into her hands. Refraining (if once again, out of impulse) from a simply self-serving act, she defines the possibility of moral integrity by renouncing her desperate desires as naturalist characters are unable to do.

In the counter-example of Howells' *Modern Instance* (1882), the behavior of both central characters seems a function of forces beyond their control. Marcia Gaylord is driven by her passion for the journalist, Bartley Hubbard, and may have "wished to resist, but she could not try."[26] If Bartley's desires are never as strong, still his unmeditated striking of Henry Bird, his impulsive departure from Equity, Maine, his self-indulgent drinking and eating in Boston, and his subsequent physical and moral deterioration all form a similar cycle of will-lessness. After they are married, much as before, Bartley and Marcia justify themselves through their separate feelings, not through shared or public codes, while the narrative itself seems to preclude the effectiveness of intention, deliberation, or will. At the novel's critical moment, moreover, when the theft of Bartley's wallet prevents his return to Marcia, the manuscript breaks off (and Howells broke down in nervous collapse) with an assertion that bewilderingly appears to confuse choice with chance: "Now he could not return; nothing remained for him but the ruin he had chosen" (277). A pickpocket's luck has effectively become the measure of Bartley's moral stature, despite his having chosen the very opposite of "ruin" in planning to return. Nothing other than sheer circumstance conspires against that choice.[27]

A pair of contradictory conclusions emerges from this brief review: that two notable texts fit alternative modes better than those assumed in traditional histories; or that scenes of restraint which are benchmarks of realism do not in fact serve to identify the mode. Before rushing to redefine Howells as a naturalist and Wharton as in this case a realist, we might reconsider what we as readers bring to such fictional scenes to help distinguish each mode from the other. Something other than evidence of restraint from action may shape our assumptions about a character's will, especially given how deep-seated those assumptions are. To find out what that something is, we need more powerful interpretive tools.

Reactive Attitudes and Moral Luck

IN DISTINGUISHING realism from naturalism, we sometimes forget that the two modes present not just similar characters enmeshed in alternative circumstances—one free, the other determined—but characters who differ themselves, and who do so in the most radical constitutional way. Part of the appeal of naturalism, in fact, lies in the contradictions it reveals between assumptions we regularly share about ourselves, as at once creatures of nature and yet as supposedly moral beings.[28] As products of pasts, we rightly suppose that behavior is partly explained through historical causes—whether economic, psychological, genetic, social, parental, or some other sort. At the same time, we assume that the force of such pasts can somehow be transcended. Much as we may resemble machines in obvious functional ways, that is, we differ from them more importantly in having a subjective sensibility. Hard as it is to know how we might be any more than the sum of what has gone into making us, we resist nonetheless being simply identified with the characteristics that result from that "making." We are after all, we insist, distinctly more than just our pasts, indeed even more than our presents might dictate.

Peter Strawson unravels this knot of altogether conflicting assumptions by pulling on a single strand: the perspective we bring to each other. Whether or not they deserve it, we offer others a "reactive" point of view that differs from the "objective" stance we otherwise assume toward things. We cannot expunge our feelings of envy, resentment, admiration, and condemnation from the judgments we also make of each other as products of external forces. We are constitutionally unable to treat others as if they were somehow simply determined, and this because of expectations that Strawson elegantly depicts: "In general, we demand of others for others, as well as of ourselves for others, something of the regard which we demand of others for ourselves."[29] So deeply rooted is this demand that we cannot conceive of life without it—of a world where determinism would have stripped those attitudes of their primary force. We need to feel our deliberations matter whether or not they really do, for as Strawson concludes, "Our practices do not merely exploit our natures, they express them" (80).

The telling feature of Strawson's analysis is his setting aside of logical "proof" to explore instead how we actually behave. Adopting

a novelist's perspective, he shows the extent to which prior assumptions of action and consequence preclude our ever attaining anything like an "objective" fact of the matter. We neither live nor think as if determinism could be true, which itself attests to the depth of our aversion to a purely external view. Still, the "objective" vantage does have a certain insistent strength, since it is so often true that we can predict behavior on the basis of cause and effect—in terms of backgrounds and dispositions, according to constitutions and circumstances. We seem in fact to live in the alternation of two conflicting views, neither of which is capable of dislodging the other. Logic immures us in the world of events while emotion everywhere strives to free us, leading Dr. Johnson to assert that: "All theory is against the freedom of the will; all experience for it."[30]

Yet there is a far greater paradox, as Thomas Nagel has recently pointed out, in this clash between two ways of viewing experience:

> between the view of action from inside and any view of it from outside. Any external view of an act as something that happens, with or without causal antecedents, seems to omit the doing of it. Even if an action is described in terms of motives, reasons, abilities, absence of impediments or coercion, this description does not capture the agent's own idea of himself as its source. His actions appear to him different from other things that happen in the world, but not merely a different kind of happening, with different causes or none at all. They seem in some indescribable way not to *happen* at all (unless they are quite out of his control), though things happen when he does them. And if he sees others as agents too, their actions will seem to have the same quality.[31]

The point is that what one actually does need not coincide with one's self-perception, and that perspectives on action therefore produce quite different kinds of actor. An internal perspective, because it generates a sense of moral responsibility, produces someone we recognize as a "self." And that category seems considerably larger than the one produced by an external perspective, which might be labeled simply "character." This distinction seems apt because our feelings about the responsible "self"—our own as well as others'—are grafted onto our sense of the amoral "character" that finds itself acting in the world.[32]

Since we construct a sense of the subjective self from something

more than our actions, it is easy to suppose that the self stands free of circumstance, at least to some extent—that, as a kind of Cartesian "ghost in the machine," it encompasses more than one's feelings and behavior. Clearly, the realists believed this, given their willingness to call to moral account those whose actions were only contingently their own. The naturalists conversely denied any hope of such release from circumstance by excluding the very category of the self, in the process making all questions of intention and subjectivity seem irrelevant. Never quite willing to ignore the realist concern for how people felt toward themselves, nonetheless they never accorded those feelings any special significance. For them, one person's moral anguish differed little from another's craving for prunes, since all they needed to define a character was a certain sequence of actions.

This tends to misrepresent, however, the challenge of depicting individuals as if they were just events in the world, if only because we treat fictional characters much as Strawson says we treat each other: as "subjective" selves to whom we extend "participant reactive attitudes." No matter how two-dimensional fictional characters might otherwise seem—whether Charlie's Angels or Camus' Meursault, Mickey Mouse or Punchinello—we assume for them capacities that their narrative depictions clearly deny. That readerly propensity suggests why the naturalists experimented with unusual strategies to reinforce a more purely "objective" perspective. For just as medical students must overcome an aversion to cutting cadavers, readers of naturalism must learn that the human body which moves in a textual world need not be a person, and that will-less characters need not be treated as if they possessed full "selves." Indeed, so fully can naturalism succeed in estranging us from these cultural assumptions that we can begin to find our own selves coming under attack.[33]

Given the constitutional difference between realist "selves" and naturalist "characters," it may seem strange that so little at first distinguishes the crucial scenes of both modes. George Hurstwood's befuddlement in *Sister Carrie* (1900)as he considers the open safe, for instance, resembles Silas Lapham's deliberations about his imminent bankruptcy.[34] Both men mull over the prospect of theft in these scenes of personal crisis, and both seem unable to alter the course of events as they unfold, wavering similarly back and forth between alternative consequences. Yet Lapham appears a responsible agent while Hurstwood is merely a victim of chance. And what seems unfair in this disparity between their reputations is not merely that

Lapham's decision is never divulged, but that he may not have made a decision at all. As he wearily admits to his wife after his night-long deliberation: "*I don't know what I'm going to say to Rogers.*" In any case, whatever decision he might have made would have been irrelevant, since the corporate letter foreclosing possibility is already in the mail.

That a vacillating Hurstwood should fail to decide is hardly cause for surprise, since the very process of indecision has the effect of draining off the self's autonomy into a determining world. A corresponding effect is produced by Carrie's hesitation on the train to New York as she hears Hurstwood's plea, and other, similar naturalist scenes might easily be adduced. What seems curious, however, is that indecision in Howells' realist novel ends by also altering nothing, as if events could be controlled no more than they would be in naturalism. Nor can Lapham's crisis be considered an anomaly: Jim has already been legally freed when Huck finally, famously opts for "hell"—a fact that undermines much of the force of his anguished resolution;[35] Isabel accepts responsibility for a marriage others have cruelly contrived—an acceptance unaltered by even her horrified discovery of the deception. In other realist scenes as well, decisions take on a futile aspect precisely to the extent that events come to seem intractable, which leaves the reader with a lingering sense that agents simply act as they must. Such circumstances may not themselves be enough to diminish responsibility, since it appears to be true that we are still moral agents despite being unable to act other than we do. Yet the logic of this position, once again, does nothing to shake our projective attitudes: those who cannot act other than they do *seem* less free than those who can. Which brings us back to the need to discriminate scenes of moral crisis from those that are not.

A clue to differences between these scenes is suggested by Nagel's stress on perspectives: Lapham's crisis occurs off-stage, succinctly summarized by a narrative voice whose indirection could not differ more from the probing eye that Dreiser's narrator focuses on Hurstwood. It is as if Howells recognized our willingness to grant to the otherwise absent Lapham—precisely *because* he is absent and only heard pacing the floor by his wife—a quality of moral rigor we withhold from a Hurstwood whose dilemma is presented with excruciating immediacy. Dreiser's narrator stresses how fully Hurstwood senses his lack of control, with the effect of confirming a determinist perspective:

"I'll look in here," thought the manager, pulling out one of the money drawers. He did not know why he wished to look in there. It was quite a superfluous action, which another time might not have happened at all. . . .

"Why don't I shut the safe?" his mind said to itself, lingering. "What makes me pause here?" [36]

The inconclusiveness of Hurstwood's reflections, his uncertainty about the source of his intentions, and the wearying length of the process all gradually deny him an integrated self. Indeed, the narrative divides the man so deeply from himself—"He did not know why he . . ."—as to make him seem little more than the intersection of desires: of greed, fear, loneliness, lust, inebriation, and so on. By contrast, Lapham's crisis seems far less interminable though it actually lasts many more hours, even as the narrative avoids any hint of true self-division by refraining from an account of his thoughts. [37]

The difference between these two narrative perspectives suggests that the closer one attends to the self, the less it tends to cohere—as if the very process of depiction somehow dismantled subjectivity, breaking the self apart piece-by-piece and absorbing it into an indifferent world. Naturalism's challenge to the reader lay, once again, not in new activities but in a new angle of vision on activities the realists assumed could only be viewed one way. Naturalism reminded realism, that is, that our reasons for wanting to believe in a "self" are of a different order from the reasons we have for believing in a "character." When persons are looked at from the outside as characters whose actions are caused, not done, the category of responsibility comes to seem simply irrelevant. It then exists as no more than a grammatical function in what has become the subjective language of the self. From an objective perspective phrased in the stripped down language of character, that issue exists as a curious paradox in our judgments of behavior, by which we hold people like Hurstwood responsible for events they did nothing to bring about. [38]

The reason we live in this paradox is because, as Nagel again reminds us, we are unable to sacrifice either the subjective or objective views of behavior—unable to see ourselves as just "selves" on the one hand, or "characters" on the other. Instead, our moral judgments regularly conflate intention with consequence, as when we blame ourselves for how things turn out even though we may be only barely at fault. Nagel offers a provocative definition of this paradox: "Where a significant aspect of what someone does depends

on factors beyond his control, yet we continue to treat him in that respect as an object of moral judgment, it can be called moral luck" (26). Think of a driver accidentally running over a child:

> If the driver was guilty of even a minor degree of negligence— failing to have his brakes checked recently, for example—then if that negligence contributes to the death of the child, he will not merely feel terrible. He will blame himself for the death. And what makes this an example of moral luck is that he would have to blame himself only slightly for the negligence itself if no situation arose which required him to brake suddenly and violently to avoid hitting a child. Yet the *negligence* is the same in both cases, and the driver has no control over whether a child will run into his path.[39]

If one had hit a dog, let's say, or a ball, one's feelings of guilt would differ, even though one had been no more neglectful in either of these cases. Ensuing effects, that is, seem to shape our understanding of causes, just as consequence alters action by providing it with a meaning. This is not to suggest that future events lead somehow to past conditions or that we actually live in a world where temporal processes could be somehow reversed. But Nagel convincingly shows that "results influence culpability" fully enough for the usual terms of responsibility to seem absurd.[40]

Given our tendency to ignore the control that things exert on behavior, and given our propensity to judge others as if they were always more or less in control, any narrative that attempts to dislodge such assumptions will focus on consequence, not intention. Writers sometimes achieve this effect by stressing unanticipated events, including accidents that alter the plot by disrupting a predictable sequence. The Swede in Crane's "Blue Hotel" simply assaults the wrong man in the barroom; in the midst of a dance in Norris' *Octopus*, Annixter unexpectedly finds himself in a gunfight with Delaney; a disconsolate Carrie frowns onstage and is thereby propelled to stardom: nothing one knows prepares either character or reader to predict what will happen, which does not derail motives as much as it makes them seem irrelevant. Another way for an author to accentuate consequence at the expense of intention is through what is in fact an unusual practice of scenic rendition: describing events before they occur and then redescribing them. The technique, mastered by Dreiser, has often seemed a sign of his lack of craft,

since this kind of repetition appears an affront to narrative economy. But as with sharp swerves in the narrative line, such repetition serves the important naturalist function of countering moral luck.

Perhaps now the contrast of "self" with "character" is apparent not as a matter of innate characteristics, but as a distinction between two sets of readerly assumptions: between projective attitudes on the one hand, and the recognition on the other of what is logically necessary. So deeply entrenched is this distinction in our ways of describing behavior as hardly to seem a distinction at all, resembling nothing so much as the connection that links causality with contingency, or that reads plots into unconnected events. No matter that the recognition was old long before Hume dismissed causality as mere custom, we keep being surprised by the need to derive consequence from contingency. Every time we try to read narrative as a mere chronicle of events, we are forced to realize that "sequence goes nowhere without [its] doppelganger, or shadow, causality."[41] Thus to recall Forster's sentence, "The king died and then the queen died of grief," we assume that the two are married to each other and that her grief was due to his death. The fact that these conclusions are neither stated nor necessary (nor perhaps even likely) is less striking than the power of our interpretive impulse, which suggests how fully texts encourage some interpretations more readily than others —whether of plots, causality, or even of selves.[42]

Insofar as we are disposed against those whose deliberations seem unrelated to their behavior, the naturalists began with a handicap few other writers have been willing to accept. That may explain why the corridors of literary history are jammed with those who act on their wills while only a handful of characters inhabit deterministic universes. We invariably extend to others capacities we have assumed all along for ourselves, and imagine for them similar selves able to choose, then act responsibly.[43] The naturalists dismissed subjectivity as irrelevant to either character or event, and denied anything like the possibility of a free-standing self. Rejecting our deepest expectations, they forestalled our interpretive premises through a rich array of narrative and stylistic strategies. To see more specifically how those strategies actually deflect our projective assumptions, we now need to turn from philosophical premises to the specifics of naturalist texts.

Repetition and Chance

DIFFICULT AS it is to distinguish naturalism from realism through scenes of restraint, it is even harder to attribute a pattern to the idiosyncracies of naturalist prose. Yet that is less crucial than gaining a sense for the immediate flavor of narratives that reveal characters as objects of circumstance—a sense gained not from overarching distinctions but from the rhetorical turns of particular texts. The chapters that follow discuss a wide range of stylistic enactments, a range that itself immmediately provokes two primary questions: How can we know in a given instance when a style is naturalistic? and, How does an author's prose enmesh characters in a narrative world that is not their own? Perhaps the best place to begin is with the feature that in quite different forms emerges most often in the following chapters —a feature so regularly criticized in naturalism as to seem a key (if inadvertent) characteristic.

Naturalist texts, so it is charged, are not simply repetitious but would need to be crafted more sparely at every level to redeem a claim on our attention.[44] Keep in mind that repetition forms a notoriously slippery premise, one about which almost anything can be stated or denied.[45] Does it reinforce or collapse possibilities, confirm a situation or introduce doubt? A hole in one is a duffer's notion of the happy workings of chance, and yet if he somehow repeats the effort, skill will appear to play a part. Or again, the chronic stutterer is unable to pronounce sounds only once, yet the aspiring pianist gains control precisely by repeating musical phrases. If recurrent patterns of behavior are often assumed to be signs of normalcy (eating at regular hours, say, or showing up for work on time), they can also by a slight twist be taken as a feature of neurosis, when behavior controls one's will according to clearly repetitive patterns. Analogously, within the province of art, recurrence is seen as essential to meaning, even as the most flagrant aesthetic defect is taken to be unvarying repetition.

Contradictory as these readings of repetition clearly are, the contradictions have less to do with repetition itself than with its control —whether artistic, athletic, or in general, behavioral. And since lack of self-control is central to a determinist vision, the repetitions of naturalism warrant more than simple critical dismissal. Not only plot and events but aspects of style seem uncontrollably repeated, depriv-

ing both characters and readers of an otherwise comforting sense of autonomy. After all, when something is repeated involuntarily, it comes to seem mechanical and gives us a helpless sense of being enslaved to forces larger than the self. John Irwin asserts that "it is those inevitable repetitions inherent in the cyclic nature of time that seem to rob the individual will of all potency."[46] Freud more peremptorily declared that "it is only this factor of involuntary repetition which surrounds with an uncanny atmosphere what would otherwise be innocent enough, and forces upon us the idea of something fateful and unescapable where otherwise we should have spoken of 'chance' only."[47] Provocative as these descriptions are, they also finally seem incomplete, since "involuntary repetition" not merely constrains the will (as Irwin suggests) or surrounds an unchanged self with its "uncanny atmosphere" (as one can infer from Freud) but subverts altogether our primary assumptions about the self. No longer sure what controls our behavior—whether desires within or conditions without—we begin to lose confidence in our own singularity. Any unforeseen repetition draws attention to our ever inadequate control, and makes us therefore aware of being enslaved to a world we have not created.

The trouble with stylistic repetition in art, then, as with daily recurrences in our lives, is the difficulty of identifying whether the repetitions are intended or not. And the trouble is only compounded by the problematic nature of intention itself, which Freud initially theorized lay behind all human behavior. Yet Freudian intention is not equivalent to artistic self-consciousness, which means we need not assume the naturalists were fully aware of the effects of their prose in order to acknowledge how much they achieved through repetitive stylistic patterns. On the contrary, it may be best to redress the balance in favor of the text, not its author, who has too often been reclaimed only to be abandoned as a realist failure. If readers have paid scant attention to the abundant recurrences in naturalist styles, it is because realist standards define those repetitions as simply the signs of bad writing. Within a traditional poetics of narrative economy and stylistic variation, naturalist texts will always fail by definition.

All one has to do, however, is suspend judgment about the supposed lapses of naturalist style for the sheer intensity of its recurrences to produce an unsettling effect. Rather than quietly confirming events and offering the reassurance of solid character, repetition

draws the categories of both event and character into question. By presenting sameness in difference again and again, from multiple points of view, it succeeds in eroding conventional assumptions about the ways in which we are in the world. So variously do naturalist texts double back—via phonic and verbal reiteration as well as the doubling of characters and plot recurrences—that the motions we otherwise ascribe to a self slowly lose their familiar appearance, first of consistency, then purpose altogether. Whether as echo or prefigurement, recollection or revenge, as helpless compulsion or willful imitation, repetition finally denies the possibility of either coherent identity or progressive behavior. Even more to the point, naturalism reveals directly through its repetitive patterns how fully character is wrenched into shape by the indifferent logic of determinism.

Unlike realist texts, which privilege a supposedly transparent style, then, naturalist prose on the face of it often seems both repetitive and awkward. Of course, no single example can suggest the diverse possibilities, but listen to this characteristic description from Stephen Crane's "Open Boat" (1897):

> In the meantime the oiler and the correspondent rowed. And also they rowed. They sat together in the same seat, and each rowed an oar. Then the oiler took both oars; then the correspondent took both oars; then the oiler; then the correspondent. They rowed and they rowed.[48]

Here, the repeated description suggests the repetitiveness of the action itself, while the alternation of oiler and correspondent as subject of successive sentences conveys the actual change in positions they undertake through the night. More importantly, the disconnected sentences and paratactic syntax, the verbal and grammatical repetitions, the limited lexical choices, all work to absorb any shaping intention or will from the text, to enforce a vision of experience as determined by forces beyond oneself.

Likewise, recall Hurstwood's pleading exchange with Carrie to "Listen to me," after he has deceived her into leaving Chicago:

> "Won't you listen to me? Listen to me a minute and I'll you why I came to do this thing. . . . Won't you listen?"

Her sobs disturbed him so that he was quite sure she did not hear a word he said.

"Won't you listen?" he asked.

"No, I won't," said Carrie flashing up . . . and again sobs of fright cut off her desire for expression.

Hurstwood listened with some astonishment. . . . "I won't stop you. All I want you to do is to listen a moment. You'll let me tell you, won't you?"

Carrie seemed not to listen. She only turned her head toward the window, where outside all was black. The train was speeding with steady grace across the fields and through patches of wood. The long whistle came with sad, musical effect . . .[49]

The assonance linking Hurstwood's demand to "listen" with the "whistle" that precedes and closes this passage is only part of a pervasive sibilance that weaves the whole together—as if to confirm the unresisting ease with which Carrie is swept eastward. Hurstwood's demand will lead at last to the argument that is its ostensible purpose, but long before then it achieves its effect of compelling Carrie to stay. The sheer repetition of the word "listen" makes his frantic performance seem to lie beyond his control, even as it also serves to deny Carrie any control of her own.

At times, the kind of assonance and alliteration that otherwise seem unintended combine with an iterative syntax to produce an even more eerie effect—one much like that which is common to biblical narrative, at least as Robert Alter describes it. Old Testament prose is never transparent but forms instead "an insistent dimension" that overwhelms characters through a process of verbal and imagistic recurrence—a process that establishes "a kind of rhythm of thematic significance, clearly suggesting that events in history occur according to an ordained pattern."[50] The naturalists likewise enforced a sense of unalterable necessity through repetition as well as through a syntax that is paratactically flat. However much particular physical environments change from author to author, text to text, characters seem similarly imprisoned in narratively static, sometimes timeless milieus.

To savor the effect of their frequently simple, often disconnected sentences—whether Dreiser's or London's, Crane's or Norris'—one need only turn to the late style of Henry James, which celebrates instead a powerful ability to reshape experience imaginatively. The

way in which clauses tumble out of grammatical thickets, or characters leap to complete (only to distort) each other's hesitant claims, or shifting perspectives illumine a series of ever fuller prospects for action: these narrative patterns seem to confirm James' philosophical pragmatism. Instead of a single narrative perspective on a world already in place, his late novels clarify multiple perspectives structuring the different worlds in which his characters live. No longer is a fixed perspective offered to the reader, who now becomes like a character compelled to make judgments in an open textual world—judgments that reveal as much of oneself as of events they purport to describe.

The naturalists sustained a vision at odds with this epistemological model by rejecting the validity of any such self-authoring impulse. Denying the premise acclaimed by late James—that separate perspectives compete for authority in an indeterminate world—they each denied as well the pragmatic precept that events are as they are described. A varied medley of contradictory voices emerges from naturalist texts more often than most have conceded, with narrators alternately bullying and pitying, speaking from omniscience or in free indirect discourse. Yet the world they narrate appears, contra James, both determinate and determined, allowing the reader to assess the disparity between that world and their moral conclusions. Experience seems fixed and unalterable, moreover, because of a characteristic syntax—of clauses that rest on an equal footing instead of linking in dependent structures. James' flexible grammar and tentative tone enforce a sense of contingency in which experience is reshaped by simply altering one's syntax. By contrast, the naturalists' flat sentences preclude any such shaping power: "everything must happen as it does happen, it could not be otherwise, and there is no need for explanatory connectives."[51] Erich Auerbach does not mean by this that parataxis defies normal rules of causation. But the absence of clausal subordination encourages us to read as if things could occur in only one way, as if only single consequences were possible and that plots therefore lacked alternatives. Where James' hypotactic prose allows one to order one's life idiosyncratically, the naturalists instead establish something like a single causal order, instilling a sense of certitude by returning us over and over to the same grammatical place.

The repetitions of parataxis produce a further effect, much like that which ensues from repeated words but better illustrated in spa-

tial terms. Just as a recurrence of physical objects blurs distinctions between this and that, here and there (or rather, this and this, here and here), so repetition of something in time dissolves the edges between then and now. An event that happens once—say, a jar placed on a hill in Tennessee—not only enables but seems to encourage a mapping of fixed coordinates. By contrast, an exact repetition confuses any single determinate order. Seeing double, like hearing an echo, disorients us by not allowing a fixed priority, and until we can assert some sequence, the unsettling effect remains. One of the results of bewilderment produced by this kind of repetition is that time itself seems suspended—an effect central to the paratactical repetitions of naturalism. They structure narratives that seem to deny their own temporality, and in the process create an aura of timelessness. Or to put it, as Bruce Kawin has, conversely: "In the continuous present there is no consciousness of repetition."[52]

Even at less immediate levels of scenic description and narrative event, the naturalists confirmed a vision of life's endless repetitiveness. Earlier, Howells had emulated George Eliot in heralding the claims of everyday life, and had staked out the region within which realists were to imagine events. The naturalists stripped autonomy from experience not by turning away from this field of vision but by having characters within it unknowingly repeat themselves and each other. Of course, characters in realism also repeat choices made and actions performed: Isabel is courted in turn by Casper Goodwood, Lord Warburton, and Gilbert Osmond, and Pansy Osmond is pursued first by Ned Rosier, then Lord Warburton. Each exchange, moreover, extends possibilities of independence and compatibility everywhere rehearsed in the novel, setting Isabel's situation in structured relief. Huck Finn's crises of conscience have a similar effect, as do the similar recurrences of other realist texts. Scenic repetition of this sort enforces our sense of personal control and psychological growth by elaborating differences within situations that otherwise seem alike. Experience is thereby opened up to the prospect of deliberation, agency, and control.

Realism encourages us to believe that because repetition is marked by difference, experience can always be viewed progressively. Divergences among separate characters, actions, and scenes are cherished over similarities, with the effect of making time seem a continuum that ever unfolds. Of course, the literary techniques of anticipation and foreshadowing violate that presumption by collapsing the future

into the present. Which is the reason, as Gérard Genette shows, that prolepsis (or foreshadowing) is invoked far less frequently than analepsis (or recollection): because prolepsis stands at odds with the "narrative suspense that is characteristic of the 'classical' conception of the novel."[53] Yet even when it does occur in the classic realist text, prolepsis never forecloses possibility. Huck "humbles" himself to Jim and declares he "warn't ever sorry for it afterwards, neither" —but we grant him no less autonomy because of this anticipatory confirmation.[54] And even when "generalizing prolepsis" confers an aura of inevitability on a text, characters still seem free to act. Isabel Archer's shy emergence from "the ample doorway" at Gardencourt anticipates her appearance five years later, "framed in the gilded doorway" at Palazzo Roccanera. The disposition that earlier prevents her from emerging into the English scene will contribute to her being "framed" into marriage to Gilbert Osmond, yet we never assume she cannot break free to control the events that control her.

By contrast, naturalist characters repeat themselves with little variation, in narratives whose advance notices undercut suspense to enforce a "plot of predestination."[55] Dreiser notably employed these techniques in his aptly titled "Trilogy of Desire," which recounts Frank Algernon Cowperwood's rise to and fall from robber baronetcy. The famous opening sequence of lobster and squid in mortal combat anticipates the shape of all the conflicts that ensue, just as Cowperwood's tireless wheeling and dealing over the course of three novels simply plays out his initial description as "a financier by instinct." Compulsive energies drive him onward through sexual as well as business affairs, at last undermining the very suspense on which realist narrative fully depends. Closure is deferred with arbitrary ease, as sequence is simply added to sequence, and the sole reason for finally bringing an end to thousands of pages is narrative exhaustion. Cowperwood may gain a predictable success by sheer force of personality, but as a victim of desire, he merely reenacts in each instance choices he cannot help but make. Ironically, Stephen Crane relies upon a similar form of exposition, different as his narratives are from Dreiser's in economy of expression and subject matter. The explosive quarrels that divide the Johnson family in *Maggie: A Girl of the Streets* (1893); the demands of the sea in "The Open Boat"; the violence of war in *The Red Badge of Courage*: a clear cyclic pattern places characters over and over in like situations. And as in Dreiser's fictional realm, Crane's texts tend to enforce a sense of completion

before any single scene begins by stressing the consequences of events prior to the account of their causes.

The effect of this anticipatory form of scenic repetition is reinforced in naturalist texts by characters themselves, who are shown not only sharing traits and behaving identically, but actively fulfilling each others' desires in exaggerated psychological form. Consider the tension in *Maggie* between Pete and Jimmy Johnson, or that in Norris' novel between McTeague and his erstwhile friend, Marcus Schouler. Sometimes, a systematically repetitive structure can compound this effect, as when *Sister Carrie* builds to the central climax of Hurstwood's theft before presenting an inverse image of the novel's first half in its second. Carrie and Hurstwood are no more free agents in New York than they were in Chicago, and although she is compelled more unremittingly by desires than he, both are equally constrained to act out simple repetitions of their pasts. She whirls to stardom as he fades to extinction in exact if more intense replication of the behavior that has characterized them all along. Her ceaseless alternation between shopping, acting, and rocking quietly in her chair—his between searching for a job and reading the newspaper as he likewise rocks—induces feelings of helplessness in them and of inevitability in the reader.[56]

Repetition conflicts, however, with a feature common to naturalism as well as to realism that emphasizes the unique, unanticipated, and unrepeatable: the workings of chance. When Hurstwood takes cash from the open safe, simple accident shuts the safe door, destroying the appearance of managerial aplomb that is the basis of his career. The Swede in Crane's "Blue Hotel" dies because he merely happens to assault a deadly gambler rather than any of the mild-mannered businessmen also sitting at the table. Chance is likewise an engine of plot in most other naturalist texts: London's *White Fang* opens with Henry fortuitously saved from a pack of wolves and the subsequent narrative alters direction by similarly random punctuations of event. Only after winning the lottery does Trina McTeague feel the first gnawings of greed, which provoke the violence that destroys both her and her husband in Norris' novel. The most notable instance and the one prepared for most exhaustively is Roberta Alden's sudden move toward Clyde in Dreiser's *American Tragedy*. Impulsively, he resists her comforting gesture and inadvertently knocks her from the boat, setting in process a chain of events that will lead to his execution. Part of the reason these episodes achieve the kind of

prominence they do is because they seem so starkly singular in narratives replete with repetition. In worlds that everywhere else repeat, these dramatic intersections of character and event deprive individuals of even the illusion of a second chance.

Such scenes at first glance appear to defy what naturalism everywhere else proclaims, that determinism rests on causal laws which preclude the existence of random events. Chance, accident, probability, fortune: any such characterization is merely a misunderstanding of the logic of events—events that, because determined, are predictable consequences of prior causes. Our limited perspectives do not always permit us to know those causes or to foresee events, but they are not therefore any less certain to occur in a determined universe. Laplace, the eighteenth-century mathematician, delivered the classic formulation of this view:

> Given for one instant an intelligence which could comprehend all the forces by which nature is animated and the respective situation of the beings who compose it—an intelligence sufficiently vast to submit these data to analysis—it would embrace in the same formula the movements of the greatest bodies of the universe and those of the lightest atom; for it, nothing would be uncertain and the future, as the past would be present to its eyes.[57]

It is unlikely the American naturalists knew of Laplace or would have agreed with this view. And had they done so, they still could not have patterned their fiction on his model of omniscience, since narrative requires the deferral of knowledge, not its complete satisfaction.[58] That is why even those naturalists who may well have realized chance was precluded by determinism nonetheless admired its dramatic possibilities. They understood how characters and readers do share an inherently limited perspective that makes some events appear accidental. The point is that even should the world run according to a logic that precludes chance, we live as if it did not out of ignorance of all the causes behind events. After all, unforeseen consequences occur all the time in the course of affairs—consequences that often seem quite arbitrary. Adopting this insight, the naturalists simply refined a literary strategy, interrupting repetitive narratives with singular events as a means of intensifying their vision of helplessness.[59]

Modal Disruptions and Literary History

THE PREMISE assumed so far has been that philosophy and style are one, or rather that they offer two ways of talking about what in narrative is the same thing. Fiction, that is, does not so much argue *for* a certain philosophy—as if characters were no more than separate voices in a Socratic dialogue—as it embodies a metaphysics in its very syntax itself. If naturalism has prompted little disagreement about either its philosophy or its styles, still, few have felt it worthwhile to explore the implications of the former or to explain why the latter seem at once inept and yet effective. The chapters that follow address both these issues, and address them jointly, by treating stylistic "flaws" as semantic strengths. But before turning to specific cases, we need to broach the larger question of narrative classification itself. If naturalism does indeed form a separate literary category, what makes a text naturalistic, and how do we know? Especially given our deep resistance to the idea of necessity, as reflected in the transformative power of our "reactive attitudes," what characterizes a determinist text and thereby distinguishes naturalism from realism?

Discussions of genre tend invariably toward the taxonomic, toward catalogues of stylistic or thematic features that make texts part of a larger set. June Howard is only the most recent of those who treat naturalism as a genre, assuring us that "particular features do indeed mark the works ascribed to naturalism." Her selection of features, moreover, outlines the "form" as it has been traditionally conceived —of brutal materials, a documentary strategy, and "recurrent images of blocked action and enforced spectatorship."[60] Others have occasionally differed about appropriate subject and character types; or they point to the proliferation of physical detail; or they cite authorial proclamations (delivered notably by Norris) of realistic techniques and romantic themes. A few now speak of the "plot of decline" in tones formerly used for "pessimistic realism."[61] In each case, however, the features adduced seem irrelevant to at least some texts that are clearly naturalistic. The formal differences between Crane's "Open Boat," for instance, and Dreiser's *Financier* suggest that no extrinsic feature defines a category capable of including them both.[62]

In a celebrated passage, Wittgenstein addressed this problem of classification by asking how we know that different games form part of a common set: "If you look at them you will not see something

that is common to *all*, but similarities, relationships, and a whole series of them at that." Then he adds: "I can think of no better expression to characterize these similarities than 'family resemblances'; for the various resemblances between members of a family: build, features, colour of eyes, gait, temperament, etc. etc. overlap and criss-cross in the same way."[63] The power of this analogy lies in allowing us to abandon the notion of special features, to rethink naturalism instead as a set of textual alignments by which different materials can be organized for a similar effect. Instead of searching for what Northrop Frye described as "analogies in form," we need to imagine the "principal operative in a number of texts" that Tzvetan Todorov claims is the basis of any genre.[64]

Yet despite its appeal for students of naturalism, Todorov's approach is less suited for describing a genre than for defining a mode. Frye himself had elaborated this distinction, claiming that modes relied on "relative or comparative terms" quite unlike the fixed features of genre.[65] In stressing the external embodiments of form, genres function much like nouns, while (to extend the grammatical analogy) modes work adjectivally. Modal descriptions, in other words, do not provide literary models or otherwise attempt to organize formal features into a taxonomic account. Paul Alpers agrees with Frye that we read fiction according to "the hero's power of action," but he moves discussion even further from possible catalogues of traits to the modal questions that readers should be prompted to ask in the face of a given text: "what notions of man's strengths, possibilities, pleasures, dilemmas, etc., are manifested in the emphases, the devices, the organization, the pleasures, etc., of this work?" Or as he later adds: "In defining mode as man's strength relative to his world (and so forth), we are not, then, specifying an attribute to be isolated and classified. Rather, we are providing questions that enable us to understand what we see and . . . to see what we are saying."[66] This way of thinking about the problem—in terms of the reader's enforced response to questions about action, event, and agency— clarifies the modal approach to naturalism I take throughout this book. Moreover, Alpers' deliberate unwillingness to specify traits and attributes makes it possible to broaden the bounds of naturalism without seeming inconsistent.

The following analyses of texts by each of four American authors rests, then, on the presumption that naturalism is a mode characterized by determinism. The implications of that philosophy affect

different people differently, prompted by texts that differ themselves in theme and plot, characterization and style. The one thing those texts have in common is a conception of men and women living as if no longer responsible for whatever they happen to do. The fact that some authors (Crane most notably) never declared they were naturalists makes identification of certain narratives seem at first problematical. In *The Monster* (1898), for instance, are the sacrifices of Henry Johnson and Dr. Trescott determined or not, and how does the novel's style help to confirm whatever decision we make? These kinds of question need to be asked of any potentially naturalist text, and imply that even an author's fervid self-declaration would not guarantee a narrative's status. The fact that none of the four wrote solely in the mode throughout his career leaves us, in any event, to decide on the basis of textual evidence itself. Difficult as that may be in practice, the decision corresponds to the principle that any sure sign of autonomous action or free will excludes a text from consideration. This is likewise the reason for excluding any other modes, kinds, or literary categories that stand at odds with determinism. Neither "tragic" nor "heroic," for instance, are appropriate descriptions of naturalist efforts, since tragedy and heroism assume capacities of characters as well as standards from the reader that are precluded by determinism.[67]

At this point, it is worth pausing to consider much that determinism plainly is not. The long-held belief that naturalism consisted of "pessimistic realism," for instance, derived from a reductive understanding of the philosophy as merely nihilistic. Granted, the phrase might be made to fit many of Crane's texts, including *Maggie*, *The Red Badge of Courage*, "The Open Boat," and "The Blue Hotel" (1898). But that is no reason to conclude that the concept of necessity need be pessimistic. The world can be determined, after all, toward the Millennium as easily as toward Apocalypse and the ability to take credit for actions is not essential to individual happiness, or perhaps even virtue. Naturalists other than Crane, then, concluded quite differently but no less logically on the basis of their informing premise. The writer differing most was Norris, who subscribed to a social Darwinism of inevitable human progress. All four of his naturalist novels—*McTeague*, *Vandover and the Brute*, *The Octopus* (1901), and *The Pit* (1903)—exclude responsibility as fully as Crane's, and yet his characters are ultimately supposed to contribute to society's amelioration.

A third attitude hearkens back to Zola's reasons for extolling the movement: an affirming belief in social reform. This group of writers believed institutions determined individuals, and that only massive social restructuring would improve the environment in which individual behavior is conditioned. Because fiction can reveal not only the effects of economic conditions but also their causes, it can direct attention to the means of social reform as well as to its ends. Instead of submitting to the jungle law of Spencer's social Darwinism, then, a naturalist author can illustrate possibilities for transcending it—as did London in *Martin Eden,* Upton Sinclair in *The Jungle,* and David Graham Phillips in *Susan Lennox: Her Fall and Rise* (1908). Clearly, this is the least consistent attitude associated with the naturalist mode since, at a minimum, a determinist premise contravenes the existence of agency.[68] Yet the lack of logical consistency is less important, at least for the moment, than is the fact that determinism should have generated possibilities so contradictory and multifarious.

The sole expectation we bring to naturalism is that characters respond willy-nilly to events in ways that demonstrate they lack any wills or might otherwise order their desires. And now we can begin to see how the wrenching styles that initially seem so estranging are precisely the means by which characters are absorbed into their fictional worlds. By contrast, realist contexts release characters on their own recognizance, as it were, assisted by readers who are encouraged to accord them full moral capacities. Despite an effective dismantling of the humanist fallacy by recent theoreticians, we still treat realist characters as persons and imagine possibilities for them outside the text, since they never seem fully defined by the fictional worlds in which they act. In James' *Portrait of a Lady,* for example, we continue to ask some form of the question with which we began: "What will she do?" Or rather, we wonder *how* Isabel will do whatever she happens to decide, knowing the choice she makes will change her much as her actions have throughout. If we can hardly imagine the same of Norris' Vandover, or Dreiser's Carrie, or Crane's correspondent in "The Open Boat," it is because the interest we have in naturalist characters ends with the text. Naturalism ever subverts that interest, turning our attention to fictional worlds into which its characters are absorbed, not to selves that stand somehow free of those worlds. The triumph of naturalism, in short, was to estrange us from the very notion of a self.

It bears stating once again that naturalism reveals the conflict of

determinism with free will as part of an ongoing tension in our views about human behavior. True as both views seem to be, they are also mutually exclusive, with causal necessity able to explain events only by explaining away the self. Free will has the effect, that is, of rescuing the autonomous self too completely from a world of things, while determinism conversely absorbs any possibility of agency into that world, making distinctions between oneself and one's circumstance disappear. Yet if neither concept can dislodge the other, together they illustrate an ongoing alternation in literary history, particularly in the changing claims of fiction during the nineteenth century. The shift from the romance through the realist novel to literary naturalism can be seen as a transition between these perspectives: that is, from the supreme empowering of an uncircumscribed self, to its gradual dissolution into realms of event. Or to consider literary history representatively, in terms of major characters: Manfred, Ahab, and Hollingsworth evolved into Dorothea Brooke, Isabel Archer, and Silas Lapham, who in turn were supplanted by Gervaise Coupeau, White Fang, and Jennie Gerhardt. Characters imagined as relatively unconstrained by the ties of class and circumstance were bound down gradually through the century and slowly emptied out.

As the naturalists discovered, imagining a determinist perspective is fraught with difficulties, largely because such a perspective denies our deepest, most necessary assumptions about ourselves. For those who study the naturalists, those difficulties are only compounded by the absence of any overall pattern to such diverse texts—with one negative exception: in all the crucial cases, the naturalists disrupted strategies familiar to the realists. By inverting their predecessors' vision of the self, they showed what determinism could involve, what living in such a world might actually mean. Isaiah Berlin once claimed that, even if we wanted to, we could not escape the illusion of free will: "I do not here wish to say that determinism is necessarily false, only that we neither speak nor think as if it could be true, and that it is difficult, and perhaps impossible, to conceive what our picture of the world would be if we seriously believed it."[69] Difficult, maybe. But if Berlin had read the naturalists, he might have agreed, not impossible.

2.

Imposing (on) Events in London's "To Build a Fire"

MORE THAN other naturalist authors, Jack London has been considered an embarrassment, a writer whose prodigious output simply confirms his lack of craft. His flat prose seems to offer an immediate, easy target of criticism, and our skepticism only grows with knowledge of his slipshod methods of composition. Given the speed with which he tossed off stories that appear suspiciously childish, most readers have simply agreed to ignore the technical aspects of his fiction. Even admirers balk at treating so inconsistent a self-proclaimed theorist as if he were nonetheless on the whole a self-consistent artist. Publicly committed to a super-race and yet to an utterly classless society, for instance, London affirmed the radical individualism of Nietzsche's will-to-power even as he was given to signing letters to Marxist friends, "Yours for the revolution!" Understandably, critics upset with the stylistic excesses of naturalism have seized upon him, out of frustration with his mud-

dled thought, his evident artlessness, and his unabated worldwide popularity.[1]

London therefore offers a perfect test case for my introductory claim that the styles of naturalism, however various, are all part of a determinist mode. The very extent to which his stories defy conventional criteria suggests how irrelevant some traditional categories are to the naturalist enterprise. This is hardly to claim, of course, that metaphysics always disproves maladroitness, even if maladroitness can sometimes be approached as a kind of after-the-fact metaphysics. To adopt that approach, however, we need to postpone for the moment any claims for London's literary status or his ultimate purpose, since such claims simply reinstall the categories brought into question by a determinist philosophy. Instead, we need to restrict ourselves to describing what happens in a fictional text—how it moves, both verbally and grammatically, and what those moves suggest about the constraints upon action and agency. The best place to begin such analysis is London's most popular story—"To Build a Fire" (1906)—especially since its strengths appear at first to be no more than inadvertent stylistic flaws.

Stylistic Dislocations

TOO OFTEN, stylistic analyses are shaped by thematic assumptions drawn from the text, and the best guarantee against invoking thematics as a guide to style is to turn first to the story's concluding paragraph. It may not even be necessary to know that an unnamed man who has repeatedly failed to ward off the Arctic cold at last slips into frozen sleep, watched over by a gradually bewildered dog:

> Later the dog whined loudly. And still later it crept close to the man and caught the scent of death. This made the animal bristle and back away. A little longer it delayed, howling under the stars that leaped and danced and shone brightly in the cold sky. Then it turned and trotted up the trail in the direction of the camp it knew, where were the other food providers and fire providers.[2]

If these lines lend a halting rhythm to the story's "sense of an ending," it is already clear that we cannot merely ascribe their odd abruptness to London's personal quirkiness. For whatever his inten-

tions may have been, there is no denying that this is a self-consciously structured prose, evident specifically in the paragraph's minor transgressions. London adamantly refuses here to subordinate clauses to one another, for instance, even though the more natural form of description clearly invites such a pattern. And as if he desired to impart to the passage a tone of even greater formality, he inverts a number of phrases with what would seem a certain self-conscious flair ("a little longer it delayed," and "where were the other food providers").

The even more convincing evidence of stylistic control appears in the paragraph's most striking feature: its multiple repetitions. Alliteration echoes a series of "l"s, "c"s, "b"s, and "t"s through to the final clause's "f-p"s, while syntax compounds that phonic stammer by trusting almost exclusively to the copulative—seven times in five short sentences. Prepositional phrases emerge additively instead of in the usual subordinated pattern (as when the dog trots "*up* the trail *in* the direction *of* the camp"); one phrase merely rewords, that is, rather than extending or developing another. Even the adverbial shifters repeat, cross-hatching the whole through a series of identical words and similar sounds ("Later"/"later"; "still"/"little longer"). Although events may thus at first appear to be given a progressive sequence, the effect is thwarted by the constant recurrence in the passage to the simple past tense—as though London deliberately wanted to avoid those temporal elaborations that would otherwise reflect a controlling narrative consciousness. Throughout, each sentence and sometimes each clause presents itself autonomously, as a single unit that announces itself only loosely dependent upon any other. Far from being a world that presents itself bound together syntactically—as equivalent, that is, to more than the sum of occasional grammatical parts—this passage confirms through its verbal and even phonemic repetitions the utter absence of any grammar at all.

We will want to pay similar attention to the texture of the rest of London's story, but other questions raised by this paragraph need to be addressed in other terms than the purely stylistic. After all, the point of listening so closely to the particulars of naturalist language is to discover how much our direct experience of it alters the assumptions we unthinkingly make about action and event. Perhaps the most obvious effect of the paragraph's verbal echoes, therefore, is to remind us that the plot itself consists of only a few basic events

reiterated over and over. On a single day, an unnamed man walks in
75-below-zero temperature, stops to build a fire and eat lunch, resumes walking, falls into an icy spring, builds another fire that is
obliterated by snow from a tree, then fails to build a third fire before
finally freezing to death. Banal as these events are one by one, they
repeat themselves into an eerie significance as the man attempts again
and again to enact the story's titular infinitive. In turn, everything
that somehow contributes to those attempts is doubled and redou-
bled, iterated and reiterated, leaving almost nothing in the narrative
to occur only once.

Moreover, just as verbal repetition succeeds in disrupting a normal
grammatical progression by breaking phrases into a series of autonomous units, so the recurrence of physical things has a curiously
disruptive narrative effect. Disconnecting objects from one another,
repetition tends to instill a static quality to individual scenes—and
by extension, to the Arctic world of which they form a part. The
story not only keeps resorting to a description of certain similar
things—the man's body, the dog, the condition of the trail—but
does so as if they lacked any ongoing relation to one another. The
textual world is broken up into discrete material objects, the reiterated reference to which lends a paralyzing quality to the story's
events. Gradually, the very notion of plot as an onward narrative
progression is drawn into question.

The unsettling effect that repetition has in "To Build a Fire" is
perhaps best illustrated in a passage of near-fatal crisis:

> Once, coming around a bend, he shied abruptly, like a startled
> horse . . . The creek he knew was frozen clear to the bottom—no
> creek could contain water in that arctic winter—but he knew also
> that there were springs that bubbled out from the hillsides and ran
> along under the snow and on top the ice of the creek. He knew
> that the coldest snaps never froze these springs, and he knew
> likewise their danger. They were traps. They hid pools of water
> under the snow that might be three inches deep, or three feet.
> Sometimes a skin of ice half an inch thick covered them, and in
> turn was covered by the snow. Sometimes there were alternate
> layers of water and ice skin, so that when one broke through he
> kept on breaking through for awhile, sometimes wetting himself
> to the waist.
>
> That was why he had shied in such panic. (71–72)

Much as it lacks in the way of exposition, the passage clearly shows that what might have seemed one paragraph's idiosyncrasies actually integrates the story. The subject—some form of H_2O—is repeated over and over, whether it occurs as "creek," "water," "snow," and "ice" fully three times apiece; or only twice as "springs" and "skin"; or simply remains the implied referent of "froze," "frozen," "bubbled," and "wetting." For both the man and the dog, that alternating substance forms a series of "traps" themselves phonemically reiterated in the cold "snaps" that never quite freeze the springs, and thereby render them fatal. Other internal rhymes reverberate strikingly throughout the text, as does an alliteration that extends onward from the hard "c"s in the second sentence (suggesting a certain crisp, chilled, possibly shivering stutter).[3] Sentences themselves repeat their structure, whether resuming from similar subjects and adverbs ("They were . . ." "They hid . . ."; "Sometimes . . ." "Sometimes . . .");[4] or dividing in the middle ("three inches deep, or three feet"; "he knew . . . but he knew"; "He knew . . . and he knew"); or turning on chiasmus ("Sometimes a skin of ice half an inch thick covered them, and in turn was covered by the snow"). The whole experience is then summarily recapitulated in the final claim that the man had "shied" away.

That one-word reiteration of the opening description has a curious effect, confirmed more fully by the complex pattern of repetitions that structure the overall passage. As in the paragraph cited earlier, such a pattern returns us to where we began, and tends to drain in the process any suspense we might otherwise have felt in the action. The very stylistic recurrences that integrate the passage deny any narrative progression. Or, perhaps more precisely, the text's very doubleness belies the singularity asserted at the opening—"Once, coming around a bend . . ." Whatever danger the scene might otherwise imply is rendered commonplace through the multiform repetitions of phoneme, word, and syntax. By precluding contingency and declaring that all that is happening will only happen again (or has itself already occurred), these repetitions evoke a realm in which human control seems irrelevant. Nothing can now be altered because everything has been so firmly set in place. Further confirming this sense that everything has already been settled beforehand is the temporal pattern suggested by the passage's overarching shift in preterite. That shift, which subtly divides the simple opening tense of "he shied abruptly" from the closing perfect of "he had shied," takes

place through a persistent concentration on past participial constructions. The predicate structure simply reinforces the sense of closure apparent from the beginning. Instead of spurring expectation onward, repetition and tense forestall action in a tableau of ever-recurring, never-changing elements.

Repetition's Narrative Effects

REPETITION ESTABLISHES a compelling pattern in London's Arctic for reasons that are neither simple nor straightforward. Most obviously, its material effect is entropic, reducing the man to the purely physical by depriving him initially of a will, then of desires, and at last of life altogether. Yet it is already clear that the process manifests itself at first not in a material realm (the realm of actions involuntarily repeated) but at a verbal level. And it does so, notably, with the word most often reiterated. "Cold" occurs in the first half of this short story more than twenty-five times with a chillingly predictable effect. For just as the narrative's focus on the physically immediate contributes to a paralyzing "tyranny of things," so the repetition of a thermal absence gradually lowers the textual temperature.[5] Or rather, the persistent emphasis on intense cold—which is no more, after all, than molecular inactivity—exposes an irreducible corporeality to the very air itself. Empty space becomes a thing.

The "tyranny of things" that develops from a repetitive concentration on the material world tends, as we have seen, to break down characteristic connections among objects as well as events. Yet repetition itself implies a more ontological stasis in terms of the story's hero, exercising its power most fully by isolating not event from event, but event from actor. The repetition of things and events creates an environment that seems to resist human intention, one in which desires fail over and over to shape results. Consequence ever falls short of anticipation, and the narrative gradually divides the man from his world by exposing the ineffectiveness of his will—not merely to reach the safety of camp by his planned time of six o'clock, but to avoid the hidden "traps" of water, then to build a warming fire, and finally to forestall the Arctic's numbing effects. The "tyranny of things" prevails over the man at first by depleting his physical resources, and at last by excluding the very possibility that he might possess any agency. As his body numbs and slowly freezes

into a thing like any other thing, he apprehends in growing panic how little effect he can have on the environment. And as this occurs, we come to realize what it means for deliberate actions not to have the results we intend.[6]

In much the same way that recurrences of plot seem to diminish a capacity for personal control (by suggesting the workings of involuntary repetition), so verbal reiterations more generally foreclose the prospects we normally assume in experience. When the man carefully builds a second fire, for instance, the warning implied by the repetitions offsets the description's calm understatement.

> This served for a foundation and prevented the young *flame* from drowning itself in the snow it otherwise would melt. The *flame* he got by touching a match to a small shred of birch bark that he took from his pocket. This burned even more readily than paper. Placing it on the foundation, he fed the young *flame* with wisps of dry grass and with the tiniest dry twigs.
>
> He worked slowly and carefully, keenly aware of his danger. Gradually, as the *flame* grew stronger, he increased the size of the twigs with which he fed it. He squatted in the snow, pulling the twigs out from their entanglement in the brush and feeding directly to the *flame*. He knew there must be no failure. (79; emphases added)

At a purely descriptive level, the flame's repeated animation ("young flame," "flame grew stronger") lends it a life and a will of its own that refuses to be controlled by the man. Yet at a more pervasive if somewhat paradoxical verbal level, the very invocation of "flame" five times in seven sentences ensures not the prospect of fiery success but rather the ephemerality of any hope. More fully confirming that effect are the fricatives proliferating through the passage, as if in partial echo of the "flame" and its predictable demise. Likewise, the reiteration shortly thereafter of the confident claim that "he was safe" establishes not the man's security but a mood of imminent peril. By translating the singular into a set, doubled language subverts linguistic authority, in the process replacing routine assurance with a mood of lingering doubt.

This verbal effect is more pronounced with words that unlike "flame" refer to capacities, not conditions. For while the narrative repetition of things makes conditions seem somehow fixed and de-

termined, the effect of repetition on emotions and other ephemeral states of being is erosive, apparently reducing them to lower levels of possibility. Agitation or happiness or lust—simply by virtue of being redescribed in the same words—appears not simply as if less spontaneous but finally as if less real. The initial assertion, that is, seems to be denied by its own reiteration. In a story devoted to the fatal consequences of all too frigid conditions, it should hardly come as a surprise that the capacity privileged above all others is a knowledge of how to forestall them—or that the word "know" occurs nearly as often as "cold." Keep in mind that "know" forms a special kind of word in everyday usage: connotations of certainty as well as of consciousness seem invoked by it, suggesting powers not only of deliberation but also of choice. By extension, it implies at least some limited control of contingency, since we commonly assume that knowledge of the past can help mediate the present and in turn shape the future. Huck and Jim "knowed" all sorts of signs in *Huckleberry Finn*, just as Lord Mark knows without being told why Kate Croy rejects him in James' *Wings of the Dove*. Claims for knowledge dictate how action is to be understood in both novels, confirming the moral considerations by which readers and characters are meant to judge narrative consequences. In "To Build a Fire," that possibility is gradually jeopardized and finally precluded by the process of repetition. Precisely because the man's knowledge is alleged with increasing frequency, it seems at first simply inadequate and then altogether irrelevant. And having in the story's first half subverted the effectiveness of knowledge, the narrative lapses from repetition into silence about what the man knows.

Compounding the effect of these singular verbal echoes is the story's repetitive syntax. Indeed, its paratactic flatness creates a world where everything is already ordered, immuring a single character not merely in a frozen Arctic environment, but in the very sentences that present him. It is as if the lack of syntactic contingency by which each sentence stands free of its neighbor reflected a more metaphysical absence of contingency whereby the future is as fixed as the past. In the process of denying its own temporality, moreover, the narrative creates an aura of timelessness. Such an effect may seem unlikely in a story that opens at 9 o'clock, pauses at 10, stops for lunch at 12:30, and ends at dusk, and in which a variety of shifters abound (such as "when," "before," "after," "at last," and "once in a while"). But this temporal precision in itself, when coupled with an absence

of singular events, effectively elides the passage of time that it pre-
tends to demarcate.

In the story's central sequence, for example, the man starts a fire
to thaw his freezing legs, and is just about to cut free his moccasin
lacings:

> But before he could cut the strings, it happened. It was his own
> fault or, rather, his mistake. He should not have built the fire
> under the spruce tree. He should have built it in the open. But it
> had been easier to pull the twigs from the brush and drop them
> directly on the fire. Now the tree under which he had done this
> carried a weight of snow on its boughs. No wind had blown for
> weeks, and each bough was fully freighted. Each time he had
> pulled a twig he had communicated a slight agitation to the tree—
> an imperceptible agitation, so far as he was concerned, but an
> agitation sufficient to bring about the disaster. High up in the tree
> one bough capsized its load of snow. This fell on the boughs
> beneath, capsizing them. This process continued, spreading out
> and involving the whole tree. It grew like an avalanche, and it
> descended without warning upon the man and the fire, and the fire
> was blotted out! Where it had burned was a mantle of fresh and
> disordered snow. (82–83)

There is no need once again to plot the multiple repetitions of this
passage, but we should not fail to notice that "it happened" echoes
the earlier disaster when the man fell into the spring ("And then it
happened"). As there, the two words contain the experience. More
to the point, we are never confused by the versatile "it" that floats
through the passage and that bobs up so variously in each of the first
four and last two sentences. Paradoxically, the very shifting of refer-
ents under the pronoun clarifies the scene, as one completed, timeless
event unfolds from a basic paratactic structure.

The real clincher, however, is the curiously immediate "Now":
"Now the tree under which he had done this carried a weight of
snow . . ." Breaking the text's completed pattern, the word seems at
first to recover us from the preterite to the immediate present. Yet
the "Now" here serves not as adverb but expletive, affixed to the
sentence for no other reason than to ease its syntactical rhythm.
Instead of moving us forward in time, it merely serves to mark time
and in doing so contributes to the narrative's pervasive timelessness.

The entire grammatical shape of the passage—including the overly simple syntax, the pronounced lack of subordinate clauses, and the subject references and verbs which effectively atomize the scene—all contribute to this atemporal effect as much as do repetition and tense. The whole resists a normal sequence from the initial "it" onwards, simply elaborating an experience that seems to us already fully completed. Here as elsewhere, the text links sections by stylistic rather than narrative causality—by a pattern of grammatical signifieds, not narrative signifiers. Actions prompt not other actions, sentences contingent sentences, so much as each doubles back on itself, in the process fostering the impression of temporal collapse.

Perhaps the best way to understand this effect is by turning to London's earlier, one-page version of the story. There the man not only has a name, but builds a fire and survives, toeless but with the hard-learned moral that one should "Never travel alone!" Clearly, the stories represent experiences that are altogether different, a difference nowhere better exemplified than in their central paragraphs:

> But at the moment he was adding the first thick twigs to the fire a grievous thing happened. The pine boughs above his head were burdened with a four months' snowfall, and so finely adjusted were the burdens that his slight movements in collecting the twigs had been sufficient to disturb the balance.
>
> The snow from the topmost bough was the first to fall, striking and dislodging the snow on the boughs beneath. And all this snow, accumulating as it fell, smote Tom Vincent's head and shoulders and blotted out his fire.[7]

Half as many words (92 vs. 183) appear in less than a third as many sentences (4 vs. 13), and yet this earlier version links compound sentences easily, reinforcing our customary sense of narrative control. Because events can be anticipated—not simply in the Arctic world but in the interdependent prose that describes what happens—contingency can be narratively controlled, the imagined effects of negligence forestalled, and responsibility affirmed as a compelling textual assumption.

By contrast, London's later version avoids participial constructions and thereby quietly erodes the basis for any such assumption. Indeed, the repetition of simple sentences only serves to corroborate the response presaged by the ominous "it happened," as if the scene

had already been fully enacted in those two words. Nothing the man can do will change an order of things fixed in such language or avert the harrowing implications of this unforeseen contingency. The explanatory connectives that authorize the didactic force of the earlier version have disappeared, replaced by a tableau-like style that excludes any hope of human agency. Zola's claim that the naturalist mode would lay bare an iron logic to events is achieved through the skewed perspective London offers on behavior, revealing how little an individual can alter causes described in a determining language.[8]

Character and Responsibility

IT WILL not do, however, simply to note the tendency of language in the story to undermine its own meaning, or even to unravel stylistic features that influence us to read deterministically. Moreover, no matter how often the word "know" is repeated (and thereby, like other words, shorn of significance), the problem of knowledge still persists, along with related issues of negligence and responsibility. We need now, in other words, to pursue more traditional questions of character in order to see how the plot also shapes a response less straightforward than first glances allow. Having rejected the old-timer's counsel before the story begins, the man can only continue to regret having decided to walk alone after fifty below. From the opening sentence, when he leaves the main trail for one that is "dim and little-travelled," we see him as he sees himself, independent-minded yet remiss—of chilling implications in the temperature as in the thin ice across which he walks, of the consequences of not building a fire as well as of building one under a spruce.[9] His mishaps are certainly unfortunate, then, but since a "close call" prompts no greater caution, we also treat him as in part responsible for the circumstances that finally destroy him. Is it fair, however, to judge him this way? And if so, why do we balk at so doing?[10]

These questions clearly drive to the heart of any determinist vision, especially given the difficulties in separating our view of the man from what happens to him. More clearly than other naturalist texts, the story draws attention to the arbitrary ties by which we associate knowledge with control, deliberation with agency. As I described in the Introduction, we project responsibility into fictional texts whether or not the capacity is warranted, and we do so much as we do in life, paradoxically holding characters to account for what

simply happens to happen to them. "To Build a Fire" forms a particularly vivid illustration of "moral luck," since we assume the man is culpable for having made an error of judgment (i.e., if circumstances had somehow confirmed his judgment, as they might easily have done, he would not have seemed to us to be at fault—although nothing he had thought, intended, or done would have been in the event any different). Notably, moreover, it is ignorance that characterizes his status as a *chechaquo*, "a newcomer in the land" who has been out before in only "two cold snaps." He ought, as he later acknowledges, to have complied with the advice of the old-timer at Sulphur Creek, "that no man must travel alone in the Klondike after fifty below." Yet although the narrator continues to stress this injunction in chiding tones, he is also forced to admit that the man was "without imagination," unable to appreciate the cold's "significance" or to anticipate the consequences of his actions. Indeed, the terms of responsibility slip from the narrator's very description, when he asserts that it was the man's "own fault or, rather, his mistake." First advancing, then withdrawing a flat statement of blame, the narrator seems compelled for accuracy's sake to translate guilt into mere inaccuracy.

Our own sense of the man's responsibility also diminishes through the story as we come to see that nothing can avert the disaster or otherwise alter events, events that result from so forceful a conjunction of character and circumstance. At the same time, our conventional conceptions of both these categories come to seem problematic. Like the narrator, we begin by wishing the man would just behave differently or show more restraint, only to realize he would literally have to be constituted differently for such a change to occur. If he were smarter, say, or stronger, or less impetuous, or followed advice: if any of these were so, we assume, he might well have been able to save his life. What his presentation makes clear, however, is that these could only be so by making him someone other than the man depicted in the story. Contrary to our normal expectation that people can always act differently than they do—that they can refrain from one activity and choose to do another instead—the unnamed man acts as he must. He is, in other words, exactly the sum of the events he enacts, no more or less, exemplifying the determinist premise that character is revealed through events, not in contrast to them. By assuming that changes in personality might somehow have altered the chain of events, we simply deny the man is who he is.[11]

Yet firmly fixed as the man's character appears to be, the circum-

stances of London's story seem somehow even less mutable, in large part because any knowledge of them has so little effect on what happens. Significantly, we never learn if the man forgot or did not know in the first place that it was hazardous to build a fire under a snow-laden tree. No matter whether he knew or not, so the narrative logic goes, the results of his trek would have been the same. The problem with such a logic is that it seems counter-intuitive, since knowledge appears to be the most determining constraint on activity, not the least. What we know or do not know would seem to dictate any possibility for action, either determined or free. Counter-intuitive or not, however, that logic corresponds to the sense of impotence we think we would feel in a deterministic world.

Or consider again a change in the man's capacities, this time from another perspective. What if he had been able in fact to imagine what the temperature meant, or had somehow anticipated the treacherous spring, or had considered the risks of traveling without a partner in this region; the story suggests that his trip would have turned out no better, even so. Judiciousness, forbearance, and circumspection all seem irrelevant when we can so readily imagine negligence leading to quite different consequences—say, the man's second fire *not* being obliterated by snow, or (as in the earlier version) his third attempt actually succeeding. Vice versa (but according to the same premise), Nagel's hapless driver might well have taken another route and still hit a child. The point is less that similar actions might have led the man to different consequences, or even that different actions could just as easily have led the driver to similar consequences, than that any consequences are always to some extent unforeseen. Our common mistake is in assuming that, since circumspection can avert disaster, greater caution will somehow decrease the hazards still further. But this ignores how much of what happens can be seen to lie outside our control, how little in fact our knowledge commands, and therefore how fully we always live in a state of unexpected contingency.

Unable to accept this condition, the narrator can only harp on the value of knowledge in the Arctic world. And much as a stress on what the man knows unsettles our faith in his wilderness lore, the narrator's larger claims have the more radical effect of drawing all knowledge into question. Grammatically as well as narratively, the text belies the assumption that causal patterns link actions with one's will, leaving the reader no better ready than the man to anticipate

when accidents will occur. Most dramatically, we remain unaware of any mistake in the five long paragraphs that detail the fire's careful construction under a tree. We too rush to assume that the cold will be at last forestalled in this instance, and when suddenly consequences clarify the error, we too are pinned as tightly as the man to a universe of "moral luck," likewise surprised only after the fact by what turns out to be something less than sin. The narrator's persistent effort to affix responsibility thus depends on a retrospective moralizing that is exposed as completely factitious.

Since knowledge appears to matter so little, regret seems altogether inappropriate, a response as irrelevant to events after the fact as the the uncertain feeling of choice is beforehand. Nor are we convinced by the man's own earnest profession of those values, which simply means that he is as fully mistaken as the narrator. Indeed, the narrative encourages us to identify with him against his own judgments, and to deny his fierce self-criticisms—if only because we recognize that his being "without imagination" has far less striking implications than the narrator didactically asserts. What we gradually realize instead is that responsibility must always seem misplaced in a world where knowledge proves so irrelevant and the will so unable to effect any change.

The sheer unknowability of consequence, which drains responsibility from the story, is reinforced by frequent references to all that the man is unable to achieve. No occasion at first occurs for such descriptions, even hypothetically, since before noon the man's desires and external events match somehow seamlessly; simply put, he keeps the pace he wants. But near mid-day, his self-assurance first gives way to doubt, and as that begins to happen the rhythm of contingency alters: "If he kept it up, he would certainly be with the boys by six." Now, conditions and the conditional begin to prevail, shifting both the man and the reader back and forth: ". . . if his feet are wet. If his feet are dry . . ."; "but now it ebbed away"; "But he was safe"; "If he had only had a trailmate"; "Even if he succeeded"; "Yet he was no better off"; "but the birch bark was alight"; "but . . . his shivering got away with him"; "But it was all he could do"; "But no sensation was aroused." This clotting of "if"'s and "but"'s occurs almost exclusively in the narrative's middle third, as the man's initial confidence turns first to doubt, then hopelessness.

At the extremes of the emotional spectrum between full certainty and utter despair, as at the beginning and end of the story, it is

irrelevant whether desire happens to align with experience. But the central section—where "things go wrong" and desire is for the first time denied—foregrounds both the man's vain hopes and what seem to him to be dire contingencies. The altered use of conditional and conjunction itself signals the shift in mood; after the story's midpoint, the sequence of "if"s and "but"s stress only prospects inimical to the man. By voicing his desire in the subjunctive, against a diminishing set of possibilities, the narrative accentuates the immutable shape that consequences give to events.

In the subfreezing Arctic, moreover, that shape is predictably a frozen one. The life-denying cold slowly enervates the man, leaving him at first bemused at the mechanical in the natural that makes his body seem somehow other: "When he touched a twig, he had to look and see whether or not he had hold of it. The wires were pretty well down between him and his finger ends." Later, "it struck him as curious that one should have to use his eyes in order to find out where his hands were." With his physical body now so clearly having become a thing apart, subjective and objective points of view begin to diverge, and to do so visibly—as he savagely beats his limbs to restore their circulation, or uses his teeth to strike matches only to cough out the flame he so painfully lights, or endures the stench of seared hands in a final fire-building attempt. However true it may sometimes be that "all a man had to do was to keep his head," that adage takes on an ironically literal significance when first the man's limbs and then his torso follow frozen toes, leaving him effectively decapitated.

His desires continue to press at the story's end as strongly as at the beginning, but by that time neither body nor actions can any longer be called his own. Or rather, he now more obviously exists in a condition that has been true of him all along: as a mere meeting of forces, more or less vital, more or less coherent. The plot, that is, at last enacts on the man's physical body a process completed long before by his narrative presentation—one in which attention is directed so fully at the world that absorbs him that no room appears to exist for a free-standing self. "Keeping his head" had otherwise seemed a matter of mere figurative self-composure, but the story turns on the profound implications of what physically is needed to compose a self, as the apparently inessential grows inanimate and consciousness slowly disintegrates.

This conclusion is nicely illustrated at the very end of the story, as

the man drifts into a sleep of death: "He did not belong with himself any more, for even then he was out of himself, standing with the boys and looking at himself in the snow. It certainly was cold, was his thought" (97). At that moment of physical release, the categories of both character and self are exploded, along with such subsidiary considerations as negligence and responsibility.[12] Refuting the customary realist conflation of the body with the will, London finally decenters the self, dissipating it through divisions between "he"'s, "himself"'s, and "his" and thereby displacing desire into the world. Of course, actually to free oneself from desire is possible only through release from the physical body, which necessarily results in death.[13]

At the grammatical level as well, London removes the man from his desires and transforms the personal into the impersonal by wrenching language and affronting usage. In the sentence quoted above ("it struck him as curious that one should have to use his eyes in order to find out where his hands were"), the pronominal disjunction between "him," "one," and "his" that otherwise suggests mere sloppy prose in this case marks the growing split between the man and himself.[14] Much as the cold dismantles him physically, the deadening maneuvers of syntax immure him in an environment that is all but paratactically fixed. Yet other aspects of his presentation likewise expose him to a textual frostbite that progressively numbs and immobilizes. Instead of actions being ascribed by the narrator to a coherent, identifiable "self," for instance, they are synecdochically assigned to parts of the man's body. At one point, his walk is described as a mere "eager nose that thrust itself aggressively into the frosty air," and at another he appears only by extension, as an ambulatory pied-à-terre—"At the man's heels trotted a dog."

Throughout the story, the man is defined by a sequence of negative formulations, as if he existed in little more than the tension derived through the contrast with what he is not; thoughts either "did not worry the man" or otherwise "never entered his head," while experience in general is asserted as having "made no impression." At those times when emotional, even automatic physiological responses *are* represented, the text offers them externally, as if they were occurring apart from and somehow happening to the man. Excluding him even more radically as a grammatical presence itself are a series of dead spatial metaphors. When he has them, for example, thoughts no longer "occurred" but entered "into his head," or sat with an almost physical weight "in his consciousness," or

"reiterated" themselves. Instead of his consciously making an effort to withdraw from the cold, it is his "blood" that is described as having autonomously "recoiled."[15] Long before the cold penetrates, however, the text incapacitates the man by denying our projected sense of him as a coherent, identifiable self.

Disabling Assumptions

IT SHOULD be clear by now that the narrative strategy of "To Build a Fire" depends upon more than a single point of view. What may be less clear, however, is that the tension between two main perspectives alters through the story and thereby itself transforms our understanding of what ensues. On the one hand, the man's limited consciousness is represented through a free indirect discourse, and as he becomes more and more panicked, the textual rhythms grow less assured. On the other hand, posed against that increasingly hysterical voice is an omniscient narrator who alternates between fiercely moralizing tones and cold impersonality. Indeed, the narrator takes an unusual tack toward his own story, and not merely because he occasionally sneers at the man's capacities or taunts his desires. As we have seen, he apparently thwarts the man's will more actively and persistently, by describing all those possibilities that can never be achieved. It is almost as if, in depicting closed options, he were delighting in the man's predicament.[16]

The fact that neither voice succeeds in finally controlling the text is less important, however, than that each persists in competing so fiercely for that control. Or so, at least, it seems in such passages as the following:

> He was sure to frost his cheeks; he knew that, and experienced a pang of regret that he had not devised a nose strap of the sort Bud wore in cold snaps. Such a strap passed across the cheeks, as well, and saved them. But it didn't matter much, after all. What were frosted cheeks? A bit painful, that was all; they were never serious.
>   Empty as the man's mind was of thoughts, he was keenly observant . . . (71)

This characteristically abrupt transition from one paragraph to the next, one voice to another, provokes a series of questions: Why allow

the man's vivid impressions to be given only to dismiss them so soon as intellectually limited? What is gained by unexpectedly adopting his pragmatic perspective and then as abruptly abandoning it? And why does the narrator elsewhere deny the man's claims with "in reality," or peremptorily refute his knowledge, or inveigh against his utter lack of imagination, curiosity, even intelligence—"The trouble with him . . ."? Were we to concur with these narratorial judgments, it would lead to the simple didactic conclusion that the man fails according to a clear set of wilderness standards; supposedly, as in the early version, he illustrates no more than a cruel moral to travel in the Yukon. Yet such an interpretation flattens out far too much in the story, and sacrifices all that we have seen of its stylistic and thematic complexity to the rough plot correspondence with an earlier version.

Part of what exposes the superficiality of so moralizing an interpretation is the very immediacy of the man's perspective, which lends an urgency to the narrative that has crucial repercussions. We as readers, after all, fail as well to anticipate the mistakes he will make and are just as surprised as he by the turn that events happen to take. Evoking his premature assessments, his frustrated desires and growing agitation, the narrative succeeds in gradually aligning the reader with the man, and thereby helps to immerse us in a deterministic universe. Distant as we may otherwise feel from someone who lacks either imagination or knowledge, we sympathize with him at those points where our wills are also denied, our own sense of foreclosure heightened. The text's persistent, repetitive rhythm affects us much as it does the man, progressively alienating us as well from our customary assumptions by absorbing us into the determinist patterns established by the text.

A curious result of the diminished sense of control that we feel along with the man is that the narrator's unrelenting critique begins to turn back on itself. Gradually, we become aware that the censure of the man calls its own terms into question—in part because it does so on occasion quite explicitly. Recall the central paragraph of the fire's disastrous obliteration, when the narrator qualifies his claim that it was the man's "own fault or, rather, his mistake." Despite the initial moralizing impulse, which recurs in subsequent observations about the man's responsibility for his plight, the hesitant retraction acknowledges how little agency in fact really matters. Even the possibility that the prose is in free indirect discourse—and that these

self-exculpating tones are the man's, not the narrator's—only helps to confirm what has been clear all along: that in subscribing to the weak moral assumptions maintained by the narrator, the man cannot escape a spurious self-indictment that only has the effect of compounding his self-alienation.

However much they may differ or share, the conflicting narrative voices are finally unable to disguise how little it is that consciousness can effect, at least in this story. "To Build a Fire" most radically subverts our expectations about the will, then, by shifting attention from thoughts to events, and in particular by presenting events as if they were happening to, even "at" the man. Left near the end as at the beginning, he forms nothing so much as a mere meeting of forces—nameless, selfless, little more than a place for things to happen—and the story comes at last to seem less a painful dismantling of an integrated ego than a revelation of how little there has been all along. At nearly every point, he finds his desire to ward off the cold is thwarted, and thwarted as much by the narrator's hectoring mode as by physical events. Yet the fact that the narrator is foiled as well— most prominently, in his repeated endeavor to hang moral tags on experience—points to what seems like a curiously unresolved tension in the story. Neither the man nor the narrator seems able to offer accurate interpretations of events or to exert control over the experience they happen to observe. In much the same way that the man's concerted efforts fail to alter the course of events, the narrator's broken syntax suggests the inadequacies of his descriptive role, revealing how little credit he can take for shaping the narrative he reports.

Still, both voices *do* exist as likely presences in the text and reinforce separate identities by the very resistance they offer to each other. It is as if their actual status was finally a matter of little or no concern. The fact that the man in particular lacks so many of the features we associate with identity comes to seem less important than that he continues to exist in the text at all. Agency may no longer be at issue, and the prospect of a coherent self has vanished, but something distinctly remains in our reading of the story, even so. What that something is has been clarified by the discussion of Strawson and Nagel, and involves the irrepressible "self" we impose on almost any narrative sequence. That "self" is not a function, then, of only familiar textual structures—of the grammatical and narrative forms so characteristic of literary realism that evoke for us the model of

responsible personhood. Indeed, London's story stands as an exemplary instance of how we arbitrarily reinsert a responsible "self" into human relations, even in the absence of enabling structures. More than simply a process of anthropomorphizing the unknown, we attribute to fictional figures capacities that cannot ever be proved and yet that far exceed the sum of particular traits or psychological processes.

Precisely because responsibility is entirely stripped from this fictional world, "To Build a Fire" forms a narrative site on which we can clearly see ourselves project habitual assumptions about moral agency. The moral category keeps reappearing, reinscribing itself through the very conflict that arises between the two narrative voices. The effect of this is to make the man seem transformed from simply a "character" to a "self"—from someone who acts as desires dictate into someone capable of restraining himself, of deciding the kinds of desires he wants, and even of choosing the type of person he thinks he would like to be. The reason the category of the self keeps reinserting itself into the text—this, despite all the narrative forces that freeze it out from so fierce an Arctic world—is that both the man and the narrator agree that the category must somehow exist. With absolutely no evidence from experience, and much to the contrary to suggest that the man is essentially powerless, they both assume (as does the reader) that he can make decisions, then act or not act directly because of them.

Of course, this paradoxical process is by no means peculiar to London's story, however differently that process occurs in other texts, as the next chapters show. Characters who at first glance seem to be flawed but nonetheless full, card-carrying "persons" appear upon closer examination to lack an array of essential attributes. The question that arises has little to do with the power of that initial illusion, since in any event we have seen how central it is to our constitutional makeup. Rather, the issue becomes a matter of distinguishing case by case how we as readers are persuaded temporarily to sacrifice such an illusion, to forego the comforting premise that others are agents as well as ourselves. What additional forms of repetition, say, or patterns of narrative voice, or syntactical maneuvers, or constructions of character, help subvert our normal projective impulses? What, in short, are the textual strategies adopted by different authors in texts more elaborate and comprehensive than London's? As importantly, how might determinism be depicted as a

psychological rather than a physical issue—as a problem not of contending accounts about a character's alleged negligence but of the psychic construction of an independent "self"? That question moves us from the natural world to a set of far stranger inner landscapes, from the philosophy of knowledge to the psychology of desire, and from matters distinctively stylistic to those more clearly behavioral. As well, the question seems constructed for the very novel often considered the triumph of American naturalism: Theodore Dreiser's *American Tragedy*.

3.

The Psychopoetics of Desire in Dreiser's *American Tragedy*

THE DEATH of Roberta Alden forms the dramatic crisis of *An American Tragedy*. Having journeyed to Big Bittern Lake with the intention of drowning her, Clyde Griffiths recoils from the act itself. Only her impulse to rise up and touch him impels him to strike out in thoughtless resistance, then to rise up himself to her aid in a series of movements that capsize their boat.

> And the left wale of the boat as it turned, striking Roberta on the head as she sank and then rose for the first time, her frantic, contorted face turned to Clyde, who by now had righted himself. For she was stunned, horror-struck, unintelligible with pain and fear—her lifelong fear of water and drowning and the blow he had so accidentally and all but unconsciously administered.[1]

The scene has a powerful dramatic energy, evoked by a disjointed syntax that masks nonetheless a surprising inconsistency: Roberta's

last appearance alive is described quite precisely as only a "first time." Yet nothing can form a first until a second time occurs, when memory is able to create repetition from resemblance. For Roberta to rise to the surface of the lake "for the first time" requires a re-surfacing that does not occur. In a novel replete with repetition, death itself would appear to be the only experience that remains starkly singular.

Two days and as many chapters later, however, another kind of rising does take place when the appropriately named woodsman, John Pole, finally drags Roberta to the water's surface. It is as if this successful repetition of the novel's most critical event was meant to accentuate the special function in this novel of repetition itself—as a narrative resurrection of the past, a kind of recitative "raising of the dead."[2] Indeed, our attention is drawn to the very power of the narrative act through the long delay in providing a referent for the earlier implied repetition. This suspension of repetition's promise denies our common faith in a natural sequence of events by bridging, even effacing the effects of represented time. The referential illusion is subverted, that is, as Roberta surfaces a second time in the text, not the lake—through the immediate re-presentation of a "first time" whose autonomous status is deferred until the woodsman's successful poling.

The idea that repetition might have such a complex effect is profoundly ironic in a novel whose multiple repetitions have seemed to most readers all too excessive, and even whose staunchest admirers have been heard to lament the lack of a ruthless editor.[3] Those same readers have nonetheless occasionally been heard to confess to the sense of "entrapment" so aptly described by Robert Penn Warren: "We live in Clyde's doom, and in the process live our own secret sense of doom which is the backdrop of our favorite dramas of the will."[4] Few, however, have sensed that this feeling is largely an inadvertent response to stylistic excesses they have otherwise shrugged off or scorned. They fail to consider, in other words, that the novel's echoing structure itself is responsible for its "sense of doom," or that the text's determinism largely depends on its multiple recurrences.[5] Given this lack of attention, few have thought to suggest that the repetitions in the novel form an interconnected pattern—that, for instance, the prefigurements and flashbacks which disrupt the narrative help to structure its ironic mode, or that in turn they shape the rhythm by which characters differ from each other and divide from themselves.

Psychological Doubles

STRANGELY ENOUGH, the lively characterization that everyone acknowledges in Dreiser's novel results from the kind of psychological doubling that few have admitted is important—a doubling more subtle than most have even thought to suspect.[6] Customarily, narratives of the double establish an aura of inevitability by posing alteregos that deprive the central figures of a sense of agency. *An American Tragedy* presents the double less obviously than such an identification suggests by paradoxically directing attention to what seems to be its most obvious occurrence: Clyde's uneasy relationship with his wealthy, look-alike cousin, Gilbert.[7] The plot of book 2 is generated by the resemblance between the two young men—a resemblance that spurs Samuel Griffiths's initial invitation to visit Lycurgus, Sondra Finchley's later interest in Clyde, and his subsequent rise to social acceptance. Indeed, according to Freud, Gilbert would seem the perfect double for Clyde, the personification of "all those unfulfilled but possible futures to which we still like to cling in phantasy, all those strivings of the ego which adverse external circumstances have crushed, and all our suppressed acts of volition which nourish in us the illusion of Free Will."[8] True as this seems at first, at least for Clyde, the cousins soon discover that the features they share ironically suggest how fully at odds they are. As no more than "manifest" doubles, their physical similarities merely mask far more significant psychological differences.

Their first meeting establishes the contrast between a "soft and vague and fumbling" Clyde and his "dynamic and aggressive" counterpart: "he entered and faced a youth who looked, if anything, smaller and a little older and certainly much colder and shrewder than himself—such a youth, in short, as Clyde would have liked to imagine himself to be."[9] Clyde desires Gilbert's Princeton education, his wealth, and easy assurance, viewing his cousin less as a distinct personality than as a fortunate set of circumstances. Gilbert with a sneer responds likewise to Clyde, dismissing him as a mere interloper raised above his station by the sheer accident of family connections. Still, the very strength of his unexplained resistance to someone who so closely resembles him suggests a fear of the double that is complemented by Clyde's own uneasiness. Each seems the other's alter-ego, as revealed most clearly in the mutually exclusive pattern of their

separate inadequacies: Clyde fails to control his conflicting desires by hardening his will; Gilbert fails to escape a will that has grown inflexible and overbearing. For both, the other becomes something like an involuntary repetition, embodying not "strivings of the ego" but what Freud described elsewhere as a return of the repressed.

The strength of that repression is revealed in the depth of their mutual resentment, evident in their parallel efforts to gain revenge upon the other. At a trivial level, Gilbert simply delights in keeping Clyde waiting, perversely delaying his cousin's appearance before him when they are scheduled to meet; Clyde similarly gloats in the knowledge that he has inadvertently disrupted Gilbert's life.[10] Yet behavior is shaped by repression and revenge far more fully than this, as confirmed in the dual plot motions of book 2: the Griffiths' casual neglect of Clyde encourages his secret dalliance with Roberta, while Sondra later befriends him merely in order to irritate Gilbert. The Griffiths slight Clyde out of nothing other than social embarrassment, hoping thereby to avoid imputations that they share his lower-class origins. He nonetheless keeps reappearing before them in dramatic enactment of a return of the repressed, and finally disrupts their lives more disastrously than even their worst fears had suggested. On the other hand, Sondra intentionally wins the affection of his double against Gilbert's will, and achieves in the process a revenge as well as self-punishment far exceeding her expectations.

Much as the cousins seem doubles of each other, their relationship lacks a daemonic power that is generally considered characteristic of psychological twinning. For that notably absent quality, we need to look elsewhere—most obviously, at the tension between Clyde and Roberta. More than is ever possible with Gilbert, she allows Clyde to project certain aspects of himself onto her—a displacement producing a burden of guilt that shapes their self-defining, self-denying relationship. As Otto Rank first noted, "the most prominent symptom of the forms which the double takes is a powerful consciousness of guilt which forces the hero no longer to accept the responsibility for certain actions of his ego, but to place it upon another ego, a double."[11] The double emerges, in other words, out of a regressive need for self-perfection—a narcissistic process that at once issues from and fosters a disposition toward paranoia. "The literary representations of the double-motif which describe the persecution complex," Rank observed further, "reduce the chief pursuer to the ego itself, the person formerly loved most of all" (74). Little as this

description matches Clyde's relationship to Gilbert, it exactly fits his affair with Roberta, an affair that eerily dramatizes the fuller implications of doubling in terms of narcissism and guilt, persecution and pursuit.[12]

Roberta hardly fits a traditional conception of the double, in part because she is so much more distinctively a character in her own right than the fictional avatars imagined by Dostoevsky, Conrad, Melville, and Poe. Still, from Clyde's point of view she comes to seem a "secret sharer," an Other that represents to the self desires at once fulfilled and frustrated. Her tacit identification with him is made through a chronological equation with his physical twin; like Gilbert, she is twenty-three, exactly two years older than Clyde. And because of the opposite sex, their psychological doubling results not from physical similarity, but from a social and economic resemblance. Her parents are virtual carbon-copies of Clyde's, "excellent examples of that native type of Americanism which resists facts and reveres illusion" (249). Both fathers are inept and fog-bound, each one the youngest and least forceful of three sons; and given equally strong wives, both Titus Alden and Asa Griffiths produce children with nearly identical dispositions. Her "warm, imaginative, sensuous temperament" (250) prompts Roberta, like Clyde, to escape a dull life at home, only to grow similarly dissatisfied at work. She too aspires to a better future, revealed in a "wistfulness and wonder" that strikingly resembles Clyde's predominant mood, and her dreams have the force of conviction that he recognizes in himself, as "a kind of self-reliant courage and determination" (246).

Similar circumstances create emotional drives that affect them alike, against their wills.[13] Caught in a whirl of helpless impulse, Clyde looks and speaks "in spite of himself," just as Roberta is "seized with the very virus of ambition and unrest that afflicted him" (247–48, 256). Spurred by loneliness and mutual desire, they can do nothing other than discover their own self-images in the other. Indeed, their first encounter alone at Crum Lake allows them successfully to conjure the other into life. In a canoe, a solitary Clyde pictures Roberta's "bright eyes" and soft face at the same time that, "looking down in the water," she strives to imagine him. Suddenly, they are together: "Almost before he had decided, he was . . . looking up at her, his face lit by the radiance of one who had suddenly . . . realized a dream. And as though he were a pleasant apparition . . . she in turn stood staring down at him, her lips unable to resist"

(265). Looked down on by others ever since childhood, uncomfortably stared at from the novel's opening pages (as he will also be through its entire last third), Clyde finds that that condition is momentarily transformed in his surprised confrontation of Roberta. Likewise she, Narcissus-like, with lips "parted in careless inquiry," has discovered a wished-for version of herself in the act of staring up at her. The uncanny embodiment of their imagined longings, the setting on water, and the joining "so intimately" in a ride that prefigures their final trip: all coalesce to suggest a deep psychological kinship.

The lake lends a fluid familiarity to a relationship that can only falter when on land, and their step from the traditional psychological setting of water onto the social shore abruptly changes their newfound ease. Nevertheless, the bond is established, leaving them both unable to think of anything but the other, both acting counter to original intentions. The pressure of psychic need, not considered volition, dictates their first walk together, then their first kiss, and finally sexual consummation. Neither one is able to control a relationship shaped so fully by desire, and at last each "yielded to the other completely. And dreamed thereafter, recklessly and wildly" (307). Now, as if to recover selves so newly and entirely displaced, the lovers separately develop the habit of staring into their bedroom mirrors, attempting to consolidate intention and desire with a self-image the other has helped to create. Two months of mutual self-abandonment have led them finally to depend on each other for a sense of self.

By the time Clyde starts to rise in the social circles of Lycurgus, Roberta has become his alter-ego. Her days and nights repeat his own early experience in town, as his indifference to her repeats society's former neglect of him.[14] Left to her room, she now embodies a part of himself rejected and cast out—that part of the ego once "loved most" and, in the usual double pattern, become the pursuer. Roberta's determination quickly grows to equal Clyde's, as the two develop into what seem like opposing fragments of a psychological whole—she expressing what he knows he should feel in the way of honorable obligation.[15] Despite lost love, Clyde cannot break free, which makes it less than ironic that Roberta should find herself pregnant only after both have finally decided to part. The pregnancy now seems not merely a natural result of their sexual union, but a kind of psychosomatic response in which psychic energies have been

bonded, with a physical consequence that symbolizes at once a mockery of love and a fulfillment of their relationship. The fetus that is destined never to become a child embodies their inability to create another outside the confines of a joint-self, a life beyond the projected other.

In his resentment of Roberta's demands, Clyde at one point silently exclaims: "Oh, why had he ever been so foolish and weak as to identify himself with her in this intimate way? Just because of a few lonely evenings! Oh, why, why couldn't he have waited and then this other world would have opened up to him just the same? If only he could have waited!" (2:12) Unusual as is this backward view, Clyde characteristically misrepresents his passion, assuming that it had resulted from a mere accident of bad timing and the pressures of loneliness. Yet his words themselves belie the very disavowal he wants to make, in the double meaning they unintentionally but nonetheless clearly convey. His euphemistic circumlocution ("identify himself with her") suggests not simply irritation at himself for having given way to sexual desire, but a larger regret that he could only achieve the assurance of a full identity by "identifying" with Roberta.

Clyde's inability to acknowledge how fully he displaces himself onto Roberta—much like her own inability to admit having projected similar desires onto Clyde—later causes his resentment to become overpowering. He cannot face up to the implications expressed in his fear of direct confrontation: "as he knew, her steady, accusing, horrified, innocent blue eyes would be about as difficult to face as anything in all the world" (2:22). What he does not realize here is that the two of them have become fundamentally one, and that Roberta's increasingly desperate pursuit of him simply reflects the energy of self-abandonment doubled. Rejecting her, in other words, Clyde seems to be rejecting himself. And as if to make the pattern clear, the murderous plan he will finally adopt incites a dream of self-destruction that anticipates his own later death: a nightmare of snakes and beasts that everywhere block his path and prevent his escape.

Perhaps unsurprisingly, therefore, emotional states more than physical events seem to dictate the closing days of book 2, where the estranged pair are reduced to little more than psychological essences. Provoked beyond measure by Roberta's importunate and finally threatening letters, Clyde listens as the "genii of his darkest and

weakest side" (2:49) suggests her murder. He feels pressed by "her crass determination to force him in this way" (2:66), and sets about luring her once again to a solitary boat on a deserted lake, where reminders of their first meeting appear in the same cloud shapes, the same fingers trailing in water, the same desultory search for water lilies. Again, that search turns inward and psychological, as the two float aimlessly along in "an insubstantial rowboat upon a purely ideational lake."[16] But now, Clyde's revulsion from Roberta becomes an all-absorbing self-revulsion, as the water seems transformed into an eerie fluid that no longer even reflects their images. Apparently oil or molten glass, it separates them both from the "substantial earth" of customary social identity. "This still dark water seemed to grip Clyde as nothing here or anywhere before this ever had—to change his mood. For once here he seemed to be fairly pulled or lured along into . . . endless space where was no end of anything . . . And the water itself . . . seemed bottomless as he gazed into it" (2:74). Roberta grows ever more shadowy and insubstantial as the scene progresses, while "he seemed to slip away from the reality of all things."

Critics have often observed that Clyde's "murder" of Roberta seems a curious non-action. Despite his reiterated plan to hit her with the camera, the event seems fully deprived of intent by what the narrative describes as a sudden "aboulia" (or "palsy of the will," 2:76). Some claim the murder is self-committed, others that Roberta abets the crime, still others that she kills herself, with Clyde as a mere accessory.[17] Yet while all agree that her death seems the product of forces beyond the individual will, none of the explanations sufficiently reveals the scene's striking inevitability; each one resurrects categories of innocence and guilt that the scene itself radically undercuts. Clyde is *not* in fact innocent from a legal point of view, since a consequence occurs that he had admittedly once intended. As the trial judge explains, the jury must find him "constructively" guilty if it lacks contrary evidence that might prove a change of heart. Likewise, Clyde is implicated from a moral perspective: no matter how his intention may have changed, he did indeed callously fail to swim to her rescue once he realized she was drowning.[18] Legal and moral terms differ, however, which ironically leads to a series of fateful interpretations. Despite the judge's instructions, an appalled jury convicts Clyde for having refused to help Roberta; the Reverend Duncan McMillan, on the other hand, later refuses to encourage the

Governor's pardon because he thinks Clyde has "sinned in many ways" (2:392). In each of these cases, the narrative draws attention to the categories by which judgment is made, categories of agency that introduce considerations altogether irrelevant to the novel. Only the reader can know that the scene of Roberta's drowning enacts a death of the double—since other than Clyde, only the reader has been present at the scene itself. The point is that such deaths resist attributions of guilt by inviting a psychologically determinist interpretation.

Rank, who argued that the double originated in narcissistic guilt, understood the paradox that "it is nourished by a powerful fear of death and [yet] creates strong tendencies toward self-punishment, which also imply suicide" (77). Exaggerating his attributes and abilities, Clyde rejects desires that do not fit his ideal, and conveniently transfers onto Roberta what he would otherwise deny in himself; that impulse helps explain why her demands express so effectively his own sense of guilt. The uncanny power of the scene at Big Bittern emerges not in Clyde's hesitant failure to help, or even in Roberta's apparent assistance in her own destruction, but in the silent acknowledgment that he is destroyed in the process of her death. More precisely, he cannot prevent the annihilation of what he cannot see: his own displaced self. Wanting first on the lake to withdraw from Roberta, then impelled by the need to "recapture her," Clyde is consumed by paralysis and ends by not acting at all. Since the demise of the double always destroys the self, Roberta's death becomes Clyde's deathknell. He too dies psychologically, unable thereafter to move beyond that moment, condemned in perpetuity to recall the lake vision, and thereby denied any comfort in even the fragments of a self he might shore against his ruin. The loneliness troubling him before he met Roberta, a loneliness assuaged only in their year-long relationship, significantly returns to plague him only after her watery death.

Narrative Repetitions

THE PRINCIPLE most clearly apparent in psychological doubling structures the novel throughout. Repetition, that is, distinguishes every other aspect of the characters' lives, including the language used to describe them. Yet no less immediately apparent than the iterative cadences of its prose is the effect of the novel's compulsive

re-presentation of scene and event.[19] To begin with, the physical activities that organize the three separate sections of the novel are each mechanically repetitive: bellhops jump up to identical requests for equivalently measly tips in the first book; collars are stamped one-by-one, day-by-day through long stretches of the second; and in the third, Clyde's relationship with Roberta is recounted over and over without variation, first in the woods, then in the courthouse, and finally in prison. The opening and closing scenes of the novel depict street preachers trailed by boys, while the parallel conclusions of books 1 and 2 describe Clyde's panicked flight from "accidents." Stark scenes of death end both these books, both of which nonetheless follow the duration of pregnancy (Esta's first, then Roberta's), suggesting in turn the powerful, ongoing rhythm of biological repetition. Life and death simply repeat themselves while things persist as they have in the past, constraining everyone willy-nilly to recurrences of which they remain unaware.

Yet these examples are far too brief to suggest the complexity of Dreiser's use of scenic repetition. When Esta leaves home in chapter 3, for example, the event is presented twice: synoptically first and then in a detailed rendition of background, motive, and consequence. That narrative pattern of summary, description, and iteration characterizes other episodes as well: Clyde's job at the soda fountain; his deception of his parents; the bellhops' dinner and drunken whorehouse visit; and countless other occasions that lead to the Governor's final refusal to grant a pardon. This stammering technique effectively establishes an aura of inevitability, by making events seem fully concluded from the beginning, before narration has even begun.[20]

Descriptions likewise offer a double view, as if by moving from outside to inside, the narrative can fix the specific context that determines an emotional response. This stress on material contexts, moreover, renders psychology secondary, since it is so dependent upon the world as to seem fully predictable. Well before his resentful impressions are given, for example, Clyde appears to an unnamed street denizen as a beleaguered child; pages prior to the account of his precocious sexual and social development, the bellhop Ratterer leers at a passing blonde. Most major characters—and in particular, Roberta and Sondra—are likewise introduced through a cinematic technique that first pans an outer perspective before zooming in on the private sensibility idiosyncratically shaped by a past. Even settings appear this way, whether the opulent Green-Davidson Hotel (and its bellhop system) or the Lycurgus Griffiths' mansion.[21]

The effects of scenic and descriptive repetition are further compounded by the narrative technique of prolepsis. Indeed, prefigurement and foreshadowing in this novel might best be thought of as anticipatory repetitions that likewise instill a sense of inevitability by linking events in the future to present expectations. The car crash that concludes book 1 has been anticipated by the fur salesman's hypothesis to Hortense Briggs: "But supposin' the next day after you take the coat an automobile runs you down and kills you. Then what?"[22] Squire warns Clyde of the fate of irresponsible bellhops and the warning is literally enacted; similarly, Gilbert cautions him of the consequences of flirting with factory girls, and his prediction is borne out. On their first chance encounter, Roberta asks, "Is it safe?" before stepping into Clyde's canoe—a question that ironically anticipates the event toward which the entire novel is pointing. Even though her hesitation is innocent, it too contributes more than a predictably unsettling atmosphere to the perils implicit in a romance on water. Just as the account of the boating accident is prefigured, so are the possibilities of a trial and a lynch mob.

Repetition, in other words, profoundly characterizes the novel's crucial event, structuring a narrative that looks forward to and repeatedly recalls Roberta's drowning. In the process, the contingency of that scene comes to seem denied, as openness, uncertainty, and possibility are gradually leached from narrative expectation. Prior to her death, Clyde entertains the various alternatives, thereby anticipating risks that will be elaborately described in the event itself. Book 3 then opens with the telephone account to Coroner Heit that initiates a series of recountings, including Mason's explanation to Clyde's landlady, his pointed confrontation of Clyde, and Clyde's separate descriptions to the lawyers Smillie, Belknap, and Jephson. Later, the actual trial testimony atomizes the event once again, in the process adding aspects unknown to either Clyde or the reader. Witnesses previously absent from the text come forward to testify to their impressions, as Roberta's death increasingly seems beyond Clyde's will, outside the possibility of change or alteration.

Each retelling of the story fixes Clyde more fully in the past, enmeshing him in a drama written by various, incomplete memories —including the reader's own. The trial testimony complicates any true recollection of the incriminating events, compelling some readers to return to book 2 in order to establish the account they have read—even as the later conflicting reports confirm Clyde's inability to do the same. At the end, he has a lonely "feeling in his heart that

he was not as guilty as they all seemed to think," but he too is finally impelled to accept his past as no longer his. Repetitions compounding repetition have enabled the community successfully to appropriate Clyde's history, first by co-opting elements of his experience to their limited terms and then by reiterating those elements into a pattern of certainty.

Likewise, the novel's recapitulations and flashbacks put Clyde at the behest of time, and reveal in the process the fundamentally ironic tenor of his life. In the transition between books 1 and 2, for instance, the narrative shifts from Kansas City to Lycurgus, New York, revealing neither the consequences of the automobile accident nor the amount of time that has since elapsed. For the duration of two whole chapters, we know only that Clyde is once again a bellhop, this time in Chicago. Although the next three chapters describe the intervening three years that bring him to Lycurgus, the proleptic narrative structure itself forecloses the realm of contingency. This narrative pattern is predictably repeated in the two days that elapse between books 2 and 3, between Roberta's death and the coroner's notification. More compellingly than in the earlier shift, the novel fills the temporal gap that separates public discovery from private torment by alternating the plot of Clyde's pursuers with that of his escape. Five chapters describe the chase, followed by three depicting his nervous flight, before chapter 9 unites the two plots in Mason's arrest of Clyde.

Time is thoroughly fragmented by this unusually doubling narrative motion, but with an equally unsettling effect: instead of thereby intensifying possibility, it tends paradoxically only to confirm what we know has already happened. Just as Mason at the very beginning of book 3 quickly identifies Clyde, so Samuel Griffiths had announced his nephew's imminent arrival early in book 2; subsequent chapters provide a host of further details, but they cannot generate any tension over a foreclosed future. Both revelations permit an ironic perspective on a Clyde who is already trapped without knowing it; denying suspense to his escapes, they reduce his plight to a sequence of forces.

At a more general level, scenic repetition weaves together the three books. Some critics think they move in terms of cause, effect, and reprise; others, that each one forms an examination into the terms of the preceding.[23] But the three can also be seen as narrative recapitulations of one another, leaving Clyde faced each time with

less secure consequences to similar actions. Freud spoke of this pattern as a "compulsion to repeat," and invoked the example of "people all of whose human relationships have the same outcome." According to him, "this 'perpetual recurrence of the same thing' causes us no astonishment when it relates to *active* behavior on the part of the person concerned . . . We are much more impressed by cases where the subject appears to have a *passive* experience, over which he has no influence, but in which he meets with a repetition of the same fatality."[24] Notwithstanding Clyde's intentions to resist sexual entanglement—first with the prostitute, then with Hortense, and lastly with Rita and Roberta—he keeps experiencing similar crises as if they were somehow different. Moreover, he never recognizes what Lycurgus shares with Kansas City, or how Roberta's accident resembles the car crash, or the way so much of his behavior passively, self-destructively repeats itself. "Behind the realm of accident," Richard Lehan observes, "is the realm of causal sequence and inevitability."[25] For the reader, if not for Clyde, the sheer repetition of event exposes that realm.

In thus presenting events, descriptive reiteration delays their course, with the effect once again of calcifying them unalterably in time. No matter how expansive the novel's review of Clyde's growth from twelve to twenty-two, each book focuses tightly upon only a few representative moments. Spanning Esta's pregnancy, for instance, from April to the January car ride, book 1 nonetheless concentrates on the dozen days when Hortense frustrates Clyde. Twice as many months are covered in book 2, which is considerably more than two times as long, but it also concentrates on representative scenes of Clyde's relationship with Roberta—on their June meeting, October consummation, December altercations, and July drowning. Book 3 is nearly as long again and documents the longest period (of nineteen months), but it attends even more narrowly to Clyde's two-month trial and incarceration. Despite the chronologically expansive rhythm of the novel, in other words, the narrative focuses on a series of experiences that seem merely more of the same. Similar episodes recur from scene to scene, book to book, in a process compounded by the narrative's separate recapitulation of the separate events themselves. The cumulative effect of these various repetitions is to brake the plot's onward flow.[26]

This retardation of temporal process grinds down everyone in the novel. In making their actions seem unnaturally slowed by a process

beyond their control, it puts them at the behest of forces clearly greater than any individual will. Clyde in particular seems constrained by narrative as well as historical forces precisely because he is caught unaware in moments that figuratively and literally repeat. His perpetually unabated enthusiasm confirms an inability to learn from experience, to master it by recognizing its repetitions and thereby possibly altering them. Unable to break from a temporal circle that tends to conflate the past with the future, he lacks the simple powers of memory that would allow him to exert intentional control. Only by recognizing the past as past, that is, might Clyde have begun to diverge from it and in the process have defined an alternative to the novel's deterministic pattern.

Against the slowed chronological rhythm of a narrative in which events and scenes endlessly recur, Clyde's obliviousness to recurrence only further imprisons him, condemning him to treat as new what the reader can see is clearly not. In book 1, for instance, he looks ever forward with an eerily frightening enthusiasm as he moves from home to soda fountain to hotel. He never recalls his first job (nor even gives notice of his departure) and forgets his family's plight as easily as Carrie Meeber does her own. Like Carrie as well he looks backs on former relationships only rarely, only out of extreme anxiety. One occasion alone in book 1 prompts any form of reconsideration: his fear that Esta will require money he has saved for Hortense. In book 2, he unreflectively moves from a Chicago hotel lobby to Lycurgus prospects, from Walter Dillard to Rita, then to Roberta and Sondra, all without a backward glance. Myra Griffiths, then Bella, disappear from the novel as easily as they slip from his consciousness.[27]

The death of Roberta therefore has a singular effect on Clyde, since it brings involuntary memory for the first time alive, and does so with a vengeance. The past now begins to assert itself in a dramatically powerful way, and when book 3 compels Clyde to reconstruct his life, he learns to fear the drowning as an episode he will never be allowed to forget. With his lawyers, he is forced to recall one past, on the witness stand to invent another, and in prison to invoke a third (by wildly imagining those who might help him to escape). Earlier, his perspective had been focused exclusively on the future — vague, unrealized, dreamy.[28] Yet the novel turns him not forward, but backward, until hope itself ends with Sondra's final letter: "the last trace of his last dream vanished. Forever" (2:383). Coercing him

gradually from his desires, the narrative at last entraps Clyde through the repetitive strategy it has enforced from the beginning.[29]

That strategy even characterizes the double edge of the narrative voice, which identifies with Clyde at one point only to hector him at another. The pattern resembles the narrator's stance toward the unnamed man in "To Build a Fire," except that the hectoring tone disappears in the second half of Dreiser's novel. Donald Pizer concludes that the narrator shifts "from contempt toward compassion" (285), although the narrator expresses no overt sympathy with Clyde's predicament and continues to mock his clear "lack of wit" (2:314). The abatement in narrative bullying, however, marks less a softened perspective toward Clyde than merely growing silence. The omniscient voice slowly disappears, refusing to declaim any more against "all religionists" (20), or "the illusions of youth" (55), or "every primary union between the sexes" (304). It no longer gleefully divulges information clearly unknown to Clyde, as it had earlier revealed the secret of Hortense's lost virginity, of the Green-Davidson's dangerous "influence," and of Sparcer's unsuspected fondlings. That voice fades, moreover, because Clyde's increasingly divided sensibility has displaced the narrator's voice in a gradual shift to free indirect discourse. Looking backward more than ahead, now turned from diminished dreams to the ineluctable consequences of a misspent past, his own double vision keys the narrative with ever greater clarity. Earlier, the narrator confirmed the inevitability of events through a sardonic ironic tone. Now, instead of a narrator's patsy, Clyde is the victim of his own perspective. It is one of the novel's consummate ironies that his characteristic vision emerges most fully and his voice is most clearly heard only as he begins to sense how little his life is finally his own to articulate.

Still, whether at the service of an omniscient voice or of Clyde's, the novel's language is patently as repetitive as everything else about it. Just as characters, events, and descriptions all overlap, so the prose itself divides and doubles, saved from utter fragmentation by a sequence of conjunctions and participial clauses that link separate phrases into parallel structure. Much as this repetitive technique suggests an uninterrupted stream of thought, the description of Clyde's sexual initiation reveals a more telling effect:

> And now, seated here, she had drawn very close to him and touched his hands and finally linked an arm in his and pressing

close to him, inquired if he didn't want to see how pretty some of the rooms on the second floor were furnished. And seeing that he was quite alone now . . . and that this girl seemed to lean to him warmly and sympathetically, he allowed himself to be led up that curtained back stair and into a small pink and blue furnished room, while he kept saying to himself that this was an outrageous and dangerous proceeding on his part, and that it might well end in misery for him . . . . And yet he went, and, the door locked behind him . . . (68)

No decision has here been made, as one action leads ineluctably to another in a prose of endlessly linking copulatives (that here ironically matches the subject represented). More generally, that syntactical pattern shapes what Ellen Moers called the novel's "sense of relentless inevitability."[30] Clyde seems deprived of personal control over his life less by events themselves than by the way those events are described. Behavior is dictated not by a conscious, predicating will, but by grammatical forces outside his self. It comes as little surprise, therefore, that the charged moments prior to Roberta's death offer more frequent syntactical repetitions than any other passage. Those moments end, of course, with the very scene in which she rises "for the first time," a scene presented through a grammar that achieves a pitch of will-less inevitability.

Making Oneself?

REPETITION COLLAPSES time and forecloses memory in *An American Tragedy* by dislocating language itself, much as occurs in "To Build a Fire" and other naturalist texts. But it weaves a special aura of necessity by putting Clyde in a double bind, one where sameness paradoxically ends by yielding difference. Contexts with similar characteristics, calling for apparent consistency of behavior, nonetheless require contradictory responses that challenge the concept of identity itself. Clyde's resemblance to Gilbert prompts both his uncle to offer him a job and Sondra to extend her invitations; yet his fellow-workers and Gilbert shun him because of that very similarity, which in turn leads to his critical misjudgment of assuming an elevated social status. As a Griffiths, Clyde clearly benefits from his uncle's legal advisors; yet because a Griffiths, he cannot submit the

obvious plea of insanity that would gain an acquittal. In a novel that relentlessly exposes a life that can only fall as it rises, Clyde finds himself everywhere affirmed yet denied, with a social definition that leads to incompatible consequences. Instead of confirming identity, the repetitions in his life only unsettle it, as desire becomes intertwined with fear, the potentially advantageous with the inherently self-destructive.

Involuntary repetition reverberates with more profound implications than this, however. Whether the repetitions of one's self occur in another, fragmenting the will, or in a series of mirroring others, thus reducing one to part of a set; whether they consist of repeated events and scenes that prove one's helplessness, or of verbal iterations that instill an aura of inevitability: collectively, these shape Clyde's narrative context as a realm of psychological constraint. Yet this series of repetitions more than merely determines him; as others have noted, they seem to make him disappear altogether. Robert Penn Warren has claimed that Clyde "always sought to flee from the self"; Richard Lehan, that he "lacks consciousness"; and Philip Fisher, most radically, that "Clyde has no self to which he might be 'true'."[31] The novel, in other words, deprives Clyde of the kind of coherent, conscious self we customarily assume for each other. Or as Ellen Moers has stated, "the thoughts that pass through Clyde's mind take up, at a guess, about half the wordage of Dreiser's long novel"—but only to establish "the thinness, the accidental indefiniteness of Clyde's consciousness."[32]

These characterizations certainly speak to our overwhelming sense of Clyde, but they also sneak into his narrative world a conception of consciousness denied by the text. Its multiform repetitions void the category of a "self" by revealing how irrelevant anything other than needs and desires are to behavior. Because Clyde lacks a will that might organize the chaos of his inner life, he thereby lacks any semblance of a self. Thus, in denying that he had *intended* to strike Roberta, he is in a way doubly correct (and this despite the fact that he had certainly *desired* her death).[33] At one level, of course, his blow with the camera was unaccompanied by an active intention, which is all that Clyde means in his testimony. But more comprehensively, he seems incapable of any larger intention, of taking a deliberate course of action in the service of a guiding purpose. Lacking the structure of character we usually associate with an independent self, he seems merely a reflexive function of his conflicting desires. In-

deed, his desires in some sense cannot ever be consistently mediated, caught as he is between the equal appeals of "pagan" and "religious" realms (5). Neither one ever puts him at ease, a mood characteristically expressed in the repeated construction "And . . . yet." Although he is fully aware of his life, his consciousness itself is curiously thin since unable to stand outside itself, beyond the dictates of the immediate present. Because unable to reflect on the past, or to direct the present, or decide on the future, his consciousness seems little more than a window on desire.

It is the novel's involuntary repetitions that contribute to this reading of Clyde's voided self. Yet no one else is any different—any less self-divided or any more able to order conflicting impulses. Hortense Briggs, for instance, acts like Clyde when she exclaims, "'Oh, what wouldn't I give for a coat like that!' She had not intended at the moment to put the matter so bluntly" (113). Similarly, Roberta misstamps a set of collars and unconsciously encourages Clyde's attention even as she resists the exposure it entails: "in the face of all her very urgent desires she hesitated, for this would take her direct to Clyde and give him the opportunity he was seeking. But, more terrifying, it was giving her the opportunity she was seeking" (275). These are only two among many instances that call responsibility into question, preparing us to ignore that category in such major "accidents" as the automobile crash, Roberta's pregnancy, and the boating scene. In each, Clyde is unfortunate, but he is much like everyone else he meets, whether his family or New York relatives, Kansas City bellhops or bar girls, Lycurgus factory workers or the various participants at his trial. They too respond to events with no greater sense of volition or self, unaware of how much they resemble the character they assume is so different from them.

Responsibility dissipates from the novel via involuntary repetition, largely because consequences loom so much larger than any intentions one may have had. Yet those repetitions have a further, more significant effect in denying that one can choose the kinds of choices one wants to make. Clyde's lawyer, Jephson, comes closest to identifying this dilemma in his courtroom confrontation of Clyde: "And it was because you were a moral and mental coward as I see it, Clyde—not that I am condemning you for anything that you cannot help. (After all, you didn't make yourself, did you?)" (2:268). The issue indeed is one of "making oneself"—of choosing the kind of desires one wants, and thereby taking responsibility for the kinds of

actions we can attribute to a self. Because Clyde cannot judge what he wants to do, his actions seem simply impersonal events outside any realm of responsibility. His very inability to resist the things and people that express his longings means he becomes what he "identifies" with, absorbed into the world only somewhat more dramatically than everyone else.[34]

"Clyde" represents a locus of urges whose very repetition increasingly reveals how little responsibility he bears. Indeed, when desire for Roberta's demise grows so strong as to threaten his moral reflexes, it can only find expression as a voice that somehow speaks through him. The supposed "Efrit" or genie that persuades him to the "way of the lake" arrives "in spite of himself" from a part of consciousness he cannot admit as his own. Consisting as he does of alternating impulses and contradictory desires, the person that is Clyde can only at last fall apart. That means, of course, that descriptions of him also become incoherent. Listen to the depiction of the act that will supposedly define Clyde for the jury, immediately prior to the passage with which this chapter opened:

> And then, as she drew near him, seeking to take his hand in hers and the camera from him in order to put it in the boat, he flinging out at her, but not even then with any intention to do other than free himself of her—her touch—her pleading—consoling sympathy—her presence forever—God!
>
> Yet (the camera still unconsciously held tight) pushing at her with so much vehemence as not only to strike her lips and nose and chin with it, but to throw her back sidewise toward the left wale which caused the boat to careen to the very water's edge. And then he, stirred by her sharp scream . . . rising . . . (2:77)

Instead of actions straightforwardly linked by a simple copulative construction, the events now form a torturous series joined by oppositional conjunctions ("but" and "yet") that keep turning clauses back against one another. As the subject of each of these sentences, Clyde is grammatically overwhelmed by clauses, lost in the shuffling movements of a countermarching prose. He disappears as a coherent, directive force in the very dissipation that occurs in the shift from predicate syntax into an attributive mode. Sentences rely on either participial, infinitive, or appositional constructions that refuse to link

Clyde at any given time and place directly with the action. He merely, so it would seem, happens to be in the same vicinity.

When Roberta dies, leaving Clyde bereft of an Other, he is left adrift both psychologically and physically. In fact, the process of the rest of the novel is one of finding in society a literal and figurative place for him. The "tragedy" of the novel (as much as is possible in any naturalist text) is that society finally does succeed in enforcing a coherent "self" upon the body that is his. Roberta's death is accounted for by a trial that constrains his desires and actions within the social construct all construe as "Clyde." That construct may not account for any of the contradictory impulses he feels, but in giving him a past and a (curtailed) future, it serves the community's available categories.[35]

In a world already "in place," with its fixed categories of selfhood, will, and desire, the unfocused energies that constitute Clyde can hardly survive. The problem is a difficult one, in part because *An American Tragedy* consistently questions the efficacy of a will that might coordinate the self's energies. Instead, Clyde finds himself repeatedly acting with repeated others in a narrative that everywhere repeats. Unable to control desire any more than he can constrain repetition, he finally is able to do nothing other than submit to execution. In the deterministic world depicted by Dreiser, life is equivalent to repetition and narrative a matter of "raising the dead." Freedom, itself always singular, lies well beyond the grave.

4.

Subversive Self-Constructions in Norris' *Vandover and the Brute*

B Y THE conclusion of Frank Norris' *Vandover and the Brute*, the once well-heeled hero has been reduced to scrubbing down rental cottages. His first day ends when a tenant asks him to clean an unlit kitchen cubby in which she discerns an "old hambone covered with greenish fuzz." But that is not all:

> Vandover crawled back, half the way under the sink again, this time bringing out a rusty pan half full of some kind of congealed gravy that exhaled a choking, acrid odour; next it was an old stocking, and then an ink bottle, a broken rat-trap, a battered teapot lacking a nozzle, a piece of rubber hose, an old comb choked with a great handful of hair, a torn overshoe, newspapers, and a great quantity of other debris.[1]

The very detail in this list of items draws attention to the whole *as* a list, reminding us of a venerable realist tradition that extends back

through Balzac to Homer.[2] Such inventories help us to fathom the world (or so we at least customarily assume), since things grouped together imply a context of values unapparent in individual items. Less than a decade before Vandover stooped beneath the kitchen sink, Huck Finn had famously catalogued the "gardens" of Bricksville, Arkansas: "they didn't seem to raise hardly anything in them but jimpson weeds, and sun-flowers, and ash-piles, and old curled-up boots and shoes, and pieces of bottles, and rags, and played-out tin-ware."[3] This horticultural survey bears the mark of Twain's inimitable style, but it also serves a familiar purpose by revealing the cultural ethos of Bricksville. For part of the moral logic of realism is that character expresses itself through just such scenes of descriptive self-fashioning, and the shabby condition of the gardens alerts us to the shoddy behavior of the town. Huck is alerted as well, of course, having learned to read the language of appearances in contexts where failure to do so threatens not only his comfort but his survival.

Vandover likewise relies on this premise and its lists function similarly, at least at first, before we realize how little they appear to refer to anything but themselves. The final description culminates a series of scenes that are just as sharply etched, but whose inconsequence is similarly confirmed in a failure to illuminate character or advance the plot. True, an inventive reader can attribute thematic significance to any list, since reading is always absorbed, as Roland Barthes has observed, "in a kind of metonymic skid" that is "the very movement of meaning."[4] Yet interpreting Vandover's items this way would only serve to mask the description's otherwise vividly odd incongruity—an incongruity that, because so vivid, seems one of its primary reasons for being. Instead of straining for thematic significance, we should ask instead why "the precision of the details" (to borrow Gérard Genette's words) so fully "exceeds the yerisimilitude of the pretext."[5] Why indeed is detail adduced with such apparent gratuitousness, unless to defy a realist metonymy by expressing how little is revealed through appearances? Irrelevant aspects of physical objects accumulate through the novel, gradually calling into question the realist logic that generates meaning from material signs. Circumstances that are carefully detailed convey nothing about individuals involved, as if descriptions in the novel were no less arbitrary than the things that were being described, things that occur deterministically.

This technique has curious implications for a novel that seems realistic, by shifting attention away from people, events, and things

themselves to the words that represent them. More generally, it makes us aware of the powerful suasions of certain forms of discourse in fostering a particular, socially encoded illusion of coherence and autonomy. Unlike any other novel by Norris (or by any other naturalist author), *Vandover* explores the implications of exceeding "the versimilitude of the pretext"—whether that pretext is aesthetic, as above, or social, or perhaps even metaphysical. It is worth noting, moreover, that these three categories are hardly unconnected. In much the same way that descriptions of things in the novel confound our habitual connotations, descriptions of events throw customary standards of judgment into doubt. Still, the bare facts are easily given: a Harvard graduate and promising painter, Vandover seems destined for success before dissipation leads to a series of disasters. He seduces a young woman who then commits suicide; squanders an inheritance on cards and alcohol; and sinks from middle-class comfort into impoverished bestiality. Ostracized by friends, unable to paint, he finally falls victim to a rare disease that makes him behave like a wolf.

Accurate as this summary is in every detail, it nonetheless seriously misreads the plot by endowing characters with capacities firmly excluded by the novel's presentation. The narrative repeatedly denies through its style its own stated censure of Vandover for having failed to live up to expectations, his own as well as others. And it does so most radically by exposing responsibility itself as an empty category. Agency is simply a social fiction, as arbitrary and invidious as any other, if somewhat more powerful *as* a fiction because it is silently self-confirming. Vandover never realizes this, or that he is destroyed less by what he does than by moralizing descriptions of his behavior —less by contingencies of an unknown future than by the terms he is given to assess his past. He, his friends, and the narrative voice each justify action by the way things turn out instead of as they were intended, which makes the process of self-definition an entirely retrospective one. Thus, the narrowly moralizing language within which his society clarifies consequence imposes a burden of misplaced guilt upon those who simply are unlucky—the stereotypical schlemiels who happen to wander into wrong places at the wrong times.

The novel dismantles two of the pillars of Vandover's social code: that intentions can be proved from the way things turn out, and that consequences stand as morally absolute. His characterization reveals instead how fully experience is shaped by a language that arbitrarily inscribes certain values into any description of behavior. Like all of

us, Vandover pieces together his life with categories borrowed from his society—although in his case, the categories of intention, will, and responsibility are exposed as irrelevant. He similarly accepts the contrast his society draws between artistic and brutish behavior, a contrast at every point undercut by the narrative presentation. Still, the curious fact remains that his view of himself is contagious, shared by a raft of readers who fail to question the illogic of his morality. Lining up alongside his erstwhile friends and an uncomfortably strident narrator, they condemn his irresolution in the very language of agency that the narrative has undermined throughout.[6] The "self" they create for Vandover is as contradictory and self-confirming as the one he assumes, if only because it conforms to a social code that continues in effect today. An inappropriate moral vocabulary encourages readers to conspire in the process of Vandover's self-destruction simply because they accept the terms of his self-definition.

Vandover and the Brute declares, far more than do novels in earlier chapters, that neither circumstance nor desire are anywhere near as restrictive as the language that describes them. Actions are limited not by physical or even by psychological constraints, but by a language that infuses them with a distinct set of social assumptions. The way that conditions are interpreted and, more specifically, the way one's story gets told determines the fate of an individual far more than does any aspect of conditions themselves. Given this premise, we can see why the novel denies that everyone possesses a self—a self prior to language, independent of circumstance, and more than the sum of conflicting desires. Characters once again form little more than bodily intersections, having been reduced to mere scenes where external events coincide with internal reflexes. All that transforms those scenes is a seemingly common-sense language of right and wrong, which introduces the comforting illusion of agency in circumstances that clearly preclude it. Before assessing those moral patterns by which characters entrap themselves, however, we first need to see how the novel works to subvert our persistent notions of personhood.

A World of Sheer Appearance

VANDOVER IS described from the beginning as alternately pliant and self-indulgent, quickly adapting to the world around him yet

ever yielding to his appetites. Initially, these impulses seem at cross-purposes, if only because fulfilling the one so often requires suppressing the other in a world where hope, envy, and regret attest to the gap between desire and circumstance. Yet circumstances allow Vandover to indulge his desires to a remarkable degree, and his early experience at Harvard anticipates his behavior throughout: "There was little of the stubborn or unyielding about Vandover, his personality was not strong, his nature pliable and he rearranged himself to suit his new environment" (17). Although he does not want to matriculate, his "yielding disposition" allows him easily to be "moulded by this new order," and the repetition of these phrases establishes a recurrent pattern in Vandover's life. With increasing ease, his "pliable character" rearranges itself in untoward circumstances, as events erode the meager resistances supposedly instilled in his youth. His life is disrupted traumatically, first by the suicide of Ida Wade following her seduction and his disregard, and then by his father's heart-broken death. Even so, he quickly becomes "accustomed" to the "new environment" occasioned by both losses. Now scorned by friends and unable to paint, he feels no more regret than he has all along, until by the end of the novel, "he had so often rearranged his pliable nature to suit his changing environment that at last he found that he could be content in almost any circumstances" (278). Even his verbal style is adaptive, and in spoken proof of his impulse ever to fit "into new grooves," he adopts Geary's slang expression, "Ah, you bet."

At the same time that Vandover accommodates himself to an ever-altering environment, he also behaves as if that environment existed simply to satisfy his desires: "Vandover was very self-indulgent—he loved these sensuous pleasures, he loved to eat good things, he loved to be warm, he loved to sleep. He hated to be bored and worried—he liked to have a good time" (32). As an undergraduate, he acts on "unreasoned instinct" in bedding a Cambridge "chippy": "The idea of resistance hardly occurred to Vandover; it would be hard, it would be disagreeable to resist" (24, 29). This description of sexual indulgence anticipates the pattern of both Vandover's academic career and his professional life—of refusing to postpone the satisfaction of any passing whim or desire. Later, rather than accept the day-in, day-out rigors of his art, he persists in a state of arrested development and thinks he "*had* to be amused" (65).

Vandover embraces a series of ever-new pleasures in his twenties,

unaware that their gratification will only further titillate desire. The process is neatly dramatized by his gradual enslavement to high-stakes gambling, an activity that had merely bored him when he first tried it. He had not realized how fully it would unite a pliant nature with a self-indulgent streak, allowing him in the very same gesture to satisfy external circumstance and inner desire. His psyche longs to spill into the world, as revealed in his "reckless desire for spending," and the risk of losing large chunks of his capital on the straightforward draw of a card allows him to erase himself psychologically.[7] Gambling, that is, simply offers the most extreme form of spendthrift behavior, and Vandover takes "a certain hysterical delight in flinging away money with both hands" (290)—until he exhausts not only an inheritance and his friends' waning patience, but his own diminished self-regard.

Gambling, that is, voids Vandover of a self that might exist autonomously, independent of either the world or of his own reflexive desires. Even the semblance of a will disappears toward the novel's end, as he transfers his wealth to a process that offers not even the vague promise of a return. Overcome by indolence, gluttony, and lust as financial pressures mount inexorably, Vandover discovers the intentions and regrets he occasionally has matter little at all. Others may attribute motives to him—he even does so to himself—but we never see how he might actually seize a semblance of responsibility from consequence. This is, of course, true as well of Carrie Meeber and Clyde Griffiths, of London's anonymous Arctic trekker and Crane's Henry Fleming: all of these characters exist as a balance of pliancy and self-indulgence, not as a constellation of special traits that distinguish them from the worlds they inhabit. On the contrary, all of them seem absorbed into their narrative worlds, precisely because they lack any selves that might be distinguished from those worlds. In *Vandover*, things turn out well or poorly as matters of circumstance, not character, and with increasing obviousness experience is defined by an unlikely equation of chance with morality. Following the unexpected suicide of Ida Wade, for instance, Vandover is snubbed by his social set, although nothing about his character suggests he could have altered the circumstances that led to her death. His social exclusion, moreover, only entrenches him further in "moral luck," by exposing him to less savory conditions that offer the risk of ever direr consequences.

Strange as it may seem that Vandover should lack a recognizable

"self," the fictional world he inhabits appears from the beginning even stranger. Objects are everywhere stripped of their usual connotations, in a peculiar process that denies any knowledge of cultural semantics from a mere reading of physical surfaces. Indeed, the narrative is strewn with surfaces that seem to merely denote themselves, in much the same way that Vandover lays claim to a body but not to a coherent "self." Or rather, just as the contiguity of pliancy and indulgence collapses an opposition between inner and outer, so objects are simply reduced to what they appear to be—no more, no less. Something of this curious semantic process was suggested in the quotation that opened this chapter, which described the motley objects recovered by Vandover from a kitchen cubby. But the process is even clearer in the long description of his home:

> It was a large frame house of two stories; all the windows in the front were bay. The front door was directly in the middle between the windows of the parlour and those of the library, while over the vestibule was a sort of balcony that no one ever thought of using. The house was set in a large well-kept yard. The lawn was pretty; an enormous eucalyptus tree grew at one corner. Nearer to the house were magnolia and banana trees growing side by side with firs. Humming-birds built in these, and one could hear their curious little warbling mingling with the hoarse chirp of the English sparrows which nested under the eaves. The back yard was separated from the lawn by a high fence of green lattice-work. The hens and chickens were kept here and two roosters, one of which crowed every time a cable-car passed the house. On the door cut through the lattice-fence was a sign, "Look Out for the Dog." (33)

In traditional realist fashion, this passage directs attention away from its simple prose rhythms to the scene it purports to describe. Yet little that occurs in the subsequent narrative requires such elaborate detail. Nothing about the trees and the birds, the yard or the library, the noises and colors, contributes to other scenes in the novel or otherwise clarifies Vandover's behavior. Indeed, the surreal ecology here—of roosters, humming-birds, and sparrows nesting in eucalyptus, firs, and banana trees—anticipates the flora and fauna of Nathaniel West's California, without at the same time linking them to phantasmagorical possibilities. The warning sign on the fence draws our notice simply because it is not a conventional "Beware" to

strangers, and because we already know the dog is Mr. Conkle, Vandover's harmless terrier. Like other signs in the novel, this one leads nowhere.

Given the inconsequence of this long sequence (at least in conventional realist terms), its point seems to be that physical description is valuable for nothing but itself—and perhaps therefore without value at all. Other contexts likewise lack any hint of the psychological dimension to be found in novels by Dickens, say, or Conrad. Circumstantial detail, in fact, provides not even a flimsy guide to plot. Vandover's various haunts and abodes give no indication of what he is like, nor do they add a characteristic luster to the novel's actions and events. Unlike McTeague's dental sign, or that novel's opening depiction of Polk Street, or the fields of wheat in *The Octopus* and Annixter's spartanly furnished ranch house, the extended descriptions of setting in *Vandover* seem altogether irrelevant, whether of Ida Wade's parlor, the Imperial Bar, or Vandover's bunk on the *Mazatlan:* "The roof was iron, painted with a white paint very thick and shiny, and was studded with innumerable bolt-heads and enormous nuts" (125). Even people's physical presences seem somehow entirely beside the point. No hint, for instance, of Turner Ravis' characteristic selfishness is disclosed in the carefully detailed appearance provided by the narrative; and although her family is described with what seems to be an uncommonly attentive concern, none of them ever materializes or even indirectly shapes the plot. Just as action fails to ensue from the operations of a shaping will, the world of people and things lacks any clear pattern of interdependency.

The significance of this unlikely process of metonymic deflation—and more generally, of the progressive voiding of connotation that occurs through the novel—emerges soon after the death of Vandover's father, when he visits the lawyer, Mr. Field: "Vandover found him in his room, a huge apartment, one side entirely taken up by book-shelves filled with works of fiction. The walls were covered with rough stone-blue paper, forming an admirable background to small plaster casts of Assyrian *bas-reliefs* and large photogravures of Renaissance portraits" (162). Again, the description seems inconsequential, since Mr. Field thereafter disappears from the novel. Only now, however, does Vandover entertain the prospect of his own accommodations: "Already he saw himself installed in charming bachelor's apartments, the walls covered with rough stone-blue paper forming an admirable background for small plaster casts of As-

syrian *bas reliefs* and photogravures of Velasquez portraits" (169). The description repeats nearly word for word the view of Mr. Field's room, and will itself be repeated when Vandover selects and furnishes his Sutter Street flat. Neither he nor the narrator identifies the lawyer's tastes with his own mimetic desire nor are the two men otherwise presumed to share any characteristic traits. Quite the contrary, the description seems intended to reveal Vandover's naive impressionability, and its reiteration simply testifies to the arbitrariness not only of his desires, but of his circumstances as well. The very lack of any greater significance to furnishings so often invoked itself confirms the overall absence of a controlling will. Lingering over the imagined and then the actual appearance of his rooms, the narrative registers little more than an inexplicable pleasure in things as simply things. Not until Vandover inexplicably copies the pattern of Mr. Field's apartment does it acquire significance—which is the sole point of this form of description: it is a repetition. Consequence again determines interpretation, whether of physical descriptions, or a series of actions, or the novel's larger narrative logic.

The Morality of Excluded Middles

VANDOVER HIMSELF is oblivious to this ubiquitous stress on consequence, or to its dire effects in a world that is always already constructed ideologically. He takes for granted the everyday notion that actions invariably result from motives, and that intentions can therefore be deduced directly from another's behavior. Individuals are to be held accountable because they supposedly control how they act, and he cherishes this premise in spite of recollections from his youth that clearly contradict it. Notwithstanding his studied stance of calm self-reflection, then, the coherent self that Vandover strives to construct stands at odds with his daily experience, so much so that he cannot help but acknowledge it in the novel's opening words:

> It was always a matter of wonder to Vandover that he was able to recall so little of his past life. With the exception of the most recent events he could remember nothing connectedly. What he at first imagined to be the story of his life, on closer inspection turned out to be but a few disconnected incidents that his memory had pre-

served with the greatest capriciousness, absolutely independent of their importance. (3)

Vandover will soon enough retreat from this astonishing observation and quietly subscribe to a belief in the psychological coherence of "the story of his life."

Yet immediately after confessing himself unable to evaluate, even to remember his past, he broaches an issue the novel continues in various forms to enact: that the chaos of our lives is wrenched into shape by a retrospective process no more accurate than the caprices of memory allow.

> As he looked back over his life he could recall nothing after this for nearly five years . . . In order to get at his life during his teens, Vandover would have been obliged to collect these scattered memory pictures as best he could, rearrange them in some more orderly sequence, piece out what he could imperfectly recall and fill in the many gaps by mere guesswork and conjecture.[8]

The business of the novel, of course, will be to do just this. Indeed, its triumph lies in focusing attention on that very narrative strategy —on the deterministic rearrangement of events "in some more orderly sequence." Vandover never again so deliberately tries to piece together his life, but that effort recurs in the imperious tones of the novel's narrative voice, which reflects his consciousness by espousing the determining assumptions he brings to bear on his past.[9] What makes those assumptions simultaneously powerful yet problematic is that they are at once unquestioned and clearly illogical, seemingly obvious yet misleading. Narrative events reveal to the reader how fully inappropriate those judgments are, but because they remain unexamined, they become for Vandover fully determining.

Informing those judgments is an ideology of the subject as the site of warring forces, imaged in Manichean terms as "an eternal struggle between good and evil that had been going on within him since his very earliest years" (215). This distinction between moral and immoral, sacred and secular, artistic and brutal, is first made explicit in Vandover's schoolboy curiosity about sex. His fellows indulge in "abominable talk," until "one day he heard the terse and brutal truth . . . But even then he hated to think that people were so low, so vile" (10). Filled now with a "perverse craving for the knowledge of vice"

(11), Vandover learns the details and "even his mother . . . fell at once in his estimation" (11). Acquiring an adult vocabulary can only be done by affirming a moral code that contaminates sexuality. Of course, Vandover fails to realize that culture alone defines any behavior as transgressive, and therefore fails to recognize the speciously melodramatic language of sin and shame.

He accepts without question the labels "pure women" and "chippies," for example, even though no one he knows fits either stereotype. Certainly, the passionate vitality of Ida Wade cannot be so reduced, and Vandover's bifurcated vision simply blinds him to her vigorous contradictions. Yet Turner and Flossie fit pat formulas no more readily than Ida, since neither conventional virgin nor syphilitic prostitute is any less a mixture of "purity" and "sin."[10] Against all the evidence, Vandover nonetheless subscribes to a binary opposition that exalts supposedly "pure" and "artistic" behavior at the expense of the otherwise "brutish." Saved by his "artistic" temperament from being "totally corrupted while in his earliest teens" (11), he judges action by a logic of the excluded middle, condemning whatever offends bourgeois sensibilities. The fact that this includes fornication, intoxication, and gambling is for the moment less important than Vandover's blithe acceptance of a standard that is so narrow, one that will arbitrarily shape his decline. The self-judgments he makes, in other words, are as inappropriate as his assessments of Ida and Flossie, and likewise encourage him to think of himself in fully inadequate moral terms. That very process leads him to condone situations he would otherwise avoid, and finally to behave in a way that will seem to confirm the very label of "brute" he abhors.

Once again, the logic structuring these judgments is neatly dualistic, much like that which defines the psychological split between Vandover's pliancy and self-indulgence. Yet whereas the collapse of that binary opposition succeeds in emptying him of a self, a similar effect is achieved in the social realm by precisely the converse process, by opposing psychological categories ever more firmly against one another. "Artistic" and "brutal" dispositions are treated as if they were mutually exclusive, instead of as jointly informing perspectives on a range of human behavior. The fact that nothing in Vandover's experience helps him to link these cultural categories together means that aesthetic and libidinal drives seem to him, as to others, radically dissociated.

Despite the fierceness with which his society maintains that disso-

ciation, the two sides of Vandover's nature are both identified with a single cash nexus. His father first rewards him with dollar bills for his painterly efforts, just as he learns "the terse and brutal truth" about sexuality looking for money hidden in an encyclopedia. Economic motives arouse his "artistic" sensibility just as they do "the brute," and reduce both sorts of behavior to the level of sheer commodity.[11] Carnal pleasures are to be paid for in the currency of restaurant dinners or hard cash itself, but are never seen as part of a reciprocating process of mutual affection. Likewise, painting for Vandover is not an expression but an exchange, as early as the teenage years when his father financed pencil copies of "ideal heads." He continues thereafter to paint both sentimental and sensationalizing canvases, oblivious to any larger connection between desire and art. Disabled from imagining scenes that might help to resolve his own personal conflicts, he unthinkingly subscribes to a commercial ethos that depends on the least common aesthetic denominator.[12] Fittingly, the job he finally takes is as a commercial decorator who paints "little pictures on the lacquered surface of iron safes" (314). Art in this society is nothing more than an inessential distraction, and Vandover's talents have found their appropriate outlet.

Everywhere else in the novel, painting is likewise presented as ornamental, merely confirming the inescapable patterns of the standing order. Ida Wade's mother, for instance, exhibits renditions of the same sort of "ideal head" that Vandover copies, and anticipates his final employment by giving "lessons in painting on china and velvet" (69, 89). By the same logic, the supposedly fine pieces acquired by the Ravises are no more than copies of copies: "oil paintings of steel engravings and genuine old-fashioned chromos beyond price to-day" (80). And Mr. Field's "photogravures of Renaissance portraits" are just as extraneous, like the similar reproductions that Vandover acquires, or the stove he buys with tiles that picture "the 'Punishment of Caliban and His Associates,' 'Romeo and Juliet,' the 'Fall of Phaeton' " (182).[13]

No one realizes how fully aesthetic power depends on "brutality," or that Vandover's "sensuous" nature is itself responsible for "his strong artist's imagination."[14] By defining the two antithetically, his society limits the range of art even as it diminishes the creative implications of sexual energy. Freud would demonstrate a radical equation of aesthetic, moral, and sexual energies by successfully theorizing that art results from sublimation, not repression. Une-

quipped to recognize this, Vandover still comes close to realizing the inadequacy of his society's artistic ideals in his shock at the *Mazatlan* shipwreck: "There was nothing picturesque about it all, nothing heroic. It was unlike any pictures he had seen of life-boat rescues, unlike anything he had ever imagined. It was all sordid, miserable, and the sight of the half-clad women, dirty, sodden, unkempt, stirred him rather to disgust than to pity" (143). Returning to San Francisco, however, he resumes his painting of "ideal heads," having once again divorced aesthetics from the "brutal" actualities of life. The very eagerness with which he continues to judge himself by that binary model attests to its dynamic force. Yet because at last unable to expunge the "brutal" from his "artistic side," he can only experience the former's repression as the latter's lingering death.

Legitimating Moral Luck

VANDOVER STAMPS his past with assumptions at once self-confirming yet self-contradictory. And that makes it less important that psychological distinctions in this novel seem somehow erased, or that fixed moral codes are inflected in action, than that any meaning is always inferred somehow after the fact, not before—that is, from consequence, not motive. Self-definition takes place, in other words, as a retrospective process that is far more clearly determining than any allegedly organic or psychological pattern. Because the after-effects of events define the feelings characters have, self-understanding in the novel is a matter of rearrangement after the fact. Perhaps no better illustration of this process can be found than Turner's explanation to Vandover of her inability to marry him:

> "What has happened hasn't made me cease to care for you, because if I had really cared for you the way I thought I did, the way a girl ought to care for the man she wants to marry, I would have stood by you through everything, no matter what you did. I don't do so now, because I find I don't care for you as much as I thought I did. What has happened has only shown me that. I'm sorry, oh, so sorry to be disappointed in you, but it's because I only think of you as being once a very good friend of mine, not because I love you as you think I did . . . [W]hen I saw how easily I could let you go, it only proved to me that I did not care for you as I

> thought I did. . . . Can't you see, it's just as if I had never met
> you." (202–3)

At first, this explanation seems nothing more than a shallow rationalization, especially since Turner had earlier vowed she would never
"break my promise to Van" (87). Yet this reading misunderstands
the process of self-perception in the novel, or at least the way characters see each other, if not themselves. Whatever intentions may
have been, however deliberate the motives for action, it is only how
an event turns out that provides any basis for judgment. Only her
present perspective can let Turner know the weight of her past
feelings, and she nicely expresses a premise central to the novel's
vision of behavior—a premise that informs others' interpretations as
much as it does Vandover's own.

Categories of guilt and responsibility can be read into events only
after the fact, as society's response to the "seduction" of Ida Wade
helps make clear. Vandover himself assumes full responsibility for
the event, confessing remorse to his father despite how little responsibility he actually bears. True, his reasons for encouraging her are
connected with his experience at Cambridge, when he was "too
diffident, too courteous, too 'slow' " to keep women more than
mildly interested (25). Yet Ida first (and knowingly so) suggests the
notorious Imperial Restaurant, and then persuades herself that it
would be fun to dine in a private room. Once there, she cheerfully
forswears regret, enjoys the champagne and the air of romance, "and
then with a long breath she abandoned herself" to Vandover's kiss
and its implications (79).

His disregard of Ida after that night is hardly to Vandover's credit,
but callousness does not make him responsible for her subsequent
suicide. The problem is that she can no more transcend a fixed social
code than he, especially one that rigidly labels her a "fallen woman."
Her death simply fits the melodramatic paradigm of Victorian culture—or so we assume, given the utter silence about her final days.
The assumption that she deliberately kills herself because of his indifference, however, smacks of the same retrospective logic that is
everywhere else dismantled by the novel. True, the unsent letter that
Ida writes just before her death is said to have "directly implicated"
Vandover—but it is significant that we never learn how "directly"
(250). And even were he responsible, the tones in which he accepts a
self-judgment of guilt seem so far in excess of their object as to draw

their moralizing terms into question: "She had consented, but he had forced her consent; he was none the less guilty. And . . . no matter if she had consented, it was his duty to have protected her, even against herself" (105).

In much the same manner, Vandover responds to his father's death with anguished self-flagellation, ignoring how little he is to blame. His confession of having "seduced" Ida, as well as the news of the *Mazatlan*'s shipwreck, may indeed have "hastened" the onset of his father's stroke. Yet by simply attributing it to his having been "so base," Vandover overreacts to effects that can only be known in retrospect (110, 216). On the one hand, a genuinely filial impulse had prompted his confession; on the other, the shipwreck clearly lay beyond his control. Still, he accepts his community's identification of motive with consequence ("he died from the news," therefore "you killed him"). Continuing for years to acquiesce to this absurd conception of guilt, Vandover comes to view his life as if beyond all redemption: "Religion could not help him, he had killed his father, estranged the girl he might have loved, outraged the world, and at a single breath blighted the fine innate purity of his early years" (219). Finally, benumbed by the disease of lycanthropy, he meekly accepts his ruined artistic career as no more than a just reward for what he has done: "It was the punishment that he had brought upon himself" (243).

Ridiculous as these judgments seem, they nonetheless make perfect sense to a Vandover unable to tell how arbitrary are the categories with which be began. His various interpretations of guilt, that is, follow straightforwardly from the moral assumptions he initially makes.[15] And the novel, in dramatizing that process, achieves its paradoxical power—at once illustrating the apparent logic of a morality that depends so fully on consequences, and yet at the same time revealing how inadequately it represents our behavior to ourselves. Because no one within such a system can recognize its self-confirming nature, no one is more capable than Vandover of transcending its fixed terms. The only thing that places him, rather than others, unduly at risk is the misfortune of having strong libidinous urges in a society that proscribes any expression of sexual desire. Jeopardized before the fact as well as retrospectively, he is victimized as much by his own proclivities as by his society's moral constraints. Charlie Geary's selfish ambition and Turner Ravis' emotional sangfroid might well in other times and places have left them at a similar

disadvantage. Here and now, however, Vandover's sensual nature leads to his demise.

Geary and Turner rise to success for no other reason than that they happen to have the psychological makeup their society prizes; they therefore never think to do other than accept its limited terms. Easily rejecting Ida Wade as a "chippy," they ensure their reputations, even as Vandover endangers his through his very capacity to suspend such a judgment. His very ability to sustain a certain degree of interpretive uncertainty exposes him to a corresponding degree of risk. Yet despite their greater security, Geary and Turner control neither their behavior nor its interpretation any more fully than he. Geary wins his way through cold-hearted greed and indefatigable energy, while Turner simply makes no mistakes. Different from Vandover with different careers, they nonetheless enjoy no more freedom of will nor is their behavior any less fully determined. And as with Geary and Turner, so with others who achieve far less in a world where success is shown to differ all too little from failure—where no one governs the consequences that always (and merely) happen to happen.

The Repressions of Language

THIS GENERAL inability to transcend a morality that ignores motive in favor of consequence commits everyone in the novel to a self-confirming pattern, no matter how self-contradictory. No one is able to conceive alternatives to the way things turn out, and Vandover is therefore like everyone else in simply accepting his decline. His erstwhile friends simply label and shun him, and he as simply accepts their judgment: "It was only a just retribution for the thing he had done" (205). Acknowledging himself the kind of person that others mistakenly condemn him to be, he accedes to an interpretation that seems at best irrelevant and at worst destructive. He as well as others is constrained by moral terms applied retrospectively, which draws our attention to the arbitrary shaping power of words themselves. Not a tool for self-definition, or even for neutral descriptions of behavior, language instead forms a medium of values in which we are immersed unawares. Vandover assumes that words reflect his experience plainly and directly—an assumption the narrative reveals is as flawed as his conviction that social morality is "natural." Yet his

very belief in these assumptions ensures his behavior will be unwittingly shaped by a language that in fact never merely describes.

At two points, Vandover experiences a suspension from the determining forces of conventional discourse. The first occurs in the *Mazatlan* shipwreck midway through the novel, when his middle-class notions of bravery and cowardice are challenged by the sheer horror of the disaster. The second instance is part of the onset of his lycanthropy, which releases Vandover from a familiar sense of the world to leave him estranged from himself: "At first the room looked unfamiliar to him, then his own daily life no longer seemed recognizable, and, finally, all of a sudden, it was the whole world, all the existing order of things, that appeared to draw off like a refluent tide, leaving him alone, abandoned, cast upon some fearful, mysterious shore" (242). The melodramatic expression confirms the extent to which his aberration debilitates Vandover not only physically, but mentally as well. Disorienting him with respect to "the existing order of things," reducing him to a state in which even "the words of a printed page would little by little lose their meaning" (273), the disease radically alters his sense of verbal logic. In fact, the wolfish attacks have an effect that resembles the reader's experience of the novel's metonymic deflation: both processes dissociate things from language and call into question normal patterns of meaning. Yet unlike the reader and despite the depths to which he is reduced, Vandover can appreciate the implications of neither the shipwreck nor his disease.[16]

Vandover and the Brute is less concerned with the socioeconomic conditions of life than with the verbal constructions by which late nineteenth-century society explains them. More generally, the novel questions the process of hooking words up with experience, beginning with Vandover's youthful embarrassment at the meaning of certain disguised sexual references. Turning vainly from encyclopedia to dictionary and then at last to his father, he tries to identify the meaning of the specialized discourse that excites his emergent sexuality, having smelt "a mystery beneath the words" used to describe "the perils of child-birth" (10). Later, he hears "a certain word, the blunt Anglo-Saxon name for a lost woman, that . . . opened to him a vista of incredible wickedness" (11).[17] This hyperbolic response is prompted by nothing more than a five-letter word, and attests to the power of language to shape expectations in ways that may seem natural, but are not.

This point is made more dramatically in the novel by the signs with which a penniless Vandover replaces the furnishings seized from his now-bare flat: " 'Pipe-rack Here.' 'Mona Lisa Here.' 'Stove Here.' 'Window-seat Here.' " (280). The scene remarkably images the extent to which language becomes its own reality, intimated earlier in the nonsense lines that characters invent to regale one another. Vandover's father jokingly places coins on his eyes and exclaims, "Good for the masses" (6). Geary later drunkenly chortles, "Cherries are ripe!"—a line that had "some ludicrous, hidden double-meaning that was irresistible" (56). Both instances announce nothing more than the delightful play of words run together, as does the behavior of the mute, stone-deaf friend of Bandy Ellis. When thoroughly soused, "Dummy" emits a series of noises that sound surprisingly like the words he has never heard, in the process inadvertently parodying any system of verbal forms. Repeatedly, occasions arise in which words are dislodged from normal contexts, although the exposure of their fully conventional status does nothing to diminish enjoyment.

The character who resists such a recognition most fervently is Dolly Haight, who at one point protests against the euphemisms his friends invoke for drunkenness. Instead, he indignantly demands the blunt truth: "Why not call things by their right name? You can see just how bad they are then" (97). Yet the novel everywhere tends to refute this very premise, showing how fully conventional discourse creates the "bad" by naming it—and, of course, creates the "good" and the "neutral" by contrast just as well. This constitutive role of language is presented most explicitly during the party at Turner Ravis' house, when her account of a broken wine glass anticipates the shattering of one in her hands, "in precisely the manner she was describing" (38). Despite Geary's reasonable explanation of why the event occurred, no one perceives that it forms an apt analogy to the socializing role of language. No one, that is, is prepared to accept so unlikely a physical event as an example of the logic by which they all create the behavior they think they are merely describing.

It has become a truism that language always mediates experience, and that transcending the logic embedded in linguistic patterns cannot be done. Whether or not such a logic more generally tends to be self-confirming, in the late nineteenth century of Norris' novel, the language of morality has that effect. And it does so most obviously in terms of activities forbidden but nonetheless largely winked at, including the fornication, intoxication, and gambling that Vandover

so enjoys. For the most part, characters drink to achieve a modest release in tension, but no matter how innocuous their subsequent behavior, it is always viewed as reprehensible. Sexual indulgence is likewise considered transgressive because so identified, although the kind of illicit encounters described by the novel hardly break any natural laws. They appear evil simply for having been labeled so by society. Because desire cannot be repressed and because sublimation is in this case so fully constrained, libidinal energies are able to emerge only in transgressive forms. Language everywhere alters behavior into a set of prescribed moral categories, defining as perverse what from other perspectives and in other times might seem only natural. For the reader to recognize how little is "natural" in any social environment is not enough to justify Vandover's self-subverting experience, and therefore his lycanthropy only more visibly allegorizes a process that threatens anyone else.

Indeed, the threat of both self-alienation and ostracism is greater than anyone imagines, as reflected in the fact that at no point is the venereal disease shared by various characters made explicit. Circulating secretly through the plot, much as it does through San Francisco society, syphilis thrives at an unspoken level, resists all antiseptic efforts, and transforms the lives of those who try most to deny its power. An apparently radiant Flossie is inexplicably moved to kiss Dolly Haight, and thereby transmits the disease to him through a tiny cut in his lip. Later, he will explain what happened to Vandover without ever "naming" his affliction. Vandover's similar affliction is less apparent though no less likely, since he has been infected by what seems to be the same source. Intimate with Flossie on numerous occasions, he may even first have infected her, and she will certainly pass on the disease to the college fullback with whom we last see her. In a world so thoroughly interdependent, even Turner bears some responsibility for the disease's silent transmission: she thoughtlessly fails to replace the broken glass with which Dolly Haight cuts his lip.

Although no further spread of disease is referred to even this obliquely, syphilis has a life of its own that invites a speculative reconstruction. The most obvious inference is that Vandover had infected Ida, which lends a commanding logic to her reasons. for having committed suicide.[18] Besides despair at his treatment of her and fear of a possible pregnancy, she may have also been horrified to discover more recent genital evidence. Lending weight to this con-

clusion is the fact that four months have passed since her drunken evening at the Imperial, but that she has only begun to feel "despondent and broke up about something or other for a week or two" (103). Better than any action could, continuing silence about the transgressions of syphilis demonstrates how the true social "disease" of the novel has been language itself. Narrative gaps and omissions not only reproduce the silent ravages of bacterial infection, but suggest more importantly the ways a repressive language encourages the spread of diseased patterns of thought. Those repressions, moreover, have effects far beyond anyone's control.

Readers are sometimes bewildered at the disparity between the fates of the three main male characters. From the beginning, Charles Geary subscribes to a double standard, but only by chance is he able to avoid situations where his desires might lead to public exposure, or where his actions and statements might come into conflict. Vandover happens to maintain a more consistent pattern of behavior, and self-indulgence therefore predictably leads to self-destruction. It is Dolly Haight, however, whose situation comes to seem paradoxical, since he is made to suffer despite having adhered conscientiously to his society's prescriptions—indeed, having hewed to a standard of relative abstinence and absolute celibacy: "You know I never had anything to do with women, Van" (304). The point of his sadly ironic example appears to be that desire itself is more or less irrelevant to what happens in one's life. Contrary to the more usual understanding of the way language works, it organizes this society both prescriptively and retrospectively, resulting in the paradox that one can never avoid the kiss of ostracism. Not only are those like Vandover saddled with desires they cannot control, but even for those like Dolly whose desires match his society's values, unpredictable consequences remain nearly all-determining.

At the end of the novel, a tired Vandover is left alone in the cottage watched over by the tenants' child: "For an instant the two remained there motionless, looking into each other's eyes, Vandover on the floor, one hand twisted into the bale rope about his bundle, the little boy standing before him eating the last mouthful of his bread and butter" (354). The image of the silently staring boy clarifies certain issues that have been present throughout. By definition, children are still in the process of ordering experience through a meaningful vocabulary, learning thereby how to define the forms a socialized self must take. Language has not yet become self-authenti-

cating in the way that adults accept as "natural," and the circular logic connecting words to experience still has the power to astonish. Still, no assurance exists that with maturity will come more than merely the illusion of control. It may be simply that we grow accustomed to the arbitrary, unnatural, even inappropriate fit that can exist between words and things, in this case between a narrowly moralizing language and otherwise richly controverting possibilities. What the boy sees but cannot know, what Vandover knows but cannot accept, is that the world defies one's desires and operates through a language one has not created. What Norris himself more particularly realized, and enacted in his first novel, is that determinism most radically constrains the will through the very words that describe one's freedom.

5.

The Spectacle of Character in Crane's *Red Badge of Courage*

STEPHEN CRANE's admirers regularly deny he is a naturalist out of what appears to be a fear of linking him with a circle of "bad" writers. Instead, they invoke for him supposedly more respectable categories, like the literary "impressionism" first admired by Joseph Conrad, or the "realism" others identify with the self-conscious craft of James and Howells.[1] Yet the "problem" of Crane persists, and it does so in part because these categories give so little sense of his singular imaginative vision, or of his obsessive fascination with behavior that lies altogether outside one's control. Repeatedly, his telltale engine of plot is an event so violent that the very possibility of agency seems precluded. Shipwrecks, blizzards, and engulfing fires, Mexican ambushes and war itself: his favored scenes insistently forestall those moments of calm reflection or deliberate choice that were, on the contrary, given such privileged status by realist authors. And like those authors described above who challenged the realists' use of

language, Crane delights in the anti-mimetic techniques that so often distinguish determinist texts.

Why is an imaginative vision so compatible with that of other naturalists consistently read as if it were not, even by those indifferent to matters of taste? More precisely, why do we attribute to Crane's characters a moral capacity that we more readily withhold from the fictional figures imagined by Norris, say, or London? The question itself sets the terms of discussion by attesting to Crane's success in getting us to disregard the absence of certain familiar human capacities. Characters in London's Arctic world may not grasp how little autonomy they have, but they realize their wills are ineffective, which contributes to our sense of their two-dimensionality. By contrast, Crane's characters are never led to doubt the strength of their wills, and this is so despite their inability to take any greater responsibility for events. Part of what makes this disjunction effective is that Crane's narratives shuttle back and forth between two basic perspectives—between external and internal views of character that reveal one's acts as either caused or motivated. The Introduction demonstrated the shaping effect of these perspectives on our understanding of plot, as either a sequence of events that seem to happen *to* people, or as personalized actions that appear instead intended *by* them. Crane masterfully explored the tension between these two by a simple expedient, lending his characters the illusion of possessing a self in a world they had not created. The very passion with which they hold to that illusion has a contagious effect, encouraging the reader to reinscribe a premise of agency into narrative contexts that are thoroughly deterministic.

Nothing is so powerful for readers and characters alike as the notion of human autonomy—of a self in control of its future because it possesses a coherent sense of its past. That comforting notion, however, is everywhere drawn into question by Crane's fiction, which anticipates prominent aspects of texts by each of the other three naturalist authors. Like London, Crane delights in contexts physically inimical to human life, and through repetition exposes the ineluctability of events and therefore the irrelevance of knowledge about them. Yet also like Norris, he foregrounds constraints inherent in our social construction of reality, which has as determining an effect on behavior as do scenes of physical violence. The heroine of his first novel, *Maggie*, for instance, is as much self-victimizer as victim, co-opted (like Vandover) by her own unself-conscious accep-

tance of the social morality that destroys her even more fully than does the physical deprivation she suffers in New York City's Bowery.[2] The far wiser Dr. Trescott of his late novel, *The Monster*, is more self-aware but no more capable of altering events or moderating their interpretation.

Of all the naturalists, however, Dreiser is the most akin to Crane —and this despite the notorious differences in their highly idiosyncratic styles. For what they share is a radical view of the socialized self and its construction, and what they similarly question are our conventional assumptions about personal agency. Both men deny the humanizing premises simply assumed by their characters, and do so through narrative patterns that may at first seem to be mutually exclusive: by dramatizing the extent to which deliberation is often estranged from action, making behavior seem to lie almost entirely outside one's control; and yet by also depicting the radical conflation of desires with the world, as if one's psychology was fully expressed in what one saw by merely looking around. Both authors juxtapose narrative perspectives with their characters' subjective views, revealing the gap between actual consequences and the futile intentions behind them, between impersonal events and the guilt or pride that characters mistakenly feel. Nothing more than circumstances enmesh characters in fictional worlds they are unable to alter.

Yet even more directly than Dreiser, Crane foregrounds the problem of action and agency by turning to characters who question, almost obsessively, what they will do. Which behavioral laws will govern how they act in crisis, his figures ask, expressing in fictional form Zola's single demand of the naturalist mode: i.e., to lay bare the determining logic of behavior by careful observation of events.[3] And precisely because his characters do have the capacity to address such questions, we tend to attribute further capacities to them they may not have. Despite how readily action in Crane can be explained via determining causes, characters do continue to believe in the power of a motivating will, and thereby they seize a presumption of agency from fictional worlds that deny it.

Far more than the fiction of other naturalists, Crane's sustains with equal cogency contradictory interpretations as deterministic yet free. His narratives swallow characters up in a maelstrom of events, and at crucial moments even foreground a necessitarian premise; but they also offer the illusion that characters have effective wills by tracing conventional possibilities for moral growth.[4] The contradic-

tion between these interpretive poles cannot be easily resolved, and certainly not without acknowledging the power of assumptions we bring to any narrative. More flamboyantly than other naturalists, Crane strips his fiction of the familiar causal tissue that reinforces those projective assumptions, in order to offer a textual approximation of the experience his characters have of events. Thus, like his characters, readers regularly slip into comforting patterns of thought unsupported by the texts they read.

Claims for agency may well be no more than self-confirming, as Crane suggests, and our comforting assumption that individual psychology is a coherent process may simply mask the state of chaotic disruption in which we live. If we can never be actually sure, at least we can try for the moment to suspend assumptions that blind us to the very possibility of incoherence. And by avoiding abstract assertions of either identity or control, we will find that Crane's characters are deprived of far more autonomy than they think. The Swede in "The Blue Hotel," like the correspondent in "The Open Boat" and Henry Fleming in *The Red Badge of Courage*: each acts only as his erratic desires happen to dictate. Each of them is further dislodged from behavior by their texts themselves, which subvert the normal connections we assume between desires and events. At times, it seems as if an orgy of incidents and feelings had melded characters together, preventing us from linking individuals to discrete experiences. More generally, even the simplest physical details are rarely used to describe a character, reinforcing a radically unconventional conception of personality—as if it were identified less with an individual body than a social system. Little as individuals are able to admit this unsettling possibility, it is everywhere established by Crane in characteristically visual terms, and perhaps nowhere more convincingly than in *The Red Badge of Courage*.

The Spectacle of War

STANDING ON Boston Common in the early 1830s, Ralph Waldo Emerson felt a tremendous sense of self-transcendence as he became for the moment like a "transparent eyeball." That famous and paradoxical image—"I am nothing; I see all; the currents of the Universal Being circulate through me"—has variously since been invoked, although never to describe the naturalist characters who best seem to

fit the description.[5] Clyde Griffiths and Roberta Alden, Vandover and London's Arctic trekker, as well as other figures only mentioned in these pages (including Carrie Meeber, Trina McTeague, and Upton Sinclair's stockyard immigrants): all seem "transparent eyeballs," lacking the opaque material of selfhood that might obtrude between their inner desires and outer events. That deficiency helps explain their usual stance of wide-eyed staring in which they identify their incoherent energies with the worlds that bear upon them.

Few other texts, however, explore this ocular fixation as profoundly as Crane's *Red Badge of Courage*, or enact so fully the paradoxical implications of repetition in Emerson's pronouncement. The novel, that is, does more than depict the kind of visual paralysis that ensues from finding oneself in a world one has done nothing to create—the claim most often defended in Marxist analyses. Such an approach, by focusing on the alienating effects of reification, invariably bolsters our initial assumptions about subjectivity and the moral self. Accordingly, even when fictional embodiments of the full Emersonian "I" are reduced to more thinly transparent "eyes"— when, as in Crane, the coherent ego is exposed as nothing but an illusion—Marxist critics nonetheless tend to recuperate that illusion as fact. The "observer becomes a participant" in fictional texts that always, so it is claimed, subvert the self-alienation they represent.[6] Whatever the case for other authors, however, Crane's version of the "participant observer" is far less assuaging than any such reading suggests. He challenges our understanding of the primary process of vision itself, revealing through narrative repetition how fully it is transformed from what seems a literal, distinctly passive experience into an active and wrenchingly figurative one. Sight always recurs as insight that is itself determined and determining. Characters who "see all," therefore, reveal not liberating possibilities for social reform, but rather the inherent constraints that are always already shaping our vision, and enmeshing us even as we presume otherwise in a self-confirming logic.

The novel itself opens with a strikingly personified view of "the red eye-like gleam of hostile camp-fires set in the low brows of distant hills."[7] As the awakening army "cast its eyes upon the roads," the novel establishes the spectatorial activity that quickly comes to dominate. Soon after, Henry Fleming's ever-vigilant gaze is first invoked—"his youthful eyes had looked upon the war" (3)—and a day later the narrative will metaphorically assert, "new eyes were

given to him." In between these opening and closing references, he is repeatedly described in distinctively spectatorial terms: "the youth stared," "the youth saw," "the youth had watched, spell-bound," a "tortured witness."[8] And at the crisis of the novel on the second day of battle, Henry appears to himself to become all-perceptive:

> It seemed to the youth that he saw everything. Each blade of the green grass was bold and clear. He thought that he was aware of every change in the thin, transparent vapor that floated idly in sheets. . . . His mind took a mechanical but firm impression, so that, afterward, everything was pictured and explained to him, save why he himself was there. (85–86)

After this respite from battle ends, the emotional and narrative pace again quickens and the syntax reverts once more to the endlessly reiterated form, "He saw . . ."[9]

Visual activity in the novel is hardly as direct as this syntax may suggest, however, conforming instead to a pair of contradictory, alternating patterns. The first consists of an awe-struck gaze so engrossing that Henry cannot resist what he sees. Absorbed into the spectacle of martial experience, he loses all self-consciousness—a feeling powerful enough at moments to reduce him to little more than reflexive motions:

> The youth, still the bearer of the colors, did not feel his idleness. He was deeply absorbed as a spectator. The crash and swing of the great drama made him lean forward, intent-eyed, his face working in small contortions. . . . He did not know that he breathed; that the flag hung silently over him, so absorbed was he. (99)

Somewhat later, this ocular absorption becomes so intense an emotional drama that it can only be presented figuratively: "The youth had centered the gaze of his soul upon that other flag" (102). Henry has reverted to a stage of unmediated identification with experience, and lacks any consciousness of himself as active agent of perception. This is the reason he loses a supposedly cowardly concern for his safety, since by the second day of battle he simply lacks self-awareness altogether.

The long gaze of wonder in which Henry is absorbed—voided psychologically as he is grammatically in the process of sheer percep-

tion—occurs most frequently at severe pitches of emotional violence. Yet this forms only one aspect of the larger process of his spectatorial dependency, since much of the time he directs his attention obsessively at others. Under the assumption that they are just as obsessively (if derisively) gazing at him, he becomes reduced to their mirroring reflections of himself. This condition of psychological enslavement to others occurs throughout the novel with an effect that is equal to the intense private moments of perceptual absorption. Repeatedly, Henry swings between alternate feelings of pride and shame, both of which seem irrelevant.

Toward the novel's end, in a scene that exemplifies the first of these responses, he amazes his comrades by the fearlessness with which he charges into battle:

> During this moment of leisure, they seemed all to be engaged in staring with astonishment at him. They had become spectators. Turning to the front again, he saw, under the lifted smoke, a deserted ground.
>
> He looked, bewildered, for a moment. Then there appeared upon the glazed vacancy of his eyes, a diamond-point of intelligence. "Oh," he said, comprehending. . . . [T]hey had found time to regard him. And they now looked upon him as a war-devil. (80)

In a thorough inversion of the earlier process by which Henry vanishes amid his surroundings, he here becomes the sole object of a completely admiring communal gaze. Yet he is no more self-constructed or autonomous than before—as much as ever the product of constraining forces that lie beyond himself. The passage's disconnected, clausal prose confirms his slow transformation from presumed subject to manifest object, as the sequence of verbs transforms someone seeing to something seen. What at first appears simply a constraining repetition of "he saw" with "he looked" is immediately inverted by the description of what "appeared" upon "his eyes," then as immediately shifted again from ocular experience to a visual trope: "a diamond-point of intelligence." The grammatical process simply corroborates his psychological transition at the center of others' attention, as his self-conception is once again governed by the way they "regard him" and "looked upon him." With little appreci-

ation for the power of their gaze, he now "lay and basked in the occasional stares of his comrades" (81).

Understandably, Henry is more fully aware of this communal gaze at moments when he fears he has become an object of derisive scorn. After his desertion, therefore, he suspects nearly everyone he sees, and especially the tattered man whose only fault is excessive good cheer: "The youth glancing at his companion could see by the shadow of a smile that he was making some kind of fun" (47). Odd as is the unnamed man's "chance persistency," his affable manner and genial questions hardly support Henry's paranoid interpretation —a paranoia that curiously compounds his apprehension about being seen with the fear that he may in this instance be seeing too little. No matter how carefully he trains his own gaze, he feels exposed to a damning inspection: "It was not within human vigilance" (48).

Nothing he does can help him avoid what he takes to be a Medusa-like stare, represented not simply by the tattered man but by all experience—or as he expresses it in panicked tones, "the dark, leering witch of calamity" (51). Narcissistically fearful of the "leer" being ever directed at him, he desperately imagines how to direct "the scrutiny of his companions" away from his presumed cowardice. Appearing to fail at that, however, he grimly imagines what will ensue once his dishonor is "apparent to all men":

> In the next engagement they would try to keep watch of him to discover when he would run.
>
> Wherever he went in camp, he would encounter insolent and lingeringly-cruel stares. As he imagined himself passing near a crowd of comrades, he could hear some one say: "There he goes!"
>
> Then, as if the heads were moved by one muscle, all the faces were turned toward him with wide, derisive grins. He seemed to hear some one make a humorous remark in a low tone. At it, the others all crowed and cackled. He was a slang-phrase. (54)

This humiliating vision of himself seen through the filter of others' scorn governs Henry's self-constitution, as "pictures of himself, apart, yet in himself came to him" (51).

So intense is this repeated feeling of watching himself from afar that it seems an outer-body experience, an all but literal enactment of the process of dissociated sensibility. Following his first battle, when self-consciousness momentarily vanishes, the experience is

vividly dramatized: "The youth awakened slowly . . . scrutinizing his person in a dazed way as if he had never seen himself. Standing as if apart from himself, he viewed the last scene. He perceived that the man who had fought thus was magnificent" (30). As Henry grows self-absorbed and increasingly complacent through the course of the novel, he will "reflect" on himself more often in versions of this posture.[10] Indeed, the passage itself anticipates the transformation yet to come in the subtle shift across an apparent repetition from literal to metaphoric sight—"he viewed" becomes "he perceived." Although the "gleeful and unregretting" account he takes of his actions in the final chapter sharply contrasts with the sense of inadequacy he felt only a day before, the prospect from which "he saw that he was good" forms much the same external vantage: "From this present viewpoint, he was enabled to look upon [his actions] in spectator fashion and to criticise them with some correctness" (106). His fresh perspective on his newly achieved identity differs little from the old—except insofar as it blinds him further to the force of his unwilled desires.

The irony implicit in the dual forms of Henry's specular enslavement is that only when fully absorbed in battle, unaware of comforming to any behavioral standards, can he perform in accord with the judgment he would have others pass on him. Only immersed in the spectacle of war can he meet his expectations, expectations cherished in a frame of mind that itself precludes his acting that way. By losing all self-consciousness and no longer figuratively standing outside himself, he functions mindlessly in a manner that others take to be heroic. Paradoxically, heroism requires something like a state of non-being, while full self-awareness necessarily rules out any such selfless behavior: "He suddenly lost concern for himself and forgot to look at a menacing fate. He became not a man but a member. . . . He was welded into a common personality which was dominated by a single desire" (26). This psychological pattern, indeed the sentences themselves, are later nearly repeated when he watches others flee: "He forgot that he was engaged in combating the universe. . . . He lost concern for himself."[11] Of course, just as this "heroism" does, panic allows him to forget reputation, likewise enabling him to forego an external perspective on his behavior.

The Red Badge of Courage emphasizes, as do few other novels, a complex exchange between the spectacle of oneself and one's altering self-conception. While that exchange would seem to privilege pow-

ers of visual discrimination, the novel denies that one can ever control one's vision, much less ever have it effectively guide one's will. "Seeing" is either a passive process that absorbs Henry into the world, or a reactive process of responding to what he imagines others are thinking. In either case, the free-standing "self" essential to classical realism disappears, along with a self-regarding, self-conscious capacity for responsibility.[12]

Loss/Laws of Character

NO MATTER how thoroughly Henry is robbed of a self by these forms of ocular enslavement, he persists nonetheless in trying to discern the laws to his behavior that might attest to a self—a psychological structure of desires controlled by an organizing will. Of course, we tend to view him differently from the way he views himself—a tendency that fills him with apprehension, as we have just seen. And because we see more of him than do his fellow soldiers, we are less impressed by his presumed self-possession than we are by the force of his desires. Still, he persistently wants to find a way to predict his behavior, and more particularly—as if in echo of Zola's naturalistic pronouncements about the effects of diverse circumstances—to know how he will act in battlefield conditions:

> He felt that in this crisis his laws of life were useless. Whatever he had learned of himself was here of no avail. He was an unknown quantity. He saw that he would again be obliged to experiment as he had in early youth. He must accumulate information of himself. (7)

Strenuously as he tries "to mathematically prove" that he will not desert, no proof can be had, and all he can do is to settle at last for Jim Conklin's communal rationale: "If a hull lot a' boys started an' run, why, I s'pose I'd start an' run. . . . But if everybody was a-standin' an' a-fightin', why, I'd stand an' fight. B'jiminy, I would" (9). No law of character emerges or is about to do so in this kind of world, in part because neither deliberation nor resolution forms a warrant for action. Behavior is almost never predictable, at least as Crane conceives Henry Fleming, because his acts are rarely intended. They emerge instead from an impersonal, interdependent nexus of

forces—sometimes physical, sometimes pyschological, but always finally social—allowing simply what happens to happen to define after the fact the way one is, shaped willy-nilly by the collective behavior of others.

Reinforcing our sense of the ways that the self is excluded from this fictional world is the absence of any scenes of restraint, of instances when Henry refrains from an action he has contemplated. The problem has as much to do with lack of deliberation as with lack of restraint, since so few actions are ever considered beforehand by Henry, who characteristically feels his "mind flew in all directions." On those rare occasions when he does deliberate and does form a resolution, the process fails to enrich our sense of his self-constraining will. Concerned to capture the enemy colors, for instance, "he was resolved it should not escape," as "hard lines of determined purpose" appear on his face accompanied by a "grin of resolution" (102–3). Yet little seems chosen or freely willed about this fit of perseverance, and nothing distinguishes it or other such scenes from sheer desire.

Likewise, when Henry refrains from twitting Wilson about his earlier timid request, the scene is presented ambiguously. He "suddenly" recalls the packet of letters that Wilson gave him for safekeeping, impulsively exclaims aloud at the memory, and then inexplicably "felt impelled to change his purpose" (70). Nothing indicates that he is choosing, like Huck Finn or Isabel Archer, to refrain after due consideration of the merits of the case—or even that he is indeed refraining from a predictable course of action. By the time "he resolved not to deal the little blow," it is clear he is compelled by the grip of pride rather than motivated by compassion. Likewise later, "he made an attempt to restrain himself" from angry outburst, "but the words upon his tongue were too bitter" (75). Even when he does on occasion maintain his resolve—as when he vows, in battle, "not to budge whatever should happen" (100)—no reason for his behavior is adduced, as if to stress his utter lack of responsibility for acting that way.

Deliberation seems shallow at best and at worst cannot be relied upon, but that is not enough in itself to prevent Henry (or us) from tracing a law to his character. The novel more certainly precludes that possibility at a behavioral level by revealing characters so unpredictable as to render identity itself incoherent. Although Henry has known Jim Conklin ever "since childhood" (10), his long-time friend

appears enigmatic not only to us but also to him: someone initially loud and boastful, belligerently trading on rumors of war, appears at the same time wise beyond his years in considering the prospect of desertion. With even greater dramatic moment, Wilson's radical change in character occurs literally overnight, from being a "loud soldier" to someone whose "fine reliance" bespeaks "a quiet belief in his purposes and abilities" (68).

These changes challenge some of our deepest assumptions about both constancy and consistency in personal behavior—and this remains so in the face of Bernard Williams' denial that "memory claims and personal characteristics" form necessary conditions for identity. Nothing, according to Williams, requires that we have the same habits, preferences, ideas, and memories today as we had yesterday to be identified as the "same" person. Still, despite his convincing logic, we do ordinarily assume that people act in a consistent fashion, that they maintain from day to day a constant configuration of beliefs, and that their identities therefore involve more or less permanent traits of character.[13] Wilson's sudden about-face may not itself surpass belief but it does contribute to the general process by which identity is brought into question by the novel.

The character who notably lacks a coherent, consistent identity is Henry Fleming, even if the narrative's free indirect discourse occasionally blinds us to this realization. He simply acts as his strongest desires at the moment happen to dictate, and their very unpredictability prevents him from telling the kind of a soldier he will be. Yet the more important question concerns what kind of a person he can be, since even were he predictable, that would not clearly make him a willing agent. Lacking a self, Henry is deprived of the power to alter his behavior, and thereby to choose the kind of person he might in any event *want* to be.[14] He admires Wilson's alteration into a kinder, better man, just as he admires the unseen "cheery soldier" who helps him back to his regiment (61). But he lacks the capacity (much as do they) to transform simple admiration into a larger volition to act like them. For much the same reason that he is unable to order his desires, he cannot direct his actions in accord with an overriding conception of himself.

All Henry can do at first is to justify himself according to a rather complacent sense of his own virtue, attributing motives to himself that are always flattering. And that all too easily becomes a matter of simply rationalizing behavior according to causes he projects back

onto experience: "He had proceeded with wisdom and from the most righteous motives" (35). Later, he hopes for the personal vindication that would supposedly ensue from his regiment's defeat, thereby proving "he had fled early because of his superior powers of perception" (52–53). Persistently, he confuses moral judgments with self-justification in a pattern sometimes openly parodied by the narrative voice: "He searched about in his mind then for an adequate malediction for the indefinite cause, the thing upon which men turn the words of final blame. It—whatever it was—was responsible for him, he said. There lay the fault" (50). Disappointed and angry, he flatly denies he can help what he's done, unaware that any resort to determinism argues him out of existence as an autonomous self.

Henry refuses to settle for this paradoxically subversive form of self-justification, having realized how little it addresses the question of what kind of soldier he will be, or otherwise reveals about his "unknown quantity." The advantage of the alternative method he adopts is precisely its greater descriptive accuracy, although in the end it will give him no greater sense of autonomous selfhood: "The only way to prove himself was to go into the blaze and then figuratively to watch his legs to discover their merits and faults" (9). This image ironically matches the pose of the unnamed man in London's story, left "looking at himself in the snow" while he slowly freezes to death. As a process of self-assessment, however, it resembles more closely the response of the garrulous old lady recalled by E. M. Forster, who when accused of being illogical, exclaimed: "Logic! Good gracious! What rubbish! How can I tell what I think till I see what I say?"[15]

Yet Henry's proposal is even more radical than this exclamation implies, corresponding to the concept of "moral luck" in which "how things turn out determines what has been done." The meaning of action, in other words, emerges now only well after the fact, not before, if with the same effect appearing to remove his actions from Henry's control. His behavior is still apparently governed by something other than a "self," since even without an "indefinite cause" he exists as no more than the things he has done. The major difference in the way he rationalizes his motives is that he begins to stand outside his actions as a means of judging them. This gradual shift in perspective releases him from narrow self-justification ("I acted that way from the best of motives") to a logic that connects his behavior with a set of larger social categories ("I am the way my actions turned out").

Despite his shift in self-appraisal, his logic remains no less circular, leaving Henry still victim of consequences rather than master of dispositions. All he can do, once having adopted an external view of behavior, is to apply fixed categories of cowardice, bravery, duty, and so on to the acts he performs. No more fully now than before does this backward-looking logic structure a self, since his experiences are simply absorbed again into the larger regimental process. As he observes (without understanding), he is a "coward" for no other reason than that his regiment happens to withstand the assault from which he flees. Later, he becomes a "hero" largely because his regiment happens to win: "It was revealed to him that he had been a barbarian, a beast . . . Regarding it, he saw that it was fine, wild, and, in some ways, easy. He had been a tremendous figure, no doubt" (80). Having tried a day earlier to assert a law to his character by moral fiat, he ends by accepting the categories imposed on himself by moral luck. The latter method may seem more effective, but it too only reveals how little self he has.

Narrating the Absent Self

THE RED *Badge of Courage* subverts any impulse to view Henry Fleming as a moral agent, establishing through its style itself deep doubts about his claims to being an autonomous actor vested with a capacity for responsibility. It does this by disrupting normal grammatical expectations for a "self" whose emotions, ideas, and actions are integrated, and who stands free of his fictional world.[16] Near the beginning of the novel, Henry overhears Jim Conklin confidently announce that "th' army's goin' t' move":

> He had burned several times to enlist. Tales of great movements shook the land. They might not be distinctly Homeric, but there seemed to be much glory in them. He had read of marches, sieges, conflicts, and he had longed to see it all. His busy mind had drawn for him large pictures, extravagant in color, lurid with breathless deeds. (3)

The effect of this sequence of simple sentences, each of which starts arrestingly afresh, is to lend to Henry a childlike air. As in Jack London's story, the passage relies on an extreme paratactic structure, with the similar effect that time itself seems temporarily forestalled.

Because sentences do not progress in a way we have normally been led to expect, our narrative sense of duration and temporal sequence is at least for the moment suspended. As well, however, and more importantly, the syntax here announces the state of its subject by its very lack of causal connectives. Henry seems to consist of a medley of conflicting energies in a world that similarly lacks any pattern, while actions are defined in a way that suggests that agency is something well beyond him.[17] Neither he nor anyone else has the power, so the prose suggests, to coordinate the conflicting desires that go into constituting themselves.

Yet if everyone is struck on first reading by Crane's notoriously eccentric narrative perspective, critics have nonetheless usually slighted its most salient feature: the way in which his descriptions invert our customary assumptions about acting in the world. The madness of war, of course, has always been deemed sufficient to explain altered consciousness, and yet Crane treats the combat setting as little more than a narrative cliché. Neither scene nor plot in themselves, that is, help explain his beguiling transfigurations, which result from a far more violent set of stylistic maneuvers. The effect of that violence is finally to reduce individuals to events, at the same time that a curious semblance of human life is breathed into things. The normal way in which we categorize people and things in the world is disrupted, as characters are made to appear from a thoroughly external and objective point of view, while the natural world conversely appears from a seemingly internal and personal perspective.

Expectations are disrupted, moreover, from the novel's very first lines through rhetorical tropes that have the effect of challenging the syntax of our thoughts. Consider the famous opening description of the monster army awakening and trembling, or this brief scene later the next day: "A single rifle flashed in a thicket before the regiment. In an instant, it was joined by many others . . . The guns in the rear, aroused and enraged by shells that had been thrown burr-like at them, suddenly involved themselves in a hideous altercation with another band of guns" (77–78). A skirmish between soldiers occurs as an "altercation" between weapons, autonomous bands of guns "aroused and enraged" into "suddenly involv[ing] themselves." Not only is experience released here as elsewhere from an appearance of human control, but it manifests a powerful life of its own that reduces individuals to dependent onlookers. Earlier, a similar description has evoked a similar sense: "The guns squatted in a row

like savage chiefs. They argued with abrupt violence. It was a grim pow-wow" (29). Unlike Henry's mode of thought—which invokes the pathetic fallacy in order to justify his actions, adducing from natural processes a supposed model for his behavior—the omniscient narrator's style establishes precisely the opposite: that those capacities we cherish as human hardly need be considered as such.[18]

Conversely, Crane's grammar tends to reduce the human to a mechanical status, and does so most obviously through forms of repetition common to naturalist prose. Descriptions are occasionally duplicated word for word within pages of each other, and accounts of events or of dialogue are likewise all but exactly repeated.[19] There is, of course, a certain thematic appropriateness to this stylistic repetition, since the experience of war that Crane presents is itself endlessly repetitive: "Also, he was drilled and drilled and reviewed, and drilled and drilled and reviewed."[20] Likewise, battle scenes repeated over two long days differ little to us, for all the sharp distinctiveness they appear to have for Henry. The collective impact of these repetitions is to produce a sense of stasis, as if no progress had been made and never could be. All that is possible is to repeat what has already been done many times before, to reiterate again what has been said on countless other occasions. The novel's conclusion confirms this sense with the news that the hard-won ground will merely be abandoned by Henry's regiment. The next day promises only more of the same—of fruitless actions described in a language incapable of making a difference.[21]

These repetitions and syntactic disruptions have an estranging effect on the reader, establishing a context within which characters exist not as agents but as machines. Even prior to that context, the effect is clearly felt in the earliest reference to Henry as a mere conjunction of parts: "There was a youthful private who listened with eager ears . . . [and then] went to his hut . . . He wished to be alone with some new thoughts that had lately come to him" (2). The compound sentences themselves, which move an elementary diction through additive clauses, tend once again to diminish their subject. Here, however, the effect results from something more than a syntactical stutter—from the description's striking reliance on a sequence of prepositions rather than adverbs. By identifying Henry's behavior through a series of separate attributes, rather than the more normal method of modified capacities, the passage transforms his dissociated sensibility into a physical fact. The preposition "with,"

in other words, links him to "eager ears" and "new thoughts," and by doing so intimates that organs as well as ideas do not cohere in a self.

As the narrative continues, this process becomes increasingly disruptive:

> The youth went along with slipping, uncertain feet. He kept watchful eyes rear-ward. A scowl of mortification and rage was upon his face. He had thought of a fine revenge upon the officer who had referred to him and his fellows as mule-drivers. But he saw that it could not come to pass. . . . And now the retreat of the mule-drivers was a march of shame to him. (90)

Henry is again shorn of the conventional markings of coherent identity, not only by the characteristic reference to him as "the youth," but by the stilted sequence of simple sentences that reveal his poor self-integration. A paratactic structure once more repeatedly returns to the same subject ("the youth," "he," "he," "but he"), dismissing a complex psychological grammar along with a complex verbal one. Likewise, the syntax of his presentation breaks him again into parts ("with slipping, uncertain feet" rather than "his feet slipped"; "kept watchful eyes" rather than "watched"; "a scowl upon his face" rather than "he scowled"; and so on). Perceptions, behavior, and thoughts seem curiously but profoundly unaligned.

Ironically, the only alignment in the passage is represented by Henry's posture, which is turned to the rear, facing backward, in bodily correspondence to his mental state. Instead of adducing possible motives, no matter how self-justifying—or even simply attempting to identify the physical causes for his present condition—Henry has by now been reduced to the logic of interpreting consequences after the fact. Return, revenge, repetition: the passage is a model of reflexivity. He is compelled bodily, emotionally, and psychologically into accepting the way things turn out as a reading of what has been. All that is left for him to do is to repeat the officer's characterization, rejecting it first only then to accept it quietly as his own interpretation ("the retreat of the mule-drivers was a march of shame").

Even more dramatically elsewhere, the narrative stresses how fully motives actually seem to ensue from behavior instead of the other way around, as we commonly assume.

Directly he began to speed toward the rear in great leaps. His rifle and cap were gone. His unbuttoned coat bulged in the wind. The flap of his cartridge-box bobbed wildly and his canteen, by its slender cord, swung out behind. . . .

Since he had turned his back upon the fight, his fears had been wondrously magnified. (32)

The description again is disjoining, as Henry metonymically flies apart in the bulging, bobbing, unbuttoning disruption of his apparel. What leads to his reintegration is the interpretive mode into which he falls, insinuated by the final sentence. Or rather, it is the ambivalent opening word of the sentence that offers a key to understanding how self-construction frequently works in the novel ("Since he had turned his back"). The word "since" intimates not just that "fears" occur *following* his flight from battle ("since" here serving in an adverbial capacity, meaning "after"), but that his fears result instead precisely from having run away (serving as a conjunction, and in this case meaning "because"). The suggestion emerges that turning his back and then running generates the fear he feels, in contrast to the more obvious causal pattern that works vice versa. Strange as this inverted process may seem, it perfectly exemplifies the paradox of "moral luck," in which our view of each other depends upon simply what happens to occur.

Even more radically, the novel suggests that the way in which characters tend to view consequences dictates the feelings they initially had, those feelings that led to their behavior in the first place. Of course, any consequence is always viewed through the frames of social convention, but here, characters casually accept a code of behavior that takes no account of motive or even of predisposing emotion. The result of this double process is to rule out the very possibility of an autonomous self, since what one is and what one feels depends on events and codes fully beyond one's control. Much as this double process defies all customary logic, moreover, it corresponds to our sense of how determinism might well work—and does so once again by disrupting our normal projective assumptions.[22]

Compounding this disruptive effect is the problematic status of the narrative voice, which slides back and forth between the free indirect discourse of Henry's atomized perspective and an omniscient third person. Seconds before he receives the gratuitous wound of his

"red badge of courage," the narrative evokes his agitated, emotionally fractured state of mind as he stumbles upon a group of fleeing soldiers:

> Soon he was in the midst of them. They were leaping and scampering all about him. Their blanched faces shone in the dusk. They seemed, for the most part, to be very burly men. The youth turned from one to another of them as they galloped along. His incoherent questions were lost. They were heedless of his appeals. They did not seem to see him. (58)

The choppy syntax here once again seems to exclude an organizing will, and powerfully evokes the consciousness of someone who lacks a self. Yet some pages later, the same syntactical pattern initially characterizes what is clearly an omniscient voice:

> The fire crackled musically. From it swelled light smoke. Overhead, the foliage moved softly. The leaves with their faces turned toward the blaze were colored shifting hues of silver, often edged with red. Far off to the right, through a window in the forest could be seen a handful of stars, like glittering pebbles, on the black level of the night. (64)

The passage brilliantly justifies Conrad's praise of Crane's "impressionist" style, even though that very brilliance raises questions about the narrative voice. After all, both diction and perspective clearly exceed Henry's modest capacities, at the same time that the syntax continues to reflect his limited processes of thought. Only gradually, that is, does the narrator abandon Henry's rudimentary constructions in favor of the compound sentences that attest to a firmer, more confident narrative control.

There are countless other occasions when the narrative voice seems colored by Henry's perspective, although at first no obvious purpose seems to be served by this. Yet the texts of other naturalists reveal similar fractures in narrative voice, sometimes cleft so sharply that the narrator seems to be hectoring characters. These dramatic divisions between alternative points of view has the effect of placing them, ironically, "in perspective," revealing their separate limitations and drawing into question any one's privileged status (as London and Dreiser showed). Conversely, here (as in Norris' novel), the

transition between assorted viewpoints and voices is entirely muted, with the result that it is more than occasionally hard to discern which is which. Part of what is achieved, however, by slipping into and out of Henry's consciousness is that he gradually becomes absorbed into the larger discursive world. The very indeterminacy in the pattern of alternating voices contributes to that overall process. Take, for instance, the pathetic fallacy, which characterizes both the narrator's animation of nature and Henry's self-rationalizations. Their separate conceptual habits are linked via a common trope—one that we share as well. What finally distinguishes Henry's usage is not his projective frame of reference, as critics sometimes claim, but rather the fact that he is so complacent about the conclusions to be drawn from his observations.

There is a more troubling aspect, however, to this confused medley of voices, one that becomes particularly apparent at moments of strained syntactical construction. Midway through the novel, Henry is mortified as he recollects his desertion: "Again he thought that he wished he was dead. He believed that he envied a corpse. Thinking of the slain, he achieved a great contempt for some of them as if they were guilty for thus becoming lifeless" (53). Logically, this way of stating the issue tends toward incoherence, since it is hard to see how one might be able to err about one's own feelings, at least as one is feeling them. Either Henry did actually have a wish for something and did in fact envy someone, or else he did not—and at the time he felt these he could not also have "thought" or "believed" he was feeling differently. The principle underlying this assertion is that an emotional state is unlike the world, since we cannot unwittingly misconstrue the contents of our own minds, while we can certainly misrepresent external events (the construction, "he thought he was in pain, but he wasn't," seems nonsensical, while "he thought it was raining, but it wasn't" is both plausible and common).[23] Yet incoherent as such mistaken self-referential claims seem to be, their appearance in the novel attests to something more than narrative incoherence. For by alerting us to a logical conflict, they help to reveal how thoroughly character is constructed through a pattern of conflicting voices. It is as if the very process of foregrounding activities supposedly attributed to oneself were intended to clarify how arbitrary the assumptions we hold about ourselves really are. Once again, the novel reveals that the process of constructing a self consists of certain habitual assumptions we do not (and perhaps cannot) think to ques-

tion—assumptions we silently impose upon texts that invite quite another way of reading.

The stylistic innovations of *The Red Badge of Courage* breach an assortment of realist conventions—so many that readers have frequently failed to realize their collective philosophical impact. More compellingly than other naturalists, Crane demonstrated how fully our assumptions about what it is like to be in the world help to create the shape of that being. He understood how little proof exists to support the conventional belief in a self able to choose, then to act responsibly. And he quietly withheld from his novel those structures—grammatical, scenic, and narrative—that enable readers to project certain comforting assumptions about agency onto fictional characters. Throughout his career, he imagined quite different kinds of plots and behavior, but he always returned to the problem of how to read ourselves into the world. Henry Fleming, in other words, provides only the most obvious example of a character who exists as little more than a vortex of emotions and desires. Maggie Johnson, the Swede in "The Blue Hotel," the correspondent in "The Open Boat," among others: all are presented as gazing subjects, denied a will by the very narratives that present them as sets of reflexive traits. For us to see them as full personalities, as agents responsible for their acts and their lives, is to submit to a cherished illusion that is everywhere exposed as far in excess of the facts. We need instead, with Crane as with others, to attend to the texture of his idiosyncratic prose. Only then will we come to realize how thoroughly the placement of words on a page can dismantle the otherwise comforting assumptions we bring to bear upon fictional characters, and as well upon ourselves in the world.

6.

Reconstituting the Subject

A NY PHILOSOPHY of determinism decrees that conclusions lie well beyond our control, the result of a narrative shape set in motion by the introductions we happen to be given. Plots predictably wind to a close as the energies of their openings dictate, with characters helpless to alter the course of events that ineluctably lead to their ends—either ostracized or hailed as heroes, frozen to death due to "negligence" or electrocuted for their "crimes." Naturalist narratives simply enact a process that has been clear all along. Yet true as this self-enfolding pattern is to the logic of naturalism, it hardly provides an appropriate model for more open-ended critical ventures. Conclusions, that is, do not have to remind those of us who *can* control our ends merely of what we have already known. They can release us instead to pursue implications in the readerly choices we have made, and the prospects opened up by those choices for reading other texts as well. Having detailed the extent to which naturalist style is neither

"bad" nor ineffective, we ought at this point to turn to larger con-texts—historical as well as critical—to speculate on some of the reasons why others have found that so hard to admit.

American naturalism has attracted a surprising amount of recent attention among critics, not least because of the revisionary work now being directed at the study of "literature"—and directed on every ideological front. Marxists, feminists, the New Historicists, and a host of other specialists—initially provoked by the exclusion of minority voices from the established canon—have rekindled inter-est in the relationship between popular culture and aesthetic value. That relationship has been a relatively troubled one at best, ever since literature became fully professionalized in the late nineteenth century and writers self-consciously addressed their work to distinct classes of audience.[1] By the middle of the twentieth century, Lionel Trilling felt the need to turn the tables against what he saw as mindless popular taste in favor of high aesthetic "ideas." Significantly, the illustrative examples he chose to use in deploring this cultural scene were Theodore Dreiser's inflated reputation and the undeserved ne-glect of Henry James.[2] More recently, following a quarter of a century in which those reputations have been firmly reversed, liter-ary historians have begun to turn attention to more popular authors, both then and now, and to the process by which reputations happen to be made, both in the marketplace and the academy. Why, these scholars wonder, do social elites prize texts by writers like James, and how do the formal terms that exclude sometimes exceedingly popular texts in fact simply mask a set of hegemonic assumptions?[3]

The answers to such questions lie well beyond the scope of this inquiry, but it does seem odd that the literary debate has so rarely drawn examples from the late nineteenth century. Naturalism offers the perfect site for that debate, after all, having captured the strange middle ground that lies between popular discourse and literary "value": its narratives still enjoy a mass audience, at least in many cases, and yet it has also been granted legitimate if grudging status by the academic establishment. Texts by London, Dreiser, Norris, and Crane have long been familiar fixtures in the American literary canon, and this in spite of their often graceless styles and seemingly simplistic philosophy. It hardly matters that within that canon those texts are treated as a passel of orphans, children of neither the Great Tradition that extends from Emerson through Faulkner nor of the popular cultural forms so often satirized by the naturalists themselves. They still are read and taught.

Yet why, especially at a time when the idea of an "American literature" has come up for grabs—when challenges to the canon have become the standard thrust and parry of literary life—why are naturalist texts most notable by their absence from the fray? Why, even at a time when naturalism has generated new critical interest, have those more interested in a national literature so regularly failed to confront the narrative and stylistic innovations introduced by American naturalism? Or again (if from another perspective), why have theoreticians interested in examining just such formal issues—those structuralists and post-structuralists who have transformed our notions of the "literary" itself by embracing familiar fairy tales and obscure Balzac, Ian Fleming and Freud—why have they also so uniformly ignored the naturalists? Such questions compel us to turn to the work of prominent historians and theoreticians, if only to understand why it is that naturalism has so often been shunted aside. In the process, it should become apparent how fully the naturalists anticipated issues we think of as our own—issues that have seemed only recently available to understanding. We may, in other words, gain a renewed respect for the imaginative responses devised by the naturalists nearly a century ago, to issues that still confound us.

Historical Placements

NATURALISM EMERGED during a tumultuous period in American history, an era of unprecedented rifts and schisms that transformed a rural agrarian republic into an urban-industrial nation, all within less than two generations. The facts behind that transformation defy all previous records—of extraordinary economic production matched by equally striking unemployment; of the final retreat of Indian tribes just as westward expansion had supposedly ended; of the launching of imperialist schemes abroad at a moment of unparalleled immigration; of unprecedented standardization in the workplace, and yet business specialization as never before. These contradictory developments have long fascinated historians anxious to understand the effects of traumatic social disruption on American identity.

The very revolt by naturalists during this period against literary realism—and their implicit revaluation of assumptions as cherished as rugged individualism, personal freedom, and the sacredness of family life—might even be adduced as evidence for changes in a national self-conception. Yet rarely has this connection occurred to

social historians. Indeed, it is as if a habitual unwillingness to accept the deterministic aspects of naturalism was itself uncannily replicated in the absence of naturalist texts from accounts of the period. Repression always returns, however, a fact borne out by the curious hypotyposis in the most ambitious of these accounts. The structure itself, that is, of arguments made by two influential recent historians reproduces the determinist logic of the very naturalist texts they choose to ignore. And precisely because their arguments differ, yet rely on similar organizational structures, the work of Alan Trachtenberg and Jackson Lears warrants our attention. Both men offer persuasive readings of a broad array of events, of idiosyncratic cultural expressions as well as of larger institutional formations, even as both also fail to draw on the fictional material that would best support their cases. Their reasons for ignoring the naturalists can in fact only be inferred, but it seems to be because they share a conventional set of "high" standards for "literary" expression. Ironically, both men subscribe to assumptions dismissed by the naturalists, assumptions about fictional narrative that blind them to the texts most appropriate for their discussions.

Trachtenberg investigates the images, myths, and figurative language of the late nineteenth century in support of his thesis that a logic of "incorporation" explains its "reorganization of cultual perceptions."[4] Just as Big Business coordinated a set of interests that before had seemed plainly opposed, so other cultural institutions now began to embody conflict, and even to foster it. "America incorporated"—a phrase that had once seemed no more than a simple contradiction in terms—grew to symbolize the larger contradictions accepted as part of institutional life. Conflict replaced consensus as the informing definition of political life in America, which had now itself most centrally become "a symbol in contention."[5] Trachtenberg offers a thick description of the period that nicely accentuates its heterogeneity, the strife and tussle and irresolution so often flattened out by historical explanation. At the same time, however, his corporate model lends a determinist tinge to events, since any potential anomaly only ends by further supporting that model. The thesis of conflict, like earlier theses that emphasized consensus, seems simply to feed back into itself, much as would a self-regulating machine. Not that anything about the period itself suggests determinism, but interpretation is governed by a thesis so comprehensive that the reader is forced to accept any new fact as evidence on its behalf.

What is latent in Trachtenberg becomes fully explicit in Lears' account, as the determinist model is transferred from the reader to the events of history itself. Americans at the turn of the century found themselves running a maze of consumer practices so ineluctable that any attempt to escape only reinforced the patterns more fully. For Lears, this commanding new "culture of consumption" is explained less by a corporate model than in terms of the advent of a "therapeutic world view"—one that promoted a broad range of intense activities as "protests" against the dehumanizing strains of modern life. These physical, emotional, and spiritual dissents induced, however, no more than a passing sense of personal "authenticity," and ironically accommodated Americans to the very society they had hoped to resist by sanctioning the cozy illusion of individual "autonomy." By exalting experience as an end in itself, and helping to replace a model of self-denial with one of self-gratification, "antimodernism" only further served the aims of modernism.[6]

Different as are these two accounts, they eerily reproduce the same determinist logic embedded so deeply in the period they describe, and in the texts they ignore. Yet even more curious than this seemingly inadvertent reduplication is the fact that the specific perspectives adopted by Trachtenberg and Lears happen to correspond with the naturalists' own most pressing concerns. Take the question of contradictions resulting from the self's "incorporation" in a body; or of challenges to the very idea of personal "authenticity"; or of the sources of desire in a larger "culture of consumption": these have long been acknowledged as the thematic centers of naturalist fiction.[7] Why then, despite their lively interest in the literature of the period, does neither historian draw this connection? The answer seems to be that they share an implicit Progressive belief that only "high" culture —and in particular, high *literary* culture—offers an incisive social critique. Both men ignore the naturalists, who would appear their most obvious supporting examples, in lieu of writers more self-consciously opposed to the forms of their era (if also less carefully attuned to them): the Howells of the eighties, the Melville of *Billy Budd*, and the Henry Adams of *The Education*.

Lears and Trachtenberg do not confront the period's most characteristic texts, finally, because they cling to a distinction otherwise transgressed so imaginatively in their own work—a distinction dividing "high" and "low" cultures that emerged, as it happens, in the nineteenth century. Bringing together phenomena as diverse as the

Beadle dime novels and Henry James, muscle-building and Weir Mitchell's "rest cure," Buffalo Bill's Wild West Show and Chicago's "White City," they nonetheless go on to reproduce the exclusionary formal terms that fence off "literature" from a market economy. Despite an enthusiasm for popular culture that leads to provocative thematic connections, they both fall back on a set of safely established, elite texts, as if those were less inflected by the culture that produced them, or somehow provided a more trenchant critique of its governing assumptions. This silent preference also precludes any sustained inquiry into possible formal analogies among the miscellaneous "texts" adduced by both historians. Realist conventions are simply reasserted, and the naturalists drop once again out of sight, into the gap between "high" and "low" culture.

The fact that structural homologies are at the heart of recent New Historicist efforts has, by the same token, already helped to revive a revisionist interest in naturalist texts. Foremost among these critics, Walter Benn Michaels has identified a consistent pattern to the assumptions shared by a wide variety of cultural practices in late nineteenth-century America, assumptions informing economic, legal, and philosophical texts that also help to explain the period's characteristic fictional shapes. The transactions, for instance, elided by Georg Simmel's monetary models, or the contractual identifications involved in Krafft-Ebing's invention of sexual perversion, or the celebration of chance in Alfred Stieglitz's account of photography, partake of the same "logic" informing the idiosyncratic texts of naturalism. The consumer capitalism that emerged at the turn of the century encouraged, according to Michaels, not simply a series of antimodern reactions but a new way of thinking about representation itself, a structure of thought expressed in texts that have usually been seen to serve quite different ends. Offering an explicit refutation of both Lears and Trachtenberg, he argues that it is not possible to stand in an adversarial relationship to one's culture, any more than fish can fight water. The structures a culture offers are precisely the structures by which we operate, and what allows us to recognize oppositional narrative strategies *as* oppositional is that they always do (because they only can) express those structures.[8]

Once again, determinism embeds itself in a modern critic's account of the period through a hypotyposis much the same as that which lurks in Lears' and Trachtenberg's histories. Michaels' approach (by his own admission) leaves little ground on which any

resistance to a society's deepest values might be able to stand, at least from within that society itself. Cultural practice at a given time does not simply *happen* to serve the essentially conservative ends of culture, but actively *has* to serve them. By default, we are always in imaginative justification of the modes that go into producing us— whether economic, social, scientific, or otherwise—and narratives therefore cannot fail to "exemplify" a primary cultural structure.[9] This model of ideological compulsion, apparent in overlapping structural homologies, enables an imaginative reading of the period in terms of "the gold standard." But it does so only by also obscuring those non-economic, non-thematic aspects of narrative fiction that form the far more obvious attributes of naturalism. The curious forms of expression that everyone finds so striking in the mode— the verbal quirks and plot rifts that have always seemed in need of repair—are once again excused by silent elision in Michaels' analysis. The point is that any such thematic analysis, no matter how effective, cannot help but smooth over disruptive narratives and estranging styles in the necessary effort of reducing them to a paraphrasable content. And in the process, naturalism's most interesting innovations are simply erased.

Michaels' insight into the "logic" of this otherwise strange set of texts is therefore gained at the cost of a kind of blindness to naturalism's most powerful agenda. The point is certainly not that thematic analysis is somehow irrelevant or unrevealing, but rather that naturalism's most striking critique is inaccessible to that approach, whether undertaken by New Historicists (who ignore the texture of "bad" styles) or by the new social historians (who ignore "bad" plots altogether). Indeed, only by confronting the "problem" of naturalism's peculiar language itself—of the verbal and syntactical idiosyncrasies that distinguish separate texts—can we come to appreciate how fully the naturalists challenged us to reconceive certain long-standing premises about the "self."

It is more than coincidence that naturalism should have anticipated attacks on the "subject" that have become an integral part of the philosophical tradition in this century. The fierce dismantling of Kantian Idealism undertaken by Nietszche, followed by Freud's disruption of the Cartesian premise of psychological coherence, has transformed our understanding of what is essential to actors, agency, even events, and indirectly altered our expectations for narrative sequence. That may itself, in a more general way, help explain why

the naturalists have recently come into favor among a small group of critics (in contrast to the historians and cultural theorists cited earlier who continue to ignore the mode). The very attention directed by critical theory to the creation of the coherent subject—and in particular, to its status as an arbitrary cultural production, not a given of nature—appears to have encouraged an interest in narratives that foreground the process of the self's self-construction. Yet the connections between naturalism and post-structuralism are closer than even this suggests. For the enduring problem faced by such different theorists as Derrida, Foucault, and Lacan has been to find a way to recast traditional conceptions of agency. And the conception each returns to is that of the fragmented "subject" constructed through language itself—indeed, determined by language that always already immures that desiring subject in its grammatical structures.

The Style of the Subject

IT IS hardly original to observe that the twentieth century has not recovered from the collapse of belief in the autonomous subject. What *is* original is to realize the naturalists were engaged in thinking through this collapse, especially since most have assumed that writers like Crane, Dreiser, London, and Norris were incapable of anything but a straightforward positivism, a naive belief in things as they seemed and in persons as they behaved. The naturalists came of age when capitalism had already created subjects who "freely" exchanged their labor for wages and "voluntarily" purchased the commodities they produced.[10] At that historical moment, however, an economy newly geared for consumption demanded a subject that stood entirely free of its social practice, the better to be guided, regulated, manipulated, and shaped by market forces. The historical paradox in this transition into fuller apparent autonomy, however, was that in literature, psychology, science, and philosophy the individual came to be seen as an ever more thoroughly fixed cultural construction—not as an agent capable of playing various parts in a vast social drama, but as a mathematical function increasingly bound by the calculus of parts he played. Instead of assuming that assorted desires and activities were organized at the behest of a personality, activities and desires now seemed capable of constructing unaided

those individuals in whom they occurred—or in Ian Hacking's phrase, of "making up people."[11]

The new society invented perversion and called it a disease, similarly inventing the pervert as a diseased person. Behavioral scientists demonstrated that certain heriditary "types" were predisposed to antisocial or criminal behavior, and "discovered" as well the racial differences that justified social inequalities. Sociologists developed theories to account for supposedly high "innate IQ" on the one hand and social "degeneration" on the other.[12] Human failings not ascribed to inherited physiological inadequacies were now thought to be determined psychologically, as hysteria, neurasthenia, nervous excitement, and even morbid introspection came to be attributed to causes that lay well beyond the bounds of the self. A range of emotional impulses formerly within a person's control were gradually assumed to lie elsewhere—in the environment, say, or one's past, or one's hereditary makeup, where they in turn controlled the person.

The attraction of the Progressive movement to large numbers of American voters lay at least partly in the rejection of traditional notions of an independent *Homo economicus*, along with the demise of political, psychological, and philosophical forms of autonomy as well. Careful management of a wide range of physiological and temperamental propensities—by newly professionalized guidance counsellors, efficiency experts, and specialists in behavior modification—would develop both individual and social capacities in the supposedly best, most productive manner. As one contemporary maintained, men are but "plastic lumps of human dough" pressed into shape on the great "social kneadingboard." Or in the more precise words of a student of John Dewey's, "the notion of a separate and independent ego is an illusion."[13] The self had at last been absorbed, in almost every conceivable way, into its social functions.

Part of the point of glancing at the historical context of American naturalism is to remind ourselves that it emerged from a set of singular historical influences—influences documented elsewhere carefully enough not to require any further review.[14] Naturalism in turn influenced major authors in the twentieth century, including prominently William Faulkner and Ernest Hemingway, but perhaps more obviously John Dos Passos, James T. Farrell, John Steinbeck, and Richard Wright—each of whom separately, distinctively helped to keep the naturalist label alive. It is worth considering, however,

that to the extent that their writing seems less wrenching or more "polished" (or even more classically realist) than the first generation of naturalists, these authors may not explore as fully the philosophical dilemma posed by the self's construction in language. Whatever the other achievements to which this later generation can rightly lay claim, its stylistic "improvements" attest to an incomplete exploration of determinism, a refusal to engage at a verbal level the contradictions in an ideology that proclaimed Americans free yet predictable.

The first generation of naturalists, more fully than those who came after, anticipated issues central to prominent writers and intellectuals of the twentieth century. From Pound, Eliot, and Joyce through to Lacan, Foucault, and Derrida, the debate has invariably been directed to the realm of language itself. Understandably, that debate has dominated recent work on fictional narrative, which has turned most prominantly (and productively) to the problem of repetition. It is, of course, a commonplace of narratological criticism that there are repetitions, and repetitions, which may make it ironic that similarities among the discussions of the phenomena are as instructive as differences between them. Indeed, the most prominent gesture repeated in analyses of repetition involves the selection of textual examples themselves. Most critics have turned to realist fiction, usually from the Victorian era, to support their conclusions. In the process, as it happens, they have recuperated the very assumptions about selfhood, responsibility, and agency that are revealed by the repetitions of naturalist fiction as dramatically insufficient.

Peter Brooks and J. Hillis Miller, in two influential recent studies, have claimed that the most fundamental and encompassing "repetition" is the very act of narrating itself: that is, narration always becomes the recreation of a story that has ostensibly occurred "once upon a time," before the process of narrating begins. "What is important," Brooks asserts, "whatever our decision about priority here, is the constructive, semiotic role of repetition: the function of plot as the active repetition and reworking of story in and by discourse."[15] Brooks extends this claim to argue for a psychoanalytic model of plot, contending that narratives rely upon a rich variety of "smaller" repetitions that serve to defer our ongoing, readerly desire for plot resolution. In doing this, they model themselves on a Freudian "masterplot" in which the primary organic desire for death is always being deferred as well. "Reading for the plot," in other

words, satisfies the desire for repetitions that "bind" our most fundamental organic energies, which are themselves "ultimately images of desire" (123).

Where Brooks self-consciously attempts to move beyond formalist criticism to a more exclusively Freudian explanation of the dynamics of narrative desire, J. Hillis Miller swerves without apology into "the words of the work."[16] Taking a deconstructive turn, he asserts that "any novel is a complex tissue of repetitions" that constitute the very reality they purport to describe (2). In his analysis of realist novels, therefore, repetition comes to characterize a broad array of sometimes psychological, sometimes emotional, sometimes simply mechanical efforts that shape our interpretations. These processes include not only the more spectacular recurrences of memory, fate, and chance, but also those less obvious, including both thematic and intertextual repetitions, and even those directly involving the reader's critical response (as he notes, "repetition cannot be analyzed without using it, in forms of language which inevitably turn back on themselves" [8]).

For all their differences, Miller appears to share one of Brooks' most basic critical assumptions: that is, that events precede any narrative about them. The category of "story" has a prior status to that of "discourse," therefore, because events supposedly exist independent of the texts that make them available to us. Despite the emphasis he places upon the generative power of language, then, Miller's investigation of repetition leads him as well to speak of the "real event," in contrast to the novelist's otherwise constructed "act of writing about it" (120). And that presumption of priority induces a similar understanding of repetition as a figure of reinforcement. Despite a broad array of texts, despite declared differences of approach, both Miller and Brooks assume that repetition fosters as much control in narrative as it supposedly does in life. It is, as Brooks asserts, "the movement from passivity to mastery."[17]

Perhaps because repetition is at once the most powerful and constraining of narrative tools, almost anything can be stated about it and, as it happens, with equal persuasiveness (a repetition itself of claims made in the Introduction). The problem, then, is not the ideas we happen to maintain about repetition—whether it actually enforces mastery or instead subverts any real control. The problem lies rather with the prior assumptions we make about the notion of a singular self. Those are the assumptions that dictate what our reading

of repetition will be. Thus, the largely conventional nature of the texts selected by Brooks and Miller shapes the kinds of conclusions they will draw about mastery, control, and autonomy, and does so before they begin. For all the innovative power to be found in their combined individual readings, they can do no more than reproduce their texts' conventional constructions of the self, which in turn confirm our own recurrent assumptions about agency and autonomy. They can only repeat, as it were, the structures of the texts they have chosen.

This book has revealed how fully naturalism engages a different conception of selfhood, and operates thereby according to a less congenial understanding of repetition. Not only does the stylistic opacity of the mode enmesh events in their textual construction (both absolutely and irrevocably), but the repetitions compound that process by drawing attention to textualization itself. For Brooks, "it is only through the postulation of repetition that narrative plot gains motivation and the implication of meaning" (254). For the naturalists, however, repetition undermines instead our belief in motivation, and erodes the more common humanizing assumptions associated with the construction of "meaning." In their most disruptive texts, they succeeded in deconstructing our conceptions of both event and of story, of action as well as of self. Their narratives do not simply repeat things that have happened before words somehow began, but instead create those events *as* events, at the same time revealing how a set of ideological premises are inscribed into any understanding of what occurs.

Radical as are the effects involved in a reading of naturalist prose, they are not altogether apparent at first—perhaps because they are so radical. By carefully listening to what Miller calls "the intimate grain of an author's language," however, we can learn to appreciate the implications involved in the construction of a philosophical "subject."[18] That process is of course never absent from any narrative, but it is more apparent in naturalism than realism precisely because of that discomfiting array of verbal repetitions, narrative recurrences, and plot foreclosures that compel us to an awareness of our own self-constructions. By failing to attend to that textual array, we allow conventional thematic structures to reinscribe themselves into the plots we read. And we thereby end up effectively countering the naturalists' attack on the reader by simply ignoring it.

London, Dreiser, Norris, and Crane each defy our customary

notions about the way we move about in the world. The fact that their naturalist texts form abrupt and sustained attacks on any reader conditioned to realist narratives has for too long been misunderstood as simple authorial incompetence. Their language was in fact a trenchant response to the dislocations of their era, a response ignored by those unaware of how thoroughly we are still the products of that history, still entrenched in the realist romance. Even those critics newly enticed by naturalism have turned away from its innovative styles, just as those who have newly completed innovative critiques of style have in turn shunned naturalism. In deliberately bridging this gap, I have meant to respond to the "immediate flavor" of naturalist prose, turning away from plot twists, scenic constraints, and the welter of descriptive details to the more complex (and confusing) medley of voices that actually establishes a determinist perspective. In naturalist texts like the four of this book, something like a stark canyon seems to divide a series of conflicting voices—and most especially, divides a largely sympathetic indirect discourse from a detached omniscient narrator, one whose fragmented syntax serves to undermine all coherent self-narrations. The repetitive tension between these two exposes the culturally determined melodrama in any character's attempt to narrate an identity into being. We may be unable to help ourselves from believing we act as essentially free agents, but what the naturalists succeed in teaching is the possible truth of an alternative vision—one that seems inconceivable the more we consider its implications, and yet one that the naturalists imagined so variously as to compel us to just such a reconsideration.

NOTES

PREFACE: TAKING DETERMINISM SERIOUSLY

1. Preface to 2d ed., *Thérèse Raquin*, trans. Leonard Tancock (Harmondsworth: Penguin, 1962), p. 22.

2. This was the focus of most definitions of naturalism through the 1970s, at least. Lars Ahnebrink made the first extensive study of the movement in *The Beginnings of Naturalism in American Fiction: A Study of the Works of Hamlin Garland, Stephen Crane, and Frank Norris with Special References to Some European Influences, 1891–1903* (Cambridge: Harvard UP, 1950). His title indicates both subject and approach, since these three writers were especially influenced by developments abroad, and transplanted Zola onto American soil.

Charles Child Walcutt substantially broadened the number of naturalist authors and argued for its indigenous development in *American Literary Naturalism: A Divided Stream* (Minneapolis: U of Minnesota P, 1956). A

decade later, Donald Pizer confirmed Walcutt's configuration with *Realism and Naturalism in Nineteenth-Century American Literature* (Carbondale: Southern Illinois UP, 1966). Both scholars agreed that naturalism was a derivative movement (of either Transcendentalism or realism), and accounted for perceived conflicts in the mode by defining it as divided between the ideal and the real (Walcutt) or the dignified and the degrading (Pizer). Both also agreed that its major themes involve "determinism, survival, violence, and taboo" (Walcutt 20), and that it is peopled with "the poor, the uneducated, the unsophisticated" (Pizer 12). See as well Walcutt's *Seven Novelists in the American Naturalist Tradition: An Introduction* (Minneapolis: U of Minnesota P, 1970).

The most common definition of naturalism has been "pessimistic realism," a phrase first used by Vernon L. Parrington in *The Beginnings of Critical Realism in America, 1860–1920*, vol. 3 of *Main Currents in American Thought* (New York: Harcourt, Brace and World, 1930), p. 325, and still invoked as a definition in the current *Norton Anthology of American Literature* (New York: Norton, 1983), p. 7. See also George J. Becker's influential, if dismissive, reading of naturalism's "pessimistic materialistic determinism," in "Introduction" to *Documents of Modern Literary Realism* (Princeton: Princeton UP, 1963), pp. 3–38.

Similar studies have defined the historical influences (Charles Darwin, Cesar Lombroso, Max Nordau) and thematic motifs (brutality, sexuality, stupidity) at work in particular novels. Robert M. Figg III provides a useful survey of this earlier critical history, in "Naturalism as a Literary Form," *Georgia Review* (Fall 1964), 18:308–16. See also Warner Berthoff, *The Ferment of Realism: American Literature, 1884–1919* (New York: Free Press, 1965); Louis J. Budd, "Objectivity and Low Seriousness in American Naturalism," *Prospects* (1975), 1:41–61; Edwin H. Cady, *The Light of Common Day: Realism in American Fiction* (Bloomington: Indiana UP, 1971); Everett Carter, *Howells and the Age of Realism* (Philadelphia: Lippincott, 1954); Harold Kaplan, *Power and Order: Henry Adams and the Naturalist Tradition in American Fiction* (Chicago: U of Chicago P, 1981); Alfred Kazin, *On Native Grounds: An Interpretation of Modern American Prose Literature* (New York: Harcourt Brace Jovanovich, 1942); Harold H. Kolb, Jr., *The Illusion of Life: American Realism as a Literary Form* (Charlottesville: UP of Virginia, 1969); Jay Martin, *Harvests of Change: American Literature, 1865–1914* (Englewood Cliffs, N.J.: Prentice Hall, 1967); and Larzer Ziff, *The American 1890s: Life and Times of a Lost Generation* (New York: Viking, 1966).

Donald Pizer, most notably, argues that the movement continues to the present in *Twentieth-Century American Literary Naturalism: An Interpretation* (Carbondale: Southern Illinois UP, 1982).

3. Haeckel, *The Riddle of the Universe at the Close of the Nineteenth Century*, trans. Joseph McCabe (New York: Harper, 1900), pp. 130–31.

4. Spencer, *First Principles* (1862; 6th ed., New York: D. Appleton, 1907), p. 299. Spencer assumed that "voluntary acts" simply occurred as a process of least resistance: "For a volition, suggested as it is by some previous thought joined with it by associations that determine the transaction, is itself a repetition of the movements which are willed, and of their sequences. But . . . the volition is itself an incipient discharge along a line which previous experiences have rendered a line of least resistance. And the passing of volition into action is simply a completion of the discharge" (219–20). As with individuals, so with societies: "Social changes take directions that are due to the joint actions of citizens, determined as are those of all other changes wrought by composition of forces" (220). See also pp. 390 ff.

5. The phrase is June Howard's, *Form and History in American Literary Naturalism* (Chapel Hill: U of North Carolina P, 1985), p. 182.

6. Among more recent critics who have considered the effects of determinism are: John J. Conder, *Naturalism in American Fiction: The Classic Phase* (Lexington: UP of Kentucky, 1984); Ronald E. Martin, *American Literature and the Universe of Force* (Durham: Duke UP, 1981); and Perry D. Westbrook, *Free Will and Determinism in American Literature* (Rutherford, N.J.: Fairleigh Dickinson UP, 1979). See also *Essays on Determinism in American Literature*, ed. Sydney Krause (Kent, Ohio: Kent State UP, 1964). For minority opinions that dismiss the relevance of determinism, see Don Graham, "Naturalism in American Fiction: A Status Report," *Studies in American Fiction* (Spring 1982), 10:1–16; Haskell M. Block, *Naturalistic Triptych: The Fictive and the Real in Zola, Mann, and Dreiser* (New York: Random House, 1970), p. 13; and Robert W. Schneider, *Five Novelists of the Progressive Era* (New York: Columbia UP, 1965).

7. Philip Fisher, *Hard Facts: Setting and Form in the American Novel* (New York: Oxford UP, 1985), p. 171; June Howard, *Form and History*, p. 182; Eric J. Sundquist, "Introduction: The Country of the Blue," *American Realism: New Essays*, ed. Sundquist (Baltimore: Johns Hopkins UP, 1982), p. 13; Alfred Habegger, *Gender, Fantasy, and Realism in American Literature* (New York: Columbia UP, 1982), p. 65; Mark Seltzer, "The Naturalist Machine," in *Sex, Politics, and Science in the Nineteenth-Century Novel*, ed. Ruth Bernard Yeazell (Baltimore: Johns Hopkins UP, 1986), p. 124; Walter Benn Michaels, *The Gold Standard and the Logic of Naturalism* (Berkeley: U of California P, 1987), pp. 172–73.

It is not irrelevant to point out that these authors sometimes appear to contradict themselves as well as each other. Fisher, for instance, earlier identifies naturalism (following Lukács) as a "specialized variant" of the historical novel (p. 16). Mark Seltzer earlier announces that "the two fundamental principles of thermodynamics—the law of conservation and the law of dissipation—operate . . . both thematically and formally in the naturalist

narrative." He later claims that "the brute is the generative principle of naturalism" (pp. 121, 138).

8. Saul Bellow, review of F. O. Matthiessen, *Theodore Dreiser*, in *Commentary* (May 1951), 11:502.

9. Philip Drew has catalogued the problems involved in representing free and determined characters, and asserts: "So thickly do the paradoxes throng that it sometimes seems as though the inconsistencies which beset even the subtlest representation of freely acting human characters were not failures in art but faithful reflections, uniquely available from a study of literature, of the confusions in which most of us labour." See *The Meaning of Freedom* (Aberdeen: Aberdeen UP, 1982), p. 17, and *passim* for a survey of six centuries of literary representations.

10. "The Dilemma of Determinism" (1884) and "The Will to Believe" (1896) depict William James' belief in indeterminism and pluralism. Yet instead of offering logical or metaphysical reasons for his argument, or even examining projective attitudes, he attempts to summarize what actually works in practical experience. See *The Will to Believe/ Human Immortality* (New York: Dover, 1956), pp. 1–31, 145–83; and *A William James Reader*, ed. Gay Wilson Allen (Boston: Houghton Mifflin, 1971), *passim*.

11. See Mitchell, "Naturalism and the Languages of Determinism," in *Columbia Literary History of the United States* (New York: Columbia UP, 1987), pp. 525–45. For a listing of literary studies, see nn. 2, 7 above. Among the better analyses of the context within which American naturalism developed are: Burton J. Bledstein, *The Culture of Professionalism: The Middle Class and the Development of Higher Education in America* (New York: Norton, 1978); Melvyn Dubofsky, *Industrialism and the American Worker, 1865–1920* (Arlington Heights, Ill.: AHM Publishing, 1975); Thomas Haskell, *The Emergence of Professional Social Science: The American Social Science Association and the Nineteenth-Century Crisis of Authority* (Urbana: U of Illinois P, 1977); Samuel P. Hays, *The Response to Industrialism: 1885–1914* (Chicago: U of Chicago P, 1957); Robert Higgs, *The Transformation of the American Economy, 1865–1914: An Essay in Interpretation* (New York: Wiley, 1971); Richard Hofstadter, *The Age of Reform* (New York: Knopf, 1955); T. J. Jackson Lears, *No Place of Grace: Antimodernism and the Transformation of American Culture, 1880–1920* (New York: Pantheon Books, 1981); Glenn Porter, *The Rise of Big Business, 1860–1910* (Arlington Heights, Ill.: AHM Publishing, 1973); Daniel T. Rodgers, *The Work Ethic in Industrial America, 1850–1920* (Chicago: U of Chicago P, 1978); Alan Trachtenberg, *The Incorporation of America: Culture and Society in the Gilded Age* (New York: Hill & Wang, 1982); Robert Weibe, *The Search for Order, 1877–1920* (New York: Hill & Wang, 1967); and Howard Zinn, *A People's History of the United States* (New York: Harper & Row, 1980). For more specialized studies, see Robert C. Bannister, *Social Darwinism: Science and Myth in Anglo-American Thought*

(Philadelphia: Temple UP, 1979); and John David Peel, *Herbert Spencer: The Evolution of a Sociologist* (London: Heinemann, 1971).

12. My approach is an attempt, that is, to respond to Isaiah Berlin's challenge: "If social and psychological determinism were established as an accepted truth, our world would be transformed . . . Our words—our modes of speech and thought—would be transformed in literally unimaginable ways; the notions of choice, of voluntary action, of responsibility, freedom, are so deeply embedded in our outlook, that our new life, as creatures in a world genuinely lacking these concepts, can, I should maintain, literally not be conceived by us." *Historical Inevitability* (London: Oxford UP, 1954), p. 75.

For an intriguing defense of the position that one should attend to textual language, not authorial intention, see Sandy Petrey's persuasive reading of Dreiser in "The Language of Realism, The Language of False Consciousness," *Novel* (Winter 1977), 10:101–13.

I. NATURALISM AND THE EXCLUDED SELF

1. Daniel C. Dennett, *Elbow Room: The Varieties of Free Will Worth Wanting* (Cambridge: MIT P, 1984), p. 13. Gary Watson anticipated this expression in his conclusion that "the problem of free will is part of the problem of finding room in the world for ourselves." See "Introduction" to *Free Will*, ed. Watson (New York: Oxford UP, 1982), p. 14.

2. Whether or not this strain is characteristically true of American literary realism, Richard Poirier makes a provocative claim: "American writers are at some point always forced to return their characters to prison. They return them to 'reality' from environments where they have been allowed most 'nakedly' to exist, environments created by various kinds of stylistic ingenuity." See *A World Elsewhere: The Place of Style in American Literature* (New York: Oxford UP, 1966), p. 29.

3. Jacques Loeb, *The Mechanistic Conception of Life*, ed. Donald Fleming (Cambridge: Harvard UP, 1912; rpt. 1964), pp. 32, xxix.

4. There is a rich theoretical literature on fictional realism, European and American, and most studies rightly agree with June Howard that "naturalism and realism share the crucial mimetic convention that narrative can and does refer to a 'real world' with a material existence somewhere outside the literary text." *Form and History in American Literary Naturalism* (Chapel Hill: U of North Carolina P, 1985) p. 11. For major statements by practitioners themselves, see the essays collected in William Dean Howells' *Criticism and Fiction* (New York: Harper, 1891); Henry James' *The Art of the Novel: Critical Prefaces*, ed. Richard P. Blackmur (New York: Scribner's, 1934); and

Frank Norris' *The Responsibilities of the Novelist* (1902; Garden City, N.Y.: Doubleday, Doran, 1926).

For more recent, general studies not mentioned in my Preface, n. 2, see Arthur E. Jones, Jr., "Darwinism and Its Relation to Realism and Naturalism in American Fiction, 1860–1900," *Drew University Studies*, Drew University Bulletin #1 (1950), pp. 3–21; Alice Kaminsky, "On Literary Realism," in *The Theory of the Novel: New Essays*, ed. John Halperin (New York: Oxford UP, 1974), pp. 213–32; Maurice Larkin, *Man and Society in Nineteenth-Century Realism: Determinism and Literature* (London: Macmillan, 1977); Harry Levin, *The Gates of Horn: A Study of Five French Realists* (New York: Oxford UP, 1963); George Levine, *The Realistic Imagination: English Fiction from Frankenstein to Lady Chatterly* (Chicago: U of Chicago P, 1981); Charles Rosen and Henri Zerner, "What Is, and Is Not, Realism?" *New York Review of Books* (February 18, 1982), 29:21–26, and (March 4, 1982), 29:29–33; and D. A. Williams, "The Practise of Realism," in *The Monster in the Mirror: Studies in Nineteenth-Century Realism*, ed. D. A. Williams (New York: Oxford UP, 1978), pp. 257–79.

5. Edwin H. Cady, *The Light of Common Day: Realism in American Fiction* (Bloomington: Indiana UP, 1971), p. 50. Cady's is only the more extreme version of a generic impulse that continues to characterize recent treatments of these texts.

6. Richard Chase, *The American Novel and Its Tradition* (Garden City, N.Y.: Doubleday, 1957), p. 199. By contrast, Catherine Belsey identifies the most prominent concern of an alternative mode: "Classic realism tends to offer as the 'obvious' basis of its intelligibility the assumption that character, unified and coherent, is the source of action. Subjectivity is a major—perhaps the major—theme of classic realism." See *Critical Practice* (London: Methuen, 1980), p. 73.

7. Mark Twain, *Adventures of Huckleberry Finn*, ed. Leo Marx (Indianapolis: Bobbs-Merrill, 1967), p. 244.

8. William Dean Howells, *The Rise of Silas Lapham*, ed. Don L. Cook (New York: Norton, 1982), pp. 290–91.

9. Henry James, *The Portrait of a Lady*, ed. Robert D. Bamberg (New York: Norton, 1975), pp. 354, 363.

10. Howells, *Criticism and Fiction* (New York: Harper, 1891), pp. 98–99.

11. Both Twain and Howells later felt this faith diminish considerably: in the 1890s, Twain experimented with first a deterministic, then a fatalistic conception of life in such uncompleted manuscripts as "The Mysterious Stranger"; Howells, even by the mid-1880s, had evinced serious doubts about the effect of moral and civic responsibility. Although no evidence exists that James suffered such doubts, the novels of his major phase explore possibilities of determinism. See Lee Clark Mitchell, "The Sustaining Duplicities of *The Wings of the Dove*," *Texas Studies in Literature and Language* (June 1987), 29:187–214.

12. Two things that will become clear in the following discussion are worth anticipating here: that I treat determinism as a metaphysical distinction, not a psychological one; and that since no proof of either determinism or agency seems convincing to me, the distinction between them is made apparent in projective assumptions and interpretive forms. The first premise logically prevents us from treating some characters in a fictional text as free, others as determined, since the presence of agency means that it exists at least potentially for everyone. An analogy exists in the concept of the soul: either everyone has one or no one does. When realist characters, like people in our lives, exhibit little capacity for agency (psychotics, for instance, or small children), we do not accept the premise of determinism but simply exclude them from normal judgment.

To repeat, voluntarism and determinism are opposed metaphysical systems that depend upon mutually exclusive categories. When we act as if they are not—assuming, for instance, that people are determined yet free, or that some people are determined while others are not—we simply show how powerful are projective moral attitudes. Far from suggesting that naturalist texts have a philosophical rigor, then, my second premise places the interpretive burden on the reader, who has an obligation to maintain a consistent set of moral expectations.

Among those who seem to me to confuse this issue, June Howard claims that two characters in London's *White Fang* "are human beasts who cannot escape determinism," while a third "in contrast, possesses self-awareness and self-control" and "not only exerts his will to control himself but in his way is a reformer" (*Form and History*, p. 58). If the former two characters are truly determined, then moral opprobrium is beside the point; if the latter can exert a will, then we might well ask what necessarily deprives the former two from doing so. In any event, "self-awareness" (and perhaps even "self-control") is irrelevant to the issue of agency.

13. Harry G. Frankfurt has argued most effectively against the principle of alternate possibilities which I have here assumed, "that a person is morally responsible for what he has done only if he could have done otherwise." See "Alternate Possibilities and Moral Responsibility," *Journal of Philosophy* (1969): pp. 829–39. My point is that our customary attitudes are not denied by even such cogent philosophical objections.

14. Dennett has rebutted, I think correctly, the notion that "determinism and deliberation are incompatible" (*Elbow Room*, p. 102). As he states, "Deliberation *is* (in general) effective in a deterministic but nonfatalistic world" (106).

15. Janet Holmgren McKay provides a useful discussion of two of these scenes in *Narration and Discourse in American Realistic Fiction* (Philadelphia: U of Pennsylvania P, 1982). According to her, Silas' "moral victory rests on procrastination rather than decisive action," while Huck's moral crisis violates "the consistency of his narrative voice" (130–31, 159).

Countless further examples of realist restraint might be adduced, but consider these prominent three: Ben Halleck, in Howells' *Modern Instance*, who refrains from courting Marcia Hubbard out of moral scruples; Maggie Verver, in James' *Golden Bowl*, who saves her marriage by restraining herself from inquiring into her husband's infidelity; and Tom Outland, in Willa Cather's *Professor's House* (1925), who refuses out of moral compunction to sell artifacts from his discovered mesa.

16. James Boswell, *The Life of Samuel Johnson* (London: Dutton, 1906), p. 363. Dr. Johnson later remarked with equal assurance: "No man believes himself to be impelled irresistibly; we know that he who says he believes it, lies" (400).

17. A. J. Ayer, "Freedom and Necessity," in *Free Will*, ed. Watson, p. 20. Gary Watson rebuts this philosophical logic in "Free Agency," *ibid.*, pp. 96–110. See also Harry Frankfurt's "Alternate Possibilities and Moral Responsibility."

18. The logic of this assertion is no less powerful for being tautological: actions either are freely chosen, which requires an agent's will, or they are determined, which requires only a strong desire. Whenever one's resolve is different from one's strongest desire, determinism requires that a character act (or not act) according to that desire. Of course, the problem of distinguishing between resolve and desire *is* the problem of free will.

Harry G. Frankfurt approaches that problem by distinguishing between first- and second-order desires, thereby separating animals, children, and other creatures from "persons," whom he defines as wanting to be different "in their preferences and purposes, from what they are." Instead of simply choosing to act, "persons" choose their choices for action and thereby select the kind of self they want. To lack such control is, in Frankfurt's term, to be a "wanton." See "Freedom of the Will and the Concept of a Person," in *Free Will*, ed. Watson, pp. 82–83, 86.

Brand Blanshard earlier made a similar claim: "The real issue, so far as the will is concerned, is not whether we can do what we choose to do, but whether we can choose our own choice, whether the choice itself issues in accordance with law from some antecedents." See "The Case for Determinism," in *Determinism and Freedom in the Age of Modern Science*, ed. Sidney Hook (New York: New York UP, 1958), p. 5. Jonathan Edwards perhaps most notably recognized this problem: "Or else we must come at last to an Act of the Will, determining the consequent acts, wherein the Will is not self-determined, and so is not a free act." See "Freedom of the Will," in *Jonathan Edwards: Representative Selections*, ed. Clarence H. Faust and Thomas H. Johnson (New York: Hill & Wang, 1962), p. 284.

For problems in Frankfurt's conception, see Gary Watson, "Introduction" and "Free Agency," in *Free Will*, ed. Watson, esp. pp. 8, 107–9; and Charles Taylor, "Responsibility for Self," *ibid.*, esp. pp. 112, 118. For an attempt to

apply that distinction to literature, see Perry D. Westbrook, *Free Will and Determinism in American Literature* (Rutherford, N.J.: Fairleigh Dickinson UP, 1979), esp. pp. 146–48.

19. This characterization of strong desires has important implications for certain kinds of naturalist texts, including the fictional studies of strong, ruthless individuals. Among prominent examples are: Frank Norris' study of Curtis Jadwin in *The Pit* (1903); Theodore Dreiser's "Trilogy of Desire," about financier Frank Cowperwood in *The Financier* (1913), *The Titan* (1914), and *The Stoic* (1947); and Jack London's *Sea-Wolf* (1904) and *Martin Eden* (1908). Donald Davidson discusses the larger ramifications of this issue in "How Is Weakness of the Will Possible?" in *Moral Concepts*, ed. Joel Feinberg (New York: Oxford UP, 1970), pp. 93–113.

William James asserted that there was no way to decide between the two views. In a powerful but distinctly illogical move he asserted that we seize freedom from the maw of determinism by simply acting as if we possess our own wills. In "The Dilemma of Determinism," he declares: "Our first act of freedom, if we are free, ought in all inward propriety to be to affirm that we are free." See *The Will to Believe/Human Immortality* (New York: Dover, 1956), p. 146.

20. *The Golden Bowl* (Harmondsworth: Penguin, 1982), p. 318.

21. Two examples of this reading are Sally Sears, *The Negative Imagination: Form and Perspective in the Novels of Henry James* (Ithaca: Cornell UP, 1968); and Philip M. Weinstein, *Henry James and the Requirements of the Imagination* (Cambridge: Harvard UP, 1971).

22. Ellen Moers, *Two Dreisers* (New York: Viking, 1969), p. 230. Harold Kaplan has observed that "the characteristic emotional flatness of naturalist fiction" is "the result of subordinating response to the movement of forces. For 'the forces' do not simply overwhelm the capacity of a human character to define himself against them; rather, they *seem* to oppose themselves to a human interest but are then discovered to be the same as the natural process that determined the character's motive in the first place and then obstructed it. In other words, nature has its fifth column within every human organism" *Power and Order: Henry Adams and the Naturalist Tradition in American Fiction* (Chicago: U of Chicago P, 1981), p. 93.

23. Harold Kaplan has tangentially noted that in naturalism, things "almost immediately become symbols of the power they generate, and *that* is their value . . . Subordinating other values, things become the signs of the power asserted in gaining them. And so a simple desire or need is translated into a sign of the power needed to satisfy it." *Power and Order*, p. 87. Philip Fisher likewise claims that "for a man inside the city his self is not inside his body but around him, outside the body," and more particularly, that Dreiser's Clyde Griffiths "gets his 'self' moment by moment as a gift from the outside." *Hard Facts: Setting and Form in the American Novel* (New York:

Oxford UP, 1985), pp. 134, 141. For Fisher, the windows that proliferate in *Sister Carrie* "define a state of the self in motion that we might call the self in anticipation," always open to desire and possibility (157).

More generally, Walter Benjamin observed that "character" and "fate" seem inseparable: "The external world that the active man encounters can also in principle be reduced . . . to his inner world, and his inner world similarly to his outer world, indeed regarded in principle as one and the same thing." "Fate and Character," in *Reflections: Essays, Aphorisms, Autobiographical Writings*, trans. Edmund Jephcott, ed. Peter Demetz (New York: Harcourt Brace Jovanovitch, 1978), pp. 305–6. Yet we do separate the two, he concedes, aligning character with freedom and fate with the world. As he states, "fate is the guilt context of the living" (308).

24. Dennett claims that "if determinism is true, then that man *could not have* performed" the act from which he refrained ("The Incompatibility of Free Will and Determinism," in *Free Will*, ed. Watson, p. 52).

25. Edith Wharton, *The House of Mirth* (New York: Scribners, 1905), pp. 515–16.

26. William Dean Howells, *A Modern Instance*, ed. William M. Gibson (Boston: Houghton Mifflin, 1957), p. 10.

27. Critics have often commented on the problematic aspects of Howells' treatment of choice in this novel, and particularly in this scene, including Kermit Vanderbilt, *The Achievement of William Dean Howells: A Reinterpretation* (Princeton: Princeton UP, 1968), pp. 76–81; Henry Nash Smith, *Democracy and the Novel: Popular Resistance to Classic American Writers* (New York: Oxford UP, 1978), p. 94; and John W. Crowley, *The Black Heart's Truth: The Early Career of W. D. Howells* (Chapel Hill: U of North Carolina P, 1985), pp. 126–28, 146–47. Richard Brodhead claims that "*A Modern Instance* demonstrates Hawthorne's continuing power to wrest control of the patterns of Howells' imaginings—and in so doing to give surprising turns to Howells' intended designs." in *American Realism*, ed. Sundquist, p. 32.

28. Lawrence Rosen has shown how questions of responsibility are mediated through culture in his comparison of Western and Moroccan assumptions. Intention is simply assumed by Moroccans from overt action, since the Western notion of an "interior self" is relatively recent. As Rosen states, following Weber, "motives and intentions are neither wholly private nor independently causal; they are culturally characteristic ascriptions by means of which the situations in which people find themselves and the kinds of people they encounter are made more or less comprehensible." See "Intentionality and the Concept of the Person," in *Criminal Justice*, ed. J. Roland Pennock and John W. Chapman (New York: New York UP, 1985), p. 68. For studies on the transition in European culture to various views of the self (e.g., romantic, psychoanalytic) see Stephen Greenblatt, *Renaissance Self-Fashioning* (Chicago: U of Chicago P, 1980), and Lionel Trilling, *Sincerity and Authenticity* (Cambridge: Harvard UP, 1972).

29. Peter Strawson, "Freedom and Resentment," in *Free Will*, ed. Watson, p. 72.

30. Boswell, *Life*, p. 210. Alasdair MacIntyre has analogously asserted that we need to be both predictable and unpredictable in certain basic ways. *After Virtue* (South Bend, Ind.: U of Notre Dame, 1981), p. 99. For an earlier vision of these possibilities, see William James, "The Dilemma of Determinism." James was concerned not with establishing new grounds of understanding—since he felt proof was not possible for either alternative—"but of deepening our sense of what the issue between the two parties really is, of what the ideas of fate and free-will imply" (145). Daniel Dennett more radically asserts: "The free will problem *may* be in large part an artifact of the methods typically used to study it" (*Elbow Room*, p. 17). He goes on, moreover, to counter Nagel's view (see pp. 75 ff.).

31. Thomas Nagel, "Subjective and Objective," *Mortal Questions* (New York: Cambridge UP, 1979), pp. 198–99. Further references appear directly in the text and are to this edition of his essays—in particular, to "Moral Luck" (1976), pp. 24–38, and to "Subjective and Objective" (1979), pp. 196–213. Nagel is responding to Bernard A. O. Williams' provocative claims in the title essay of his *Moral Luck: Philosophical Papers, 1973–1980* (New York: Cambridge UP, 1981), pp. 20–39.

32. Amelie Oksenberg Rorty provides a useful taxonomy of such terms in "A Literary Postscript: Characters, Persons, Selves, Individuals," in *The Identities of Persons*, ed. Amelie O. Rorty (Berkeley: U of California P, 1976), pp. 301–23. Rorty claims that "personhood" is a step shy of "selfhood," and that "the idea of a person is the idea of a unified center of choice and action, the unit of legal and theological responsibility. Having chosen, a person acts, and so is actionable, liable." On the other hand, "since they choose from their natures or are chosen by their stories, neither characters nor figures need to be equipped with a will, not to mention a free will" (309). It is worth noting that Rorty's taxonomy suggests a historical evolution, while Nagel is presenting simply a synchronic analysis.

Bryan S. Turner offers the perspective of symbolic interactionism: "The 'I' is the response of an individual in a total fashion to the variety of attitudes of others; the 'me' is the organized attitudes of others. The self is thus the complex union through interaction, symbol and gesture of the I and the me . . . . The self is fundamentally sociological not biological, since the self is little more than a principle for the organization of gestures." See *The Body and Society: Explorations in Social Theory* (New York: Basil Blackwell, 1984), p. 32.

Leo Katz, from a legal perspective, observes that "what makes a bodily movement into an act is not perhaps the fact that it is preceded by a 'volition,' but that it is accompanied by a very characteristic experience, which for lack of a better word, we may call the experience of acting." See *Bad Acts and Guilty Minds: Conundrums of the Criminal Law* (Chicago: U of

Chicago P, 1987), p. 127; also p. 134. From the perspective of drama criticism, Michael Goldman has remarked: "Action allows us to think of what happens around us not just as events but as deeds, and to think of our private selves as somehow issuing forth into the world." *Acting and Action in Shakespearean Tragedy* (Princeton: Princeton UP, 1985), p. 5. See also Erving Goffman's attempt to unravel paradoxical social attitudes about character, in "Where the Action Is," *Interaction Ritual: Essays on Face-to-Face Behavior* (New York: Pantheon, 1967), pp. 149–270.

33. Bertolt Brecht is, of course, the proponent of "alienating the familiar" in theater, and his advice to the actor is instructive for an analysis of naturalism: "In order to produce A[lienation]-effects the actor has to discard whatever means he has learnt of getting the audience to identify itself with the characters which he plays." See "A Short Organum for the Theatre," in *Brecht on Theatre*, ed. and trans. John Willett (New York: Hill & Wang, 1964), pp. 192, 193.

34. For a discussion of Dreiser's focus on the "sub- or semi-conscious instead of introspective," see Gordon O. Taylor, *The Passages of Thought: Psychological Representation in the American Novel, 1870–1900* (New York: Oxford UP, 1969), p. 13.

35. Laurence B. Holland first observed this narrative problem in "A 'Raft of Trouble': Word and Deed in *Huckleberry Finn*," *Glyph* (Baltimore: Johns Hopkins UP, 1979), 5:69–87.

36. *Sister Carrie*, ed. Neda M. Westlake (Philadelphia: U of Pennsylvania P, 1981), p. 267.

37. A fuller analysis here would require an examination of the quite different realist scenes in *Adventures of Huckleberry Finn* and *The Portrait of a Lady*—both of which in fact briefly stress the process of deliberation. In the case of *Huck Finn*, that concentration does seem to me to undercut his autonomy—even though the narrative devotes only a short paragraph to his deliberations.

38. Lewis Beck likewise defines this distinction as an opposition between two perspectives, that of actor and spectator. "The process of giving and revising accounts of action is easier to observe when it is another spectator who tries to account for the actions of an agent. . . . For the actor, the assessed reasons are grounds for further practical reasons, but for the spectator they are grounds for prediction." *The Actor and the Spectator* (New Haven: Yale UP, 1975), p. 85.

39. P. 29. Or as he asserts of a list of historical figures notable for their decisive actions: "It is tempting in all such cases to feel that some decision must be possible, in the light of what is known at the time, which will make reproach unsuitable no matter how things turn out. But this is not true; when someone acts in such ways he takes his life, or his moral position, into his hands, because how things turn out determines what he has done" (29–30).

I should note that Nagel's example of the driver is originally Bernard Williams', who coined the phrase "moral luck" (pp. 28 ff.). To my knowledge, only two recent scholars have considered these ideas in relation to literature. Robert Hopkins treats the problem of "moral judgment under uncertainty" in "Moral Luck and Judgment in Jane Austen's *Persuasion*," *Nineteenth-Century Literature* (September 1987), 42:143–58. Martha C. Nussbaum offers a more procovative treatment in *The Fragility of Goodness: Luck and Ethics in Greek Tragedy and Philosophy* (New York: Cambridge UP, 1986). Nussbaum defines "luck" not as random or uncaused events: "What happens to a person by luck will be just what does not happen through his or her own agency, what just *happens* to him, as opposed to what he does or makes" (3). Her larger thesis is that removing "luck" from life is to deny the possibility of "the livable life," since goodness depends precisely upon contingency, upon things remaining to some extent outside one's control.

George Henry Lewes anticipated this view over a century ago in *Problems of Life and Mind*, 3d Series (London: Trubner, 1879), 1:106–7: "Spinoza thought that men believe themselves to be free because they are conscious of their actions but ignorant of the causes. Yet there is something more in it than this. For we are ignorant of the causes which determine the particular direction in the growth of leaves and limbs, the colours and dispositions of animals, etc., yet we never doubt that causes are in operation, and that for each particular detail a particular determinant was needed. What is this something more? It is our conception of a Personality, which is not limited to the momentary feelings, and not exhausted in the individual act. The mere feeling does not suffice. We are conscious of certain operations of our organs, which we do not assign to volitional impulses. In a voluntary act there is the intervention of the *we*: that is to say, accompanying the feeling of the act itself there is a vague feeling of the act as one manifestation of a variously manifesting Self. This conception of a Self or Personality as superior to and directing each particular manifestation is another aspect of the relation of Organism and organs. Once formed, it comes to represent an abstract Will which dominates concrete volitions; so that although each particular volition is assigned to a motive, and is thus admitted within the rigorous limits of determinism, the motives themselves are said to be under the power of a Will which is not determined."

40. Dennett seems to agree with Nagel: "We simply do not exempt someone from blame or praise for an act because we think he could do no other" (*Elbow Room*, p. 133). See also n. 13.

41. Frank Kermode, "Secrets and Narrative Sequence," *Critical Inquiry* (1980), 7:83–84. For fuller discussion, see his *The Sense of an Ending: Studies in the Theory of Fiction* (New York: Oxford UP, 1967), pp. 18, 30, 48–51, 63–64, 89, 139.

42. E. M. Forster, *Aspects of the Novel* (1927; rpt. New York: Harcourt, Brace, 1955), p. 86. The sentence is invoked as an example of "plot," which

differs from "story" in the addition of the phrase "of grief." As Shlomith Rimmon-Kenan observes, however, "there is nothing to prevent a causally-minded reader from supplementing Forster's first example with the causal link that would make it into an implicit plot." My point is that all readers are in fact "causally minded." Compare the other example Rimmon-Kenan offers: "Milton wrote *Paradise Lost*, then his wife died, and then he wrote *Paradise Regained*." See *Narrative Fiction: Contemporary Poetics* (London: Methuen, 1983) p. 17. For another exploration of these issues, see Seymour Chatman, *Story and Discourse: Narrative Structure in Fiction and Film* (Ithaca: Cornell UP, 198), esp. ch. 2, pp. 43–95; and "Toward a Theory of Narrative," *New Literary History* (1974), 6:306.

Hans Meyerhoff intriguingly asserts: "Only by presupposing the principle of causality, therefore, can we distinguish between an objective and subjective ordering of temporal sequences in the world." *Time in Literature* (Berkeley: U of California P, 1955), p. 19. A broad survey of just such considerations, which came to my attention after finishing this book, is Peter J. Rabinowitz's *Before Reading: Narrative Conventions and the Politics of Interpretation* (Ithaca: Cornell UP, 1987).

43. For a discussion of the necessity of secrets in the construction of subjectivity, both for characters and readers, see D. A. Miller, *The Novel and the Police* (Berkeley: U of California P, 1988), esp. ch. 6, "Secret Subjects, Open Secrets," pp. 192–220. As Miller states: "It is as though the only way to underwrite the self, in the sense of insuring it, were to under-write the self, in the sense of merely implying it. The Novel protects subjectivity not by locking it in, in the manner of a box, but by locking it out, since the story always determines the destiny of *somebody else*" (215).

44. Even their defenders have tacitly agreed with this charge, as in Charles Child Walcutt's claim that "style is therefore no criterion of naturalism." "Naturalism and Robert Herrick: A Test Case," in *American Literary Naturalism: A Reassessment*, ed. Yoshinobu Hakutani and Lewis Fried (Heidelberg: Carl Winter, 1975), pp. 75–89. Only a few recent critics have confronted the "problem" of naturalist style, and even then by way of excuse. Rachel Bowlby, for instance, claims "the episodic structure of naturalist novels" is justified in terms of the new consumer mentality. Plots lack narrative connections because the naturalists were "spectators of spectatorship." See *Just Looking: Consumer Culture in Dreiser, Gissing, and Zola* (New York: Methuen, 1985), pp. 13–15.

45. Kierkegaard was certainly not the first to observe that "all life is a repetition," or that "recollection and repetition are the same movement, except in opposite directions." But most subsequent studies have been influenced by his *Repetition* (1843; trans. and ed. Howard V. and Edna H. Hong, vol. 6 of *Kierkegaard's Writings*, Princeton UP, 1983, p. 131); note, for instance, Mircea Eliade's discussion of the relation between repetition

and timelessness, in *The Myth of the Eternal Return: or, Cosmos and History*, trans. Willard R. Trask (Princeton: Princeton UP, 1954), esp. pp. 34–36, 85–90, 123. E. K. Brown recognized repetition as "the dominant device" of the novel, in *Rhythm in the Novel* (Toronto: U of Toronto P, 1950). Of recent writers, see especially Robert Alter, *The Art of Biblical Narrative* (New York: Basic Books, 1981); Peter Brooks, *Reading for the Plot: Design and Intention in Narrative* (New York: Knopf, 1984); Gérard Genette, *Narrative Discourse: An Essay in Method*, trans. Jane E. Lewin (Ithaca: Cornell UP, 1980), esp. ch. 3, "Frequency," pp. 113–60; John Irwin, *Doubling and Incest/ Repetition and Revenge: A Speculative Reading of Faulkner* (Baltimore: Johns Hopkins UP, 1975); Bruce F. Kawin, *Telling It Again and Again: Repetition in Literature and Film* (Ithaca: Cornell UP, 1972); J. Hillis Miller, *Fiction and Repetition* (Cambridge: Harvard UP, 1982); and Edward W. Said, "On Repetition," in *The World, The Text, and the Critic* (Cambridge: Harvard UP, 1983), pp. 111–25.

Shlomith Rimmon-Kenan has most succinctly illustrated the problems of repetition as "a perplexedly double-edged phenomenon" in "The Paradoxical Status of Repetition," *Poetics Today* (Summer 1980), 1:151–59.

46. Irwin continues: "Yet it is not just repetition that is involved here, it is recollection as well—that awareness of repetition that, like the Medusa's gaze, paralyzes the will, that awareness that the memory of what has occurred in the past is at the same time the foreknowledge of what will be repeated in the future, the debilitating sense that time is a circular street and that recollection is prophecy" (*Doubling and Incest*, p. 69). As I argue below, however, it is amnesia, not recollection, that paralyzes the will. Recollection allows at least the possibility of difference, while to forget is invariably to repeat. See, however, Irwin, p. 60.

47. Freud, "The Uncanny" (1919), in *Studies in Parapsychology*, trans. Alix Strachey. *Collected Papers* (New York: Collier Books, 1963), 10:144.

48. *Great Short Works of Stephen Crane* (New York: Harper & Row, 1958), p. 281.

49. Dreiser, *Sister Carrie*, pp. 276–77. See also Hurstwood's response when he reads of Carrie's stage success "'Well, let her have it,' he said. 'I won't bother her.' It was the grim resolution of a bent, bedraggled but unbroken pride" (449). Of course, his resolution is broken even as it is undermined here by alliteration; he will later approach Carrie for money outside her stage door.

50. As Alter goes on to say, "there is in the biblical view a causal chain that firmly connects one event to the next, link by link, and that, too, accounts for a good deal of recurrence in the narrative shaping of the events." See *The Art of Biblical Narrative* (New York: Basic Books, 1981), pp. 180–81.

51. Erich Auerbach makes this claim for French epic in *Mimesis: The*

Representation of Reality in Western Literature, trans. Willard R. Trask (1946; rpt. Princeton UP, 1968), p. 101.

52. Kawin makes a number of similar claims, including: "Clearly, repetition is felt to have the power to negate time just as it has the power to punctuate, create, or transfigure time. Its very quality of *being the same thing again* makes us doubt that this thing was ever not here." *Telling It Again and Again,* p. 104; see also pp. 69, 92. Analogously, Debra Fried has remarked about funerary inscriptions, that "the formulaic stutter of the repetitive lines denies a sense of temporal progression or possibility." "Repetition, Refrain, and Epitaph," *ELH* (Fall 1986), 53:620–21. See also Shlomith Rimmon-Kenan, "The Paradoxical Status of Repetition," p. 158.

Taking a thematic perspective, June Howard observes that naturalism privileges inaction: "The image of immobility . . . seems to recur obsessively in naturalism." She then adds, "the recurrent images of blocked action and enforced spectatorship in American naturalism suggest that Lukács' characterization of the genre in terms of observation and description embodies a profound insight into the nature of the form." *Form and History,* pp. 111, 114.

53. Genette, *Narrative Discourse: An Essay in Method,* p. 67. As he goes on to state, "thus we will find very few prolepses in a Balzac, a Dickens, or a Tolstoy." Genette coined the words prolepsis and analepsis "to avoid the psychological connotations of such terms as 'anticipation' or 'retrospection'" (39–40). See his fuller discussion of the various functions of prolepsis, including the "paradigmatic function" served by "generalizing prolepses" (72).

54. Mark Twain, *Adventures of Huckleberry Finn,* p. 105.

55. The phrase is Tzvetan Todorov's description of the shape of Homeric narrative, and is cited by Genette in characterizing the "certain load of 'predestination' [that] hangs over" those novels which begin proleptically. See Todorov, *The Poetics of Prose* (Ithaca: Cornell UP, 1977), p. 65; and Genette, *Narrative Discourse,* p. 67.

Some critics claim that scenic repetition functions in naturalism as it does in realism. Donald Pizer, for instance, asserts that "the 'ladder' of Drouet, Hurstwood, and Ames" in *Sister Carrie,* like the sequence of women in *An American Tragedy* (from the prostitute to Hortense to Roberta and Sondra), represents a refinement and growth of the central characters (*Novels,* pp. 66–67, 240–43). Other readers make similar claims for Henry Fleming in *The Red Badge of Courage* or Martin Eden. My own reading is that the similarity among these characters is privileged over any differences, and that interpretations of "growth" are therefore mistaken projections of moral attitudes.

56. Walter Benn Michaels explores the "economy of desire" of the novel, explaining Carrie's success versus Hurstwood's failure as a function of her strong desires versus his "inability to want badly enough." See *The Gold*

Standard and the Logic of Naturalism (Berkeley: U of California P, 1987), pp. 31–58.

57. Pierre Simon, Marquis de Laplace, *A Philosophical Essay on Probabilities*, trans. from 6th ed., Frederick Wilson Truscott and Frederick Emory (New York: Dover, 1951), p. 4.

George Henry Lewes wrote, in 1879: "When we say something happens by chance, we do not mean that it had no conditions; we mean that the conditions are unforeseen, unknown—out of the regular order of appearance" (*Problems of Life and Mind*, p. 103). In 1900, Ernst Haeckel more forcibly stated that "the general law of causality . . . teaches us that every phenomenon has a mechanical cause; in this sense there is no such thing as chance" (*The Riddle of the Universe at the Close of the Nineteenth Century*, trans. Joseph McCabe (New York: Harper, 1900), p. 274). William James anticipated this claim in 1884: "The stronghold of the deterministic sentiment is the antipathy to the idea of chance," which he thought "a purely negative and relative term." That is, chance simply meant "not controlled, secured, or necessitated by other things in advance of its own actual presence" (*The Will to Believe*, pp. 153–54). As a postulate for agency, this position has been forcibly discounted by most philosophers, who recognize that chance or random actions do not support a voluntarist argument. Still, literary critics often mistake narrative logic for a larger philosophical one. Thus, Walter Benn Michaels: "Only the presence in the universe of something like 'absolute chance,' with the corresponding presence of a certain irreducible even if minimal arbitrariness in all cause-and-effect relations, makes freedom possible" (*The Gold Standard*, p. 231).

58. Peter Brooks offers the fullest, most compelling elaboration of this view, that "narrative is hence condemned to *saying* other than what it *would mean*, spinning out its movement toward a meaning that would be the end of its movement" (*Reading for the Plot*, p. 56).

59. Georg Lukács famously asserted: "The key question is: what is meant by 'chance' in fiction? Without chance all narration is dead and abstract. No writer can portray life if he eliminates the fortuitous. On the other hand, in his representation of life he must go beyond cross accident and elevate chance to the inevitable." "Narrate or Describe?" in *Writer and Critic and Other Essays*, trans. and ed. Arthur D. Kahn (New York: Grosset & Dunlap, 1970), p. 112. This seminal essay thoroughly dismisses naturalism, but in terms which continue to challenge. For material omitted from *Writer and Critic*, see Part 2 of S. Altschuler's translation of the essay, entitled "Narration vs. Description," *International Literature* (1937), 7:93–98.

Erving Goffman offers an intriguing discussion of the role of chance and risk-taking in daily life—and of our understanding of character in terms of these activities—in "Where the Action Is," *Interaction Ritual: Essays on Face-to-Face Behavior* (New York: Pantheon, 1967), pp. 149–156.

60. Howard, *Form and History*, pp. 10, 114. To be fair, Howard some-

times seems to share in the Wittgensteinian model I will develop below (in her commitment to "meaningful affiliations," p. 30); but she more regularly subscribes to a counter-logic of extrinsic features. Her discussion of "American naturalism as a genre and not simply as the reflex of a philosophical position" (36) clearly differs from my approach. For other studies of naturalism as a genre, see my Preface, n. 2.

61. The first phrase is Philip Fisher's (*Hard Facts*, p. 171). For discussion of the second, see the Preface, n. 2. And for the different taxonomies of naturalism, see the Preface, n. 7.

62. In one of the earliest serious treatments of the issue (and still an essay worth reading) Philip Rahv asserted: "I know of no hard and fast rules that can be used to distinguish the naturalist method from the methods of realism generally. It is certainly incorrect to say that the difference is marked by the relative density of detail. . . . A more conclusive test, to my mind, is its treatment of the relation of character to background." See "On the Decline of Naturalism," *Partisan Review* (November-December 1942), 9:487.

63. Ludwig Wittgenstein, *Philosophical Investigations*, trans. G. E. M. Anscombe (3d ed.; New York: Macmillan, 1953), No. 65–67, pp. 31–32. Or as Leon Katz concludes: "In other words, the sundry items that are referred to by a single word may have nothing in common at all, save the label. Any two or three of them will have a lot in common, of course, but not the group. They are like the members of the Hapsburg dynasty: each reigning monarch greatly resembled his predecessor. But there is no trait all Hapsburgs shared—not even the famous Hapsburg lip" (*Bad Acts*, pp. 90–91).

64. Frye's work is still the best beginning for anyone interested in questions of genre and mode. Unlike many of those who speak of naturalism as a genre, moreover, he prefers to consider it as a mode, taking care to base generic distinctions upon "the radical of presentation," which allows (strictly speaking) only four genres: "Words may be acted in front of a spectator; they may be spoken in front of a listener; they may be sung or chanted; or they may be written for a reader." See *Anatomy of Criticism: Four Essays* (Princeton: Princeton UP, 1957), pp. 95, 246–47. Tzvetan Todorov challenges Frye's claim to provide a scientific study of literature in his own analysis of what I take to be a mode, not a genre, in *The Fantastic: A Structural Approach to a Literary Genre*, trans. Richard Howard (Ithaca: Cornell UP, 1975), p. 3.

For further discussion, see Mikhail M. Bakhtin, *Problems of Dostoevsky's Poetics*, trans. R. W. Rotsel (Ann Arbor: Ardis, 1973), esp. ch. 4, pp. 83–149; Jacques Derrida, "The Law of Genre," trans. Avital Ronell, *Critical Inquiry* (Autumn 1980), 7:55–81; Paul Hernadi, *Beyond Genre: New Directions in Literary Classification* (Ithaca: Cornell UP, 1972); E. D. Hirsh, Jr., *Validity in Interpretation* (New Haven: Yale UP, 1967), esp. pp. 86–88, 109–10; Peter

J. Rabinowitz, *Before Reading*, pp. 176–93; and the essays collected in *Theories of Literary Genre*, ed. Joseph P. Strelka (University Park: Pennsylvania State UP, 1978), esp. John Reichert, "More Than Kin and Less Than Kind: The Limits of Genre Theory," pp. 57–79; and Horst S. Daemmrich, "The Aesthetic Function of Detail and Silhouette in Literary Genres," pp. 113–22.

65. Frye, *Anatomy of Criticism*, p. 49. Alastair Fowler has provided an exhaustive survey of genres that, like Todorov's, disagrees with major aspects of Frye's work. Fowler notably takes a Wittgensteinian tack in his study, examining "the implications of treating genres not as permanent classes but as families subject to change" (v). My adducing of the grammatical analogy of genres and modes is taken from his *Kinds of Literature: An Introduction to the Theory of Genres and Modes* (Cambridge: Harvard UP, 1982), pp. 106–7. See also his "Genre and the Literary Canon," *New Literary History* (1979), 11:97–119.

66. See Frye, *Anatomy of Criticism*, p. 33; Alpers, "Mode in Narrative Poetry," in *To Tell a Story: Narrative Theory and Practice*, ed. Robert M. Adams (Los Angeles: William Andrews Clark Library, 1973), pp. 23–56.

Lilian R. Furst offers an incisive instance of how one might thus approach naturalism: "In many ways it is an intensification of Realism . . . But it was not just a matter of choosing more shocking subjects, earthier vocabulary, more striking slogans or more photographic details. The true difference lies much deeper: at its core is the imposition of a certain, very specific view of man on Realism's attitude of detached neutrality." Furst and Peter N. Skrine, *Naturalism* (London: Methuen, 1971), p. 8. "All that is required," Robert M. Figg III, states even more compellingly, "is that the novel reflect a relatively strong illusion of determinism." He does not, however, pretend to show how this is done. See "Naturalism as a Literary Form," *Georgia Review* (Fall 1964), 18:314.

67. Harold Kaplan is therefore mistaken in claiming that *Sister Carrie* is a "naturalist tragedy" or that *The Red Badge of Courage* celebrates "naturalist heroism" (*Power and Order*, pp. 88, 122). See also Thomas A. Gullason, "Stephen Crane: In Nature's Bosom," in *American Literary Naturalism: A Reassessment*, pp. 37–56; and especially Donald Pizer's comprehensive analysis of the "tragic themes which are at the heart of American naturalism," in *Twentieth-Century American Literary Naturalism: An Interpretation* (Carbondale: Southern Illinois UP, 1982), p. 6.

68. Walcutt nonetheless attempts to defend this position in *American Literary Naturalism*, pp. 23–29.

69. Berlin, *Historical Inevitability* (London: Oxford UP, 1954), p. 33.

2. IMPOSING (ON) EVENTS IN LONDON'S ''TO BUILD A FIRE''

1. For an informative, if controversial, biography that confirms the fears even admirers have about London, see Irving Stone, *Jack London, Sailor on Horseback: A Biographical Novel* (1938; rpt. New York: Signet, 1969). Carolyn Wilson assesses his confusions in "'Rattling the Bones': Jack London, Socialist Evangelist," *Western American Literature* (August 1976), 11:135–48.

2. Jack London, "To Build a Fire," in *Lost Face* (New York: Macmillan, 1910), p. 98. Subsequent references to this edition appear directly in the text.

3. One complexly patterned rhyme occurs later, with the "tingling" and "stinging ache" that is "excrutiating" (86). And while this passage happens to lack many examples, alliteration occurs nearly as frequently throughout as at its conclusion. A small, random sample of such instances includes "day dark" (63), "spat speculating" (65), "numb nose" (67), "warm-whiskered" (67), "dropped down" (69), "first faraway signals of sensation" (85–86), "fetched forth" (86), "freezing feet" (86), and "day drew" (97).

4. Another notable instance occurs on pp. 74–75, where in one paragraph, each sentence, sometimes each phrase, begins with the formulation "He [transitive verb] . . ."

5. The phrase is Harry Levin's, who aptly invoked it to define the materially importunate worlds of realism. Part of my argument, however, is that in naturalist texts the illusion of things matters enough for absence to be thematized directly; it dictates behavior with as straightforwardly "tyrannous" an effect as presence. See "Society as Its Own Historian," in *Contexts of Criticism* (Cambridge: Harvard UP, 1957), p. 186; also, "What Is Realism?" pp. 67–75; and "On the Dissemination of Realism," in *Grounds for Comparison* (Cambridge: Harvard UP, 1972), pp. 244–61.

6. It bears repeating that this is not philosophically necessary, but merely narratively persuasive. Harry G. Frankfurt has cogently argued that one need not be able to effect one's will to be morally responsible. See "Alternate Possibilities and Moral Responsibility," *Journal of Philosophy* (1969), pp. 829–39.

7. Jack London, "To Build a Fire," *The Youth's Companion* (May 29, 1902), 76:275. Susan Ward has observed that London's style was considered innovative by contemporaries, and that he moved to a shorter, simpler style in the decade from 1899 to 1910. See "Toward a Simpler Style: Jack London's Stylistic Development," *Jack London Newsletter* (1978), 11:71–80.

8. For Zola's views, see the essays collected in George J. Becker, ed., *Documents of Modern Literary Realism* (Princeton: Princeton UP, 1963), esp. pp. 159–229.

9. Earle Labor provocatively asserts that the story's opening sentence already suggests the man's doom, in *Jack London* (New York: Twayne, 1974), p. 63.

10. Joan D. Hedrick, at least, thinks so, claiming that this and another story deal with "unnecessary death—death that could have been avoided had the protagonists the imagination to perceive their finitude and their need to rely on others for mutual support and protection." *Solitary Comrade: Jack London and His Work* (Chapel Hill: U of North Carolina P, 1982), p. 49. On the other hand, Earle Labor regards the man as a "tragic hero," who finally "achieves true heroic stature" (*Jack London*, pp. 65–66). James I. McClintock, in *White Logic: Jack London's Short Stories* (Cedar Springs, Mich.: Wolf House Books, 1976), takes an alternative view that the story "is London's most mature expression of his pessimism," and that "man is inherently too limited to explore life's mysteries and live" (116).

11. Thomas Nagel has also asserted that since we are not responsible for creating ourselves, we cannot be held liable for what our constitutions lead us to do. Conversely, one cannot praise as virtuous a person who refrains from immoral action if the person is so constructed as not to be attracted to such an act. Not getting angry in provocative circumstances is not a moral virtue if a person happens not to be an easily angered person. *Mortal Questions* (New York: Cambridge UP, 1979), pp. 32–33.

12. For a radically different reading of the man's death and its significance for the story, see Charles E. May, "'To Build a Fire': Physical Fiction and Metaphysical Critics," *Studies in Short Fiction* (Winter 1978), 15:19–24.

13. Bryan S. Turner addresses some of the paradoxes involved in the conjunction of self and body, in *Body and Society* (New York: Blackwell, 1984): "Our bodies are an environment which can become anarchic, regardless of our subjective experience of our government of the body" (7). And he adds: "In writing this study of the body, I have become increasingly less sure of what the body is. The paradoxes illustrate the confusion. The body is a material organism, but also a metaphor; it is a trunk apart from head and limbs, but also the person (as in 'anybody' and 'somebody'). The body may also be an aggregate of bodies, often with legal personality as in 'corporation' or in 'the mystical body of Christ.' Such aggregate bodies may be regarded as legal fictions or as social facts which exist independently of the 'real' bodies which happen to constitute them. There are also immaterial bodies which are possessed by ghosts, spirits, demons and angels. . . . The body is at once the most solid, the most elusive, illusory, concrete, metaphorical, ever present and ever distant thing—a site, an instrument, an environment, a singularity and a multiplicity" (7–8).

14. This pronominal division occurs earlier, and to similar effect. See, for instance, the last sentence in the full paragraph quoted above, p. 76.

15. The passage reads: "The blood of his body recoiled before it. The

blood was alive, like the dog, and like the dog it wanted to hide away and cover itself up from the fearful cold" (80; also p. 89).

16. The free indirect discourse accorded the dog forms a third voice that appears less obviously—at the end of the story, for example, in the concluding paragraph quoted at the beginning of this chapter. At other times, the man's "throat sounds" and uncharacteristically threatening movements are clearly rendered from the uncomprehending, instinct-ridden perspective of the animal (cf. pp. 76–77, 90). The way in which that perspective is characterized strongly resembles the man's, which contributes to the reduced view of him as a distinctly human self. The man's efforts to entice the dog to him, for instance, elicit this response: "Something was the matter, and its suspicious nature sensed danger—it knew not what danger, but somewhere, somehow, in its brain arose an apprehension of the man" (90). Moreover, the accuracy of instinct, in contrast to the ineffectiveness of knowledge, forms a minor theme through the story and is confirmed in the concluding scene. Still, this third narrative voice is at once less prominent and less critical to the story's development than the other two.

3. THE PSYCHOPOETICS OF DESIRE IN DREISERS *AMERICAN TRAGEDY*

1. Theodore Dreiser, *An American Tragedy*. 2 vols. (Garden City: Sun Dial Press, 1925), 2:78. Subsequent references to this edition occur directly in the text, with only the second volume indicated by number.

2. J. Hillis Miller has made this claim for Virginia Woolf's *Mrs. Dalloway*, in *Fiction and Repetition: Seven English Novels* (Cambridge: Harvard UP, 1982), p. 178. Significantly, the raising of Roberta from the lake is also a literary repetition of the recovery of Zenobia's drowned body near the end of Hawthorne's *Blithedale Romance*.

3. Ironically, Dreiser did in fact omit actual historical recurrences in fictionalizing the 1906 Chester Gillette-Billy Brown murder. As well, he dropped chapters from an early draft that described what he thought was the excessively repetitive background of Clyde's parents.

4. Robert Penn Warren, *"An American Tragedy,"* *Yale Review* (1962), 52:8.

5. For one dismissive example, see Charles Thomas Samuels, "Mr. Trilling, Mr. Warren, and *An American Tragedy*," *Yale Review* (1964), 53:629–40. More sympathetically, Richard Lehan has observed that "as in Zola's novels, Dreiser's fiction takes place in a world of limits, controlled by what Dreiser called the 'equation inevitable.' This is the term Dreiser used to convey his belief in the circularity and repetitiveness of life which stemmed from antagonistic forces canceling each other out." See "American Literary

Naturalism: The French Connection," *Nineteenth-Century Fiction* (1984), 38:553. Lehan anticipates some of my observations on repetition in his earlier full-length study, *Theodore Dreiser: His World and His Novels* (Carbondale: Southern Illinois UP, 1969), ch. 10, pp. 142–69. For other explanations of Dreiser's view of life (in terms of his style), see Ellen Moers, *Two Dreisers* (New York: Viking, 1969), p. 204; and Donald Pizer, *The Novels of Theodore Dreiser: A Critical Study* (Minneapolis: U of Minnesota P, 1976), pp. 235, 243, 259.

6. Readers have not tended to notice how often characters form doubles of Clyde and Roberta, or pursued Robert Penn Warren's observation that even "apparent digressions are really mirrors held up to Clyde's story, in fact to Clyde himself: in this world of mirrors complicity is the common doom" ("American Tragedy," 12).

As in London's "To Build a Fire," repetition has an erosive effect upon identity, making the two lovers disappear in the multiple reflections offered by others. The self's characteristics proliferate, making them no longer characteristically the self's. Among secondary figures, the bellhops at the Green-Davidson; the fellow-boarder, Walter Dillard; the haberdasher, Orrin Short; the prosecutor, Orville W. Mason; the defense attorney, Alvin Belknap; the Reverend Duncan McMillan; and Clyde's nephew, Russell: all repeat characteristics and experiences that Clyde thinks of as uniquely his. Similarly, Roberta is mirrored by Mrs. Elvira Griffiths, Esta Griffiths, Hortense Briggs, even Sondra Finchley. Their varying relationships with Clyde anticipate and repeat each other, despite all his attempts to avoid "the danger of repeating" (303). His and Roberta's doubles end by driving them only closer, into mutual self-annihilation.

For discussion of these other "doubles," see Richard Lehan, *Dreiser*, pp. 153–55; Donald Pizer, *Novels*, pp. 252–53; and Strother B. Purdy *"An American Tragedy* and *L'Etranger," Comparative Literature* (1967), 19:264. René Girard provides a broader context for understanding the dynamics of the novel in his claim: "This disconcerting return of the identical exactly where each believes he is generating difference defines this relationship of the doubles, and it has nothing to do with the *imaginaire*. Doubles are the final result and truth of mimetic desire, a truth seeking acknowledgement but repressed by the principal characters because of their mutual antagonism. The doubles themselves interpret the emergence of the doubles as 'hallucinatory.'" See "The Underground Critic" in *"To Double Business Bound": Essays on Literature, Mimesis, and Anthropology* (Baltimore: Johns Hopkins UP, 1978), p. 41.

7. Donald Pizer finds this resemblance "one of the few discordant melodramatic devices in the novel," an instance where "melodrama moves in the direction of allegory" (*Novels*, p. 246). Ironically, however, as Richard Lehan points out, Chester Gillette resembled his nephew, Harold Gillette,

quite strikingly (*Dreiser*, p. 147; see also p. 163). Lauriat Lane, Jr., first analyzed this relationship in "The Double in *An American Tragedy*," *Modern Fiction Studies* (1966), 12:213–220.

8. See "The Uncanny" (1919), p. 41, in *Studies in Parapsychology*, trans. Alix Strachey, *Collected Papers* (New York: Collier Books, 1963). On "manifest" doubles, see Robert Rogers, *A Psychoanalytic Study of the Double in Literature* (Detroit: Wayne State UP, 1970), p. 19; also Ralph Tymms, *Doubles in Literary Psychology* (Cambridge: Harvard UP, 1949); Albert J. Guerard, "Concepts of the Double," in *Stories of the Double*, ed. Guerard (Philadelphia: Lippincott, 1967), and Claire Rosenfield, "The Shadow Within: The Conscious and Unconscious Use of the Double," in *Stories of the Double*, pp. 311–31.

9. 1:186. The first contrast is made by Gilbert's mother (221), but the judgment is more or less shared (and repeated) by the prostitute Clyde visits (67), Clyde's mother (122), and Roberta (259).

10. Compare Hortense Briggs' and Rita Dickerman's similar success in delaying Clyde (80, 208), which likewise suggests a need to control and subdue. In these cases, however, the tactic of delay occurs not because he is Clyde, but because he is any swain to be kept dangling.

11. Rank goes on to state: "This detached personification of instincts and desires which were once felt to be unacceptable, but which can be satisfied without responsibility in this indirect way, appears in other forms of the theme as a beneficent admonitor . . . who is directly addressed as the 'conscience' of the person." See *The Double: A Psychoanalytic Study* (1925) trans. Harry Tucker, Jr. (Chapel Hill: U of North Carolina P, 1971), p. 76 (also p. 33).

12. In a footnote, however, Rank resisted describing cross-sexual doubling: "The significance of the pursuer's possibly being of the other sex in the picture of paranoia cannot be discussed here" (74). Irving Howe is nearly alone in having detected this bond between Clyde and Roberta: "The part of him that retains some spontaneous feeling is doubled by Roberta, thereby strengthening one's impression that Clyde and Roberta are halves of an uncompleted self, briefly coming together in a poignant unity." "Afterword," *An American Tragedy* (New York: New American Library, 1964), pp. 824–25. But Howe does not develop this observation. See also Richard Lehan, *Dreiser*, pp. 164–65.

13. Like the automobile crash and accidental meeting with his uncle that result in Clyde moving to Lycurgus, Roberta arrives in town through a series of similarly fortuitous events: a younger sister's marriage, the closing of the Biltz factory, and Grace Marr's casual invitation.

14. The sole exception to his consistent blindness occurs when Clyde at one point can "almost see himself in Roberta's place" (369).

15. Robert Rogers has defined the double as an "opposing self" (*Psycho-

analytic Study, p. 62). In this sense, my reading of Roberta implicitly denies Donald Pizer's claim for her increased "emotional maturity" (*Novels*, p. 258).

16. 2:70. Ellen Moers not only claims that the world of the novel grows increasingly unreal, but that Big Bittern Lake absorbs all the waters of the novel (*Two Dreisers*, p. 283).

17. For statements expressing each of these three, see: Robert Elias, *Theodore Dreiser: Apostle of Nature* (1948; rev. ed. Ithaca: Cornell UP, 1970), p. 222; Strother B. Purdy, "*An American Tragedy* and *L'Etranger*," *Comparative Literature* (1967), 19:257; Paul A. Orlov, "The Subversion of the Self: Anti-Naturalistic Crux in *An American Tragedy*," *Modern Fiction Studies* (1977), 23:472; Ellen Moers, *Two Dreisers*, p. 285; and Philip Fisher, "Looking Around to See Who I Am: Dreiser's Territory of the Self," *ELH* (Winter 1977), 44:747. Fisher incorporates most of this essay verbatim into *Hard Facts: Setting and Form in the American Novel* (New York: Oxford UP, 1985), but does not include its last four pages.

18. Donald Pizer has laid out nicely the legal and moral terms of Clyde's involvement in Roberta's death (*Novels*, pp. 271–72). For a more speculative analysis, see Leo Katz's discussion in *Bad Acts and Guilty Minds*, pp. 201–9. He first compares the case with an account of a man "out driving thinking about how to kill his uncle [and whose] intention to kill his uncle makes him so nervous and excited that he accidentally runs over and kills a pedestrian who happens to be his uncle" (204). Since the man isn't guilty of murder, Katz argues, neither is Clyde. Katz then develops the problem of intention, pointing out that "the act triggering Roberta's death was not merely noncriminal but *commendable*—it was aimed at saving Roberta's life" (206).

19. This has been partially described by Richard Lehan, "Dreiser's *An American Tragedy*," *College English* (1963), 25:188, 191; Lehan, *Dreiser*, pp. 164–65; and Donald Pizer, *Novels*, pp. 282–83.

20. Richard Lehan has further described the novel's structure: "*An American Tragedy* employs the familiar block method with a great mass of accumulated material being arranged into blocks or units, each scene repeating and then anticipating another. Each individual scene parallels the structure of the novel as a whole . . ." Lehan then adds in a footnote: "We spiral down on Clyde, and movement of each scene, as of the novel, is from the general to the particular" ("*An American Tragedy*," p. 191).

21. For a description of Dreiser's borrowing from the cinema, see Moers, *Two Dreisers*, p. 232, and Pizer, *Novels*, pp. 286–87.

22. See p. 117. The car crash is also recalled by Clyde, and by Mason at the trial; see 2:50, 267. Of a somewhat different order of repetition, Mason tells Titus Alden of his daughter's death, reminding us of Clyde asking directions on that same doorstep only weeks before.

23. See Richard Lehan, "*An American Tragedy*," p. 191; Donald Pizer, *Novels*, pp. 234–35; and Philip Fisher, "Looking Around," p. 747.

24. Sigmund Freud, *Beyond the Pleasure Principle* (1920), trans. James Strachey (New York: Norton, 1961), p. 16.

25. "*An American Tragedy*," p. 164.

26. No one, to my knowledge, has commented on the fact that the novel's time scheme is not merely vague, but actually confused—which also has the effect of slowing time. Since days and dates are given at various points, a universal calendar can confirm certain years for the course of the narrative; but there still remain too many vivid internal conflicts. Roberta, for instance, dates one letter to Clyde, "Saturday, June 14th," which places the year of her death as 1919 or 1924 (given the style of automobiles, the slang, and other identifying details of the period). Yet she dates a letter two weeks later, "Wednesday, June 30th," which occurred only in 1920 and 1926. As well, Clyde's December datebook allows too few days between his Christmas party with Sondra and his meeting with Roberta. The novel's time scheme, in other words, is as fictional is everything else—and this is true whether one attributes the confusion to Dreiser's sloppiness or his deliberate intention (categories that simply reinscribe the novel's concerns back into any critique of it).

27. Brief exceptions to this general pattern do occur, as when Clyde fears his past will become known, or wonders "What had become of Hortense?", or dwells in Lycurgus on "happier scenes," the "few gay happy days he had enjoyed in Kansas City" (200, 209, 263). Near Big Bittern, he and Roberta will independently recall their walk of a year before. Yet these rare recollections encourage Clyde only once to change his mind, when having first considered running from Roberta—"as in the instance of the slain child in Kansas City—and be heard of nevermore here" (2:13)—he resists flight and steels himself to remain: "No, he could not run away again." Ironically, his one attempt to avoid repetition becomes the major instance in which he courts it.

28. Clyde had notably attempted to escape the possibility of repetition when he telephoned Roberta during her last month out of fear of the evidenciary impact of her letters. The reading of her letters at his trial does in fact convince the jury to convict. By bringing her lonely anguish alive once again, they throw both Clyde and the reader back into an earlier time and thereby make its process seem slowed.

As many critics have remarked, "dream" is repeated over a hundred times, more often than any other word in the novel. See William L. Phillips, "The Imagery of Dreiser's Novels," *PMLA* (1963), 78:580–81; Lehan, "*An American Tragedy*," p. 189; and Moers, *Two Dreisers*, p. 277.

29. Haskell M. Block has claimed: "The relentlessness and inevitability of the sequence of events in the courtroom are an analogue on a smaller

scale of the coercive movement of the novel as a whole." See *Naturalistic Triptych: The Fictive and the Real in Zola, Mann, and Dreiser* (New York: Random House, 1970), p. 69 (also pp. 71–72). My conclusion disagrees with two of Pizer's judgments: that "the trial is not fictionally repetitious . . . The details therefore contribute to a sense of ironic density rather than to an effect of repetition"; and that "the closing section of *An American Tragedy* is the weakest of the novel" due to its "repetitious detail" (*Novels*, pp. 274, 276).

30. Moers, *Two Dreisers*, p. 276. Donald Pizer usefully analyzes the prose, but interprets its effect differently (*Novels*, pp. 287–89). See also Lehan, "*An American Tragedy*," p. 191.

31. Warren, "*An American Tragedy*," p. 14; Lehan, "*An American Tragedy*," p. 190; and Fisher, *Hard Facts*, p. 140.

32. Moers, *Two Dreisers*, p. 230.

33. He is, in Harry G. Frankfurt's term, a "wanton." See ch. 1, n. 18. Warwick Wadlington argues a contrary interpretation of Clyde, in identifying the novel with the mode of pathos. "Pathos and Dreiser," *Southern Review* (1971), 7:414.

Leo Katz helps unpack the problem of action by offering hypothetical cases where "the intention that caused the action doesn't really 'explain' the action." As he imagines: "Suppose Clyde's real intention had been to push Roberta to the ground and then to shoot her. He would still have been seized by panic, his hand would still have jerked, Roberta would still have stumbled backwards, the boat would still have careened, and she would still have drowned. Again, by changing his intention, Clyde would not be changing the action that it brings about. Because of this, it makes more sense to say that the actor's action happens to coincide with his intention that then fulfills it. And without such fulfillment, one would be loath to speak of an intentional action" (*Bad Acts and Legal Minds*, pp. 207–8).

34. Philip Fisher has nicely observed that "Clyde is never intimately sculpted by his actions. He does not seem to do them. Every decisive event in his life is an accident, a mistake or a confusion. In the existential sense, he does not 'do' his life. For that reason his acts are not essential to who he is" (*Hard Facts*, p. 148). My claim, however, is that no "essential" Clyde exists outside the events of his life. Richard Lehan likewise describes Clyde's "mechanistic" appearance ("*An American Tragedy*," p. 188), while Ellen Moers outlines "the gradual desubstantiation of Clyde himself" (*Two Dreisers*, p. 280). See Charles Thomas Samuels ("Mr. Trilling," p. 635) for another version of this will-versus-psyche dilemma.

35. Strother B. Purdy claims that "though society is the villain of both novels, it is also the victor. It organizes chance into something resembling determinism" ("*An American Tragedy*," p. 264). From a different angle, Warwick Wadlington observes that "pathos is imprisoning, leading to a

vision of a series of inescapable, concentric prisons—the self, society, nature" ("Pathos," p. 415).

4. SUBVERSIVE SELF-CONSTRUCTIONS IN NORRIS *VANDOVER AND THE BRUTE*

1. Frank Norris, *Vandover and the Brute* (Lincoln: U of Nebraska P, 1978), p. 351. Subsequent references are cited parenthetically in the text. First published posthumously in 1914, *Vandover* was completed by 1895 according to James D. Hart. See *A Novelist in the Making: A Collection of Student Themes, and the Novels "Blix" and "Vandover and the Brute,"* ed. James D. Hart (Cambridge: Harvard UP, 1970), pp. 27, 47.

2. The best investigaton of the function of descriptive detail in narrative is still Erich Auerbach's survey in *Mimesis: The Representation of Reality in Western Literature*, trans. Willard R. Trask (Princeton: Princeton UP, 1968). See in particular his analysis of Balzac's description of Mme Vauquer: "The series of things mentioned . . . reveal no trace of composition; nor is there any separation of body and clothing, of physical characteristics and moral significance" (471).

For an account of the emergence of lists in the novel, see Hugh Kenner, "The Comedian of the Inventory," in *The Stoic Comedians: Flaubert, Joyce, and Beckett* (Berkeley: U of California P, 1962), pp. 30–66. James Guetti has claimed that reading, seeing, and knowing are interconnected: "Seeing becomes knowing by a constant process of accumulating and digesting images on the way to some ultimate reduction or abstraction of them. We follow from image to image to arrive at a 'larger,' more comprehensive image that will rule them all." Moreover, "the illusion of realism requires continual verbal variation because such variation is necessary to imitate the conditions of the seeing-knowing process that is usual with us in actual life." *Word-Music: The Aesthetic Aspect of Narrative Fiction* (New Brunswick: Rutgers UP, 1980), p. 2.

3. Mark Twain, *Adventures of Huckleberry Finn*, ed. Leo Marx (Indianapolis: Bobbs-Merrill, 1967), p. 165.

4. Barthes is describing "the birth of thematics" in *S/Z: An Essay*, trans. Richard Miller (New York: Hill & Wang, 1974), p. 92. June Howard offers an instance of one who describes this list thematically, asserting that it "demonstrates" Vandover's "degradation"; she then goes on to invoke Norris' alleged obsession with dirt, in *Form and History in American Literary Naturalism* (Chapel Hill: U of North Carolina P, 1985), p. 68.

Few have taken even this trouble with Norris' prose style, however, and perhaps the most dismissive is Warner Berthoff, who claims, "It is as if Cole Porter had written novels," in *The Ferment of Realism: American Literature,*

1884–1919 (New York: Free Press, 1965), p. 225. His specification of Norris' flaws is nonetheless instructive: "He can not write credible dialogue (or dialect, which he unwisely attempts); he can not describe appearances convincingly; the whole tendency of his conveyor-belt sentences, pieced together like exercises in a grammar workbook, is to obscure rather than substantiate the matter at hand. His development of plot and incident is always arbitrary, fantastic without being interesting. Human character appears to baffle him totally; his own characters, distinguished principally by the presence or absence of 'virility,' act out the parts assigned them with comic-strip predictability." And so on. See also Michael Davitt Bell, "Frank Norris, Style, and the Problem of Naturalism," *Studies in the Literary Imagination* (1983), 16:93–106.

5. Genette, *Figures of Literary Discourse*, trans. Alan Sheridan (New York: Columbia UP, 1982), pp. 185–86. Genette more generally anticipates some of my points in his essay, "Flaubert's Silences," pp. 183–202. Compare his claim, about another passage, that "from the point of view of the rules of realistic narration, this description . . . is as little 'in situation,' as unjustified, dramatically and psychologically, as possible" (197).

Georg Lukács has claimed that in Zola, novelistic detail is irrelevant: "An arbitrary detail, a chance similarity, a fortuitous attitude, an accidental meeting—all are supposed to provide direct expression of important social relationships." Since they do not do so, however, the failure proves the historical decline of the novel from Balzac and Dickens: "The description of things no longer has anything to do with the lives of characters. Not only are things described out of any context with the lives of characters, attaining an independent significance that is not their due within the totality of the novel, but the very manner in which they are described sets them in an entirely different sphere from that in which the characters move." Lukács rightly realizes that the result of this technique is to make both characters and readers "merely spectators." But he sees this as a narrative debility, rather than essential to a determinist vision. See "Narrate or Describe?" in *Writer and Critic and Other Essays*, trans. and ed. Arthur D. Kahn (New York: Grosset & Dunlap, 1970), pp. 115, 132.

Ironically, Norris himself criticized the realism of Howells for doing what he does so well: "Realism stultifies itself. It notes only the surface of things." See "A Plea for Romantic Fiction," in *The Responsibilities of the Novelist* (1902; Garden City, N.Y.: Doubleday, 1928), p. 164.

6. Warren French claims, for instance: "Even in the unsatisfactory form in which it has reached us, *Vandover and the Brute* is obviously a tract against self-indulgence." *Frank Norris* (New Haven: Twayne, 1962), p. 52. See also Stanley Cooperman, "Frank Norris and the Werewolf of Guilt," *Modern Language Quarterly* (September 1959), 20:252–58; June Howard, *Form and History*, pp. 63–69, 91, 95, 96, 101; Edwin Haviland Miller, "The Art of

Frank Norris in *Vandover and the Brute,*" *Markham Review* (Summer 1981), 10:54–63; Donald Pizer, *The Novels of Frank Norris* (Bloomington: Indiana UP, 1966), pp. 33–52; and Robert W. Schneider, "Frank Norris: The Naturalist as Victorian," *Midcontinent American Studies Journal* (Spring 1962), 3:13–27.

7. For an examination of Vandover's spendthrift behavior, see Walter Benn Michaels, *The Gold Standard and the Logic of Naturalism* (Berkeley: U of California P, 1987), 139–80. See also William B. Dillingham's examination of the link between gambling and chance in Norris' fiction, in *Frank Norris: Instinct and Art* (Lincoln: U of Nebraska P, 1969), pp. 79–82.

8. P. 5. Barbara Hochman has examined the "lack of simple *narrative* coherence" in Vandover's efforts to tell his own story, and relates this to Norris' engagement with "the problematics of the self," in *The Art of Frank Norris, Storyteller* (Columbia: U of Missouri P, 1988), pp. 29, 41.

9. Joseph R. McElrath, Jr., argues against reading the narrative voice of *Vandover* as Norris' own judgment, in "Frank Norris's *Vandover and the Brute*: Narrative Technique and the Socio-Critical Viewpoint," *Studies in American Fiction* (1976), 4:27–43. The following discussion is indebted to McElrath's cogent analysis, as is Don Graham's reading in *The Fiction of Frank Norris: The Aesthetic Context* (Columbia: U of Missouri P, 1978), pp. 16–42. David Wyatt comes close to this view in support of his claim that "for Norris, plot is the thing that knocks character down." See "Norris and the Vertical," *Southern Review* (Autumn 1983), 19:761.

10. See McElrath, "Narrative Technique," esp. pp. 33–34.

11. P. 11. Mark Seltzer claims that "Vandover's degeneration [is] precipitated by his discovery of the obstetrics article," and that his "brute" forms "a strikingly perverse case of obstetrics." See "The Naturalist Machine," in *Sex, Politics, and Science in the Nineteenth-Century Novel: Selected Papers from the English Institute, 1983–84*, ed. Ruth Bernard Yeazell (Baltimore: Johns Hopkins UP, 1986), p. 131. See also June Howard, *Form and History*, p. 64.

12. For a different view of the role of art in the novel, see Don Graham, *Fiction*, pp. 16–42.

13. Magazine reproductions hang in nearly every parlor in the novel, but the transformation made by either Ida or her mother of a similar object deserves comment. It is "a large and striking picture, a species of cheap photogravure, a lion lying in his cage, looking mildly at the spectator over his shoulder. In front of the picture were real iron bars, with real straw tucked in beyond them" (71). This anticipation of the eclectic mixed media pieces of Robert Rauschenberg constitutes less a rejection of sentimental art than a reinforcement of its pathos. The dominant cultural aesthetic is resisted but finally accepted, prefiguring Ida's acceptance of contemporary social morality in her later suicide.

14. At only one point does the narrative voice register a self-conscious

equation between the two: "It was the sensitive artist nature in him that responded instantly to anything sensuously attractive. Each kind and class of beautiful women could arouse in Vandover passions of equal force, though of far different kind" (52). But this is a fleeting identification that Vandover never engages.

15. For three alternative readings, see Don Graham, *Fiction*, pp. 35–42; Joseph R. McElrath, Jr., "Narrative Technique," p. 41; and Donald Pizer, *Frank Norris*, p. 41.

16. For a scientific explanation of lycanthropy, see Donald Pizer, *Frank Norris*, pp. 36–39; and William B. Dillingham, *Frank Norris*, pp. 73–74.

17. Of analogous importance is the pocket library with which Bandy Ellis satisfies his "curious passion for facts and statistics" (46). On various occasions, he self-consciously refers to his collection of miniature guides, including a reference diary, information card, vest encyclopedia, and pocket calendar (see pp. 55, 72, 89).

18. James D. Hart first offered this hypothesis, in *A Novelist in the Making*, pp. 42–43.

5. THE SPECTACLE OF CHARACTER IN CRANE'S *RED BADGE OF COURAGE*

1. Over thirty years ago, Stanley B. Greenfield perceptively observed: "An examination of the criticism of the novel reveals errors ranging from inadvertent though disturbing misstatements of fact to quotations out of context and gross distortions of sense." "The Unmistakable Stephen Crane," *PMLA* (1958), 73:562. James Nagel provides a good source for Conrad's and other similar comments about Crane, as well as aggressive resistance to the label of naturalism for Crane, in *Stephen Crane and Literary Impressionism* (University Park: Pennsylvania State UP, 1980).

Richard Chase claimed Crane was a "romancer, and his naturalism remains relatively poetic, abstract, pure, and impressionistic." "Introduction" to *The Red Badge of Courage and Other Writings* (Boston: Houghton Mifflin, 1960), p. x. James Trammell Cox declares Crane was a "symbolist rather than a naturalist" in "Stephen Crane as Symbolic Naturalist: An Analysis of 'The Blue Hotel'," *MFS* (1957), 3:148. Frederick C. Crews asserts: "Where he chiefly differed from the naturalists was in his abrupt metaphorical style and his radical conciseness," in his "Introduction" to *The Red Badge of Courage* (New York: Bobbs-Merrill, 1964), p. xiii. J. C. Levenson calls the novel "realism slightly embellished," in "Introduction" to *The Red Badge of Courage*, CEAA text (Charlottesville: UP of Virginia, 1975), p. xiv.

Donald Gibson claims that only *Maggie* is naturalistic among Crane's works, in *The Fiction of Stephen Crane* (Carbondale: Southern Illinois UP,

1968), p. xvi. And Marston LaFrance asserts that "Crane's irony . . . proclaims that he does not believe human irresponsibility is even inevitable or determined by anything other than the wilful dishonesty of human beings." *A Reading of Stephen Crane* (New York: Oxford UP, 1971), p. 40. See also his similar claims in "Stephen Crane Scholarship Today and Tomorrow," *American Literary Realism* (1974), 7:125–35.

2. For discussion of this novel, see in particular Frank Bergon, *Stephen Crane's Artistry* (New York: Columbia UP, 1975), esp. pp. 66–75.

3. For Zola's views, see ch. 2, n. 8.

4. See, e.g., Frederick C. Crews, "Introduction" to *The Red Badge of Courage* (New York: Bobbs-Merrill, 1964), p. xx; Andrew Delbanco, "The American Stephen Crane: The Context of *The Red Badge of Courage*," in *New Essays on "The Red Badge of Courage,"* ed. Lee Clark Mitchell (New York: Cambridge UP, 1986), pp. 64–65; J. C. Levenson, "Introduction" to CEAA edition of *The Red Badge of Courage* (Charlottesville: UP of Virginia, 1975), esp. pp. xliv–xlvi, lxviii ff.; Donald Pizer, "*The Red Badge of Courage*: Text, Theme, and Form," *South Atlantic Quarterly* (Summer 1985), 84:302–313; Eric Solomon, *Stephen Crane: From Parody to Realism* (Cambridge: Harvard UP, 1967), p. 97; Max Westbrook, "Stephen Crane: The Pattern of Affirmation," *Nineteenth-Century Fiction* (1959), 14:219–29.

5. Georg Lukács' thesis inadvertently bears on Crane's characteristic narrative technique. Posing Scott, Balzac, and Tolstoy against Flaubert and Zola, he claims the former narrate while the latter merely describe: "In Flaubert and Zola the characters are merely spectators, more or less interested in the events. As a result, the events themselves become only a tableau for the reader, or, at best, a series of tableaux. We are merely observers." And later: "Thus every epic relationship disappears in the descriptive style. Lifeless, fetishized objects are whisked about in an amorphous atmosphere. . . . Description debases characters to the level of inanimate objects." People are transformed "into conditions, into still lives," so he asserts: "Corresponding to the false breadth assigned the external world is a schematic narrowness in characterization. A character appears as a finished 'product' perhaps composed of varied social and natural elements." Lukács' categories privilege the epic, but if what he states is true, Crane's reliance on description has its powerful effect precisely by reducing characters to conditions. See "Narrate or Describe?" in *Writer and Critic and Other Essays*, trans. and ed. Arthur D. Kahn (New York: Grosset & Dunlap, 1970), pp. 116, 133, 139.

6. Thus, Carolyn Porter asserts of American realist texts: "The contemplative stance of the detached observer, by virtue of the extremity to which it is taken, is undermined from within." See *Seeing and Being: The Plight of the Participant Observer in Emerson, James, Adams, and Faulkner* (Middletown, Conn.: Wesleyan UP, 1981), p. 52. Porter defends American writers from

the traditional charge that they engaged in ahistoricist celebrations of pure perception so as to escape the implications of their social visions.

From a similarly Marxist perspective, June Howard declares that "enforced spectatorship" and "the paralysis of the observer" are distinguishing features of naturalism, which finally aligns with a reformist movement. See *Form and History in American Literay Naturalism* (Chapel Hill: U of North Carolina P, 1985), esp. pp. 114, 125. Significantly, both Porter and Howard rely upon Georg Luckács' late analyses of reification and narrative technique.

7. *The Red Badge of Courage: An Episode of the American Civil War*, ed. Henry Binder (New York: Avon, 1982), p. 1. All subsequent references to the novel are included in the text. For discussion of reasons for using this edition, see Binder's essay, entitled "The 'Red Badge of Courage' Nobody Knows," in *ibid.*, pp. 111–58. J. C. Levenson provides a close reading of the opening paragraph in his "Introduction" to the CEAA edition of *Red Badge*, p. xiv. See also James Nagel, *Impressionism*, p. 54.

8. See pp. 83, 108, 31, 34, 45, 47. These examples can be multiplied. Sergio Perosa has pointed out that there are "no less than 350" verbs directly indicating perception, "no less than 200" expressions that suggest visual sensation, and numerous other auditory and sensory verbs, in "Naturalism and Impressionism in Stephen Crane's Fiction," *Stephen Crane: A Collection of Critical Essays*, ed. Maurice Bassan (Englewood Cliffs: Prentice-Hall, 1967), pp. 88–89. See also Nagel, *Impressionism*, p. 44.

9. Pp. 97–99. Sergio Perosa has bserved that "the rhythm of perception is ceaseless and pressing, continual and almost obsessive" ("Naturalism and Impressionism," p. 89). For an alternative, persuasive reading of this process in the novel, see Amy Kaplan, "The Spectacle of War in Crane's Revision of History," in *New Essays*, esp. pp. 95–98.

10. See, e.g., pp. 21, 38, 47, 71–74, 94, 106.

11. P. 57; also 86. James Trammell Cox has appositely observed that "man's relationship to his universe is paradoxical. He becomes least an animal when most an animal." See "The Imagery of 'The Red Badge of Courage,' " *MFS* (1959), 5:210.

12. James Guetti interprets the connections in *Red Badge* between seeing and knowing, visibility and intelligibility, as evidence of classical realism. See *Word-Music: The Aesthetic Aspect of Narrative Fiction* (New Brunswick: Rutgers UP, 1980), pp. 123, 127–28.

13. See Williams, "Personal Identity and Individuation," and "Bodily Continuity and Personal Identity," in *Problems of the Self: Philosophical Papers, 1956–1972* (New York: Cambridge UP, 1973), pp. 1–18, 19–25.

14. For further development of this idea, see Harry G. Frankfurt's discussion linking free will with "the concept of a person" (ch. 1, n. 18).

15. Cited by E. M. Forster in *Aspects of the Novel* (1927; rev. New York: Harcourt Brace, 1955), p. 101.

16. W. H. Frohock has explored the "modern" effect of Crane's "typical sentence" in "*The Red Badge* and the Limits of Parody," *Southern Review* (1970), 6:137–48. Neil Schmitz makes a more radical claim that "there are no things for Fleming, only words," since for him "reality is a verbal contrivance, simply what one is motivated to articulate." In "Stephen Crane and the Colloquial Self," *Midwest Quarterly* (1972), 14:444–45. Frank Bergon's is the most precise analysis of language in Crane, working from the assumption that Crane's prose is "marked by silences; its essential subject always borders on the inexpressible." As he adds: "Considered only in terms of language and syntax, Crane's style is one which interprets life as fragmented and unpredictable, something about which it is difficult to form express conclusions" (*Artistry*, p. 28).

17. In private correspondence, Douglas Gordon has observed that agency is excluded from this passage stylistically, starting with the first sentence: "he had burned" may technically be an active verb, but our "burnings" are beyond our control. The second sentence then jumps out of Henry's mind, while the "linking verbs" of the third "subvert the sense of Henry actively judging matters for himself." When he does at last act, in the fourth sentence, the actions are "fairly pallid" ("He had read . . . he had longed"). The last sentence simply puts him "at the mercy of his mind."

18. Compare the opening description of Henry's bunk: "The sun-light, without, beating upon [the roof], made it glow a light yellow shade. A small window shot an oblique square of whiter light upon the cluttered floor. The smoke from the fire at times neglected the clay-chimney and wreathed into the room. And this flimsy chimney of clay and sticks made endless threats to set a-blaze the whole establishment" (2). Or again: "The little flames of rifles leaped from [the trees]. The song of the bullets was in the air and shells snarled among the tree-tops. One tumbled directly into the middle of a hurrying group . . . Other men, punched by bullets, fell in grotesque agonies" (85).

19. Henry Binder and Steven Mailloux agree with Hershel Parker's claim that this is a textual fault. See chapter 6 of Parker's *Flawed Texts and Verbal Icons: Literary Authority in American Fiction* (Evanston: Northwestern UP, 1984), pp. 147–79; and chapter 7 of Mailloux's *Interpretive Conventions: The Reader in the Study of American Fiction* (Ithaca: Cornell UP, 1982), pp. 159–91. For an example of nearly exact repetition of a whole paragraph, see pp. 3, 6.

20. P. 6. Crane invokes a similar stylistic pattern in rendering the repetitive rowing experience of the men in "The Open Boat," as quoted above in the Introduction. See also Bergon, *Artistry*, pp. 86–92.

21. Eric Solomon seems the first to have commented on the duplicated structure of the novel, in *Stephen Crane: From Parody to Realism* (Cambridge: Harvard UP, 1967), esp. pp. 76 ff. But see also Bergon, *Artistry,* pp. 76–81.

22. Donald Pease offers a deconstructive reading of narratives in the novel, which "do not follow battles and provide needed explanation; instead they precede and indeed demand battles as elaborations and justifications of already narrated events." See "Fear, Rage, and the Mistrials of Representation in *The Red Badge of Courage*," in *American Realism: New Essays*, ed. Eric Sundquist (Baltimore: Johns Hopkins UP, 1982), p. 160.

23. Part of what it means to "have" a feeling, in other words, is to have it irrefutably. That is not to deny that feelings sometimes change, or appear less severe from other perspectives, or are often mixed and contradictory. Yet even mixed feelings are so not because they are less certain *as* feelings but because they do not fit the cultural map of our emotional landscape. To enjoy a bitter-sweet taste, for instance, or to feel both guilty and pleased, or to have a "love-hate" relationship, is to be no less certain than we otherwise are about our feelings—although these feelings happen to be expressed oxymoronically simply because of the way our language works. In these cases, as we commonly say, we just don't have the precise words to express what we feel.

The confusion we experience on this issue results from our assumption that supposedly refutable feelings can be lumped together with the category of mixed feelings. We mistakenly treat claims of the former sort ("he believed that he envied a corpse") as if they were the same as the latter ("he felt both guilty and pleased"). Yet the former implies not ambivalence, but uncertainty—that when he was feeling envious he was mistaken *in* the feeling, and was not really feeling it at the time. This is not a state of emotional conflict, of feeling ambivalent because of the sometimes problematic fit between our language and our emotions. Rather, it is a logical problem of self-reference, of the impossibility of being in uncertainty about the feelings we have at any given moment (even, perhaps especially, our feeling of uncertainty about our feelings). Moreover, this has nothing to do with self-correcting references or later revisions to the state of one's earlier feeling (I am assuming through all of this, of course, that no confusion exists about the language itself—that people are not simply ignorant, that is, of the meaning of certain terms, such as "dead" and "corpse").

6. RECONSTITUTING THE SUBJECT

1. This is a controversial claim, since a developing conflict among different audiences was already apparent by mid-century. Hawthorne's notorious outburst against "that damn mob of scribbling women" might be taken as representative of an early stage in this divergence. But only after the Civil War did it become entrenched. For two excellent studies, approaching the issue from alternate perspectives of popular (American) readership and elite

(English) authorship, see Christopher Wilson, *The Labor of Words: Literary Professionalism in the Progressive Era* (Athens: U of Georgia P, 1985); and Allon White, *The Uses of Obscurity: The Fiction of Early Modernism* (London: Routledge & Kegan Paul, 1981).

2. See Lionel Trilling, "Reality in America" (1940/1946), in *The Liberal Imagination: Essays in Literature and Society* (1950; rpt. New York: Doubleday, 1953).

3. For two of the more influential of these studies, see Janice Radway, *Reading the Romance* (Chapel Hill: U of North Carolina Press, 1984); and Jane Tompkins, *Sensational Designs: The Cultural Work of American Fiction, 1790–1860* (New York: Oxford UP, 1985).

4. See Trachtenberg, *The Incorporation of America: Culture and Society in the Gilded Age* (New York: Hill & Wang, 1982), p. 3.

5. P. 8. It is worth observing that Trachtenberg's account itself represents part of the historiographical transition that has taken place over the past forty years, from histories of consensus to those of conflict. Indeed, the arc of Trachtenberg's own career mirrors this transition. Compare the thesis of *Incorporation of America* with that of his first book, expressed as a question about the Brooklyn Bridge: "Might it not serve an even higher function as a reconciliation, a bridge between the opposite impulses of love and power? Might it not in the imagination heal the most serious breach in the age?" See *The Brooklyn Bridge: Fact and Symbol* (Chicago: U of Chicago P, 1965), p. 139.

6. T. J. Jackson Lears, *No Place of Grace: Anti-Modernism and the* Transformation of American Culture, 1880–1920 (New York: Pantheon, 1981). See also the essays collected in *The Culture of Consumption: Critical Essays in American History, 1880–1980,* ed. Richard Wightman and T. J. Jackson Lears (New York: Pantheon, 1983).

7. As Trachtenberg claims: "any account of [the influence of corporate life on thought and expression] must include subtle shifts in the meaning of prevalent ideas, ideas regarding the identity of the individual, the relation between public and private realms, and the character of the nation" (*Incorporation*, p. 5).

8. Michaels, *The Gold Standard and the Logic of Naturalism* (Berkeley: U of California P, 1987).

9. This is a point made explicitly by Michaels in his "Introduction: The Writer's Mark" (see esp. pp. 26–27), but it also forms part of a rhetorical strategy he effectively exploits. See *Gold Standard*, esp. ch. 5, pp. 139 ff.

10. For the best discussion of this development, see Louis Althusser, *Lenin and Philosophy and Other Essays*, trans. Ben Brewster (London: New Left Books, 1971).

11. Hacking, "Making Up People," in *Reconstructing Individualism: Autonomy, Individuality, and the Self in Western Thought*, ed. Thomas C. Heller

(Palo Alto: Stanford UP, 1986), pp. 222–36. For a central statement of man as "a recent invention" of language, see Michel Foucault, *The Order of Things: An Archaeology of the Human Sciences* (New York: Random House, 1970).

12. See Gina Lombroso-Ferrero, *Criminal Man, According to the Classification of Cesare Lombroso* (1911; rpt., Montclair, N.J.: Patterson Smith, 1972). According to Lombroso, "The ability to distinguish between right and wrong, which is the highest attribute of civilized humanity, is notably lacking in physically and psychically stunted organisms" (28). For discussion of the "scientific" developments discussed in this paragraph, see Stephen Jay Gould, *The Mismeasure of Man* (New York: Norton, 1981).

13. Cited by Daniel T. Rodgers, "In Search of Progressivism," *Reviews in American History* (December 1982), 10:125. See also Rodgers' excellent study of attitudes toward labor, time, and activities in general during the Progressive period, in *The Work Ethic in Industrial America, 1850–1920* (Chicago: U of Chicago P, 1978).

14. For studies of the historical context of American literary naturalism, see Preface, n. 11.

15. Brooks, *Reading for the Plot: Design and Intention in Narrative* (New York: Knopf, 1984), p. 25. He later goes on to assert that "narrative always makes the implicit claim to be in a state of repetition, as a going over again of a ground already covered" (91). For a judicious assessment of Brooks' argument, see Jules Law, "Desire Without History," *Novel* (Fall 1985), 19:91–94.

16. Miller, *Fiction and Repetition: Seven English Novels* (Cambridge: Harvard UP, 1982), p. 20. Further references to this edition will be included parenthetically in the text.

17. Brooks continues, in a significantly hypothetical mode: "*If* repetition is mastery, movement from the passive to the active, and *if* mastery is an assertion of control over what man must in fact submit to—choice, we might say, of an imposed end—we have already a suggestive comment on the grammar of plot, where repetition, taking us back again over the same ground, could have to do with the choice of ends." *Reading for the Plot*, p. 98, my emphases.

18. Miller, *Fiction and Repetition*, p. 19.

INDEX

Actions: as intended, not caused (unlike events), viii, 1-2, 14; non-action, 7, 62; subverted in naturalism, 35, 39-44, 63, 74, 98-99, 106-10; *see also* Choice; Deliberation; Intention; Self

Agency: characterizes literary realism, vii-ix, 2-3, 5, 10-12, 15-16, 32, 41, 43, 76; as a cultural construction, 140n28, 141n32; modern critiques of, 123-26, 137n12; as opposed to determinism, v, 8, 14, 32-33, 57, 83, 117, 137n12, 138n18, 141n30; as a philosophical problem, 134n9, 135n1, 137n12, 155n18, 157n33; as a projective assumption, x, xv, 9, 13-19, 44-45, 97, 113, 116, 133n4, 135n12, 142n38, 150n6; refuted in naturalism, xi-xii, xv, 6, 11-12, 16-17, 22-23, 30-32, 39-40, 43-53, 59-63, 67-74, 77-78, 80, 82, 88-90, 94-99,

106, 108-13, 164n17; requiring self-consciousness, 104, 143n39; *see also* Choice; Intention; Knowledge; Self

Ahnebrink, Lars, 131n2

Alpers, Paul, 30

Alter, Robert, 23

Althusser, Louis, 166n10

Auerbach, Erich, 24

Ayer, A. J., 8

Barthes, Roland, 76

Beck, Lewis, 142n38

Becker, George J., 132n2

Behavioral laws, *see* Determinism

Bellow, Saul, viii

Belsey, Catherine, 136n6

Benjamin, Walter, 140n23

Bergon, Frank, 164n16

Berlin, Isaiah, 33, 135n12